The Evans Symposium

The Evans Symposium

Witchcraft and the Gay Counterculture

&

Moon Lady Rising

Arthur Evans

40th Anniversary Release
2018

With an Introduction by Bo Young
Forewords by Murray Edelman & Bob Barzan
Afterword by Hal Offen

WHITE CRANE BOOKS
NEW YORK

iv

White Crane Institute
22 County Route 27 • Granville NY 12832
www.whitecraneinstitute.org • www.gaywisdom.org
editor@gaywisdom.org

Witchcraft and the Gay Counterculture was originally published by Fag Rag Books, Boston, MA, 1978

The Evans Symposium was published in hardcover as a White Crane Book, Granville, NY, November 2018, and in paperback, December 2018

Cloth cover:
ISBN-13: 978-1-7322844-0-1
ISBN-10: 1-7322844-0-7

Paperback:
ISBN-13: 978-1-7322844-1-8
ISBN-10: 1-7322844-1-5

Book layout by Toby Johnson.

Cover by Dan Vera

Introduction

The Arthur Evans lectures, which had taken place over the period of a couple of weeks in one summer in San Francisco, 1974, represented, in part, the collected material that Arthur had gathered into the book we all know as *Witchcraft and the Gay Counterculture*.

Every word of that book resonated in me, personally, like a tuning fork and it became part of my pantheon of fundamental reads along with Mark Thompson's trilogy of *Gay Body*, *Gay Spirit* and *Gay Soul* books, Randy Connors' *Blossom of Bone*.

In 2007 White Crane began publishing books as a way to expand our outreach as a 501(c)(3) educational corporation. Initially, what prompted this expansion of our publishing undertakings was seeing a copy of Andrew Ramer's classic *Two Flutes Playing* on sale on Amazon for $97.00! We contacted Andrew and were off to the races.

But even as we worked to produce that first book, in the back of my mind always, was the idea of finding out if Arthur Evans had published all of the material from his 1975 San Francisco lecture series. And if he hadn't, maybe we could work together to produce and publish a "sequel" to his groundbreaking original, *Witchcraft and the Gay Counterculture*.

In fact, there was more material, and in 2007 I approached Arthur to see if we could work together to assemble the unpublished material and produce what was originally conceived of as a sequel to *Witchcraft*. He was excited by the idea and started work almost immediately. Throughout 2009 Arthur and I spoke on the phone on a regular basis and he began sending me the chapters of what he was calling "Moon Lady Rising."

We did not have a contract with him yet, so in 2007, Dan Vera and I flew out to San Francisco to attend John Burnside Harry Hay's surviving partner of forty years, 90th birthday celebration and to visit with Arthur's. I was going to offer to buy him a new computer since he had told me that he was having issues with the old one he was working on. We didn't really have a lot of money to play with at the time, but this was an important enough work that we were willing to make that investment in Arthur and his work.

We had a lovely lunch in the Castro with Arthur and left him with the contract and copies, saying he could send one back at his leisure. I got back to New York and waited. Arthur continued to send chapters. 2010 came, but no contract and I finally decided to call him and see if there was a problem.

Alas, there was. Arthur had decided that, as he put it, as much as he enjoyed working with us and how much he appreciated the support we were offering, he needed to say no. All that he had, he said by way of apology, was his writing, and he decided he was going to self-publish the new book. To say that we were disappointed doesn't begin to cover it. But I respected his decision and after a decent period of mourning, let it go.

And then Arthur died.

In due time I spoke to Arthur's literary executor, Hal Offen, who granted permission for this book. And I thank him here for this privilege. Originally, the plan was to publish a second book, a sequel. Arthur worked on it in that way, as I mentioned, sending me a manuscript, chapter by chapter, for a book he titled *Moon Lady Rising*.

But with Arthur's death it seemed to more important to combine the two, to bring the entirety of the material that comprised the lectures — the symposium — that Arthur convened so many years ago back together, under one cover, again, as a body of work.

We maintain the separation of material so as to accurately represent the work, as Part Two of this book, *Moon Lady Rising*, and retain his titles, notes and references. To the best of my knowledge, this represents the entirety of Arthur Evans' seminal work on the subject of the cultural roots of homosexuality in western society that was presented in the symposium he presented in San Francisco in 1974.

There are many discussions and debates about the origins of the modern Radical Faerie movement, to which this book is closely connected. Credit, in part, can certainly be ascribed to Arthur's original circle work with Murray Edelman in San Francisco; Harry Hay, John Burnside and Don Kilhefner and their collaboration in Los Angeles and the desert Gathering must be factored in; others still, Donald Engstrom and groups of gay men in the Midwest. And there must be others whose work contributed to this movement but remain unknown to the movement known as the Radical Faeries. Because that, in the final consideration is what it is.

What seems clear is that there was — and remains — a zeitgeist of gay, lesbian, bisexual and transgendered people that erupted over the past 50 years. No one force, no one individual could have produced the society and culture we are witness to today. Furthermore, no one can stop it.

Witchcraft and the Gay Counterculture played an essential role in grounding the movement across time and cultures. Typical of Arthur, the title was an "grabber" and among the emerging theorists of the LGBT movement it was, as they say, controversial. It remains controversial and is sometimes dismissed for the "bias" Arthur showed in his interpretations, ignoring the inherent heterosexual bias that has bedeviled us for centuries. And why not read between the burry lines of history and see same-sex love just as easily as one might assume opposite sex attractions?

For this reader, the text amounted to a Rosetta Stone with which to understand western European sexualities and culture. It opened the door to reading about same-sex love in every society, culture and era around the world. It introduced many to the works of Will Roscoe *(The Zuni Man-Woman; Queer Spirits: A Gay Man's Myth Book; Changing Ones: Third and Fourth Genders in Native North America;* and *Jesus and the Shamanic Tradition of Same-Sex Love, et al.)* and Randy Connor (*Blossom of Bone*) and to a world in which I could see that I had a connection and roots.

In the back of my mind as I worked on this project, I had a conundrum around the title for this book. I wanted to be sure anyone looking at it would immediately be aware that this isn't simply a retread of *Witchcraft and the Gay Counterculture.* The addition of *Moon Lady Rising* material represented a collection of the entire series of lectures Arthur had presented. I watched videos of Arthur talking about his work and he spent a good part of one video talking about the Platonic Symposium, from which a good part of Arthur's ideas arises.

And I realized that the lectures he presented were a form of symposium. So this book is now *The Evans Symposium* that includes all the material Arthur presented in San Francisco back in those days.

I invited three of Arthur's intimate friends to share something of their relationship:

Murray Edelman, Arthur's long-time friend, who was responsible for financing the original publication of *Witchcraft and the Gay Counterculture* to write a new introduction to Part One of this edition, which is that same material. *Witchcraft and the Gay Counterculture* might very well not have made it into print without Murray's support.

Bob Barzan, founder of White Crane Journal, and also an old friend of Arthur's, wrote the introduction to the new material, Part Two which Arthur titled *Moon Lady Rising.* It was through our mutual friendship with Bob that I became friends with Arthur. This book would not have been possible without his assistance.

And finally, Hal Offen, Arthur's long-time friend and literary executor to write a post script to this volume. As I mention previously, it is through Hal's good graces that this collected work has come to fruition.

My own friends played important roles in getting this project into the world. The book design and layout are author and former White Crane publisher Toby Johnson's tireless and patient work.

For many years I worked with Dan Vera to produce White Crane after Toby's era until Dan set off into a brilliant career as a poet. The cover art is by Dan, who, clearly, also does beautiful watercolor work.

Around the time of Dan's departure, the late Mark Thompson and his partner Malcolm Boyd came into my life. Dan and I did a retrospective collection of Malcolm's writing, *A Prophet in His Own Land.*

And after that, Mark became my daily, trans-continental partner. He and I spent hours on the phone every day, going over manuscripts and collecting material for *The Fire in Moonlight* All told, we did three books together, including work on this book. Malcolm was a constant presence as well, dropping me notes on Los Angeles Episcopal Diocese stationery every other week or so. The two of them were stalwart fans of *White Crane* and served as Board members for those years. They were some of the dearest and most brilliant friends I have ever had. Malcolm was in his 90s when he died. But Mark was merely in his 60s, and they were vibrant 60s at that. His untimely, sudden death was a body blow, and my life is poorer without him.

I sincerely thank them all.

A word about the use of the term "faerie" in this edition: Bradley Rose created an etymological chart that traced the development of the term ("fairy") that he called "Faerie Tongues." It was originally posthumously published in Bradley Rose's *A Radical Fairy Seedbed*. And as can be seen in the title of his book and his subsequent usage, he seemed to be undecided if not conflicted about which was the better modern usage. White Crane published the chart in the Radical Faerie anthology, *The Fire in Moonlight* [ISBN-13: 978-1-938246-04 ed. Mark Thompson, Richard Neely, Bo Young]. We include it here for your reference.

Early usage among the modern Radical ("root") Faeries has been divided. Some circles use the spelling "fairy" and others "faerie." In the interest of historic accuracy, we have chosen to let each use stand as the writer spelled it at the time they used it. If they changed spelling, it will appear as such here. If they didn't, it won't.

Finally, I would like to dedicate this edition to, the late Eugene V. Kettner, a supporter of White Crane Institute for years and from whom we received the funds with which to finally produce this book.

Bo Young
Granville, New York
2018

Contents

Faerie Tongues
by Bradley Rose

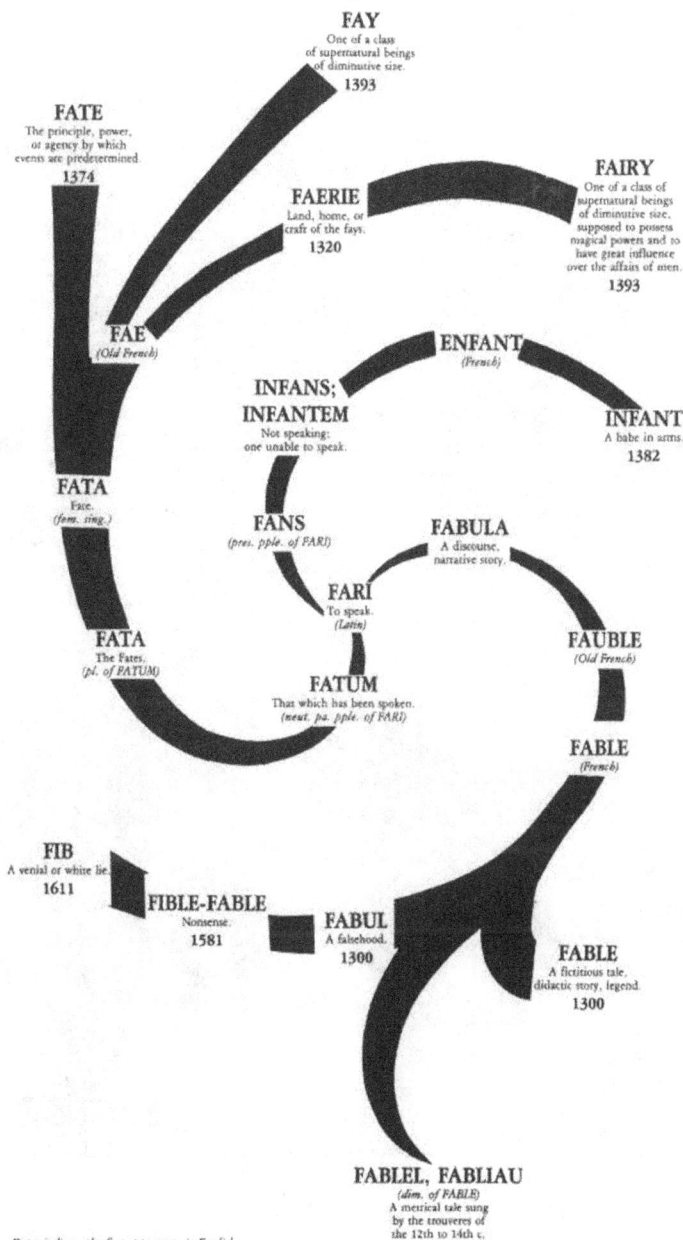

FAY
One of a class
of supernatural beings
of diminutive size.
1393

FATE
The principle, power,
or agency by which
events are predetermined.
1374

FAIRY
One of a class of
supernatural beings
of diminutive size,
supposed to possess
magical powers and to
have great influence
over the affairs of men.
1393

FAERIE
Land, home, or
craft of the fays.
1320

FAE
(Old French)

ENFANT
(French)

**INFANS;
INFANTEM**
Not speaking;
one unable to speak.

INFANT
A babe in arms.
1382

FATA
Fate.
(fem. sing.)

FANS
(pres. pple. of FARI)

FABULA
A discourse,
narrative story.

FARI
To speak.
(Latin)

FATA
The Fates.
(pl. of FATUM)

FAUBLE
(Old French)

FATUM
That which has been spoken.
(neut. pa. pple. of FARI)

FABLE
(French)

FIB
A venial or white lie.
1611

FIBLE-FABLE
Nonsense.
1581

FABUL
A falsehood.
1300

FABLE
A fictitious tale,
didactic story, legend.
1300

FABLEL, FABLIAU
(dim. of FABLE)
A metrical tale sung
by the trouvères of
the 12th to 14th c.

Dates indicate the first appearance in English.

Photo by Sal Russo

Witcheraft and the Gay Counterculture

Arthur Evans

A Radical View of Western Civilization
and Some of the People It Has Tried to Destroy

40th Anniversary Release
2018

WHITE CRANE BOOKS
NEW YORK

Arthur Evans
Mask of Dionysos by John Soares
December 1997

My Friend Arthur

Murray Edelman

I met Arthur in San Francisco in 1973 in Buena Vista Park. He was leaving the cruising area and I was arriving. I recognized him from his pictures and we had been told about each other by David Goldman, a mutual activist friend, so we eagerly made plans to meet. David told us we had a lot in common; we did, and we watched that grow over many years.

We had both moved to the city after being swept into the beginnings of the Gay Liberation movement in our home cities. He was an early member of the Gay Liberation Front, a founder of the Gay Activist Alliance (GAA) and a very visible force in New York and hence nationally. I had founded the Chicago version of the Gay Liberation Front and had my share of arrests, but I was in awe of what Arthur had done. I encourage the readers to look up the YouTube Arthur Evans Memorial Video to see his activist side.

We had many more walks in park and afternoons of tea.

We learned that we both came to San Francisco with a deep yearning. Our movement work had exposed the emptiness of the values we had been brought up with. I grew up Jewish in a Christian dominated culture. I never fit in sexually or spiritually. I internalized my alienation and believed in these values although they didn't serve me. Arthur's response was anger which fed his activism and could still turn a mild conversation between us into a rant against Christianity and the values it offered.

But it became more than just a rant, as he started to use his amazing intellect and academic training (a Masters in Philosophy from Columbia) to put that anger into research and to develop, in effect, an expose of Christianity.

I have fond memories of the gleam in his eye when he told me how he had traced the "faerie" epithet all the way back to a people that were wiped out by Christianity, and then months later he was in total rapture when he led me step-by-step with his evidence about why Joan of Arc was a practitioner of "the old religion." I had just finished by PhD at the University of Chicago in Human Development, so I was not a slouch intellectually, but he sure turned my head around. I had bought the thinking of the time thought that Gay oppression had come out of capitalism, Arthur was showing that it came out of Christianity and their conquest of the old cultures. He was the first for me to connect the Christian holidays with the celebrations of the earth-based religions and of course the Crusades.

At some point, Arthur started talking about making his research into a book. He couldn't think of any publisher than would come close to his work, so he wanted to self-publish. He couldn't afford to do it because he was living on welfare. So I ended up loaning him $1,500 so he could publish the first edition. He eventually paid me back in installments over 10 years. I was so proud of supporting him that I was unconcerned about getting it back. But he was a man of his word.

In early 1975, shortly before *Witchcraft and the Gay Counterculture* was to come out, Arthur decided to give a series of lectures on the book at what was our Gay community center on Page St. The place was full with around 200 men quite a few women. They were enthusiastic about getting a historical perspective being expressed. It is hard to convey what a shift his ideas brought. Our movement had no sense of history or perspective. We framed everything in terms of the liberation struggles of the day. We were alienated from religions but we didn't necessarily see them as the clear cause of our problems.

After the second or third lecture, I suggested to Arthur that we start a group to explore the issues and ideas he was talking about. He said he had thought of that, but didn't know what we would do. I told him that if there were unfilled time, I could lead exercises based on my experiences in my weekends. Others also talked to Arthur, and on a couple of weeks later I was invited to join seven others in his apartment;

Someone suggested that we pass an amulet around whoever held it would have the floor and others would listen. He had recently been part of a group that had one that. We agreed to do that share our needs and visions for the group. During the sharing Timo Butters suggested the name Faerie Circle and it instantly became our name. So in October, 1975 at 604 Ashbury we met as a modern day Faerie Circle and conducted a "Heart Circle"

We remained loosely structured. A ritual, or circle would be called and it was spread by word of mouth. The first ritual was in someone's home a couple weeks after the meeting. It was my first spiritual ritual, but I mostly remember my sexual connection. Being sexual with a new person in the context of spirit and ritual was truly amazing, far deeper and explosive than anything before it. There was the comfort of having known him for a long time, being connected in our hearts, and yet discovering each other for the first time.

Another ritual was at Land's End in San Francisco. About twenty of us formed a circle near the popular cruising area on a weekday. Somehow this ritual evolved. Each person would chant their name three times in whatever way felt good, we would then repeat it back three times, then the next. We kept going around and increasing the speed. It was like we took off. I have tried repeating that ritual at gatherings but it was never the same.

But the most significant ritual for me was when some Faeries called for our group to go to the Sutro baths on a specific weekday night. The bath house had the usual amenities, but with outdoor space. On that night around 50 of us gathered in the outdoor Jacuzzi, some with towels and some without. We were pressed together and chanted "OM" and then related sounds.

It was like being in another world. The sexual vibe of the bathhouse, the naked men pressed together, along with the spiritual connection touched me at all levels. It was like stepping into a new world; the feeling was akin to my first gay demonstration. I was forever changed; I experienced something that I would never forget. The year I was using my psychological training to trying to replicate that experience at the Baths for guys that were just drawn in by the vision in my leaflet. We did a couple of other nights at the bathhouse and rituals at other locations in the SF area, but by late 1978, our Faerie Circle ran out of steam in late 1978. I was so inspired by my bath experience that I used my experience leading groups to create "A Different Kind of Night at the Baths" that was open to gay men interested in a deeper physical connection at the bath house. In 1979 I accepted an attractive offer to work in New York for only 18 months, but then it kept getting extended.

I would return to SF periodically and would have lunch with Arthur to catch up with our lives. He would tell me of his research and next book with that gleam in his eye. I would tell him of my explorations with mushrooms, shamans, ayahuasca the Naraya, a Native inspired dance, and other adventures. He would listen with rapt attention and I could feel a bit of envy from him as I would describe my ecstatic experiences. Yet every offer to include him in one of these ceremonies was refused. At one point I had arranged for him to come to the Naraya at the Faerie sanctuary in Wolf Creek as an Honored Guest, but he left it as a "maybe," someday.

Another frequent topic in our lunches was the Radical Faeries and Harry Hay. In August, 1979 I attended the first "Spiritual Gathering of Radical Faeries" in Benson, Arizona. I saw it as an extension of our SF group and eagerly brought my experience. On the last night I led a ritual for the full gathering at the swimming pool based on our Faerie Circle bathhouse night. It was a grand success. I really enjoyed being the conduit between our earlier discoveries and this new emerging group of Faeries.

Arthur and I watched with excitement as this gathering spread all over the country. But that became tempered as we learned from others that Harry Hay was the "Founder of the Radical Faeries." Arthur became furious that the leadership acted and wrote as though our Faerie Circle never existed. There are some heated exchanges been Harry and Arthur in the White Crane archives for any history buffs. A few months before Arthur passed, I visited him on a trip to San Francisco. At our lunch he told me of his heart problem and his decision to not do anything about it. He was offered the possibility of a surgery that had a chance to correct the problem, but it could also leave him as a vegetable. He just didn't like the odds. He wanted to die with dignity even if it meant sooner rather than later. He went over all the details in the same way he would explain his historical research, but the gleam wasn't there, but his sense of humor was. He wanted my support, in part because I was a statistician and could understand making a decision under uncertainty.

Before I left San Francisco, I paid what I expected would be my last visit to Arthur in his apartment, this time with a close friend who I will refer to as the Green One, a dedicated Faerie, witch and a big fan of Arthur's. Arthur started by raising his hands, and mocking the voice of a guide in trance, imbued with reverence, pronounced: "Here we are at the birthplace of the Faeries. It started in October, 1975 right here in this very room."

For Marty Robinson, a Free Spirit, who taught through personal example and direct action. Marty's tremendous influence on the early Gay movement in New York has been slighted, now that academics, professional politicians, and other liberals have taken over the show. But his time, and ours, will come again. Thanks for everything, Marty.

INVOCATION FOR STRENGTH

Isis. the rainbow of sapphire mysteries
you are the calling i hear from
the wind in my bones.
oh mother of life
begotten from your womb of light
we rise now out of the masculine death
that is jehovah's enslavement
in the fullness of sweet woman's blood
and fairy rage —
our touch blossoms.
like the tides of earth we are strong
to come again.

i believe in the goddess
the movement for life.
thorned by our genderless
brightening for our powerless
and suckling our struggle.
by the rose in my chakras
i tap the androgyne.
with you our love is revolt
with you we are each
atoms of significance.

Diana
my lover of amazons
my triumph of faggot witches.
feed us the lunar nectar
between poems and tears
between silence and celebrations,
and guide us to destroy
the machinery that alienates us.
then shall our captors parasite
upon themselves.

oh Kali
the source the destroyer the
return: in pain's dignity
your face is behind our faces.
we are strong
to come again.

Moonrose Shaundel Angeles

Introduction: Whatever Happened to Gay History?

O nce upon a time, Mayor John Lindsay of New York "invited" all city employees to Radio City Music Hall so they could contribute money to his bid to become President of the United States. When His Honor arrived at the theater, he had to enter by the back door because of an angry demonstration out front by the Gay Activists Alliance. When he finally made his way to the stage, he was brought to a shocked stop by the actions of Cora Rivera, a Lesbian, and Morty Manford, a Gay man. The two chained themselves to the balcony railing and shouted: "Why don't you support Gay rights?" Startled, Lindsay gave up trying to make his fund-raising pitch and walked off, as the audience rumbled in confusion. Gay activist Ernest Cohen hurried to the balcony railing and poured down a shower of leaflets explaining the disruption: While passing himself off as a liberal, Lindsay refused to support a simple Gay-rights bill before the City Council.

Despite past efforts by Gay people at polite education, there had been a conspiracy of silence in the New York news media around Gay rights. The intent of this disruption was to force the Gay rights issue into the arena of public discussion. As it happened, one television station did give the event competent coverage (although referring to Cora Rivera as "an *apparent* Lesbian"). But more typical of past experience was another station that completely falsified the news. The announcer not only failed to mention the zap, but falsely added that Lindsay was well received and "completed his speech as scheduled." His account was a total fiction.

This was not the first time that professional journalists had falsified the news. Earlier *The New York Times* printed a comprehensive list of bills introduced into the legislature — listing all bills except those dealing with Gay civil rights. And in its yearly feature on homosexuality (by the medical editor), the *Times* made no mention of GAA's militant political activity. In the eyes of most professional journalists, Lesbians and Gay men were nothing more than a tiny minority of perverts.

Historians, just like professional journalists, have falsified the Gay story, and just as badly. Writing in 1971, a leading authority on Gay history said:

> Almost everyone who has written about gay life has called it pretentious, absurd, pitiful or repugnant. The great majority of homosexuals seem to vouch for the accuracy of its depiction in *The Boys in the Band*, a play replete with jealousy, competitiveness,

insecurity, malice, tantrums, and hysterical mood shifts (Karlen, 526).

A similar type of venom can be found just beneath the surface in the writings of so-called liberal historians. A good example is the widely read work of a liberal Anglican priest. He concludes his whitewash of the church's atrocities against Gay people with this statement: "Homosexual perversion, therefore, is not itself a fount of corrupting influence, but only, as it were, the ineluctable consequence of a corrosion which has already left its mark upon marriage and family life and, if not checked, may ultimately undermine the whole social order and lead to sexual anarchy" (Bailey, 166).

Just as bad is the liberal approach found in the popular historical study by a Danish psychotherapist. While assuring the reader that he is most fair-minded, the author concludes by saying that there is no such thing as Gay history and that men who are exclusively Gay suffer from an "inability to adjust themselves heterosexually" (Vanggaard, 52).

The professionals have suppressed Gay history, just as they have suppressed the truth about Third World people, women, the poor, the imprisoned, and the insane. They have been co-opted, not only by being bought off, but in a more insidious way. Through their long "training" they have lost the ability to see other realities than the official ones, and have internalized within themselves the values of the ruling classes. Intellectually and spiritually, they have been anesthetized.

We will have to write our own history, and when I say "we" I mean any of us who have the interest and energy to do so. We must demystify ourselves from the illusion that only well-paid professionals can do this work. In many ways, trained professionals, including Gay ones, are the least suited to teach us, for they have been most assimilated into the lifestyles and values of the ruling classes.

This book is an attempt to record some of the things that professional historians usually leave out. It is one-sided, in that it is mostly concerned with the victims of Western civilization, rather than their rulers. It is subjective, in that it reflects my own personal value judgments and emotions. It is arbitrary, in that it picks and chooses among all the source material, accepting a few things here and there, but rejecting most as biased or unreliable.

The book, however, is as true as any other historical work. It is true because *all* historical works are one-sided, subjective, and arbitrary. Every historian works this way. The real falsehood occurs when historians hide their values, emotions, and choices under a veneer of "objectivity." A work of history cannot be assessed apart from the values of the person who wrote it.

This book may horrify professional historians. They will probably object to my use of myths as historical sources. Yet myths can have historical worth if we learn how to evaluate them, just as *The New York Times* can have historical worth if we know how to evaluate it. They will be offended by my qualified acceptance of the theory of matriarchy. Yet current feminist writers are showing that *male* prejudice has greatly distorted the writing of history. They will be angered by my contempt for academic professionalism and its methods. Yet whole new insights often emerge, even in the physical sciences, despite rather than because of the professionals.

There is no such thing as *the* authoritative Gay history, but as many Gay histories can exist as there are Gay visions. May they all be written.

1 Joan of Arc:

Transvestite And Heretic

On May 30, 1431, in the town of Rouen, France, a peasant woman named Joan of Arc, age nineteen, was burned alive at the stake as a relapsed heretic. The immediate reason for her death was that she was found wearing men's clothing in her prison cell. This fact about Joan's execution may surprise those who view her as a traditional Christian saint. But the records of the time show she was hardly traditional.

After 1425, when she started her drive against the English invaders of France, Joan of Arc was an adamant transvestite. On May 23, 1430, she was captured by a sell-out French faction. They sold her to the English, who charged her with heresy and handed her over to the Inquisition. At the trial, Joan's judges were horrified by her transvestism. Article twelve of her indictment read:

> Jeanne, rejecting and abandoning women's clothing, her hair cut around like a young coxcomb, took shirt, breeches, doublet ... tight-fitting boots or buskins, long spurs, sword, dagger, breast-plate, lance and other arms in fashion of a man of war (T. Douglas Murray, 345-346).

When brought before the court, Joan refused to promise to wear women's clothing, even though her refusal meant she couldn't receive communion. What's more, she insisted that her transvestism was a *religious* duty, saying: "For nothing in the world will I swear not to arm myself and put on a man's dress; I must obey the orders of Our Lord" (T. Douglas Murray, 87).

To the judges, it was bad enough that Joan had been wearing men's clothing. But to say this was a religious duty was heresy! The following was one of the chief charges brought against her:

> Jeanne attributes to God, His Angels, and His Saints, orders which are against the modesty of the sex, and which are prohibited by the Divine Law, things abominable to God and man, interdicted on pain of anathema by ecclesiastical censure, such as dressing herself in the garments of a man, short, tight, dissolute, those underneath as well as above .... To attribute all this to the order of God, to the order which had been transmitted to her by the Angels and even by Virgin Saints, is to blaspheme God and His

Saints, to destroy the Divine Law and violate the Canonical Rules
(T. Douglas Murray, 346).

The English drew attention to Joan's transvestism and urged the church to condemn her for that reason. The King of England, Henry VI, even got involved on this point. In a letter he wrote about Joan, he said: "It is sufficiently notorious and well-known that for some time past a woman calling herself Jeanne the Pucelle [the Maid], leaving off the dress and clothing of the feminine sex, a thing contrary to divine law and abominable before God, and forbidden by all laws, wore clothing and armour such as is worn by men" (W. S. Scott, 52). The sell-out French faction that had captured Joan called her homasse, which was a derogatory word in Old French meaning masculine woman (Lightbody, 60).

Not only did Joan wear men's clothing as a religious duty, but in the eyes of her judges she did something else just as bad— she acted masculine. Contrary to the Christian view of womanhood, she was bold, self-assertive, strong willed, and contemptuous of her captors. In article sixty-three of the original indictment, the judges condemn her for "allowing herself a tone of mockery and derision such as no woman in a state of holiness would allow" (T. Douglas Murray, 363). The judges were horrified that Joan had rejected the traditional woman's role: "She disdains also to give herself up to feminine work, conducting herself in all things rather as a man than as a woman" (Murray, 348). The fact that Joan had led male troops in battle and had even given them orders seemed to her judges another sign of heresy: "In contempt of the orders of God and the Saints, Jeanne, in presumption and pride, hath gone so far as to take command over men" (T. Douglas Murray, 359).

The judges were interested in Joan's relationship with other women. In the summer of 1424, Joan had left her parents against their will and went to live with another woman, La Rousse ("The Red"), who lived in Neufchateau. La Rousse, it turns out, was an innkeeper, which is interesting since inns in the middle ages were often brothels. In article eight, the judges accused Joan of hanging out with prostitutes: "Towards her twentieth year, Jeanne, of her own wish, and without permission of her father and mother, went to Neufchateau, in Lorraine, and was in service for some time at the house of a woman, an innkeeper named La Rousse, where lived women of evil life, and where soldiers were accustomed to lodge in great numbers. During her stay in the inn, Jeanne sometimes stayed with these evil women" (T. Douglas Murray, 344).

The judges also questioned Joan about her relationship with another woman, Catherine de la Rochelle. Joan admitted to the judges that she had slept in the same bed with Catherine on two successive nights, but that her reason for doing so was religious. Joan claimed that Catherine told her she often had visions of "a lady" at night, and Joan said she wanted to see this lady too. Whatever her reason, Joan admitted to sleeping twice with Catherine (W.S. Scott, 97).

The judges were interested in Joan's sex life, and had her examined by a panel of women to determine if she was a virgin. They reported that she was.

Joan's behavior at her trial was hardly that of a Christian saint. When she was asked to swear to tell the truth on the Gospels, she repeatedly refused. Usually, after much haggling back and forth at each session, she would give in (partially) by swearing on the missal (which is the liturgy). In addition, Joan adamantly refused to recite either the Lord's Prayer or the Creed, although she was asked to do so many times. Her judges thought this refusal was significant.

The mystery of Joan deepens as we look at other aspects of her life. Before her capture, whenever she appeared in public she was worshipped like a deity by the peasants, a practice she never discouraged. The peasants believed that she had the power to heal, and many would flock around her to touch part of her body or her clothing (which was men's clothing). Subsequently her armor was kept on display at the Church of St. Denis, where it was worshipped.

The area of Lorraine, where Joan grew up, was famous for the lingering paganism of its people. In the century before Joan's trial, the Synod of Treves had condemned the peasants of Lorraine for believing in "all kinds of magic, sorcery, witchcraft, auguries, superstitious writings . . . the illusions of women who boast that they ride at night with Diana or Herodias and a multitude of other women" (M. Murray, *God of the Witches*, 177).

The peasants who lived in Joan's own neighborhood retained memories of prophecies from the old Celtic religion that had existed there before the introduction of Christianity.

One of these ancient prophecies concerned a wooded area called Bois Chesnu that was near Joan's house. The prophecy, which was well known and was attributed to Merlin the sorcerer, said that a maid would come forth from Bois Chesnu, perform many marvels, and unite the French people (W. S. Scott, 76, note).

In certain parts of Europe where Celtic beliefs survived, the word "Maid" or "Maiden" was a religious title, signifying a type of divine being who had the power to cure people (Hope, 35). The old French word for this title was *La Pucelle*, which was sometimes applied by French Christians to the Virgin Mary. When Joan was asked by what title she called herself, her standard reply was "Joan the Maid, Daughter of God."

Joan's judges believed that she had not been raised as a Christian, but as a pagan. "In her childhood, she was not instructed in the beliefs and principles of our Faith, but by certain old women she was initiated in the science of witchcraft, divination, superstitious doings, and magical acts. Many inhabitants of these villages have been known for all time as using these kinds of witchcraft" (T. Douglas Murray, 343).

The judges spent a lot of time questioning Joan about her supposed relations with beings called "fairies" — a fact that has puzzled many modern commentators. Near Joan's home was a huge old beech tree (in Latin, fagus tree). Rumor had it that the fairies sometimes came and danced around this tree at night. By Joan's time, the tree was considered sacred to Our Lady of Domremy, but suspicion remained that it had once been a holy spot in the old pagan religion. Near this tree was a spring where the peasants often went to be cured of diseases.

Joan denied ever seeing fairies at the tree, but did admit to participating in celebrations around it as a child. Her admission on this point, which the judges considered incriminating, is as follows:

> Not far from Domremy there is a tree that they call 'The Ladies Tree' —others call it The Fairies Tree' .... It is a beautiful tree, a beech [fagus], from which comes the 'beau mai' [the maypole] .
> . . . I have sometimes been to play with the young girls, to make garlands for Our Lady of Domremy. Often I have heard the old folk — they are not of my lineage -say that the fairies haunt this tree .... As for me, I never saw them that I know of . ... I have seen the young girls putting garlands on the branches of this tree, and I myself have sometimes put them there with my companions; sometimes we took these garlands away, sometimes we left them. Ever since I knew it was necessary for me to come into France, I have given myself up as little as possible to these games and distractions (T. Murray, 20-21).

On April 2, 1431, all charges of witchcraft were dropped against Joan (see entry under "Joan of Arc" in Robbins). The court apparently felt that it could not prove (short of a confession forced by torture) actual practices of conjuring demons. Besides, the Inquisition had not yet been authorized to deal with witchcraft in and of itself. This would not happen until 1451 (Robbins, 272). The court had enough evidence to condemn her anyway, in view of her claim that her transvestism was a religious duty and her belief that her personal visions were more important than the institutional authority of the church.

Joan was subjected to unending psychological abuse and threatened with being burned alive. By April 24, 1431, she could stand the pressure no longer and recanted. She promised to submit to the institutional authority of the church and said she would stop wearing men's clothing. The court showed her mercy, as Christians understand it: she was sentenced to life imprisonment on bread and water.

On May 30, Joan again resumed the wearing of men's clothing. It's not clear from the records whether she did this deliberately or was tricked into it by her guards. In any event, as Margaret Murray observes, "the extraordinary fact remains that the mere resuming of male garments was the signal for her death without further delay. On the Sunday she wore the [male] dress, on the Tuesday the sentence was communicated to her, on the Wednesday she was burned, as an 'idolator, apostate, heretic, relapsed'" (M. Murray, *The Witch-Cult*, 274). This fact is extraordinary because the laws that regulated the wearing of clothing never made transvestism a capital offence. Apparently, in the opinion of her judges, Joan's resumption of male clothing was a sign of relapse into "heresy."

A clue to the importance of Joan's transvestism comes from a decree of the faculty of the University of Paris. On May 14, 1431, the faculty condemned Joan and urged that she be burned as a heretic (medieval academics, like their modern counterparts, were mostly mouthpieces for the values of the ruling class). The *reason* for the faculty's condemnation of Joan's cross-dressing is striking. They said that by doing it she was "following the custom of the Gentiles and the Heathen" (W. S. Scott, 156). This should stop us and make us ask, "*What* custom? *What* heathen?" Just what are these academics referring to? Before we answer these questions, however, we first have to examine one more angle —

During her military career, Joan's closest friend, personal bodyguard, and most devoted follower was a man named Gilles de Rais (1404-1440). Gilles de Rais was widely reputed during his lifetime to be a homosexual. In 1440, the Bishop of Nantes publicly charged Gilles de Rais with violating the immunities of a certain priest; conjuring demons; and sodomy. At the insistence of the bishop, a concurrent civil trial was begun in which Gilles was accused of massively molesting and murdering children, mostly young boys. In the language of the Inquisition's indictment, Gilles was said to be a "heretic, apostate, conjurer of demons . . . accused of the crime and vices against nature, sodomy, sacrilege, and violation of the immunities of Holy Church" (see entry under "Gilles de Rais" in Robbins).

At first Gilles denied everything and spoke contemptuously to his judges. Then he and some of his closest friends and servants were tortured by methods rather like those used by the CIA today. Gilles confessed everything his judges wanted to hear. On October 26, 1440, nine years after the burning of Joan of Arc, Gilles de Rais was publicly strangled.

Historians are divided over what was really going on in the trial of Gilles. One of the problems involves his relationship to his family — who were upset at the way he was squandering their money. Gilles was one of the richest nobles in Europe, but he was blowing the money away on everything that caught his fancy. He spent so much that he started selling off family estates to pay for his debts. This selling of the family inheritance was too much for his relatives. In 1436, they got the King of France to issue a decree forbidding him to sell any more family land. In September of 1440, a priest tried to take possession of one of the estates that Gilles owned outside the King's jurisdiction and had sold for debt. Gilles beat up the priest and arrested him. The priest than collaborated with Gilles' relatives and with the Bishop of Nantes, who stepped forward and made his charges.

But there are other factors besides economics. In general, slanderous charges of child murder or child molestation have been used in the past by patriarchal religions against people who practice a dissenting religion. For example, such charges were leveled against Christians in ancient Rome, against Jews in Christian Europe, and against Jesuit missionaries in China. It is extraordinary that this same type of slander is widely used today against Lesbians and Gay men. ("We can't let them be teachers because they'll convert our children"; "They practice strange rites among themselves"; etc.).

We know that Gilles was a practitioner of magic before he was arrested. At the time of his arrest and thereafter, some pretty strange things happened. On the day he was to die, there was a large public demonstration on his behalf (James, 154). This is hardly the type of thing to happen for someone regarded as a child-molester!

After he was executed, a fountain was erected on the spot where he died. For many years thereafter, nursing mothers would visit this fountain and pray to it to increase their flow of milk. Every year on the anniversary of his death, the parents of Nantes ritually flagellated their children in his memory (Murray, *God of the Witches*, 195).

So we see that with Joan and Gilles we have a very strange set of circumstances. On the one hand, we have a peasant woman who practiced transvestism as a religious duty; who was masculine in appearance and behavior; who admitted to sleeping in the same bed with another woman; who was worshipped in her own life time; and who came from an area where pagan traditions were still strong. On the other hand, one of her closest friends was a man who was commonly known as a homosexual and a sorcerer; and whose place of execution was popularly regarded as a fertility charm.

To most straight historians, these strange circumstances mean very little. They usually dismiss the trial of Joan as a phony political frame-up and regard Gilles as "a vicious sexual pervert" (Russell, 263). Despite this shallow straight approach, we will follow up other historical clues.

For one thing, the emphasis on transvestism at Joan's trial is important because transvestism played a major role in the religion of Europe before Christianity. The historian Pennethorne Hughes puts it this way: "The wearing of clothes appropriate to the opposite sex was always one of the rites of witchcraft, as it has been and is of primitive [sic] peoples, during their fertility festivals, throughout the history of the world" (Hughes, 108).

Links between witchcraft and transvestism appear regularly in the history of Christian Europe. In the sixth century, the Christian writer Caesarius of Aries denounced the pagan practices of ritual transvestism and the wearing of animal costumes. Sixth and seventh century synods repeatedly condemned transvestism during the popular New Year's holiday, where men were dressed as women— "a masquerade probably originating in a fertility rite of some kind" (Russell, 58). In the ninth century, a Christian guidebook prescribed penance for men who practiced ritual transvestism (Russell, 74). A thirteenth century inquisitor in Southern France denounced female worshippers of the goddess Diana along with male transvestites (Russell, 156-157).

Ritual transvestism associated with the old holidays continued in Europe down to modern times. "May Day sports perpetuated the practices, including even transvestism, and…in Wales, there existed, into the nineteenth century, a peasant dance and march with a garland, led by a dancer, [a horned god figure] called the 'Cadi'" (Hughes, 125). Similarly in twentieth century England such celebrations as the Helston Furry Dance, the Morris Dances, and the Peace Egg Mumming Play continue the tradition (Hughes, 211-212). In the Hogmanay celebration in Scotland, "the boys wore skirts and bonnets, the girls hats and greatcoats" (Hughes, 212). The Feast of Fools, a remnant of the old pagan religion, has persisted into modern times, with clerics "wearing masks and monstrous visages at the hours of office.

They dance in the choir dressed as women, or disreputable men, or minstrels. They sing wanton songs" (Hughes, 111). Today many Gay people throughout Europe and America observe Halloween as a Gay holiday with transvestite celebrations. Originally, Halloween was one of the great holidays of the old religion — the Night of All Souls.

Besides transvestism, a second clue to understanding Joan's history is her association with "fairies." Pennethorne Hughes observes that "the people who until the late Middle Ages were called fairies by one name or another were often those, who until the seventeenth century, were called witches" (Hughes, 76). Everyone knows "fairy" as a derogatory word for Gay men. Many other anti-Gay words have historical connections with heresy or witchcraft.

The word "bugger" comes from a group of twelfth and thirteenth century Christian heretics. Hughes observes that:

> this particular name became associated with the homosexual practices which the heretics were held to encourage... Hence they were known as Bulgari, Bugari, Bulgri, or Bourgres, a word which, as it is delicately put, 'has been retained with an infamous signification in the English, French and Italian vernaculars'"(Hughes, 66).

Gay men were once called "punks" in Britain. Until recent times in Yorkshire, a festival was annually held on the Night of All Souls. Local people themselves call the festival "Punky Night" or "Spunky Night," and some participants are called "punks" (Hughes, 211).

The history of the word "faggot" reveals the intimate connection between Gay men, heresy and witchcraft. Both witches and heretics were regularly burned on bundles of sticks called "faggots." In the popular speech of the time expressions popped up like "fire and faggot" or "to fry a faggot," suggesting that the victims themselves were called "faggots." "Faggot" even became "the embroidered figure of a faggot, which heretics who had recanted were obliged to wear on their sleeve, as an emblem of what they had merited" (Oxford English Dictionary). The word "faggot" comes from the Latin fagus, which means beech tree. Fagus in turn derives from the Greek *phagos* or *phegos*, which originally meant any tree bearing edible nuts or fruit (in Greek, phagein means "to eat"). In classical Greek, phagos especially referred to oak trees. Burning witches and heretics on bundles of faggots may have originated from a religious link with trees (especially beech and oak)— which were sacred in pre-Christian Europe. The old fairy tree near Domremy where Joan of Arc first heard her voices was a fagus tree.

Margaret Murray offers an interesting interpretation of these clues. In 1921, Murray, a professor of Egyptology at University College in London, unsettled conventional historians with the publication of The Witch-Cult in Western Europe (still available as a paperback). Murray approached the subject as an anthropologist: she collected transcripts from witch trials (mostly from Britain, where torture was rare), went through the evidence for common themes, and compared the results with existing mythological and archaeological knowledge of early Western Europe. Murray claimed that "witchcraft" was a lingering pre-Christian religion and that various pagan cults continued to exist underground until recent times. In examining the evidence about Joan of Arc and Gilles de Rais, she concluded that both were members of such a cult — a supposition which clarifies many strange incidents surrounding them.

In addition to Murray's view, we have seen that Joan of Arc and Gilles de Rais were probably Gay. Of course, our evidence, like most historical evidence concerning sexuality, is circumstantial. But Joan was certainly not an orthodox Christian: she refused to recite the Lord's prayer; she viewed transvestism as a religious duty; she rejected the authority of the church; she accepted deification in her own lifetime; she admitted to sleeping in the same bed with another woman; and she boldly asserted her womanhood. Similarly Gilles de Rais was well known for his sorcery and suspect for sodomy.

Most "respectable" historians (usually straight males) have rejected Margaret Murray's views. But straight historians provide no context for understanding Joan, Gilles, or Gay history. Their writings mainly concern the straight-identified ruling classes and ignore the people. What we need instead is a people-oriented context for Gay history, especially in relation to heresy and witchcraft. In what follows, we will create such a context by exploring certain themes of sexuality and religion from prehistoric times, through the middle ages, and up to modern times. In this way, Joan of Arc, Gilles de Rais and other parts of our hidden history will no longer be unexplainable mysteries.

2 WHO WERE THE FAIRIES?

Human beings are animals. In the earliest ages, the sex life of humans resembled that of other animals. Today people are alienated from both their sexuality and their animal nature, but in the beginning this was not so.

Animals do not live in neat little nuclear families, as the mass media often claim. Instead, the mating instinct is separate from the sexual impulse, and the heterosexual bond is limited and weak (Briffault, I: 212ff). For "higher" animals such as mammals, heterosexual fucking usually occurs only when the female is in heat; otherwise, the two sexes often live separately — females and young in one group, and males in another. Some mammals even live in separate *herds* of male and female, such as reindeer, elk, antelope, buffalo, bats, elephants, seals, walruses, moose, boar, squirrels, as well as certain monkeys, orangutans, and gorillas (Briffault, I: 122-23). Usually females alone raise and protect the young. When rearing is done by pairs of both sexes, as among many birds, the pairing usually lasts for only one season. Pairings that last longer are rare (Briffault, I: 171). Monogamy and the nuclear family are almost unknown in nature.

The strongest emotional bond among mammals is that between mother and child, not between mother and father. The need for adult companionship is usually satisfied by members of the same, not the opposite, sex. Both female and male homosexual behavior is common in the animal world, especially among "higher" mammals (Ford and Beach, 139ff). Except when the female is in heat, physical distinctions between the sexes are deemphasized. Animals of one sex often take on the appearance and mannerisms of the other sex, and "the development in the male of instincts and psychical modifications of female origin is widespread in the animal kingdom" (Briffault, I: 137).

Among humans, early social forms resemble these animal practices, as can be seen in surviving stone and iron age societies. There, men and women associate more often socially with members of the same sex; sometimes the sexes live in separate common houses. For example, such separate housing arrangements have existed among the Moto, the Bassa Komo of Nigeria, the Hottentots, the Zulus and the Aranda of the Upper Congo. Among the Aranda, the sexes once even lived in separate villages (Briffault, I: 509-13). In many of these common houses, homosexuality is regularly practiced, and "in such cases the first homosexual intercourse is a rite of friendship" (Van Gennep, 171). Even when the custom of separate houses isn't found, the sexes in nature societies still tend to live their daily lives apart. "In all the North American Indian tribes there was scarcely any social intercourse between the men and the women; the sexes lived their lives separately" (Briffault, I: 510).

In the earliest forms of human society, marriage was much different from what it is today. When a man married a woman, he often married all her sisters as well, and she, all his brothers (Briffault, I: 629ff). "However rare collective sexual organizations may be at the present day, they are by no means so rare as might be supposed . . . . there is scarcely a portion of the habitable globe where those forms of sexual association or the evidence of their recent existence are not to be found" (Briffault, I: 765).

Women had a high status in the oldest societies. In cases where men and women *did* live together, the husband often left his people and went to live as a stranger in his wife's household (matrilocal marriage). Thus the wife was in a relatively secure position. "The practice of matrilocal marriage was the original form of marriage union, and is coeval with the origin of humanity" (Briffault, I: 307). Inheritance rights passed from the mother, not the father (matrilineal descent). Consequently, "in the great majority of uncultured [sic] societies women enjoy a position of independence and of equality with the men and exercise an influence which would appear startling in the most feministic modern civilized society" (Briffault, 1: 311). Sexist white observers have misunderstood the role of women's labor in early societies. For example, Native American women were viewed as oppressed because of their lives of hard work, which ran counter to European notions of feminity. But their right of access to essential labor was the very basis of their independence (Briffault, I: 317, 328).

Taboos and ceremonies around menstruation have also been misunderstood. These taboos are simply an extension from the animal world, where *all* species limit access to females when they are menstruating, giving birth, or nursing. Menstruating taboos were originally invented by *women* and were used as vetoes against male advances during these times. In fact, the most severe taboos are found in those societies where "the women exercise an almost despotic power over the men" (Briffault, II: 400, 404).

White male observers usually misinterpret the role of *males* in nature societies. While talking to leaders of the men's groups and ignoring the women, they reach the false conclusion that the society as a whole is organized by males. The chief, who is only the leader of hunters and warriors, is interpreted as being a king or president (Briffault, I: 492). But male activities like hunting and warfare are only a part of tribal life. The labor and activities of women are at least as important as that of men. True, among nature societies we find examples where women are treated harshly, even brutally. But where such brutality exists, as among certain tribes in Australia and Melanesia, there is evidence of a previous matrilocal system that has since broken down (Briffault, I: 334).

The first shamans (or healer priests) in nature societies were women (Briffault, II: 518). The first male shamans imitated women by taking on their roles and wearing their clothing. Wherever patriarchy has overthrown matriarchy, even in nature societies, the previous religious power of women is feared as something diabolical. The priestess is turned into the witch (Briffault, II: 561). Unfortunately, Robert Briffault, whose book I have been citing so far, freaks out over homosexuality, which he dismisses as "the indulgence of unnatural vices" (Briffault, II: 533). And so he can't imagine there could be a link between cross-dressing shamans and homosexuality. But we will see later there is such a link, and that as the priestess was turned into the witch, so the Gay male shaman was turned into the heretic.

In stone age Europe, humans probably lived pretty much like people in surviving nature cultures. For example, archaeology suggests that a shamanistic religion was practiced and that women had high status. From as early as 30,000 BC we find an abundance of female figurines and cave drawings that show women leading religious ceremonies (Rawson, 13ff). From about 5, 000 BC, the heads and necks on many of these figurines are stretched out to form smooth dildos, so that the composite figure is that of a fat female with a dildo emerging from the top (Rawson, 18). We know from the practices of existing nature societies in Africa and India that such implements were often used in ritual Lesbian acts where an older woman initiated a younger (Rawson, 18 & 71). In addition, the oldest deity worshipped by the Celts, Germans, and Anglo-Saxons of Western Europe was a Great Mother goddess who was associated with womb-like caves.

Many bisexual figurines have been found from the stone age — notably in Trasimeno, Italy; the Weinberg Caverns, Bavaria; the Jordan Valley; and Pembrokeshire, Wales (Rawson, 17). Among surviving nature societies, bisexual deities often indicate bisexual religious rites (Baumann, *passim*). Many cave paintings show pictures of nude men with erections dancing together in groups without women. Among nature people, a man's cum is often thought to embody ancestral religious power, "and this probably explains one male initiation ritual . . . during which adult male initiates have anal intercourse with novices" (Rawson, 48).

Animals (especially horned ones) also play a large part in stone-age art, and male human figures appear wearing animal skins. These figures are probably shamans, since nature societies often identify themselves collectively with the animals they eat (totemism) and imitate their behavior, including their sex life, in religious rites.

At the end of the stone age and the beginning of the bronze age (around 4,000 BC), sacred places came to be marked by the presence of huge stones, called megaliths. They extended from Ireland, through Brittany, to Portugal, Italy, Malta, South Arabia, India, Malaya, Sumatra, Indonesia and the Pacific Islands (Rawson, 42). These sites were apparently sacred to the Great Mother and often marked burial spots for the dead (von Cles-Reden, 11). Some writers, pointing to surviving beliefs in re-incarnation, think the megalithic tombs were viewed as "magical reservoirs" of souls waiting to be reborn (Rawson, 43). They could be right, since the tombs certainly were thought to have great fertility powers. In historical times, women believed they could get pregnant by visiting them at night. In some medieval witchcraft trials, there were persistent reports that sabbats were being held at a few of these spots (Grinsell, 77, note 18).

Into this world of matriarchal Europe, there eventually moved a new people, the Celts. They spread across Europe, coming from the east, and set up a civilization that extended from Turkey in the West, through Central Europe and even into the British Isles. The Celts came in waves, beginning around 1500 BC. Conquering local tribes, their society became increasingly militaristic and patriarchal (Hatt, 63-84). By 500 BC, a national Celtic culture emerged, fused from the cultures of both the conquerors and the conquered. As such, it stood midway between the two worlds of matriarchy and patriarchy (Markale, 16-17).

One legacy of the older ways was the continued high status of Celtic women. They were independent and chose their sexual partners freely (Hope, *passim*). Both marriage and divorce were by mutual agreement, and a wife maintained her own property apart from her husband's family (Markale, 32-35). Many types of marriage existed, including marriage for a specific length of time; marriage between one wife and one husband; between one husband and many wives; and between one wife and many husbands. If a woman had greater wealth, she and not her husband was considered head of the family (Markale, 36-7). This sexual openness continued well into Christian times. Around 395 AD, the Christian propagandist Jerome complained that "the Irish race do not have individual wives and . . . none among them has a spouse exclusively his own, but they sport and wanton after the manner of cattle, each as it seems good to them" (Hope, 295).

Women played an important role in Celtic myths, as shown by the *Tain Bo Cuailnge* — a pre-Christian Irish epic finally put into writing in the eighth century.

Thomas Kinsella, a translator of the *Tain*, writes, "probably the greatest achievement of the Tain and the Ulster cycle is the series of women . . . on whose strong and diverse personalities the action continually turns: Mebd, Derdriu, Macha, Nes, Aife" (Kinsella, xiv-xv). The *Tain* depicts the arts of war as the special province of women. Men learning to fight went to school under women, who were at the same time sorcerers (Markale, 38). The medieval saga *Kulhwch and Olwen*, drawn from Celtic traditions, describes a group of women called *gwiddonot* who fight in battle and utter prophecies. "They are amazons who live in a settled house called *Llys of Gwiddonot*" (Chadwick, *The Celts*, 136). Some sources suggest these women were Lesbians (Markale, 39).

Celtic men were notorious for their homosexuality. In the first century BC, the historian Diodorus Siculus said about Celtic men:

> Although they have good-looking women, they pay very little attention to them, but are really crazy about having sex with men. They are accustomed to sleep on the ground on animal skins and roll around with male bed-mates on both sides. Heedless of their own dignity, they abandon without a qualm the bloom of their bodies to others. And the most incredible thing is that they don't think this is shameful. But when they proposition someone, they

consider it dishonorable if he doesn't accept the offer! (Diordorus, III: 5, 32, 7).

Celtic religion, like Celtic social life, also reflected earlier matriarchal traditions. The most ancient Celtic deities were three goddesses whom the Romans called Matres or *Matronae* — 'The Mothers." They were versions of the Great Mother, who was worshipped as early as the stone age (Chadwick, *The Celts*, 168, and Rawson, 45). Altars to the Mothers have been found all over Europe. Stories about them persisted into medieval times fn the King Arthur legends, where the goddess Morrigan (the Great Queen in Ireland) became the figure of Morgan Ia Faye (Morgan the Fairy). Finally, the Mothers were turned into fairies, as indicated by the Welsh word for fairies, *y Mamau*, which means "the Mothers" (Hope, 32).

The newer forces of Celtic patriarchy and militarism brought new gods who challenged the ancient matriarchal traditions, but even after these changes, the Mothers retained their importance among Celtic peasants and women. They were the overseers of nature: goddesses of earth, moon, plants, animals and sex. Their worship included ritual sexual promiscuity, even with animals, and their chief priests were women (Rawson, 44; Hope, 166-167). The two types of deities continued to exist side by side. The Celtic upper classes converted to patriarchal gods, while the lower classes maintained the old religion (Hope, 43).

One manifestation of the Celtic Mother was the bear goddess Artio who was widely worshipped. "The name *Art*, 'Bear', occurring in names such as *Artgenos*, 'Son of the Bear', occurs widely in Welsh and Irish personal names and in toponymy" (Ross, *Britain*, 349). The name persisted into Christian times. Lady Alice Kyteler of Kilkenny, Ireland, was accused in 1324 of having ritual sexual intercourse with a "demon" named Robin, son of Art. Hers was the first trial for heresy and witchcraft in Ireland.

The Mother Goddess made her influence felt even within traditional Christianity. Some of the earliest churches in Ireland, Britain and German Switzerland have nude figures of a woman carved above the front door. She squats, looking down on the incoming worshipper with an intense stare, and has both hands on the lips of her cunt, which is greatly enlarged. These figures are known as sheelagh-na-gigs, and "they are, in fact, portrayals of the ancient goddess" who was "long-remembered in the traditions and festivals of the people" (Ross, *Celtic and Northern Art*, 104). In France most of the great sanctuaries of the Virgin Mary are located on sites that previously were consecrated to a Celtic Mother goddess (Markale, 17).

One Celtic male deity is as old as the Mothers. This is the horned god, "one of the most basic of the Celtic god types, "whose worship goes back to the stone age (Ross, Celtic and Northern Art, 83; Bober, 40). He is often associated with the Mothers, as well as sex, animals and nature. He also seems to have links with male shamans. His great antiquity is shown by a stone age painting in Ariege, France, which shows a man dancing in the hide of an animal and wearing the antlers of a stag. And in the eighteenth century, construction workers inside Notre Dame Cathedral in Paris uncovered a four-sided Celtic stone altar dating from Roman times and bearing the figure of a bearded male deity with antlers. The stone was inscribed with the word *Cernunnos*, which means "The Horned One" (Bober, 28ff).

The horned god was especially linked with male sexuality and often appears with an erect cock. Moreover, when erect, he is sometimes portrayed in the company of men, not women. A drawing of the horned god from Val Camonica, Italy, shows him holding a ceremonial collar ring in one hand and a horned serpent in the other. He is being worshipped by a man, and the man has an erection (Bober, 18; Ross, *Celtic and Northern Art*, 84). This picture is reminiscent of early art scattered throughout Europe. The men often have erections and appear together in groups without women (Ross, *Celtic and Northern Art*, 81). In view of the Celts' notoriety for homosexuality, these facts suggest a Gay element in the worship of the horned god.

The horned god was also lord of the dead and the underworld (Bober, 44). To the Celts, who believed in reincarnation, darkness and death were parts of the cycle of life and rebirth, and death was the very place where the creative forces of nature brought about new life. Because of this connection with the underworld the horned god was often shown as black in color (Ross, *Britain*, 137). But this blackness was not considered evil, as Christians later viewed it.

The depiction of the Celtic male god as an animal with horns is understandable in view of the economy and religion of the times. Stone age Europe was dependent for its very existence upon the hunting of reindeer, red deer, and elk. Among the first animals to be domesticated were sheep and goats. Ancient Europeans, like all nature people, worshipped the animals they depended on, in contrast to modern "civilized" people who objectify and destroy animals with all the impersonal violence that only scientific industrialism can devise.

The Celts dated the feast days of their religion according to the changing of the seasons, the breeding habits of animals, and the sowing and harvesting of crops. As in Judaism, feasts began on the night before the holiday. The four greatest Celtic holidays (with their Irish names) were *Samhain* (November 1); *Imbolc* (February 1); *Beltaine* (May 1); and *Lugnasadh* (August 1) (Chadwick, *The Celts*, 181). These holidays were celebrated with ritual sexual promiscuity (Hope, 166-167).

As it happens, these dates correspond exactly with the holidays later attributed by medieval Christians to witches. The Christians called these days, respectively, Halloween, Candlemas, Walpurgisnacht, and Lammas. Two other holidays were also celebrated by both Celts and witches: the winter solstice, December 21, surviving as the Feast of the Fools; and the summer solstice, June 23, surviving as Midsummer Night. Shakespeare's *A Midsummer Night's Dream*, written in the late sixteenth century, has echoes of this holiday. The play is full of magic, fairies, human and animal sexuality. It features a leading character named Puck, or Robin Goodfellow — a descendant of the horned god (Kott, 213-236).

After the Roman conquest of the Celts in the first century BC, the Celtic druids urged their tribes to resist Roman imperialism. They organized rebellions and prophesied that Roman power would be overthrown. "We may probably regard the druids as the most formidable nationalist and anti-Roman force with which Romans had to contend" (Chadwick, *The Druids*, 72). The Romans responded by conducting a campaign of propaganda against the druids and the Celts, attempting to portray them as bloody barbarians (Chadwick, *The Druids*, 25). In churning out this propaganda, the Romans were like the early American colonists who painted the native Indians as "savages" so they could feel justified in murdering them and stealing their land. Unfortunately, some modern scholars have been taken in by these anti-Celtic tirades.

The Celts of Europe were not the only people who carried on matriarchal religious traditions. In Asia Minor we find "the Great Mother of the Gods," who was associated with animals, sex and nature (Showerman, 230ff). Her priests were both women and men. The men castrated themselves, grew long hair, and wore the clothing of women (Showerman, 236-237). They were called "teachers of orgies," "sorcerers," and "cave dwellers" (Showerman, 236 & n. 55). Male followers of the religion were later called "effeminate" by Greek writers (Showerman, 294-295).

The Great Mother of the Gods was worshipped with sacred orgies. Participants of the rituals played flutes, castanets, cymbals, and drums, calling these the "strings of frenzy" (Showerman, 238). Homosexual and heterosexual acts of all kinds took place at these rituals. As one academic (a tightassed homophobe) puts it, there were "revolting sensual rites, the presence of the hermaphroditic element" (Showerman, 247). A man who wanted to become a priest of the Great Mother attended the orgies, and in an ecstatic and frenzied trance, castrated himself (Showerman, 238-239). This castration was entirely voluntary, and was undertaken only by those who wished to be initiated as priests.

After the Roman conquest, the cult of the Great Mother of the Gods spread across Europe. In every location, the conquered people saw in the Great Mother the same deity their ancestors worshipped. She was most popular among the lower classes, who retained much of the ancient matriarchal traditions. The Roman upper classes distrusted her. They especially disliked the fact that she was popular among women and slaves (Showerman, 295 & 300).

Among the Romanized Celts of Western Europe, the worship of the Great Mother spread under the Latin name of Diana (the Greek Artemis) (Turcan, 48ff). The Celtic preference for the Roman Diana is easy to understand, considering the history of her worship. The official deities of Greece and Rome (the Olympians) were really latecomers. They overthrew an older set of three Greek goddesses connected with the moon. Like the Celtic mothers, the goddesses presided over agriculture, hunting and domestic arts, and were worshipped with sexual orgies (Graves, passim). By late Roman times, they were absorbed into the figure of Diana, who was originally goddess of the new moon (Graves, 1: 83, n. 1). In an alternate form, they also survived as the three Fates. Again like the Celtic Mothers, they were turned into fairies by the medieval Christian world ("fairy" coming from the Latin *fata*, meaning fate).

The Greek Fates and the C:eltic Mothers also find their counterparts among the ancient Anglo-Saxons. The oldest Anglo-Saxon deity is the goddess Wyrd (Fate), who was one of three sisters (Branston, 64-65). They later became known as "the weird sisters" ("weird" originally meant fateful). This tradition survived at least until 1605, when they were mentioned in Shakespeare's *Macbeth* (Branston, 66). According to Christian tradition they were associated with witchcraft, and Shakespeare portrayed them as androgynous, as witnessed by Banquo's remark, "You should be women, yet your beards forbid me to interpret that you are so." Belief in these three goddesses was almost universal in ancient Europe. "It is evident that the conception of the three Fates goes back to Indo-European times and that the ancestresses of Wyrd, the Norns [Iceland], the Parcae [Italy], and the Moirai [Greece], were three all powerful figures of at least six thousand years ago" (Branston, 70).

Throughout the entire Mediterranean area, the oldest religious tradition in many cultures was the worship of a great goddess, often associated with sexual rites. She had many different names: Ashtoreth or Astarte in Palestine; Tanit in Carthage; Ma in Cappodocia; Aphrodite in Cyprus; and Isis in Egypt (Showerman, 247; Lethbridge, 19). Roman writers were well aware of this Mediterranean tradition. For example, in Apuleius' *The Golden Ass* (2nd century AD), the hero Lucius prays to the moon, calling her *Regina Caeli*, "Queen of Heaven," a title later given to the Virgin Mary. When Lucius falls asleep the goddess appears to him and reveals her true power:

> Look, I have come, Lucius, moved by your prayer. I am the mother of the nature of things, the mistress of all the elements, the original progeny of the ages, the supreme divinity, queen of the departed souls, chief of the deities of heaven, the manifestation in one of all the gods and goddesses. By my commands, I regulate the bright vault of heaven, the health-giving sea breezes, the bereaved silence of the dead. The whole world venerates my single name in many forms, with varied ritual, with a name linked to many others. And so the Phrygians — the first born of all humans — call me Mother of the Gods at Pessinus; native Athenians call me Cecropean Minerva; the sea-tossed Cyprians, Paphian Venus; the Cretan archers, Diana Oictynna; the tri-lingual Sicilians, Stygian Proserpine; the Eleusinians, the most ancient goddess Ceres. Some call me Juno, others Bellona. Here I am Hecate, there Rhamnusia. And both Ethiopias, which are illuminated by the beginning rays of the rising sun god, as well as the Egyptians, who are strong in the teaching of antiquity and who revere me with special ceremonies, call me by my true name — Queen Isis" (Apuleius, Book XI, Section 4).

In both Asia Minor and Celtic Gaul many statues of Artemis (or Diana) have been found with a singular feature: they show a woman with many rows of naked tits and surrounded by animal figures (Turcan, 49). In some stone-age caves, groups of stalagmites can be found, such as at Pech Merle, that are painted like tits with pictures of animals around them. The statues of Artemis are similar to these strange figures and "must embody echoes of that same ancient Mother of the Animals whom we can first identify in Pech Merle" (Rawson, 15).

During the early days of Christianity, Artemis was worshipped in the city of Ephesus in Asia Minor. Her cult was one of the chief impediments to the missionary effort there of Paul of Tarsus. The new testament book of Acts describes the severity of the struggle between the two religions. The pagan worshippers of Artemis rioted against Paul, shouting "she whom Asia and all the world revere may soon be stripped of her magnificence" (Acts; 19, 23-29).

The people of Asia Minor worshipped Artemis with sexual rites that included homosexuality. For this reason most of Paul's denunciations of a high status for women, free sexuality, and homosexuality — when read closely— turn out to be denunciations of *idolatry*. In *Romans*, Paul writes:

> They claimed to be wise but turned into fools instead; they exchanged the glory of the immortal God for images representing mortal man, birds, beasts, and snakes. *In consequence, God delivered them in their lust to unclean practices*: they engaged in the mutual degradation of their bodies, these men who exchanged the truth of God for a lie and worshipped the creature rather than the creator. Their women exchanged natural intercourse for unnatural, and the men gave up natural intercourse with women and burned with lust for one another (*Romans* l; italics added).

In other words they were practicing the old sex and nature religion. As Christianity rose to power in the Roman Empire, the worship of the Great Mother was one of the most powerful forces to resist it. Christian propagandists bitterly attacked this old religion and singled out for abuse its effeminate priests. Augustine condemns

> effeminates consecrated to the Great Mother, who violate every canon of decency in men and women. There were to be seen until just the other day in the streets and squares of Carthage with their pomaded hair and powdered faces, gliding along with womanish languor, and demanding from shopkeepers the means of their depraved existence (Augustine, 286).

Once Christianity was made the official religion of the Roman Empire, Mother worship was outlawed. 'The prominent part the Mother played in the last struggle [against Christianity] probably made her sanctuary one of the first pagan edifices to fall before the fanaticism or rapacity of the Christian party as soon as all restraint was removed" (Showerman, 312). Attacked, with its temples looted and destroyed, Mother worship went underground, but did not die.

Many ancient cultures worshipped horned gods, in addition to a mother goddess. Behind all these gods was a common ancestor that went back to the stone age. In pre-Christian times he appeared under many different names. In the Greco-Roman world he was Dionysus, Bacchus, or Pan; in Crete, the Minotaur; at Carthage, Baal Hammon; in Asia Minor, Sabazios; and in Egypt, Osiris. He usually had the horns of a goat or a bull and was worshipped with rites that included sexual orgies, animal masquerades, and transvestism. As with Pan, the lover of Diana, he was often linked with a goddess who was mistress of wild animals, the forest, agriculture, and sexuality.

Among the ancient Greeks, as with the Celts, the horned god was associated with homosexuality. One ancient bowl shows Pan, with cock erect, chasing a young male shepherd, which the German scholar Reingard Herbig describes this way:

> The god pursues at quick pace and with utmost excitement a beautiful shepherd boy. The meaning of the picture is unmistakeably underlined by the addition of an accessory that should be symbolically understood, a Priapus herm [a phallic image]. Here Pan is really everything that fits his original essence: masculine drive seeking release, which here, following the early Greek preference, devotes itself to 'the beautiful boy' (Herbig, 37).

As ancient Greece became "civilized" and fell under the influence of patriarchal institutions, the worship of Pan was denounced and repressed. The new order couldn't handle the religion's open sexuality, transvestism, feminism and emotionalism. The struggle between the rising Greek patriarchy and the old traditions underlies Euripides' play *Bacchae*. The plot revolves around a revival of the worship of Dionysus (same as Pan) and the attempt to suppress the religion by King Pentheus of Thebes, who is an urban law-and-order type, the ancient Greek equivalent of Richard Nixon. Dionysus himself appears in the play as an effeminate young man. King Pentheus arrests him, not knowing who he is, and cuts off all his long hair. In retaliation, Dionysus drives Pentheus mad, for Dionysus is lord of the emotions. Pentheus in his madness dresses up as a woman and attempts to spy on one of the orgies of Dionysus' religion. When the King gets to the orgy, the women worshippers (including the King's own mother) are driven into a frenzy by the rites. Mistaking Pentheus for a lion, they attack him and tear him to pieces. His mother returns to Thebes with the head of this lion in her apron, only to discover on becoming sober that she has torn off the head of her own son. The moral of the play is clear: the new order is repressing aspects of human behavior that are sacred to the god of ecstasy. The price of this repression will be a madness that tears the new order itself apart.

Historically the worship of the horned god was responsible for the rise of theater in Western civilization. (So there has always been a connection between theater and Gay men.) In ancient Greece, Dionysus was first worshipped in a ritual of masquerading, song, dance, and sex by a group of people called the chorus. In time, a few persons emerged from the chorus who played special roles and were called actors. Eventually the religious and sexual aspects of the ritual were forgotten and the ceremony became a play, enacting out a previously written script. It's no accident that the word "tragedy" comes from the ancient Greek *tragoidia*, meaning "goat song."

After the Roman conquest, various concepts of the horned god blended together, just as they did in the case of the Great Mother. We find him appearing under the names of Priapus, Attis, Adonis, Dis Pater and Tammuz. But the relationship of the horned god to the Mother changed as the patriarchs gained more control throughout the world. At first he was born from the Mother and subordinate to her, but finally he became the world's sole creator (Campbell, 86).

The triumph of Christianity brought bad news for the horned god. Since he kept company with the Great Mother and her sex rites, the church made every effort either to suppress or change him to suit its own needs. He became identified with the Christian ruler of the underworld — Satan — and was viewed as evil, even though the Celtic god of the dead was not considered evil. In the Jewish religion, Satan had been an adversary only to humans, never to God himself. The new testament went beyond this view, but the personality of the devil was still fuzzy. In 447 AD, the Council of Toledo settled this question once and for all by picturing the devil as cosmic evil personified (Robbins, 132).

With the doctrine of the devil established, the church took many of the "bad" traits of the horned god (such as sexuality) and gave them to the devil (Schoff, *passim*). The old horned god was turned into the devil himself, and from that time forward, Christian art depicted the devil as having horns, cleft hooves, furry legs, and an erect cock — the very characteristics of the horned god (Ross, *Britain*, 132). Soon the old teutonic fertility spirits were likewise changed into subordinate "devils" (Russell, 46). To medieval witchhunters the figure of the devil became sex personified. The Malleus Maleficarum, a manual used for detecting witches, stated, "the power of the Devil lies in the privy parts of men" (*Malleus*, 26).

The "good" aspects of the horned god were taken and applied to figures in Christianity. For example, in the book of *Revelations* we find Christ pictured symbolically as a horned animal and called "the Lamb" (V:6ff).

The doctrine of the devil also affected Christian attitudes toward the color black. As the Celtic lord of the underworld, the horned god was pictured as black. This was not an evil color since the Celtic underworld was a place of rest before reincarnation, whereas the Christian underworld was a place of hell and damnation. As a result, black to the Christians became an evil color, connoting sin, death, and the Devil. Later, when Christians from Europe encountered people whose skin was black, the Christians viewed them as sinful and devilish. This attitude was not the only cause of Christian racism, as we'll see, but it was one factor.

In the British isles, an ancient name in folklore for the horned god was Robin or Robin Goodfellow. In one 17th century picture, Robin is shown surrounded by a ring of dancers. He has hooves, a goat's horns, and an erect cock. In one hand he carries a candle; in the other a ritual broom (Murry, *God of the Witches*, 97). Robin also figured in witch trials as well as folklore. We've already seen that Lady Alice Kyteler was accused of having sex with a black demon named Robin, son of Art.

Matriarchal traditions persisted through Celtic, Roman, and early Christian civilizations, even though they were suppressed more vigorously in each succeeding epoch. The Roman period saw a fusion of the Great Mother with Diana, the Fates, and the Celtic Mothers, just as there was a blending of Pan, Robin, Dionysus, Adonis, and the Celtic horned god. When the Christians took over, a part of the Great Mother, although greatly desexualized, squeezed through as the Virgin Mary, while the horned god was banned as the devil. Though outlawed, the worshippers of this matriarchal mix — which Margaret Murray calls the old religion — persisted underground and were known in folklore as fairies, named after the fateful goddesses whom they worshipped. Later in the medieval period, various remnants of the old religion were to emerge again, only this time they were called heretics and witches. As we'll see, their greatest "crime" was that they experienced the highest manifestations of the divine in the free practice of sexuality.

3 Homosexuality and Class Warfare

The mass media have long given us an impression of the Stone Age as a time of terror, violence and war. Stone Age people are often depicted as ape-like creatures who went around clubbing each other over the head. Their societies are usually described with pejorative words like "primitive," "barbaric," "savage," and "low" (in contrast to modern industrial society, which is called "advanced," "civilized," "cultured," and "high").

Despite this Hollywood view of history, Stone Age culture was actually rather peaceful. The testimony of archeology is overwhelming on this point: the people who lived in the Stone Age did *not* practice organized warfare (Hawkes, 265). Paintings and art work from the period do not depict warlike activities, weapons are not found in burial areas, settlements are completely unfortified. It may be surprising but is nonetheless true that "war is a comparatively late development in the history of humanity" (Dawson, 239).

Organized warfare did not arise until the appearance of cities, class conflict, government hierarchy, and private property. Indeed, it is precisely those societies in history that have been the most "civilized" that have waged the most frequent and terrible wars. No Stone Age society even approaches the savagery of Nazi Germany against Jewry or "democratic" America against the Vietnamese.

What we know about the people who still live in close contact with nature confirms our knowledge of the peacefulness of the Stone Age. For example, organized warfare was extremely rare among the native North Americans prior to the Christian invasion (Driver, 355). Admittedly, the North American Indians did engage in duels and feuds. But until the white Christians "instructed" them in warfare, they did not develop a permanent military organization, special fighting regalia, or militaristic ceremonies. (The situation was different with middle and south American Indians who were partially *urbanized*.)

People have mistakenly associated nature societies with war because so-called barbarians have come in conflict with urbanized and stratified societies as in the "Gothic invasions" of the Roman Empire. But the "barbarians" were usually tribes who lived on the periphery of urbanized societies and who imitated their methods. In the case of Rome, outlying "barbarians" had long been admitted into the Roman army before the tribes they came from attacked Rome. Roman militarism had been seeping into their cultures for centuries.

The Stone Age was striking for other reasons besides its peacefulness. As best we can determine from archaeological evidence and from comparison with existing Stone Age cultures, there was communal ownership of property by the tribe or the clan, government by voluntary consensus without any hierarchical superstructure, an absence of class domination and no rigid division of labor (Hawkes, 265 ff.). Of course, it is tempting to dismiss this as a utopian fantasy since we are so accustomed in our own society to self-aggrandizement, government repression, class domination and rigid soul-killing division of labor that is either idiotic or based on years of zombie-like institutionalization ("education"). We have become so conditioned through universities, factories and offices to be feelingless, brain-dominated, self-seeking billiard balls that we cannot conceive of a society run otherwise. But the evidence will not go away. Human beings once lived differently.

Women had a very high status in the Stone Age, as we have seen. Archeology, myth and comparison to still-existing nature societies all point to their dominant position. "There is every reason to suppose that under the conditions of the primary Neolithic way of life, mother-right and the clan system were still dominant [as they had been in the Paleolithic period], and land would generally have descended through the female line. Indeed, it is tempting to be convinced that the earliest Neolithic societies throughout their range in time and space gave woman the highest status she has ever known" (Hawkes, 264).

Around 4000 B.C. an extraordinary change took place, beginning first in the Near East and spreading gradually from there into Europe. At this time there emerged a new era — the Bronze Age, which involved much more than the making of bronze implements. For the first time in history, social groups came into existence that were controlled by males and were based on military exploits. In the Stone Age, humans had survived by foraging, farming and hunting. Now came people who survived by warfare. The political and economic life of the human race was completely upset by these male invaders (Woolley, *passim*). In place of the earlier tribal communalism, a new institution came into being: the state (Woolley, 360).

The new states lived off the labor of agrarian people and economically exploited them. Class divisions developed, and slavery was imposed where formerly there had been free labor. People became separated from the immediate, direct life of nature, and intellectual activity was stressed at the expense of emotional gratification. Most important of all, the status of women fell, as did the great importance of the mother goddess. "Urban life, the strengthening of intellectual powers and of individuality and selfconsciousness, male rulers and priests, military conquests, were to combine to lower the status of the goddess in all her manifestations in the centers of ancient civilization" (Hawkes, 343).

Many scholars believe these male-dominated warrior groups evolved from Stone Age hunters (usually male). By some process, the male hunters in certain of the earlier societies developed into a separate caste devoted not to hunting but to warfare. The change, once made, became self-perpetuating: peaceful Stone Age tribes were either conquered by the new militarists or were forced to become militaristic to defend themselves.

In the new social order, private property made its first appearance in history (possibly as the seized booty of warfare; Engels, *passim*). Strict hierarchies, always characteristic of military societies, emerged, as did a new sense of morality characterized by obedience and self-discipline. The beginnings of class warfare lie in this period, as the new order of warriors tended to constitute an urban-based aristocracy that held sway over the peasants.

The older Stone Age traditions that had existed time out of mind eventually reasserted themselves against the Bronze Age innovations. The new military class was too small, and the old peasant culture too large and old, to allow for the annihilation of Stone Age ways. The conquerors tended to be absorbed into the customs of the conquered. An equilibrium was eventually reached, and societies stabilized into new forms that embodied practices and beliefs of both the older Stone Age and the new Bronze Age. Such, for example, were the ancient civilization of Sumer and the oldest kingdoms in Egypt. There, even though organized warfare had now come into being, "it was exceptional and of a rudimentary type" (Dawson, 238). Although the status of women was lower than in the Stone Age, women still maintained a position far higher than they do under the primitive conditions of modern industrialism (Davis, *passim*).

Bronze Age civilization still retained much of the old love of sexuality, especially in religion. Archeological evidence is abundant on this point, both from the new cities and from the countryside. For example: "In searching for some positive features of Bronze Age religion our attention is caught by the strange phallic figures in the rock-carvings of Northern Europe. Whatever the meaning of these figures may be, they unquestionably show that sexuality played a great part in that cult and belief of which they are expressions" (Runeberg, 247). In literary evidence from Bronze Age Egypt, homosexual behavior is idealized as an activity of the gods (Licht, 449). Nearly everywhere the worship of the Great Mother and the horned god continued right along side that of the new militaristic dieties.

One very important example of Bronze Age civilization is the culture that emerged in Crete. From 3000 B.C. to 2000 B.C. waves of immigrants from Asia Minor mingled with the local Stone Age people of Crete and created a new civilization called Minoan, named after the legendary King Minos.

Minoan civilization reached its peak in the period from 2000 B.C. to 1600 B.C. During this time, women had a very high status. They are depicted in Minoan art work as participating equally with men in feasting and athletic contests. In addition, Minoan society was peaceful. Scenes of war are rare. "The emphasis is on nature and on beauty" (Hammond, 30). The two chief deities of the Minoan religion were a great mother goddess associated with animals (such as the snake) and the horned god (in the form of a bull). Later Greek tradition particularly associated Crete with public homosexuality, and several ancient authors claimed that it was the historical source of homosexuality in Greece (Symonds, 4).

Olive tree and crescent sacred to the Moon Goddess (Minoan gem)

On the Greek mainland itself, the local culture originally showed the same peaceful characteristics. "It was peaceful, agricultural, seafaring, and artistic, and its religious beliefs, if we may judge from the steatopygous [fat-assed] female figurines, were focused on a mother goddess and may have been associated with a matriarchal society or at least with one which was not strongly patriarchal" (Hammond, 37).

An analysis of early Greek literature shows that the society of the mainland was matrilineal, not patrilineal, and that the characteristic religion was one of shamanism (Butterworth). As we have seen, shamanism is frequently associated with ritual homosexuality, both male and female. There is also evidence of transvestism in the rituals of early Greece as well as the sexual worship of earth deities (Butterworth, 145ff.).

All this was changed at the end of the Bronze Age. There were great upheavals in Crete and Greece. About 2500 B.C. and thereafter, maledominated militaristic tribes started entering parts of the mainland. They worshipped male sky gods, the Olympians, and were organized socially into a partriarchy (Hammond, 39). These new invaders spoke Greek, a language that was previously unknown in the area.

The invading patriarchal Greeks disrupted life in both Crete and Greece. They established a capital at Mycenae in Greece (from which they were called Mycenaeans) and at Cnossus on Crete. They developed bureaucratic institutions, plunged the entire Aegean Sea area into warfare, and violently opened up new markets for their trading interests (Hammond, 42ff.). By the end of the 15th century B.C., all the leading settlements of Crete had been burned (possibly accompanied by a volcanic eruption).

During this period, the status of women declined. Succession to religious rites, political power, and property became patrilineal, not matrilineal. In religion, the status of the Great Mother fell, and the power of Zeus and Ares (the god of war) increased. 'The matrilineal world was brought to an end by a number of murderous assaults upon the heart of that world, the *potnia meter* [Revered Mother] herself. The opposition to the *potnia meter* seems to have been closely connected with the cult of Ares" (Butterworth, 51). Ares was the only Greek god who was not famous for his homosexual love affairs (Symonds, 10).

After 1400 B.C., patriarchal Greek culture was widely established throughout the Aegean. In the late 13th century B.C., a great convulsion of war rocked the Greek settlements around the Aegean, including but not limited to the famous Trojan War. The ruling patriarchal states destroyed each other, and migrations of new peoples moved into Greece.

In the 12th Century B.C., during all this turmoil, a new tribe of Greekspeaking people moved into Greece, dispossessing the previous warlords of their power. These people — the Dorians — are of special interest because of their attitude toward women and homosexuality.

The early Dorians, whose capital was established at Sparta, are often negatively depicted as boorish and militaristic, in contrast to their rivals, the Athenians, who are usually praised. This depiction is at odds with the facts and has been largely inspired, I believe, by academics' dislike of the Dorians' love for Gay sex.

It is true that the early Dorians were militaristic, but they were actually *less* militaristic than the previous Mycenaeans. For example, the Dorians were not dominated by a miltaristic aristocracy, and they had no government bureaucracy devoted especially to war, as did the Mycenaeans. 'The Dorians, whose tribal organization did not preclude the arming of all their people, attacked and overthrew the Achaeans [another name for Mycenaeans], who were only a small, armed, ruling class ruling over the Greek agricultural population, which was largely unarmed" (Wason, 30).

The Dorians maintained many of the most ancient traditions of the earlier ages, especially with respect to women. For example, unlike the situation in the previous patriarchy, "there is ample evidence to show that the status of women among the early Dorians was one of freedom and honour — a survival, perhaps, of a matriarchal period" (Carpenter, *Intermediate Types*, 107). Among the Dorians, women ran and wrestled naked in public with men. They had fuller power over property than anywhere else in Greece. They had the power to publicly praise or censor men, who greatly feared their criticism (Carpenter, 106ff.).

Among other Greeks who had lost the earlier traditions, women were not allowed to dine with their husbands. The could not call their husbands by name, but only "lord." They lived secluded in the interior of the house (Mueller, 297).

Homosexuality had a high status among the Dorians. In fact, it was more highly regarded there than it was at Athens during the later classical period. Male homosexuality at Sparta took the form of *paiderestia* — the love of an older more experienced man for a younger inexperienced man. *Paiderestia* was a form of religious, military, educational and sexual training. The experienced man initiated the inexperienced man into men's mysteries. It was through the institution of *paiderestia* that the Dorians transmitted their cultural values. It made learning into an intimate personal, emotional and sexual experience. The more experienced man was called eispnelas, which means "inspirer," and the inexperienced man was called aitas, which means "hearer" or "listener" (Mueller, 300-301). In Crete, where the same cutoms prevailed, the corresponding terms were *philetor* ("lover") and *kleinos* ("renowned one") (Mueller, 302).

Paiderestia had a religious origin, as we discover in a remarkable study by the German scholar E . Bethe. Bethe points out that cum was originally viewed as a sacred substance, conveying a man's soul-power (468). The "inspiring" that took place among Dorian men was the transference of cum, which was viewed as a holy and religious act (463).

Unfortunately, little is known about the Gay sex life of women at Sparta, due to the sexist prejudice of Western historians. It's very probable, however, that similar religious and sexual relations existed among women in view of their high status. Plutarch, writing in the first century A. D., said of the women of Sparta: "the unmarried women love beautiful and good women" (Lives, v.1, 18, 4). We know that even in the non- Doric island of Lesbos in the 6th century B.C., Sappho praised and practiced lesbianism and that she and her lovers worshipped Aphrodite, the great goddess in her capacity as the protector of love. When the Christians came to power in the early Middle Ages, they deliberately set about destroying most of Sappho's works.

From what has been said about the Dorians, we can see the falsehood of two lies often repeated by historians: 1) that male homosexuality is historically associated with contempt for women; and 2) that homosexuality was a late development in Greece. To the contrary, Doric *paiderestia* is a reflection of familiar shamanistic and religious concepts that date back to the Stone Age. The Dorians, though coming later than the Mycenaeans, remained much closer to the earlier sexual traditions. As for the contempt-for-women myth: "It completely founders on the fact that precisely in Sparta and Lesbos, where boy-love and girl-love are best known, the sexes, as best we can tell, associated more freely with each other than in the other Greek states" (Bethe, 440).

In the 12th century B. C., as we have seen, Mycenaean power collapsed, and Greece was thrown into chaos. Invading tribes had learned well the military methods of the Mycenaeans, which they now imitated (including, eventually, the Dorians as well). Militarism was again on the rise, and another revolution occurred in human affairs — the Iron Age. With the advent of the Iron Age, the power of male-dominated armies increased in politics, and powerful city-states with imperialistic ambitions came into existence.

After 1000 B.C., the city-state emerged as *the* typical political unit. Cities became economic centers, and a "new type of people" began making themselves felt in politics — traders, seafarers, artisans, and merchants (Wason, 52). An urban-based bourgeoisie developed and struggled for power with the older class of land-magnates and warlords. Monarchies tended to be replaced by republics, still in the form of city-states. The various city-states were constantly at war with each other, struggling to build up their own commercial and military empires. Slavery became widespread in Greece for the first time (Wason, 44).

The effect of this urbanism, militarism, and growing bourgeois ambition was predictable. "Civilization" (that is, *urban* culture) increasingly lost touch with the nature religion of the peasants, who formed, together with the urban slaves, the lowest level in the new economic order. The status of women fell because male-dominated activities like war, trade, and government service were now the crucial activities on which urban society depended for its survival. A negative turn developed in the attitude toward sexuality in general and homosexuality in particular. Sex was no longer part of the public religion of the urban upper classes.

The final outcome of this turn of events is well illustrated in Athens during the classical period (after 500 B.C.) During this period Athens was almost constantly at war: against the military empire of Persia, against Sparta, even against its former allies. During the same period, the status of homosexuality fell. It was no longer practiced as a means of public education or viewed as an expression of public religious sentiment. It had become a *private* affair, something done in the privacy of one's house between consenting adults.

In the late classical period, Greeks got out of touch with the religious origins of homosexuality. Educated writers reacted with surprise and contempt when they encountered it in more "primitive" societies, especially when male transvestism was involved. Herodotus describes such behavior among Scythian shamans as "a disease of effeminacy" (*theleia nosos* — quoted by Carpenter, 24). Classical Greek civilization became contemptuous of the effeminate man — which is not surprising in view of their contempt for women and the importance of war (hence masculinism) to their economy and politics.

This change in attitude toward homosexuality is strikingly evidenced by an event that occurred in 399 B.C. — the trial and condemnation of the philosopher

Socrates. Few straight academics have understood the real issues involved in Socrates' confrontation with the establishment of his day. They usually describe Socrates as an advocate of unpopular ideas who was executed by people who felt threatened by them. In part this is true. But there is much more: Socrates' Gayness and his religion. In the second half of the 5th century B.C., a reaction had developed against educational homosexuality. This reaction was led by the Sophists (Bethe, 439). The Sophists were independent professional academics who taught practical skills and knowledge for money and who believed in book learning. They viewed the relationship between teacher and pupil as a purely objective, mercenary one. They rejected the traditions of the old nature religion, where learning was through the oral tradition and where sexuality played an important part in the relationship between teacher and student.

Socrates hated the Sophists. He was horrified by the idea that teachers should make money out of conveying knowledge. He rejected book learning. He believed that the only way to learn was through personal *dialogue.* He believed that sex was an important part of the educational process (he had famous affairs with his pupils, like Alcibiades). Finally, he insisted that his vocation was a holy one and that he was personally inspired by some spirit or god (in Greek, *daimon* — usually used to denote nature spirits, and almost never applied to the Olympians). These characteristics of the Socratic method of learning are all typical of shamanism: the sexual relationship between teacher and pupil; the emphasis on learning through personal oral communication rather than through books; the aura of a divine being. Of course, Socrates was not a shaman in the same way that shamans existed in the Stone Age, but he was following that tradition in so far as it had managed to survive in urbanized, militarized Athens.

Socrates infuriated the Sophists. He attacked their economic prerogatives, their bookishness, and their repressive attitude toward sexuality. In the end, the Sophists won out. Socrates was condemned to death for corrupting the young men of Athens and for believing in gods that the state didn't believe in (Plato, *Apologia,* 24B). The new moralism of the Iron Age could no longer be resisted.

After the advent of the Iron Age, the entire Mediterranean area became a world of deep class divisions and ever-increasing urbanism. Small groups of warlords and their attendants settled in fortresses, which later became cities, and held sway over the masses of peasants. Economic growth depended on warfare. By the end of the fourth century B.C., most Greek city-states had become "military tyrannies ruling over an enslaved population and resting in the last resort on mercenary armies" (Rostovtzeff, 6).

Throughout the entire Mediterranean, rival states fought for supremacy. In the end, the city-state of Rome proved to be the most ruthless and violent of all and succeeded in conquering nearly all the rest.

The nature of the Roman state and Roman society has been greatly misunderstood, especially in regard to sex. Most people still think that the Romans did little else than sit around at banquet tables and devote themselves to orgies. This view, which is based on Christian propaganda, is a distortion. Roman society — when viewed in the context of the cultures before it— was actually hostile to sensual pleasure. Admittedly, in the eyes of the early Christians it seemed hedonistic. But we must never forget that the standard of judgment used by Christians was one of the most sexrepressive in the history of the world.

The dominant value system of Rome, both early in the republic and later in the empire, was one of self-discipline. The virtues praised in public and taught in school were the virtues of self-sacrifice to the state, obedience to hierarchical authority, and suspicion of pleasure and sex.v It was no accident that Rome had these values. Rome was a highly artificial state created and maintained through military violence. The foundation of the expanding Roman economy was quite simple: "The Romans enslaved the enemy and maintained their lands" (Levy, 62). War was the essence of the Roman economy. The property seized from the defeated tribes and nations became state property and was divided up among the most aggressive of the Roman warlords who became absentee landlords. The defeated peoples themselves were often shipped off to Rome where they formed an army of slave labor (Levy, 62). Roman warlords developed masculinist values because these values validated their warlike activities and supported the economy.

As might be expected, women and Gay men, especially effeminate Gay men, suffered under such a regime. In 186 B. C., the Senate banned the practice of the Bacchanalia, which was an ancient sex and nature ritual in honor of Bacchus, a variant of the horned god. The historian Livy has preserved a Consul's argument in favor of this ban, including his condemnation of the high status of women and Gay men in the Bacchanalia and its subverting influence on Roman militarism:

> A great number of adherents are women, which is the origin of the whole trouble. But there are also men like women, who have joined in each other's defilement ... Do you think, citizens, that young men who have taken this oath can be made soldiers? Are they to be trusted when they leave this obscene sanctuary?" (Partridge, 54).

There were extensive prosecutions under the ban, and about 7000 people are reported to have been arrested (Partridge, 55). The class nature of this oppression is evident when we realize that the ancient worship of Bacchus was most popular with the lower classes (Finley, 82).

The status of women fell under the militarized Roman patriarchy. Under original Roman law, a man's wife and children were considered his personal property to dispose of as he will, as if they were so many tables and chairs. This extreme situation was later tempered, however, but not because of anything Roman. It resulted from the influence of the more lenient customs of conquered peoples on Roman legislation itself (Bury, V. 2, 403).

Around 169 B. C., the Scantinia or Scatinia law was passed, which outlawed pederasty and made it punishable by death (Meier, 180). The emperor Augustus re-affirmed this condemnation and also made adultery a public crime. The anti-gay laws of Rome were primarily designed to control the behavior of the lower classes and were often ignored or flaunted by the members of the upper classes. Although homosexuality was tolerated in the upper classes, however, it had clearly lost the great social and religious significance it once had in earlier ages. It was now often associated with guilt, self-deprecation, and cruelty.

This decline in the status of homosexuality is illustrated in the case of the emperor Hadrian and his lover Antinous. When Antinous died in 120 A.D., Hadrian ordered statues erected to him throughout the Empire. Some historians compare this act to the repressive mentality of modern industrial society and see it as showing a high status for homosexuality at Rome. In reality, however, when the event is compared to *earlier* ages, we see that homosexuality had fallen in esteem. This falling off is well explained by one historian as follows:

> To Hadrianus the relationship with Antinous was a personal matter, respected by the society in which he lived in the same way as other serious emotional relations. But whatever ethical and esthetic component there was in the relationship was an individual and private matter between the two. Pederasty was no longer a means employed by the state in the education of the young, controlled by its highest authorities and an obligation for the best men to take upon themselves. It was not institutionalized any longer, had no place in the cult, and its symbols had ceased to be the generally recognized expressions of the noblest aims of the communal life of the society" (Vanggaard, 131).

The longer the Roman state existed, the more militarized it tended to become. "As the army in its new shape was the greatest organized force in Rome, its chiefs were bound not only to represent the military strength of the state but also to become its political leaders" (Rostovtzeff, 26). As early as 49 B. C., Julius Caesar, the militarist who defeated the Celtic tribes of Western Europe, seized power at Rome in a military coup d'etat. The republic became a military dictatorship. Even though Caesar was subsequently assassinated, the new form of government stuck.

It was during this period of the increasing militarization of the Roman state that Christianity first came into being — a fact of great significance for women and Gay men, as we'll shortly see.

The oppressive class structure of Rome was reflected in the relationship between city and country. Warlords, bureaucrats, manufacturers, academics, and other members of the upper classes took up residence in the cities, whose growth was deliberately fostered by imperial policy. In Western Europe, the emperor

Augustus tried to suppress the tribal system of the Celts in favor of urbanizing them (Rostovtzeff, 51). The new class of the urban bourgeoisie supported these efforts in return for being granted a "privileged position among the masses of the provincial rural population" (Rostovtzeff, 83). The result of these developments was that the oppressed classes of the empire were rural classes, either still on the land of absentee landlords or living dispossessed in cities.

These rural-based classes held on to the old religious and cultural values, which included elements dating back to the matriarchal period. They held on to their old languages and steadfastly resisted efforts to make them accept Greek and Roman culture. It was only the privileged classes in the cities that spoke the official languages of Latin and Greek; the rest of the population spoke Celtic, Iberian, Illyrian, Thracian, etc. (Rostovtzeff, 298). In reality, the Greek and Latin literature that modern academics hold up before us as the basis of Western civilization is the voice of a minority of oppressors.

The city-based oppressing classes looked down on the tribal, rural cultures as "half civilized or uncivilized" (Rostovtzeff, 180). They especially disapproved of their loose sexuality. The emperor Tiberi us had the image of the sex goddess Isis (a version of the great mother) pulled down and thrown into the Tiber (Partridge, 60). Increasingly, Roman poets and other molders of public opinion mentioned homosexuality in a context of scorn, ridicule, and satire (Gibbon, V. 2, 377).

Despite this cultural repression, the old traditions sometimes even penetrated into the upper classes. The most famous example is that of Elagabalus, a priest in a sex and nature cult, who became emperor of Rome in 218 A. D. As Emperor, he often appeared in public in drag, practiced ritual sex with members of both sexes, and publicly declared one of his male lovers to be his husband. The sentiments of the ruling classes were outraged. He was assassinated by an indignant Praetorian Guard in 222 A. D. His body was mutilated, dragged through the streets of Rome, and thrown in the Tiber River. "His memory was branded with eternal infamy by the senate" (Gibbon, V. 1, 129).

THE MASSACRE OF THE DRUIDS

The rise and triumph of the Roman patriarchy brought with it a profound change in human values. At first gradually, and then in a great rush just prior to the triumph of Christianity, a wave of grim asceticism swept across Greco-Roman civilization. "It pervaded philosophy and religion. Like a mighty tide it swept onward, especially from the first century B.C., from the East over the West, gathering momentum as it forced its way into every serious view of life. Every great teacher from Plato to John the Baptist, from Paul to Plotinus, axiomatically accepted asceticism as an essential of and qualification for religious life" (Angus, 216-217). In the new system of values, sex and the body were degraded. "Copulation in itself became a sin . . . Matter was looked upon as evil or as the seat of the evil principle; the whole business of life was to release the soul from the contact and pollution of matter, from the body, its bane" (Angus, 222).

The cause of this cultural phenomenon was the ever-increasing militarism of the Roman state. In the late Empire, the army became a separate caste consisting of huge numbers of soldiers with an elaborate bureaucratic organization. Together with the emperor, it was the largest single consumer of goods and services produced in the empire (Rostovtzeff, 149). All important political decisions came to be dictated, either directly or indirectly, by the needs of the army. Emperors were made and unmade at the behest of various factions of the army. The legendary last words of the emperor Severus to his sons sum up the whole scene: "Be united, enrich the soldiers, and scorn the rest" (Rostovtzeff, 354).

This utter militarization ot society encouraged asceticism. In the first place it gave rise to the "cult of discipline" — the idea of stern self-sacrifice on behalf of the state. Secondly, and more important, it resulted in a strangulation of local political life (Halliday, 41). Decisions were made at the top, and often with great violence. Ruinous civil wars were frequent, whenever the various factions of the army couldn't agree on an emperor. The economy was dangerously unstable, depending as it did on war needs. Government became increasingly rule-bound, top-heavy, bureaucratic, and out of touch with peoples' needs. All freedom of expression was squelched. A system of secret police was formed to spy on the population. People simply had no control over their lives. Daily life became dangerous, and the best the average person could hope for was to be left alone. Ascetic religion became an opiate for the pain, enabling people to stifle their real needs and feelings, and thus avoid the suffering of constant frustration. The government was well-disposed to ascetic religion because it kept the people quiet and obedient.

It was within this historical setting that Christianity entered the stage. From its very start, the Christian religion was one of the most ascetic religions of the empire. Jesus the Nazarene, believing that the world was about to end, called upon his followers to renounce all interest in worldly things and to prepare for the age to come. Paul of Tarsus based his entire theology on the concept of sin and saw sin in practically every form of human sensuality . The new religion fed on and re-enforced the sense of despair that was growing in the Roman state:

> In not a few respects Christianity was a new reflection of that pessimism which pervaded the ancient world in the centuries immediately before and immediately after the beginning of the Christian era. It adopted, but transformed in so adopting them, many of the characteristic sentiments of Greek and Roman philosophic pessimism ... by cultivating certain practices like asceticism, mortification, and celibacy (Thompson, 61-62).

In one important way, however, Christianity differed from the other ascetic religions: it strongly emphasized corporate organization. Ascetic movements that were non-Christian were never well organized, nor were they generally intolerant of other religions . The Christians, on the other hand, were totally intolerant of any religion but their own and were very effectively organized (Gibbon, V. 1, 383). In fact, it was because of their fanaticism and zeal for organizing that the Christians were originally perceived as a threat by the Roman establishment. Consequently they were sporadically persecuted in the first and second centuries.

Christianity had another important peculiarity. In contrast to the old sex religions, Christianity was from its very first an *urban* religion. The word "Christian" first came into use in Antioch, a large metropolis in Asia Minor. "Early Christianity was a religion of towns and cities; it was urban, not rural. It spread from city to city, from province to province, along the highways of trade and commerce by land and by sea" (Thompson, 56). The first Christians were members of the new urban classes: artisans, craftspeople, shopkeepers and tradespeople (Thompson, 57). Urban oriented, they tended to equate rural living with everything non-Christian. The word "pagan" comes from the Latin *paganus*, which means country dweller. Augustine labeled his ideal Christian community the city of God and subtitled his book of that name "Against the *pagani.*"

Early in the third century A.D., Christianity spread rapidly in the army, as soldiers responded to the Christian emphasis on discipline, organizational order and obedience. A contending religion, Mithraism, had also grown rapidly in the army as early as 60 B.C. (Taylor, 251-252). Christianity absorbed much of the militaristic spirit of this religion and even some of its holidays (such as December 25th, the birthday of Mithra, the son of the sun god, and Sunday, the day of the sun, in contrast to Saturday, the Jewish sabbath). During this period, with the conversion of soldiers and the absorption of Mithraism, Christianity began to change from a loose federation of cells into a unified, centrally-controlled hierarchy of bishops and archbishops (Gibbon, V. 1, 421)

The emperor Constantine emphasized the militaristic traits of Christianity and incorporated them into army life. The cross was adopted as a *military* symbol and placed on shields and banners. Goths and Germans were recruited in the army and made to march behind the sign of the cross . The first two letters of the word "Christ" in Greek were formed into a logo and stamped on coins with the inscription *in hoc signa vinces* ("By this sign shall you conquer") (Gibbon, V. 1, 644, 656).

On becoming emperor, Constantine proclaimed himself the protector of Christianity, made Christianity a legal religion throughout the empire, systematically appointed Christians to high-level bureaucratic jobs in the government and army, encouraged people to donate money to the church, and finally converted to the new religion on his death bed. He was the first Roman ruler to realize that a religion well-entrenched in the army and ascetic in outlook could be very useful in controlling the state: "The passive and unresisting obedience which bows under the yoke of authority, or even of oppression, must have appeared in the eyes of the absolute monarch the most conscpicuous and useful of evangelic virtues" (Gibbon, V. 1, 640).

The Christian emperors following Constantine consolidated his policy. Christianity became the state religion; all other religions were banned. The rich and powerful converted in great numbers to Christianity and donated vast amounts of money to the church. Bishops became more than religious officials; in many parts of the empire, both east and west, they absorbed the powers and functions of government officials, generals, and judges. They also became absentee landlords of huge estates. For example, the fifthcentury bishop of Cappadocia owned almost all the land in the province of Cappadocia (Thompson, 82).

The church itself increasingly assumed the powers of government, developing an elaborate bureaucracy (Thompson, 77). As the largest landowner in society, the church also became the largest slaveowner and advocate of slavery. The church pushed slavery beyond its earlier form in the secular Roman empire (Thompson, 86). Christians systematized a whole set of slave laws which later facilitated the enslavement of non-white people in the 17th and 18th centuries. "It was that most Christian of emperors, Justinian, whose codification of the Roman law ... provided Christian Europe with a ready-made legal foundation for the slavery they introduced into the New World a thousand years later" (Finley, 88-89).

And so Christianity became more than just a religion. It became a system of power and property. The ruling warlords and absentee landowners of Roman civilization converted to Christianity and made it their own, as society moved away from the ancient economy towards medieval feudalism. The church itself emerged as the most potent corporate body in society, holding in its hands not only the keys of Peter but also the government and the major means of production.

As these changes were taking place, Christian propagandists called for the destruction of paganism because of the prevalence of homosexuality in the religions of the old nature cultures. Augustine, one of the most influential writers, repeatedly called attention to this love of sexuality and urged that it be destroyed. He was particularly incensed by the worship of the Great Mother, whose chief priests were Gay transvestites. After ridiculing various rural sex gods, he says, 'The same applies to the effeminates consecrated to the Great Mother, who violate every canon of decency in men and women. They were to be seen until just the other day in the streets and squares of Carthage with their pomaded hair and powdered faces, gliding along with womanish languor, and demanding from the shopkeepers the means of their depraved existence" (Augustine, 286).

Constantine declared pederasty a capital offence; the emperors Valentinian and Theodosius applied the penalty of being burned. Justinian initiated a pogrom against Gay men, whom he rounded up in large numbers, tortured, and burned. An ancient author notes: "Some he had castrated, while in the case of others he ordered sharp reeds inserted into their genital openings and had them paraded as captives through the forum" (Theodosius of Melitene, quoted by Bury, 412, note 5). The charges of homosexuality became a tool for hunting down political dissidents, as it would be later in the Middle Ages (Gibbon, V. 2, 378). In the fourth century A. D., the emperors Valentinian and Valens undertook a witch-hunt for practitioners of "magic." "From the extremity of Italy and Asia the young and the aged were dragged in chains to the tribunals of Rome and Antioch. Senators, matrons, and philosophers expired in ignominious and cruel tortures" (Gibbon, V. 2, 856).

The triumph of Christianity thus represented the triumph of the worst patriarchal elements of Roman civilization. It was the final triumph of urban-based male militarists and their followers, who increasingly rose to power first under the republic and then under the empire. Once victorious, they adopted a new patriarchal religion, banned all other religions, appropriated to themselves all the means of production, reduced the rest of the population to slavery, enforced a universal code of blind obedience to authority, degraded women, and suppressed sexuality.

In the past, victorious patriarchal groups always reached some accommodation with the older matriarchal and rural traditions which continued to exist and mold society in an important way. But things were different after 300 A.D. For the first time in Western history, the patriarchists attempted to root out and utterly destroy everything connected with the old rural-based sex religions. Their successors continued the same tactics of terror later in the middle ages in their attacks on witches and heretics.

The repressive institutions and values established by these patriarchists became the basis for the development of industrialism. The new cities that emerged in the late middle ages came to birth in the context of a profound Christian contempt for rural living. "Christianity . . . reinforced the prejudice against the countryside in making the countryman (*paganus*) into the pagan, the rebel against the word of the Christian god" (*Fontana Economic History of Europe*, V. 1, 71). This is not surprising since the new towns first formed around the fortresses of Christian warlords and the buildings of Christian monasteries.

These new towns owed their existence to violence and repression against the countryside. They became an "abnormal growth, a peculiar body totally foreign to the surrounding environment." As the countryside itself gradually became industrialized, peasants were wrenched away from rural servitude to become slaves in urban workshops (*Fontana*, V. 1, 18, 180). The mentality of the new towns was typically Christian: they displayed a love of order, discipline, punctuality and self-restraint. These attitudes were "indispensable to the growth of capitalism and to the industrial revolution" (*Fontana*, V. 1, 94).

Another Christian legacy to industrialism was the objectification of nature. In the old religion, trees, rocks and plants were viewed as living beings with which people could personally communicate. Often they were worshipped as gods. Christians viewed these natural beings as so many objects to be used by the highest order of creation: humankind. The new urbanism reinforced this belief. Christians lived within the walls out of touch with natural beings, which now became "resources." One result of this attitude was the rapid deforestation of Europe. 'The great forests of Europe ... were regarded as as enemy to be hewn down" (Thompson, 610). As might be expected, these practices led to an acute shortage of lumber, especially in England. There, this state of affairs led in turn to the adoption of coal for manufacturing activities, a practice that "put England well on the road to the Industrial Revolution" (*Fontana*, V. 2, 12).

The evolution of monasteries laid the foundation for the development of a money economy. In the 4th century A. D., monasteries were incorporated and allowed to own corporate property (Thompson, 139). The discipline, asceticism and orderliness of the monasteries enabled them to acquire great wealth in a short period of time. "Religiously the monks were intense fanatics, economically they became avaricious" (Thompson, 141). Bulging with wealth, monasteries became the earliest banks of the middle ages. Although Christian law at this time forbade usury, the monasteries were exempted. "A common argument was that, as the monastery was a corporation, and not a person, no sin was attached to the taking of usury" (Thompson, 638).

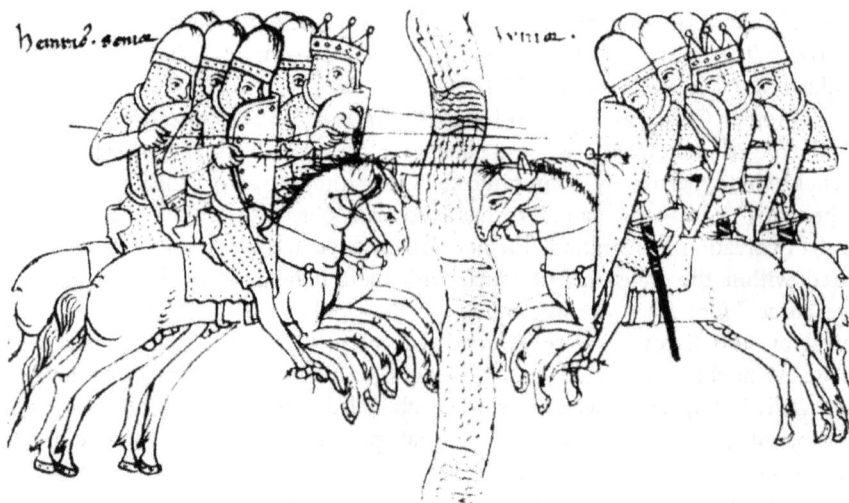

Soldiers fighting in twelfth century Germany.

Another important step along the industrial road was Christian militarism. By the middle ages, the church had become a great military power. Bishops, abbots, and even Popes were warlords who often personally took to the field of battle (Thompson, 655-657). The Christian love of war, together with the Christian intolerance of any other religion, led to the development of the crusades, beginning in the 11th century. The crusades were the first great impulse of European imperialism. They brought foreign markets under Western control, encouraged the development of cities, created a money economy in place of the natural economy of barter, and fostered the development of a new class, the bourgeoisie (Thompson, 397).

It was in the same mood of religious militarism that Europe undertook a second wave of expansion in the 16th century, the so-called voyages of discovery to the new world. In reality, they were imperialistic expeditions with two goals: to spread the Christian religion and to get gold (Gilbert, 30). These European invaders annihilated the cultures of the native peoples they encountered (all of whom were non-white), and gave special attention to wiping out their sacred Gay transvestites. The gold and silver bullion stolen from the nature peoples was returned to Europe, where it provided the basis for the financial expansions of European businesses. In the succeeding centuries, white Europeans enslaved millions of people from nature cultures to provide the forced labor necessary to support the growing industrial monster. The enslaved victims, who were non-white, were viewed as less than human beings. "These dark-skinned peoples lacked both the Christian culture which Europeans considered essential for salvation, and the technology to resist European mastery" (Gilbert, 288).

The violence of Christian militarism was also internalized in Europe itself. The most famous example of this was the never ending hunt for heretics and the mobilization of armies to wipe them out. In the time of the early Christian emperors, a campaign was begun "to despoil the pagan temples of their property" (Thompson, 71). The seized property was used to pay for the increased cost of government bureaucracy, and bishops became financial speculators with the proceeds (Thompson, 71, 77). In the later middle ages, the hunt for witches and heretics was an example of the same thing. Witch-hunting became a major industry in the middle ages. The crusade against the Albigensians turned into "a series of gigantic buccaneering expeditions" (Thompson, 490). The King of France supported the crusade because he wanted to bring the southern provinces within his power, thereby unifying the French state and establishing direct trade routes with the East (Thompson, 492). In a separate incident with another French King, the Templars were charged with homosexuality and deprived of their property in order to build up the French Treasury and underwrite war expenditures. Everywhere heresy-hunting helped provide the needed capital for building up the apparatus of the emerging state.

The entrenched militarism of Christian civilization led to the development of a huge arms industry where modern methods of production were first practiced on a wide scale. "It is characteristic of the early modern period that until far into the 17th century the best examples of large-scale industrial organization were state-owned factories producing war materiel" (Gilbert, 51). The modern factory system is thus a direct descendant of Christian militarism.

The real beneficiary of Christian militarism was a new institution that became the epitome of institutionalized violence—the nation state. This happened because the business of war increasingly became the specialty of secular princes and the new economic forces that supported them (the bourgeoisie). The nation-states they created eventually came to have a monopoly on institutionalized violence, and so ended up with a monopoly on political power as well.

Although Christian violence was responsible for the birth of the modern nation-state, the state nonetheless engaged in a savage struggle with its parent. In time, the state was victorious. The rule of clergy was replaced by the rule of politicians. Scholasticism was replaced by science. Government bureaucracy took over from church hierarchy. But underneath there remained the same class domination, urbanism, militarism, racism, exploitation of nature, and repression of women and sexuality.

The triumph of the nation-state brought with it a shift in Christian values, coinciding with the rise of Protestantism. Lutheranism, the first successful form of Protestantism, came into being because certain petty states in Germany were willing to use their armies to resist Catholic military power. Luther never forgot this debt and continually supported the secular power's authoritarianism. For example, in 1525 Luther urged the state to suppress with violence the rebelling peasants, whom he compared to mad dogs (Gilbert, 155). Lutheranism became a profoundly reactionary religion, whose members were drawn mostly from the upper and middle classes (Gilbert, 156).

In Calvinism, the successful accumulation of money was viewed as a sign of God's grace; alienated labor was a "calling"; and self-interested calculation was a sign of rationality. The bourgeois thrust of Calvinism has led some writers like Max Weber to conclude that Protestantism prepared the way for the rise of capitalism. But as we have just seen, the entire Christian tradition was working to this end for a thousand years.

The really different thing about Protestantism is that it tried to purge Christianity of influences it had picked up from paganism. The so-called Reformation was in reality a reaction against the Renaissance, where pagan influence (including a looser sexuality) had had a major impact on Western culture. Protestants emphasized the anti-sexual, anti-woman writings of Paul of Tarsus. They detested anything that suggested sensuality. In some cases, they entered existing churches, smashed the organs, broke the statuary, and white-washed the murals (Gilbert, 136). Significantly, they rejected the worship of Mary, whose cult was a survival within the Christian patriarchy of earlier matriarchal values.

The Puritans were the most fanatical of the Protestants. John Knox attacked the status of women in his pamphlet "The First Blast of the Trumpet Against the Monstrous Regiment of Women" (Partridge, 116) . Thomas Hall published a pamphlet called "The Loathsomeness of Long Haire" (Partridge, 118). Puritans insisted on sexist dress codes. "The Puritans attempted, for reasons which should not be too obscure, to masculinize men as far as possible, and correspondingly, to defeminize and make negative members of the opposite sex" (Partridge, 117-118).

All the major sects of Protestantism agreed on severely repressing sexuality; on inculcating unquestioned obedience to authority, both of the state and of the male head of the family; and on scorning non-Christian and non-white cultures. The rising bourgeoisie eagerly embraced these values and translated them into public policy, where they remain to this day.

And so the story of human history in the West has been the sickening spectacle of increasing patriarchal power, first gradually in the Bronze Age, then with a sudden leap in the triumph of Christianity, and finally overwhelmingly with the onrush of industrialism. Corresponding to this rise has been a fall, first in the status of women, then of rural people, then of Gay people, then of non-white people.

Everywhere the old nature cultures are gone. The Celts are gone, conquered by Caesar. The peasants of Europe are gone, having been murdered, enslaved, or transformed into an urban proletariat. The Indians are gone, wiped out on orders from the Pope and from Washington. The Third World has been going every day. They are all gone, and in their place has come that son of the city of God, that all-conquering Leviathan, the new industrial state.

And that's how it happened that straight white males got control of our lives.

Medieval Gnostic religious symbols.

4 HERETICS: WOMEN, BUGGERS AND FREE SPIRITS

hristianity was not always well defined. The established doctrine of today's church was originally just one of many competing views. It prevailed because it was favored by the ruling interests of the time. All other views were suppressed. Among the earliest repressed views were popular movements trying to combine paganism with the new testament. The most famous example, Gnosticism, arose in first-century Asia Minor (western Turkey). Gnostics believed that knowledge gained through personal mystical experience (*gnosis*) was more important than the dogmas of faith (*pistis*) (Vanggaard, 150; Obolensky, 3; Runciman, 7). In the tradition of the Great Mother, many Gnostics believed in a goddess: Helen, Barbelo, Silence, or Wisdom (Quispel, 73-74). Gnostics generally believed that the things of this world and the world itself were evil. Many rejected Jehovah the Creator as an evil demon.

Gnostics were ascetics in a way hard for modern people to understand. They believed in denying this world and purifying themselves, but sometimes practiced sexual indulgence as a means of purification. Occasionally they seemed to believe that the best way to transcend "evil" was to experience it. They were sensitive to pagan asceticism, which unlike Christianity included both self-indulgence and self-denial. For example, the ancient rites of the Great Mother involved sex orgies, yet they were presided over by celibate priests. Rejecting the old testament god, Gnostics sympathized with the victims of this god's wrath. "Sects arose that paid reverence to Cain, to the Sodomites, and the Egyptians" (Runciman, 10).

Orgiastic sex rites appeared among some Gnostics and scandalized traditional Christians. Roman authorities used these practices to discredit Christianity as a whole. Traditional Christians consequently condemned the Gnostics and denied any connection with them. In 177 AD Irenaeus, missionary to the Celts, condemned a group of Gnostics for their promiscuity. In the third century, Bishop Clement of Alexandria denounced Gnostics for holding orgies, as did the historian Eusebius (Cohn, *Demons*, 9; Benko, 113). An account of such practices by Epiphanius, a fourth century monk and former Gnostic, claimed that men and women had sex in common and worshipped cum and menstrual blood as the body and blood of Christ (Benko, 110). According to Epiphanius, Gnostics believed in sexual pleasure but not procreation, because birth divided up the worldsoul. Salvation consisted in the gathering together and return to Barbelo, the Great Mother, by means of communal sex rites (Benko, 110; 117-118). Many historians believe that Epiphanius' sex reports were untrue (Cohn, *Demons*, 9ff). Yet his reliability on other matters of Gnostic faith is generally accepted (Benko, 111).

In 242 AD a Mesopotamian Gnostic, named Mani, began teaching that Gnostic believers were divided into two categories: the leaders (or elect) and the followers (or hearers) (Runciman, 15). Both women and men were leaders in Mani's religion, in contrast to traditional Christianity, which prohibited women from being priests. Leaders were also forbidden to own personal wealth, again contrary to the Christian tradition of rich priests and bishops. Mani believed in one good god and one evil god (Jehovah). Salvation meant escaping from the control of Jehovah and renouncing all material possessions and earthly power, even for the church. Mani's religion spread rapidly and under the name of Manichaeism (or Manichaeanism) became a serious rival to traditional Christianity. Augustine, later Bishop of Hippo, was a Manichee for nine years before converting to Christianity. He accused the Manichee leaders of libertinism, and claimed that this was the reason for his conversion (Cohn, *Demons*, 17). Later, Christian writers called any popular movement "Manichaean" whenever it displayed a belief in more than one god, a prominent leadership role for women, and a pagan sense of asceticism.

In the latter part of the fourth century a Manichaean type heresy (known as Massalianism) appeared in Syria and Asia Minor. The Massalians (or Messalians) were Christian Gnostics whose leaders were both women and men (Runciman, 23). They believed that a period of strict self-denial was necessary for them to reach a purified state, at which point sin was no longer possible. Once in this state, believers no longer required self-denial and could engage in any sex act without sin (Obolensky, 50). "The Messalian doctrines were the extreme expression of the longing to comprehend mystical revelation through sensual experience" (Laos, 72). By the tenth century, Massalian beliefs reached Bulgaria, where they gradually fused with Bogomilism, a heresy named after a priest called Bogomil. The Bogomils believed in two gods, rejected the church hierarchy, and preached passive resistance to government authority (Laos, 53-56; Runciman, 74-75; Obolensky, 126ff).

At first they were strictly puritanical but in time came closer to the Messalians. "Under the increased influence of Massalianism, the Bogomils entirely lost their reputation for puritanism and had become associated with the most extreme form of sexual indulgence" (Obolensky, 251). Both groups were persecuted by traditional Christians.

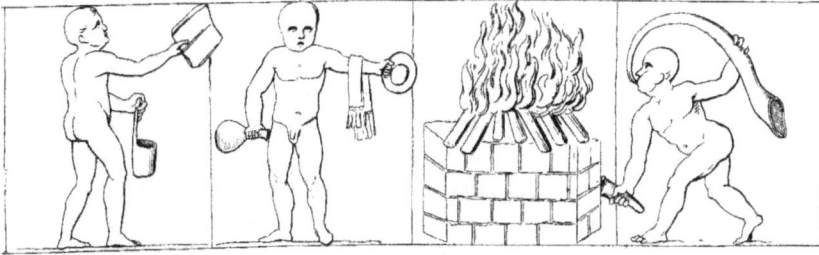

Under the heat of persecution, the Bogomils allied themselves with the masses of Bulgaria, where paganism was still powerful. Boris, the king, hadn't converted to Christianity until 864 AD (Loos, 41). His attempt to impose Christianity on the people resulted in a civil war in which he eventually defeated and blinded his rebellious pagan son. Boris and his Christian successors were "bitterly resented by the common people of Bulgaria, who were obstinately attached to their own pagan customs and worship" (Loos, 42). The Bogomils became political, "espousing the cause of the serfs against their masters, of the oppressed against the oppressors"(Obolensky, 141).

Some historians have denied that the erotic Massalians had any connection with the Bogomils. They believe that the word "Massalian" didn't refer to any actual heresy, but was used as a general term of abuse against the Bogomils (Cohn, *Demons*, 18, note). But evidence shows that the name did have a definite technical meaning. It occurs repeatedly from the very beginning in accounts of Bogomilism. It is used in this manner by Theophylact, Patriarch of Constantinople, in 950 AD; the priest Cosmas, around 969; the theologian Euthymius Zibagenus around 1100; Anna Comnena, daughter of the Byzantine emperor, in 1148; and the council of Tirnovo in 1211. Anna Comnena wrote:

> For two very evil and worthless doctrines which had been known
> in former times, now coalesced; the impiety, as it might be called,
> of the Manichaeans, which we also call the Paulician heresy, and
> the shamelessness of the Massalians. This was the doctrine of the
> Bogomils compounded of the Massalians and the Manichaeans"
> (Anna Comnena, 412).

In the early 14th century, when Massalian influence was at its greatest, a Bogomil monk named Lazarus appeared in Tirnovo, the capital of Bulgaria. He advocated nudism and sexual freedom as ways to salvation. Arrested, but refusing to recant, he was consequently branded on the face and exiled (Runciman, 97). Another Bogomil, Theodosius, advocated orgiastic sex, but his fate is not recorded. Most Bogomils did not share these views, but they were an example of where Bogomil teaching could lead. The Bogomils were strict vegetarians, rejecting any food that was created as a result of heterosexual sex. As with the Massalians, women were prominent in their leadership (Loos, 53-59; Obolensky, 117-140). In the eleventh century, Bogomil practices and teaching emerged from Bulgaria and swept across Europe. In the west, these heretics were known as Cathars, from the Greek *Katharoi*, meaning "the Purified Ones." Within a hundred years, the Cathars managed to organize a rival church, create a counter-civilization in southern France, and raise armies in their own behalf.

From their first appearance in the west, Cathars were associated with practicing ritual sex. An early example of what was probably Catharist heresy appeared in Orleans, France, in 1022. According to the earliest account:

> They adored the devil, who first appeared to them as an Ethiopian [that is, a black man], then as an angel of light, and who daily brought them much money. In obedience to his works, in private they completely rejected Christ and secretly practiced abominations and crimes of which it is shameful even to speak, while publicly they pretended to be true Christians (Wakefield and Evans, 75).

A later account by an arrested participant reported that believers were offered a "heavenly food" and told "often you will see with us angelic visions, in which sustained by their consolation, you can visit whatsoever places you wish without delay or difficulty" (Wakefield and Evans, 78). The report said they met secretly at a certain house until a demon descended in the form of an animal, at which point the lights were extinguished and there was an orgy. If a child was born from these sexual acts, it was killed, then burned, and its ashes saved for making the "heavenly food".

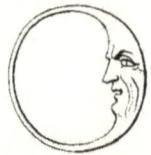

Most historians regard these early reports either as sick fantasies or as stereotypes used by the church to crush dissent (Lerner, 34; Cohn, Demons, 20).

But the first view ignores evidence from folklore, and the second, the fact that such stereotypes were not widely used by the church until the thirteenth century.

These early charges make some sense if considered in the context of heresy, paganism, and folklore. The Celts worshipped a black horned god, whom Christians later identified with the Devil. The heretics in question flourished in Orleans, once part of Celtic Gaul, where ancient traditions persisted until the time of Joan of Arc (the Maid of Orleans). Throughout the middle ages, church writers continually condemned the wearing of animal costumes at peasant rituals. Even in the twentieth century, Portuguese peasants have dressed in cats' skins to do ritual dances (Alford, 356). In shamanist religions a priest often dresses up as the animal god who is being invoked.

The heavenly food of the heretics was said to be sustained by angelic consolation. The only sacrament later attributed to known Cathars was the *consolamentum* ("consolation"), thought to be administered by leaders possessing the souls of angels. As for the child murder charges, the Catholic Church has always claimed that those who perform abortions are committing murder. Women accused later of witchcraft were often abortionists. In pagan times a new-born infant was not assumed to be a person until the mother (or family) formally accepted it. If the infant was deformed, or simply unwanted, it was killed or abandoned in the wilderness. Among nature people, this attitude towards newborn infants is the general rule and is widely observed among animals, who will abandon, kill, or even eat the unwanted young. The heretics at Orleans probably performed some abortion rite, especially since Cathars considered giving birth as a grave sin.

Long before the Inquisition created its stereotypes, Cathars had a reputation of tolerance toward lesbianism and male homosexuality. In 1114 the French abbot Guibert of Nogent wrote about two brothers, Clement and Evrard, whom he knew personally. He said they were heretics who had a large following among the local peasants in Bucy-le-long:

> They condemn marriage and the begetting of offspring through intercourse. And surely, wherever they are scattered throughout the Latin world, you may see them living with women but not under the name of husband and wife, in such fashion that man does not dwell with woman, male with female, but men are known to be with men, women with women; for among them it is unlawful for men to approach women (Wakefield and Evans, 103).

The followers of Clement and Evrard were accused of holding orgies in cellars and killing any children that might be born among them (Wakefield and Evans, 103). On trial before the Bishop of Soissons, one brother confessed, but refused to repent, while the other brother denied the accusations. Both were burned.

Charges of lesbianism and male homosexuality henceforth became routine against Cathars. "This, the first explicit allegation of homosexuality, also became a commonplace in later trials. Variations on the phrases *vir cum viris* [the man with men] and *femina cum feminis* [the woman with women] appear again and again" (Russell, 95, note). The word for Cathar in most European languages carne to be the word for homosexual: in German, *Ketzer*, in Italian, *Gazarro*, and in French, *herite*. In several languages the word for Bulgarian (the heresy originated in Bulgaria) also came to mean homosexual: Italian, *Bulgaro*; French, *Bougre*; and the English, *Bugger* (Russell, 238-239; Hughes, 66). Heresy and homosexuality became so interchangeable that those accused of heresy attempted to prove their innocence by claiming heterosexuality. A thirteenth century weaver accused of heresy replied: "Gentleman, listen to me! I am not a heretic, for I have a wife and I sleep with her. I have sons" (Wakefield, 213). When the people of Toulouse rebelled against the heresy-hunting Dominicans, "the cry was, they were unjustly accusing decent married men of heresy" (Wakefield, 213).

Mere suspicion of homosexuality was enough to condemn a person for heresy, even though the person was not known to have believed in or taught any heretical doctrine. In 1381 an epileptic German beggar named Brother Hans was thought to have magical powers. Arrested and tortured by the inquisition, he confessed that he was a "perverter of young boys" (Lerner, 145). He was consequently burned at the stake for *heresy* even though no doctrinal dispute was involved.

Since the same words often came to mean both heresy and homosexuality, we sometimes have trouble knowing exactly what was meant by the legal codes of the times. In 1272 the laws of Orleans, Anjou, and Marne called for death by burning of anyone guilty of "bougerie." Historians are still debating whether this refers to homosexuality, heresy, or both (Bailey, 141-142). As a result of this confusion, a person's sexual orientation became a test of religious orthodoxy and political loyalty. "Heresy became a sexual rather than a doctrinal concept; to say a man was a heretic was to say that he was a homosexual, and vice versa" (Taylor, 131).

Straight historians rarely believe the Gay sex charges made against Cathars. But their own homophobia, which affects the way they deal with the evidence, is revealed by their very language. One noted medieval historian calls Lesbians "perverts," while another calls Gay sex acts "nasty sexual aberrations" (Lerner, 119; Wakefield, 41).

There is good reason to accept a connection between Catharism and Gay sex: the Cathars' special view of morality. Cathars did not believe in Hell, purgatory, or damnation, but like many ancient peoples believed in reincarnation. For them, souls continued to be reborn as animals or humans until they escaped from the cycle of life. Eventually all souls will escape, and no one will be damned. Cathars held that there was only one sin; that occurred when the angels, led by the evil god Jehovah, rebelled and were thrown out of heaven (Borst, 175; Laos, 140). These angels became human souls weighted down with matter, and so were continually reborn. Only when they regain their original angelic state, brought about by a complete renunciation of the world, will they escape from the cycle of rebirths and return to the good god.

Cathars believed that only a tiny minority were able to attain this angelic state. These were the *Cathari*, the "perfected ones." They led completely ascetic lives and were worshipped as angels. There was only one way to become a perfected one: through an initiation rite called *consolamentum* ("consolation"), a laying-on of hands. Once receiving this sacrament, perfected ones were expected to live a life of strict self denial (Loos, 142). As a result, Cathars usually put off receiving the rite until just before death (Wakefield, 36). Most Cathars had not taken the *consolamentum* and lived by a different moral code from the perfected ones. There was no point for them in doing penance, practicing asceticism, confessing. And, in fact, Cathars rejected all Church sacraments, including penance. The only thing that really counted was getting the *consolamentum* before death, and *then* leading a totally ascetic life.

The perfected ones feared procreation, since that would ensnare yet another angelic soul in matter. Sex must not lead to birth. Lesbianism and male homosexuality were therefore safe forms of sex, if sex must be practiced at all. "So long as it did not lead to the conception of children they positively seemed to encourage sexual intercourse or at least not discourage it — a complete reversal of the Catholic view" (Runciman, 152).

Although Cathar *leaders* were austere, many *followers* believed that until they received the *consolamentum* sex acts not resulting in birth were permissible (Borst, 182). Many of them told Christian inquisitors at Toulouse and Turin that they didn't think homosexuality was a sin (Borst, 182, notes). "Even the most hostile depositions against the later Bogomils and Cathars declare that the Initiates led personally blameless lives, but that they associated with and seemed to encourage Believers who led lives of remarkable immorality" (Runciman, 176).

Cathars were also strict vegetarians. They refused to eat meat, eggs, cheese, or any milk products (Wakefield, 38). Because animals were viewed as reincarnated souls, killing an animal for food was akin to killing a human. Also, procreation — even in the animal world — was the work of the evil god. As with the Bogomils, women played a large role among Cathars. Women and men were viewed as equals; many women became Cathar leaders. Cathar women also fought in battles. A woman catapultist killed Simon de Montfort, leader of the Catholic army that attacked Cathars in southern France. Catharism scorned the institution of marriage, and was one of the few religions to have no marriage rites. In fact Cathars considered marriage to be no better than prostitution (Wakefield, 33). Catharism was tolerant toward other religions. Cathar-controlled areas were among the few safe places for Jews. In southern France, a fusion of Cathar and Jewish thought produced the Kabbala, a book of Jewish mysticism (Wakefield, 61). Cathars had an encouraging attitude towards the arts. Cathar areas in France were the very ones where troubador poetry developed, a poetry marked by sensuality and bawdyness (Briffault, 3:488 ff; Wakefield, 56-57, notes). After the Cathars were suppressed, this tradition continued, although in a less openly erotic form. In time it had a tremendous impact on the development of modern Western poetry. Catharism was essentially a religion of the lower classes and was spread from town to town by itinerant weavers. In 1157 these weavers were condemned for preaching against marriage, and practicing promiscuity (Runciman, 121; Russell, 128; Loos, 117; Cohn, *Millennium*, 153).

Because of its close association with the lower classes, Catharism gave rise to pagan offshoots — which I call the Cathar left wing. Some Cathars worshiped the sun as a god. Between 1176 and 1190, a man named Bonacursus, a Cathar who had converted to Catholicism, said of some Cathars at Milan: "They hold that the devil himself is the sun, Eve the moon; and each month, they say, they commit adultery" (Wakefield and Evans, 173). Here the sun is called the devil, but among Cathars the devil was viewed as a god. In 1350, Armenian speaking heretics were reported to be worshipping the sun (Russell, 93, n.49). Armenia was a known Cathar stronghold. During the war between the Cathars and Catholics in France, Cathar leaders took refuge in a fortress long rumored to be a pagan temple of the sun (Wakefield, 173), and notes).

Among some Cathars the evil god came to be highly regarded. Heretics in Austria, Brandenburg, and Bohemia in the early fourteenth century were accused of worshipping "Lucifer" (Russell, 177-179; Lerner 25-26; 30-31). The word *Lucifer* literally means "the light bearer" in Latin, and this was applied in pagan antiquity to the sun and the morning star (Venus). Among medieval Christians, it was used as another name for the devil. This usage arose from a misunderstanding of *Isaiah*, where the King of Babylon is compared to the morning star: "How have you fallen from the heavens, 0 morning star, son of the dawn!" (Isaiah, 14:12). In the Latin translation of this passage, "morning star" was rendered by *Lucifer*, falsely making it appear that Isaiah was talking about Satan being thrown out of heaven. From this double meaning as light bearer and devil, the word *Lucifer* was easily used to describe the god of sun-worshipping Cathars, since Christians viewed sun worship as demon worship.

Practices of the Cathar left wing triggered frequent Christian charges that Cathars had sex orgies, killed infants (abortion), and worshipped a demon. The charges appeared before the creation of the Inquisition and continued into later times. Typical of them all is an anonymous letter from 1390 describing a group called "Luciferans":

> First they worship Lucifer and believe him to be the brother of God, unjustly driven from heaven ... they sacrifice their children to him ... they meet together in underground locations ... They indulge in promiscuous cravings and abominable wantonness (Lea, 1:206).

Cathar belief that the Devil was a god — plus the traditional notion that the Devil was above all concerned with sex — would naturally lead to orgiastic rituals, especially for Cathars who remained close to ancient pagan traditions. In addition, ritual sex was a part of Gnosticism, which was the historical root of Catharism. And later heresies, building on Catharism, denied the existence of any moral law. Seen in this way, ritual sex was part of a lasting heretical tradition.

In the thirteenth century a new heresy arose. People formed independent communal groups, either all male or all female. They gave up all their property (if they had any to begin with) and traveled around the country begging for bread. They rejected any form of church regulation or control. The women were known as beguines and the men as beghards (hence the English word *beggar*). Within some (but not all) beguine and beghard communities, a heresy came to birth known as the Free Spirit, which later took off on its own. From the very start, beguines, beghards, and Free Spirits were accused of being Lesbians and Gay men (Lerner, 39, 70-71, 117). In 1339, two men — John and Albert of Brunn — joined the Dominican order after renouncing their previous participation in the Free Spirit. They claimed that as Free Spirits they did not consider any passion of the flesh, including sodomy, to be sinful (Lerner, 108-110). In 1367, a German Free Spirit, John of Ossmannstedt, was questioned by the Inquisition. He eagerly responded without any coercion and declared that those who are truly free "can be subject to no authority" (Lerner, 136). He said people should act on their sexual feelings, even if incestuous, and rejected any distinction between holiness and pleasure, saying, "as for the sacraments, a Free Spirit did not have to confess because he was without sin and a game of chess could reveal God as well as the Eucharist if one took more delight in it because God is found in pleasure" (Lerner, 138). The Free Spirits held that "one of the surest marks of the 'subtle in spirit' was, precisely, the ability to indulge in promiscuity without fear of God or qualms of conscience." Since God could be experienced through sex, the sex act itself took on "a transcendental, quasi-mystical value" (Cohn, *Millennium*, 189). Many academics do not take Free Spirits seriously. One historian dismisses John of Ossmannstedt as psychopathic: 'There are some personalities that so enjoy being in the spotlight that they will do or say anything to remain bathed in it. John might have been of this type, or he may have been slightly deranged" (Lerner, 138). Another academic labels Free Spirits "aberrant," "paranoid megalomaniacs," "schizophrenic," and "nihilistic" (Cohn, *Millennium*, 149, 151, and 185).

The Ranters as imagined by their contemporaries.

Free Spirits lasted until the seventeenth century in England, where they were known as Ranters. One of them, Abiezer Coppe, was a member of a group called My One Flesh. He sometimes wrote ecstatic spiritual passages filled with Gay images:

> Eternal kisses, have been made the fiery chariots, to mount me swiftly into the bosom of him who my soul loves (his excellent Majesty, the King of glory). Where I have been, where I have been, where I have been, hug'd, imbrac't, and kisst with the

kisses of his mouth, whose loves are better than wine, and have been utterly overcome therewith, beyond expression, beyond admiration (Cohn, *Millennium*, 370-371).

Coppe condemned the people of Sodom not for their homosexuality, but because they "called Angels men, they seeing no further than the forms of men" (Cohn, *Millennium*, 363). Although Ranters supported Cromwell's revolution, they were suppressed once the revolutionaries came to power. In 1650, Parliament passed a law forbidding Ranters to advocate that certain kinds of human actions, including sodomy, were not sinful in and of themselves (Cohn, *Millennium*, 326). This was not the only time in history that advocates of sexual freedom supported a revolutionary cause, only to be silenced once the revolutionaries came to power.

By the fourteenth century, some Free Spirits had come to the conclusion that private property was as contrary to economic justice as the church was contrary to true religion (Cohn, *Millennium*, 193). In 1317, John of Durbheim, the bishop of Strassburg, began a persecution of Free Spirits, charging that they urged poor people to steal from the rich on the grounds that all property should be owned in common (Lerner, 86). Protestant leaders were no less upset by the link between Free Spirits and the lower classes. In 1525, Martin Luther condemned the unlettered Free Spirit Loy Pruystinck of Antwerp because of his close association with thieves, prostitutes, beggars and craft workers (Cohn, *Millennium*, 177-178). Many Free Spirits carne to the conclusion that only the poor could get to heaven. For them, "apostolic" became synonymous with "poor" (Cohn, Millennium, 162-163). Abiezer Coppe had his God say, "And as I live, I will plague your Honour, Pompe, Greatnesse, Superfluity, and confound it into parity, equality, community" (Cohn, *Millennium*, 361).

There has been a continuous tradition of pagan-influenced rebellion within Christianity itself. This tradition includes Gnosticism, Manichaeism, Massalianism, Bogornilism, Catharism, the Free Spirit and others — movements that have been called heresies within the restrictive framework of traditional Christianity. In many cases where they appeared, these movements displayed five important features: 1) Belief in more than one deity; 2) a prominent leadership role for women; 3) a pagan sense of asceticism, including both self-denial and self-indulgence; 4) hostility to the wealth and power of the church; and 5) a tolerance for Gay sex. The underlying force that nourished these heresies was the surviving paganism of the lower classes. Soon the church would move against this paganism itself and call it "witchcraft."

Out *magazine.*

Drawing by Krista Van Laan by permission of Out magazine

5 Tђe Sαcᴚeᴅ Oᴚgᴉes of Wᴉᴛcђcᴚαfᴛ

Dhile some so-called "heretics" tried to combine paganism with Christianity, others (especially lower-class country people) retained pagan rites in their old pre-Christian form. In the early middle ages, church synods repeatedly condemned surviving pagan rites, including the ceremonial use of sex images (Russell, 55 & 58, notes; Cohn, *Demons*, 157; Summers. *History*, 99). Christians were also troubled by the surviving worship of the Great Mother, who was most often honored under the name of "Diana, the goddess of the pagans." Condemnations of her worship persisted from the early middle ages until the 16th century. The earliest accounts tell of sex rites, describe surviving statues of the goddess, and report strong popular resistance to Christianity, even to the point of killing missionaries (Russell, 57; 58, n. 21; 61, n. 25; Cohn, *Demons*, 212; Grimm, 237). In the late 9th century, one hostile writer gave this description:

"It is also not to be omitted that some wicked women perverted by the devil, seduced by illusions and phantoms of demons, believe and profess themselves, in the hours of the night to ride upon certain beasts with Diana, the goddess of the pagans, and an innumerable multitude of women, and in the silence of the dead of night to traverse great spaces of earth, and to obey her commands as of their mistress, and to be summoned to her services on certain nights. But I wish it were they alone who perished in their faithlessness and infidelity. For an innumerable multitude, deceived by this false opinion, believe this to be true, and so believing, wander from the right faith" (Russell, 76).

Due to the widespread and ancient nature of her worship, the goddess had many other names beside Diana. In Germany and France, she was called Holda or Holle. In Norwegian and Danish lands, she was Hulla, Huldra, or Huldre. In Switzerland and Austria, she appeared as Berchta, Bertha, or Perchtha. Elsewhere, she was known as Faste, Selga, Selda, Abundia, Satia, Befana, and Befania (Grimm, 221-225; Russell, 49, note). Whatever her name, she was usually regarded as a powerful deity, ruling over the weather, animals, sexuality, spinning, weaving, plant life, and the abode of the dead.

Hundreds of years before the Inquisition's great witch hunts, some Christians already viewed worshippers of the Great Mother as witches, contrary to the view of certain historians that these early accounts had nothing to do with witchcraft (Cohn, *Demons*, 212). In the early 11th century, Burchard of Worms called the night-riding goddess "the witch Holda" (Russell, 81). And in Germany, the word *hollefahren* (from *Holle* and *fahren*, meaning to travel) came to mean *witches'* travel (Grimm, already cited).

Other Christians, especially the "well educated," tended to laugh off these accounts. The 12th-century philosopher John of Salisbury reported the popular belief of his time in a night-riding goddess who held meetings where infants were killed (abortion again?). Ridiculing such stories, he exclaimed, "it is clear that these things are put about from silly women and from simple men of weak faith" (Cohn, *Demons*, 219). Like many of his modern academic counterparts, John felt that the experiences of women and "uneducated" men had little relevance to history.

The specter that the intellectuals tried to laugh off would not go away. In 1249, William of Paris described the people's belief in a deity — Abundia or Satia — who traveled at night with a band of followers to whom she gave prosperity (Ginzburg, 49). In 1270, Jean de Meung, author of sections of *Roman de la Rose*, relayed the popular notion that people roamed at night with Dame Habonde and that one-third of the world joined them (Russell, 135). In 1279, Bishop Auger de Montfaucon condemned women who rode at night with Diana, Herodias or Bensozia (Alford, 355). In 1320, an English Franciscan asked in disgust: "What is to be said of these wretched and superstitious persons who say that by night they see most fair queens and other maidens tripping with the lady Diana and leading the dances with the goddesses of the pagans, who in our vulgar tongue are called *Elves*?" (Russell, 175).

Authorities soon had a ready answer about what to do with these wild fairies. By the 14th century, the church increasingly came to interpret this type of activity as the work of "demons." Dominican Jacopo Passavanti wrote:

> It happens that demons taking on the likeness of men and women who are alive, and of horses and beasts of burden, go by night in company through certain regions, where they are seen by the people, who mistake them for those persons whose likenesses they bear; and in some countries this is called the *tregenda* [which has come to mean "witches' sabbat" in modern Italian]. And the demons do this to spread error, and to cause a scandal, and to discredit those whose likenesses they take on, by showing that they do dishonorable things in the *tregenda*. There are some people, especially women, who say that they go at night in company with such a *tregenda*, and name many men and women in their company; and they say that the mistress of the throng, who leads the others, are Herodias, who had St. John the Baptist killed, and the ancient Diana, goddess of the Greeks (Cohn, *Demons*, 215-216).

As Christian intellectuals became more convinced that these practices were led by demons, they became less inclined to laugh them off as they had earlier. In 1370, the Inquisition at Milan indicted a woman for being a member of the "society of Diana" (Russell, 210). In 1384, an Italian peasant named Sibillia was brought to trial before a secular court (and later before the Inquisition at Milan). She freely admitted that she belonged to a society that went out every Thursday night with "Signora Oriente" and that they "paid homage to her" (Russell, 211). Sibillia said she never confessed these things because it never occurred to her that they were sinful (Kieckhefer, 22). She was reprimanded and sentenced to wear two red crosses as penance. Six years later in 1390, Sibillia was again before the Inquisition. She admitted to the same practices, saying they went back to her childhood and again insisted they were no sin. Now, however, she admitted that the name of God was not used at the celebrations for fear of offending Oriente (Russell, 212). In the same year of 1390, Pierina de Bugatis was tried for similar charges before both a secular court and the Inquisition at Milan. At their celebrations, she said, people weren't the only ones who appeared, but also animals and the souls of the dead. She claimed that she traveled with a group of women who robbed the houses of the rich, while bypassing those of the poor. She also claimed that Signora Oriente ruled their society as Christ ruled the world (Russell, 213).

The manner in which professional historians have reacted to the trials of Sibillia and Pierina is a good indication of how history has been ignored, suppressed, and distorted by straight white males with Christian values. As Norman Cohn sees the trials, "something that hitherto has happened only in the minds of silly old women has taken on an objective material existence" (Cohn, *Demons*, 217). As usual, Cohn resorts to sexist and ageist stereotyping, and just ignores the evidence. He even rejects other historians on the same grounds. For example, among the many reasons he can't stand Margaret Murray's approach to witchcraft, is that "by the time she turned her attention to these matters she was nearly sixty" (Cohn, *Demons*, 109). We find a different kind of prejudice in the historian Jeffrey Russell. He admits that the experiences of Sibillia and Pierina were in some sense real, but he can't bring himself to admit that they were an example of anything *religious*. He says what we are dealing with here and in similar cases is merely "old folk tradition" or at best "strange fertility rites" (Russell, 212-213).

To historian Richard Kieckhefer, the practices of Sibillia and Pierina may be religious, but they could *never* be considered pagan. "It would be misleading to speak of them as conscious or deliberate pagan survivals, since the participants seem to have viewed themselves as Christians, despite the reservations that churchmen evidently held" (Kieckhefer, 22). Here we have not only a misinterpretation of the evidence, but a complete falsification of it. Where do the women say they regard themselves as Christians? What they said is that they didn't regard the things they did as *sinful*. And what on earth does Kieckhefer mean by "the reservations that churchmen evidently held"? He makes it sound like their inquisitors had some polite second thoughts in a dinner-table discussion of theology. We aren't dealing with mere *reservations* here. These women were accused of *heresy*!

Despite the prejudices of historians like these, evidence abounds for the continuation of pagan religion right into the 15th century. Around 1421, Gobelinus Persona told of the popular belief of his time that Domina Hera flew through the night between Christmas and Epiphany and brought an abundance of good things to people (Lea, v.L 176-177). In 1428, the earliest Swiss witch hunts by inquisitorial methods began. In these trials, people were tortured into confessing that they worshipped "the Devil" instead of Diana or Herodias (Cohn, *Demons*, 225-226). In 1435, the inquisitor Johann Nider reported that peasant women imagined themselves to fly with Diana after rubbing their bodies with an ointment (Cohn, *Demons*, 219-220). Similar tales were later recounted by Bartolommeo Spina and Johann Weyer, a physician. In 1439, Thomas Ebendorfer in his book *De decem praeceptis* condemned the popular practice of leaving food and drink out at night for Perchta or Habundie (Ginzburg, 51). In 1487, Tomas de Torquemada, the Grand Inquisitor of Spain, declared, "Diana is the Devil" (RusselL 235, note).

We can clearly see the transition from Diana-worship to Devil-worship in the witchcraft trials of the 16th century. In 1525, a woman named Wypat Musin from Burseberg in the Tyrol was tried for "superstition." She confessed that two years before, on the night of one of the four quarterly feasts of the year, she had seen a multitude of dead souls being led by Frau Selga, the sister of Frau Venus (Ginzburg, 58). In 1532, Domenica Barbarelli confessed to traveling and dancing with Diana, whom she called "Mistress of Play" [*Domina Ludi*] (Ginzburg, 36, n. 3). In 1573, a Swiss woman with the significant nickname *Seelenmutter* ("Mother of Souls") was arrested. She was tried by a secular court for "non-Christian fancifulness" and burned as a witch (Ginzburg, 59).

The best documented case of how the Inquisition turned the followers of the Great Mother into witches occurred in Friuli, Italy, in the 1570s. At that time a group of people were uncovered called the Benandanti (that is, the wanderers). They admitted, without coercion or torture, that at certain times of the year (the beginning days of the four seasons), they went into trances. In this state, they had the experience of leaving their bodies and doing things that reveal a curious mix of Christian and pagan beliefs. When they were in the out-of-the-body state, they traveled in company with animals and carried fennel stalks, which they used as weapons against another group of spirits, who were evil and who carried stalks of sorghum (Ginzburg, 4). They called these evil spirits "witches" and said they themselves were fighting for the faith of Christ (Ginzburg, 34).

The Italian scholar Carlo Ginzburg has shown that the Benandanti were in fact remnants of a shamanistic cult. This cult existed continuously among segments of the peasant population since the days of paganism (Ginzburg, 40 ff). The Benandanti originally worshipped a Diana-type goddess who was mistress of vegetation and growth and also queen of the dead. She was the center of a religion that was widely spread throughout Europe. During the change of the seasons, her followers celebrated the changes as a ritual conflict between different nature spirits (Ginzburg, 39). In the course of the centuries, the Benandanti absorbed certain Christian beliefs. Some of them came to the conclusion that what they were fighting for at the seasonal feasts was the faith of Christ.

By the 16th century, these rituals were no longer acted out but were experienced only when the believers went into trances. Nevertheless, the Benandanti insisted over and over again that their experiences were real (Ginzburg, 20). Many modern historians, who have had Christian/industrial values burned into their brains, just don't know what to make of these and similar shamanistic experiences. We find Norman Cohn suggesting that the Benandanti suffered from catalepsy (Cohn, *Demons*, 124). He thinks that the experiences of shamans in general are "all purely imaginary" (Cohn, *Demons*, 222). Of course such trances involve psychological effects, and of course fantasy is an essential part of them. But that doesn't mean that we should refuse to see reality in them — perhaps a kind of reality that industrial civilization is blind to and would even prefer didn't exist.

In addition to having visions, the Benandanti were healers. In fact, the Inquisition first got wind of them because they were healing people. On March 21, 1575, a priest spoke to the Inquisition at Friuli. He said he had come upon a certain Paolo Gasparutto who claimed to heal people through the power of vagabonds who traveled at night carrying fennel stalks. Through their questioning of Gasparutto, the Inquisition uncovered the practices of the Benandanti (Ginzburg, 3 ff). The remarks about fennel stalks bring to mind the ancient worship of Dionysus. Dionysus was a version of the horned god and an associate of Cybele, the Great Mother (see Chapter 2). Both he and the Great Mother were worshipped by women and by men dressed in women's clothing. These worshippers carried wands made of giant fennel stalks (*narthex*) with a pine cone on the end (see Euripides' *Bacchae*). (The modern Italian word for fennel is *finocchio*, which also happens to mean "homosexual.") Once the Inquisition realized how widespread the practices of the Benandanti were, they launched a broad attack against them. Members of the cult were arrested, only now they were tortured into confessing what the Inquisitors wanted to hear. And what the Inquisitors were interested in was not Diana, but the Devil (since they viewed Diana as a demon). The upshot was that the Benandanti were continuously tortured until they said that they were witches and that they worshipped the Devil. By 1618, many of the Benandanti, under this extreme physical and psychological torment, actually came to view themselves as Devil-worshipping witches (Ginzburg, 108 ff). Hence the evidence concerning the Benandanti is conclusive proof that paganism survived very late in Europe and that Christians turned these pagans into witches.

The last stage in the transformation of paganism into witchcraft occurred when the night-riding followers of Diana became the witches who fly through the night on broomsticks. As we'll see later, the pagans sometimes used hallucinogenic drugs that gave them their visions of flying. These drugs were taken in the form of an ointment rubbed over the body and absorbed through the skin. To the inquisitors, this became the witches' salve that enabled them to fly through the night.

Evidence for the transformation of Diana into the Devil has been preserved in some of the existing peasant dialects of Europe. So, for example, in Sardinia, *Jana* (derived from *Diana*) means "witch." In Asturias, *Dianu* means "devil," and the same for *o Diana* in Galicia, and *Dianho* in parts of Portugal (Alford, 359).

We find broken-down remnants of Diana-worship even into the present day. In 1935, a visitor in Portugal reported that she was present in the town of *Janas*, which had been built on the site of an ancient pagan temple. She observed a public feast day that still had traces of paganism. The peasants brought their cattle in from the fields and walked in a big circle counterclockwise around the church. The older women arrived riding on donkeys. People made small votive offerings out of wax in the form of cattle and placed them on the altar. The visitor heard persistent rumors that a cock was killed in the church and the cattle sprinkled with its blood, although she herself did not witness this (Alford, 359-360).

In most of the accounts dealing with Diana, her followers usually seem to have been women. But similar rites existed among all-male groups with a male god. As with Diana, the leader of the male troops had many different names, depending on the location in Europe. Among the most common were Herne the Hunter, Herla the King, Herlechin, Herlequin, Harlequin, Hellequin, Hillikin, Berchtold, Berhtolt, Derndietrich, Quatembermann, and Kwaternik (Russell, 49, note & Ginzburg, 58, n. 2). In my opinion, this male figure is a survival of the Celtic horned god. As we saw in chapter 2, the Latinized name for the Celtic horned god was *Cemunnos*, which means "The Horned One" (Bober, *passim*). The ending *-os* on this word is the suffix that Greek and Old Latin added to most masculine nouns borrowed from other languages. So the original, de-Latinized form was probably *Cernunn*. Now, the prefixes *Cer-* and *Her-* are interchangeable IndoEuropean roots that both mean "horn." Hence a variant spelling of the same name is *Hernunn*. This last word, I suspect, was the original Celtic ancestor of *Herne*, which is one of the oldest names for the male figure we're dealing with. A variant spelling of *Herne* was *Herla*. From *Herla* comes *Herla, the King*, and from *Hera, the King* comes *Herlequin* and *Harlequin* (see "Harlequin" in the *Random House Dictionary*). Medieval depictions of Harlequin confirm these speculations based on language. They usually show him wearing a forked cap having two drooping horn-like appendages.

In the Latin literary tradition, Harlequin was turned into the figure of the Fool, as, for example, he appears in late Italian comedy. He is usually shown dressed up in bright clothes, and this is the traditional appearance of Harlequin on the Italian stage. His manifestation as the Fool is interesting, because in the middle ages a holiday survived from paganism called the Feast of Fools. It usually took place around January 1st (the festival of Janus — the brother of Diana), and was characterized by drinking, feasting, sex orgies, and transvestism (Russell, 51, 58-59; Rawson, 74).

The word "Fool" as applied to Harlequin didn't originally mean silly or stupid, but rather frenzied or ecstatic or mad, akin to the French word *folie*, which means madness or lunacy. This latter meaning is certainly in line with the ecstatic nature of the Feast of Fools. The rites of Harlequin originated from the countryside and the forest and impressed Christian observers with their wildness. This impression is conveyed through the words by which Christians described the followers of Harlequin. They were variously known as *sauvages, selvatici, selvaggi, selvatici*, and *homines selvatici*, meaning "wild men" from the root *silvus*, meaning forest (Russell, 49, note). Throughout the middle ages, we find numerous reports about troops of men following Harlequin at night. As one example, consider the historian and monk Ordericus Vitalis. In the 11th century, he reported in his Church History that these beliefs existed in Bonneville, France. A priest late one night was said to have witnessed a large crowd on horses and on foot, among whom were many who had recently died. On seeing this sight, he replied: "This is doubtless the troop of Harlechin, of which I have heard but never believed" (Lea, v. I, 171). This account recalls the Benandanti, who often said they saw the dead as well as the living.

Harlequin Disguised as Diana
Seventeenth century print

By the fifth century, Christian intellectuals had transformed the pagan horned god into the Devil, and Christian law began defining the old teutonic fertility gods as "devils" (Russell, 48). The church called these spirits *incubi* (that is, demons who lie on top) or *succubi* (demons who lie on the bottom). In the eyes of the church, they were devils who could take on the body of a man or woman at will and have sex with humans of either sex. For example, in the seventh century, Isidore of Seville said that the Teutons worshipped a spirit that lived in the woods called *Scrat*, which in Old English means hermaphrodite. He claimed that among the Latins they were called *incubi* (Wright, 75). Around 1218, Gervais of Tilbury noted that many people claimed to have seen nature and forest spirits that the ancient Celts called *Dusii*, but that the people of his day (that is, Christians) called incubi (Lea, v. L 173). Around 1455, Felix Hemmerlin reported that in Denmark and Norway demons frequently appeared in human form and were called Trolls. He added:

> And due to habit, they are not frightened by men, but men practice obeisance to them, who even still are called *incubi* and *succubi* and are mingled [that is, have sex] in human form with the sons and daughters of men (Lea, v. I, 160).

These examples show that the church did not just invent incubi and succubi. Behind the concept were minor pagan gods, sometimes hermaphroditic, that were believed to have sex with human beings. As the practitioners of paganism came to be viewed as witches, the church emphasized more and more the importance of *incubi* and *succubi*.

In 1484, Pope Innocent VIII issued a bull attacking *incubi* and *succubi*:

> It has recently come to our ears, not without great pain to us, that in some parts of upper Germany, as well as in the provinces, cities, territories, regions, and dioceses of Mainz, Koln, Trier, Salzburg, and Bremen, many persons of both sexes, heedless of their own salvation and forsaking the Catholic faith, give themselves over to devils male and female (Kors, 108).

The issuance of this bull marked a turning point in the history of witchcraft. It gave strong papal support to the growing view that witchcraft in and of itself was a form of *heresy*, and thus subject to the Holy Inquisition. "It established once and for all that the Inquisition against witches had full papal approval and thereby opened the door for the bloodbaths of the following century" (Russell, 230). It is from the date of this bull that we mark "the European witch-craze."

Few historians have analyzed the sexual dimension of Innocent's bull. His *reason* for classifying witchcraft as a heresy was that "devils" were having sex with humans of both sexes. Such people were guilty of "forsaking the Catholic faith" — in Latin, a fide *catholica deviantes*, literally "deviants from the Catholic faith" (Lea, 1:161). The western view that sexual non-conformity is "deviance" originated in religious orthodoxy. Modern psychiatrists, in taking up this view, have assumed the role once played by priests and inquisitors in suppressing dissent.

Because Christians believed incubi and succubi to be evil spirits without bodies, they ran into an embarassing theological quibble: How could beings without bodies have sex? Caesarius of Heisterbach, a thirteenth century monk and historian, offered a memorable answer in his *Dialogus*: demons collected all the cum that was ejaculated "contrary to nature" and used it to make bodies for themselves! (Lea, 1:152) In whatever form demons obtained their bodies, sex with them was a crime. "Intercourse with a devil was held the equivalent of buggery, for which the penalty was burning" (Robbins, 467). Margaret Murray in *The Witch-Cult in Western Europe* proposed that *incubi* and succubi were actually humans impersonating pagan gods who had sex with both *male* and female followers. After examining many charges brought against witches, Murray concluded:

> The evidence of the witches makes it abundantly clear that the so-called Devil was a human being, generally a man, occasionally a woman. At the great Sabbaths, where he appeared in his grand array, he was disguised out of recognition; at the small meetings, in visiting his votaries, or when inducting a possible convert to join the ranks of the witch-society, he came in his own person, usually dressed plainly in the costume of the period (Murray, 31).

Sex played a big role in the surviving traditions of paganism. Many accounts hint of sex rituals, transvestism, and nature worship, sometimes in association with sacred areas that are known to date back to the Stone Age or the Bronze Age. For example, church condemnations of both ritual transvestism and the worship of images of sex organs are frequent (see calendar at rear of book). Concerning surviving sex worship in general, we have a lot of evidence. In the 11th century, the German church historian Adam of Bremen reported that the god Fricco — represented by a huge dildo — was still being worshipped in Upsala, Sweden, and that the day Friday was sacred to him (Wright, 26). In the 13th century, we find several reports concerning acts of worship around dildos. In 1268, there was a spreading cattle disease in the Scottish district of Lothian. *The Chronicle of Lanercost* reported that some members of the clergy urged that an image of Priapus (that is, a dildo) be raised up in order to protect the cattle (Wright, 31). In 1282, in Inverkeithing, Scotland, a parish priest led an Easter dance of little girls around a dildo (Wright, 31-32). Some historians laugh off this last account, but if we bother to take the original text seriously, we find out the priest's motivations. When challenged by the bishop, *the priest said it was the ancient custom of the country* (Wright, 31-32). The bishop apparently believed him, because he was allowed to keep his job. Can you imagine what would happen if a Catholic priest did that today in Boston?

In the 14th century a group of Armenians, probably Cathers, practiced sun worship and held orgies (Russell, 93, n. 49). In 1353, Boccaccio's *Decameron* mentioned a secret society called "rovers" (reminiscent of the Benandanti) that met twice a month for feasting and orgies (Russell, 193). In 1375 an Italian woman, Gabrina Albetti, was brought to trial at Reggio for teaching other women to take off their clothing at night and pray to the stars. She was condemned by a secular court, branded, and her tongue was cut out (RusselL 210). In the 15th century, John Zizka charged that Bohemian heretics called Adamites were practicing nudity, ritual dances around fires, and sodomy (Lerner, 123). This report probably referred to pagan practices, since fire dances were a regular feature of the pagan holiday that survived under Christianity as the Feast of St. John the Baptist (Midsummer Eve).

Around 1455, Pope Calixtus III forbade religious practices that were still being celebrated in his day in caves decorated with. horses. One art historian thinks this refers to Stone-Age caves, since these often had animals painted on them and were originally used as shamanistic religious sites (Rawson, 10).

In the 16th century, we find more links between stone-age and bronzeage sites and charges of witchcraft. In 1514, the Englishman John Panter was accused of visiting a location annually on the eve of the Feast of St. John the Baptist for the purpose of consulting demons. The place he went to was in the parish of Doulting, near a location of 12 bronze-age burial mounds (Grinsell, 73). In 1566, John Walsh of Netherburg in England said he consulted "fairies" that resided in large heaps of earth and that he got his power of witchcraft from them. These heaps were prehistoric burial mounds (Grinsell, 73-74). In this same century, blatantly pagan practices continued even within some churches. In 1562, a large wood and leather dildo was worshipped in the Catholic church of St. Eutropius at Orange and was publicly seized and burned by Protestants (Wright, 51).

In 17th-century England, many bronze-age monuments were reputed to be the sites of witches' sabbats and were mentioned repeatedly in witch trials. In northwestern France, the sites of bronze-age monuments were often associated in folklore with witches' sabbats. Some burial mounds were even named from witchcraft, such as one in Brabant called *Le Lieu du Sabbat* ("The Place of the Sabbat") (Grinsell, 76-77).

These reports bring to mind stories about magic mounds in Italy. In 1630, Diel Breull of Assia said that he had traveled to the Mound of Venus, where he met Frau Holt, who was a protector of the fertility of the land. In 1632, Breull was tortured by the Inquisition into confessing that he had worshipped the Devil there (Ginzburg, 64-65). In 1694, a group of people called the Brotherhood of John were tried in Leopoli. They said they had visited the souls of the dead on the Mound of Venus and had the power to evoke them (Ginzburg, 64).

Paganism even continued into the 18th century. On December 30, 1781, an eyewitness account told of a church in Isernia, Naples, where the phailic god Priapus was still worshipped under the name of St. Cosmus. People placed wax models of cocks and balls on his altar as votive offerings (Hamilton, 18-21). In 1794, the minister of Callander in Pertshire, Scotland, claimed that pagan rites were still being practiced in his area (Hope, 73). In Brittany, people continued to hold sex rituals at the site of bronze-age monuments until the 19th century. And they didn't give up the practice without a struggle, for "until the last century the Church fought vigorously and with varying success against pagan and often obscene practices associated with the megalithic monuments" (von Cles-Reden, 260).

Even as late as the beginning of the 19th century, the names of the old deities were still used in some places. The goddess Demeter was worshipped under her own name and in the form of an ancient statue at Eleusis, Greece, until 1801. The cult was put down at that time by two Englishmen, Clarke and Crips. They formed an armed guard and went in and forcibly removed the goddess, causing a riot among the peasants (Briffault, v. III, 182).

The feasts of the ancient pagan gods were often celebrated with sex orgies. We shouldn't be surprised, therefore, to find Christian inquisitors linking witchcraft with sexuality. When people were arrested on suspicion of witchcraft, they were questioned at great length about their sex lives. Often they were tortured into confessing to every possible form of sexual activity. As one historian says: 'The curiosity of the judges was insatiable to learn ail possible details as to sexual intercourse and their industry in pushing the examinations was rewarded by an abundance of foul [sic] imaginations"(Lea, II:916-917).

In the 16th and 17th centuries, people who were suspect of being sexually unorthodox might easily find themselves accused of witchcraft, just as earlier, such people could easily find themselves accused of heresy. At lnnsbruck, Austria, the notorious witch-hunter Henry Institoris was uncertain whether a defendant had killed someone through poison or witchcraft, "though he inclined toward the latter suspicion on the peculiar grounds tht the suspect had a history of sexual laxity, and was thus no doubt prone to such base activities as witchcraft" (Kieckhefer, 49-50). During the peak of the witch-hunting craze, the great majority of people accused of witchcraft were women. This is understandable since women were the chief transmitters of the ancient pagan traditions. Under the earliest forms of paganism, women had enjoyed a great deal of sexual freedom. Their association with loose sex and paganism resulted in the creation of the Christian stereotype of women as sexually depraved.

This stereotype comes out quite clearly in the *Malleus Maleficarum*, an official 15th-century handbook for prosecuting witches. The authors of the *Malleus* ask themselves why more women are witches than men, and reply in the best tradition of male supremacy that "since they are feebler both in mind and body, it is not surprising that they should come more under the spell of witchcraft" (*Malleus*, 44). The authors continue their line of reasoning by claiming that women are more sexual than men, and therefore more likely to be controlled by the Devil: "But the natural reason is that she [woman) is more carnal than a man, as is clear from her many abominations" (*Malleus*, 44).

Their underlying attitude toward women's sexuality is well summed up in these words: "A woman is beautiful to look upon, contaminating to the touch, and deadly to keep …. All witchcraft comes from carnal lust, which is in women insatiable" (Malleus, 46-47). In the worst periods of the witch craze, a woman could find herself hauled before the Inquisition and accused of being a witch merely because she had a reputation for enjoying sex. The same thing could happen to a man if he had a reputation for being Gay. Unfortunately, professional historians have not given the latter fact much attention. This is because they often have an attitude toward homosexuality very similar to that found among medieval Christians.

Male homosexuality and witchcraft were often linked together, just as Gay sex was earlier linked with heresy. Some scholars may be confused on this point because of the view of homosexuality in the *Malleus Maleficarum*, which was the first witch-hunters' handbook to carry the Pope's approval. According to the *Malleus* homosexuality is so disgusting that not even demons would do it! In the words of the *Malleus*:

> And it must be carefully noted that, though the Scripture speaks of *Incubi* and *Succubi* lusting after women, yet nowhere do we read that *Incubi* and *Succubi* fell into vices against nature. We do not speak only of sodomy, but of any other sin whereby the act is wrongfully performed outside the rightful channel. And the very great enormity of such as sin in this way is shown by the fact that all devils equally, of whatsoever order, abominate and think shame to commit such actions (*Malleus*, 29-30).

The *Malleus* concludes by saying that anyone who commits a Gay sex act after the age of 33 is probably beyond all hope of salvation:

> Indeed many say, and it is truly believed, that no one can unimperilled persevere in the practice of such vices beyond the period of the mortal life of Christ, which lasted for thirty-three

years, unless he should be saved by some special grace of the Redeemer (*Malleus*, 30).

Unfortunately for Gay people, the Inquisition did not follow the *Malleus* in believing that the Devil was above homosexuality. In 1582, the Inquisition at Avignon, France, delivered this judgment against a group of condemned witches: "You men have fornicated with *succubi* and you women with *incubi*. You have wretchedly committed genuine sodomy and the most unmentionable of crimes with them by means of their cold touch" (Lea, v. I, 485).

Homosexuality and witchcraft became so closely associated that the two were often linked together in popular tracts on the subject. In 1460, an anonymous tract appeared during the trial of accused witches at Arras, France. It made this accusation:

> Sometimes indeed indescribable outrages are perpetrated in exchanging women, by order of the presiding devil, by passing on a woman to other women and a man to other men, an abuse against the nature of women by both parties and similarly against the nature of men, or by a woman with a man outside the regular orifice and in another orifice (Robbins, 468).

In 1589, an anonymous pamphlet of 15 pages appeared in Paris accusing King Henry III of France of being a homosexual and a witch (Summer, *Popular History*, 164-165). In Lisbon in 1612, homosexuality and witchcraft were so intermixed that authorities were confused over whether sodomites should be executed under the civil procedure for criminals or under the religious procedures for witches (Lea, v. II, 485). In many witchcraft trials, defendants were tortured into confessing that Gay sex acts took place at the sabbat. In 1615, the accused witch Gentien le Clerc was tried at Orleans. He was made to confess that "after the Mass, they dance, then lie together, men with men, and women with women" (Murray, *Witch-Cult*, 249).

During the peak of the terror, judges, theologians, and intellectuals routinely combined charges of witchcraft with lesbianism and male homosexuality. A good example is Henry Boguet, who personally tried a great many cases. Around 1619, he wrote in his book *Discours des Sorciers*:

> You may well suppose that every kind of obscenity is practiced there, yea, even those abominations for which Heaven poured down fire and brimstone on Sodom and Gomorrah are quite common in these assemblies (Summers, *History*, 157).

In 1620, a Portuguese inquisitor named Manuel do Valle de Moura published a book on witchcraft. He said that in Portugal the Inquisition got jurisdiction for prosecutions of sodomy and that no one who was convicted escaped the stake (Lea, v. II, 481-485). In 1625, the Jesuit Paul Laymann published a book on morals called *Theologia Moralis*, which claimed that adultery and sodomy were crimes that led to witchcraft (Lea, v. II, 680).

The association between Gay sex and witchcraft was not limited to continental Europe. In 1661, the Irish woman Florence Newton was brought to trial and accused of aggressively kissing and bewitching a young servant woman, Mary Longdon (Robbins, 352-353). In 1670 in Scotland, Thomas Weir, a respected 70-year-old bachelor, stunned public opinion by confessing, at his own initiative, to witchcraft, fornication, and sodomy (Robbins, 534).

By the 16th century, the Inquisition had created a witch stereotype. According to this stereotype, a witch was a person who had the power to bewitch people, was bound to the Devil, flew through the air at night, conspired to overthrow Christian civilization, and attended periodic meetings where wild sex rites were held (Cohn, *Demons*, 147). People were arrested on suspicion of witchcraft and were often tortured until they confessed to practicing everything in this stereotype. As a result, many people were burned who had absolutely nothing whatsoever to do with any of these things.

The stereotype of the witch was a fantasy developed by the Inquisition, but it was a fantasy based on a certain reality. Evidence for the survival of sex and nature worship abounds in both Gnostic heresy and peasant traditions. Witches existed, but they were not Devil-worshipping monsters hell-bent on destroying the human race. They were simply remnant practitioners of broken-down strains of the old paganism. They healed, went into trances, had visions, and celebrated bawdy rites in honor of the magical powers of sex and nature. Like the pagans of antiquity, they did not make a distinction between sex and religion. For them, sex was one manifestation of religious power. In the eyes of patriarchal Christians, that was heresy and the same thing as worshipping the Devil.

6 The Medieval Counterculture

The old religion had a coherent world view. Behind its many forms there lay a basic outlook on life, a way of feeling and experiencing nature and other people, that was passed down from generation to generation. This world view was manifest first in ancient paganism, then in medieval heresy, and finally in witchcraft. Although the old religion and Christianity influenced each other and in some cases even fused, the root beliefs and social forms of the old religion formed a genuine counterculture, radically opposing the way traditional Christians lived and thought.

The old religion was polytheistic. Its most important deity was a goddess who was worshipped as the great mother. Its second major deity was the horned god, associated with animals and sexuality, including homosexuality. These and other deities were worshipped in the countryside at night with feasting, dancing, animal masquerades, transvestism, sex orgies, and the use of hallucinogenic drugs. Sensual acts were at the heart of the old religion, since theirs was a worldly religion of joy and celebration. The testimony of the witches themselves, when uncoerced, bore witness to this joyousness. Pierre de Lancre, a seventeenth-century judge, reported: "Jeanne Dibasson, twenty-nine years old, tells us that the sabbat is the true paradise, where there is more pleasure than one can express" (Murray, *Witch-Cult*, 25). Sometimes, motivated by a desire to discredit paganism, inquisitors tortured witches until they denied their joy and said the celebrations were disgusting. In so doing, the inquisitors were like some modern psychiatrists who "treat" Gay patients into saying that Gay life can't possibly be happy.

Women were the chief priests and leaders of the old religion, performing the roles of prophet, midwife, and healer. Women priests impersonated the goddess and acted in her name. Although groups of male priests also existed (such as the Druids), they never suppressed the religious role of women. The material substructure of the old religion was a matriarchal social system that reached back to the Stone Age.

The old religion was a religion of the countryside and forest, rather than of the city. In the earliest period, references to any church or temple were rare, becoming more frequent only under the later influence of patriarchy and Christianity. Followers of the old religion lived rural lives in direct dependence on nature and felt a sense of community with all plant and animal life. In the stone-age world from which paganism emerged, no "government" existed except for the people themselves. Even in the early medieval period, their culture was devoid of institutionalism as we now know it. In later European history, witchcraft retained this characteristic hostility to institutional authority. "In the history of Christianity, witchcraft is an episode in the long struggle between authority and order on one side and prophecy and rebellion on the other" (Russell, 2).

Both ancient pagans and later witches were learned people, possessing a vast storehouse of knowledge about herbs, plants, animals, signs of the weather, astronomy, and medicine. This knowledge, along with their myths and poetry, was transmitted by word of mouth from one generation to the next. Learning was thus a matter of close personal dialogue. Originally the old religion knew nothing of books or the bureaucratic control of knowledge by universities. Only as Christianity became more powerful did bookishness find its way into the old religion.

The Christian religion, in its traditional forms, was opposed to these features of the old religion. Christians worshipped only one god, described in terms that suggested male heterosexuality ("God the Father"). This god existed in grand isolation above nature, which he created and dominated, whereas the deities of the old religion always remained subordinate to nature. The Christian god was also completely intolerant of any other deity or spirit. Christian hatred for people who worshipped deities other than their "one true god" goes back to Jesus the Nazarene, who compared such people to weeds:

> The weeds are the followers of the evil one and the enemy who sowed them is the devil. The harvest is the end of the world. The Son of Man will dispatch his angels to collect from his kingdom all who draw others to apostasy, and all evildoers. The angels will hurl them into a fiery furnace where they will wail and grind their teeth. (*New American Bible, Matt.*, 13: 38-42).

While the old religion was tolerant of all forms of sex, traditional Christianity condemned every form of sex except monogamous heterosexuality sanctified by marriage. Jesus the Nazarene had no sex life at all, and Paul of Tarsus constantly condemned adultery, fornication, and homosexuality, both male and female. "The earlier religious element most particularly pursued and repressed by Christianity was the naive and quite beautiful adoration of the sexuality of nature and of human beings" (Legman, 103-104). Wherever traditional Christianity has come to power, it has used the power of government to repress sex. Whenever Christian missionaries have encountered so-called "primitives," the first thing they've done is to make the people feel guilty about sex, nudity, and the very fact of having a body. The major forces behind the American homophobe Anita Bryant were a coalition of churches, synagogues, and right-wing political groups.

Christianity's hatred of sex was matched by its hatred for women. The Christian god was always addressed as "He," and no women were found among the disciples of Jesus the Nazarene. Women have always been excluded from the priesthood. Paul of Tarsus stated:

A woman must listen in silence and be completely submissive. I do not permit a woman to act as a teacher, or in any way to have authority over a man; she must be quiet. For Adam was created first. Eve afterward; moreover it was not Adam who was deceived but the woman. It was she who was led astray and fell into sin (*I Tim.*, 2: 11-14).

During the 16th and 17th century witch hunts, inquisitors singled out women as dangerous. Many times women were condemned precisely because they were associated with sex. The heterosexual men who controlled Christianity viewed sexual feelings as sinful; since women aroused these feelings, they too must be sinful. The condemnation of women was a natural consequence of the condemnation of sex.

In contrast to the anarchistic values of the witches, Christianity was obsessed with obedience to established institutions. Typical of this tradition was the attitude of Paul of Tarsus:

Let everyone obey the authorities that are over him, for there is no authority except from God, and all authority that exists is established by God. As a consequence, the man who opposes authority rebels against the ordinances of God; those who resist thus shall draw condemnation down among themselves (*Romans*, 13: 1-2).

The concept of hierarchy was spread throughout the Christian world by Dionysius, the Pseudo-Areopagite, "the father of Christian mysticism." In his theology, the hierarchy of the church was a symbol of the hierarchy of heaven, which was a symbol of the mystical inner structure of God. The only way for Christians to know God was to obey those who occupied the next highest rung in the church's hierarchy, since hierarchy in and of itself was an image of divinity. Dionysius made obedience more than just a moral duty; it became the means of grace itself, as bureaucracy was raised to the level of a mystical principle. Later, Protestantism threw off the concept of the hierarchical dispensation of grace, but retained the idea of the mystical importance of its own hierarchy. As a result, in both Catholicism and Protestantism, church and hierarchy have become synonymous.

Christianity viewed learning as a bookish practice, and set up a system of universities across Europe. Learning became impersonal and objective, consisting of the study of documents and books in a classroom under the control of a central bureaucracy. The church carefully outlawed and destroyed those books that the faithful were forbidden to read. The effect of these practices was to separate reason from feeling and to make learning into an objective, intellectualized pursuit conducted within the confines of an institution. Learning became bureaucratized.

Christianity and the old religion differed in the way they viewed nudity, hair, drugs, and animals. Among the Celts, nudity was never regarded as shameful since the nude body was respected as a source of religious power. Celtic warriors sometimes fought nude in order to increase their magical powers on the battle field (Chadwick, *The Celts*, 134). The chief deities of the old religion were generally shown nude, and the male deity had an erect cock. Small lead amulets, depicting both male and female genitals, continued to be used as good-luck charms by the peasants in Europe long after Christianity became the official religion (Hamilton).

Christianity's contempt for the nude body was logically connected to its hatred of sex. In the old testament the first fall into sin is connected with the shame Adam and Eve felt over nudity:

> Then the eyes of both of them were opened and they realized that they were naked; so they sewed fig leaves together and made loincloths for themselves (*Genesis*, 3:7).

When the god Yahweh appeared in the Garden of Eden, Adam hid: "I heard you in the garden; but I was afraid, because I was naked, so I hid myself" (*Genesis*, 3:10).

The new testament continued in the same vein, and several statements of Jesus the Nazarene have encouraged some Christians to become fanatically ascetic:

> What I say to you is: anyone who looks lustfully at a woman has already committed adultery with her in his thoughts. If your right eye is your trouble, gouge it out and throw it away! Better to lose part of your body than to have it all cast into Gehenna (*Matt*, 5: 28-29).

In the third century, both the letter and spirit of this statement was followed by Origen, a church father, who castrated himself to avoid sexual temptation.

Medieval Christians were morbid about nudity. Some even refused to bathe because that would involve undressing. Stories were circulated about early Christian saints who had never bathed in their whole lives. The inevitable result of this type of thinking was widespread disease, particularly skin disease, which constantly plagued the middle ages. In Christian art of the middle ages, the genitals are rarely shown, and the human form usually appears emaciated and anti-sensual. A common motif is the tortured or mutilated body of some Christian martyr. The major emblem of medieval Christianity — the agonized body of Jesus the Nazarene nailed to a cross — sums up the whole Christian mentality: crucify the body for the sake of the soul. During the Renaissance, Christian artists began to show a more positive body image. The underlying cause, however, was the revival of pagan Greek values; it had nothing to do with Christianity *per se*. The so-called "Reformation" was a revolt against this revival, leaving as its legacy the artistic sterility of modern Protestantism.

The old religion prized body hair. Celtic stories and poems frequently praised the beautiful long hair of both men and women. Among the ancient Germans, Holle (a great mother goddess) was associated with long hair, giving rise to a German expression for a man with long unkempt hair: *Er ist mit der Holle gefahren*, meaning "He's been traveling with Holle" (Grimm, 223). Fairies, too, were associated with long hair until very late times. Longhaired fairies dressed in green were reported in Danffshire, Scotland, until 1793 (Hope, 14).

Medieval Christians associated long hair with the Devil. William of Auvergne, thirteenth century philosopher and Bishop of Paris, said that women must cover their hair in church because "the beauty of the hair strongly excites the lust of incubi" (Kors, 152). Paul of Tarsus thought long hair was acceptable for women, but unnatural for men: "Does not nature itself teach you that it is dishonorable for a man to wear his hair long, while the long hair of a woman is her glory" (*I Corinthians*, 11:14). Although tolerating long hair on women, he insisted they cover it in church: "Any woman who prays or prophesies with her head uncovered brings shame upon her head. It is as if she had her head shaved. Indeed, if a woman will not wear a veil, she ought to cut off her hair" (*I Corinthians*, 11:5-6).

The old religion celebrated its rites with hallucinogenic drugs. Throughout the history of witchcraft, references are made to drug taking. Walter Map, a twelfth century ecclesiastic, stated that he knew certain heretics who served innocent people a "magic food" that affected their minds (Russell, 131). Johann Weyer, a sixteenth-century physician who opposed the oppression of witches, wrote: "The experiences of witches are delirious dreams induced by drugs wherewith they confect their ointments" (Lea, II: 505). Weyer identified several substances in the witches' so-called flying ointment as hallucinogens. .

Thorn apple (Datura)   *Mandrake (Mandragora)*

Margaret Murray was the first modern scholar to suggest that witches used hallucinogens. Her suspicions have been confirmed by Michael Harner, who concludes that the witches' ointment contained atropine and other alkaloids, "all of which have hallucinogenic effects" and which can be absorbed through the skin (Harner, 128). Some historians reject Harner's conclusions, but their reasons usually boil down to simple prejudice against drug takers. Norman Cohn ridicules Harner because his book "was published just as the craze [!] for psychedelic experiments and experiences was building up" (Cohn, *Demons*, 118).

Henbane (Hyoscyamus)   *Deadly nightshade (Atropa belladonna)*

The role of hallucinogens in the witches' religion is interesting in view of the ancient worship of Dionysus (the horned god of the Greco-Roman world), who was also the god of drunkenness. Wine was originally viewed as a religious hallucinogen, giving participants in the sacred orgies visions similar to those reported by witches. The ancients viewed wine as a magical power distilled from the life forces of plants. By drinking wine, the worshippers of Dionysus became *entheos*, "filled with the god," literally drunk with divinity.

The old religion had a reverent attitude toward animals. Both major deities — the great mother and the horned god — were animal-oriented. The great mother, as mistress and protector of animals, was called "Diana" by Christians because of her similarity to the Greco-Roman animal and moon goddess. Besides his horns, the male god had cleft hooves and furry legs, and his worshippers dressed in animal skins. So common was the practice of animal masquerades in the middle ages that detailed condemnations were issued against them. Theodore, the seventh-century Archbishop of Canterbury, wrote:

> If anyone in the kalends of January goes about as a stag or a bull; that is making himself into a wild animal and dressing in the skin of a herd animal, and putting on the head of beasts; those who in such wise transform themselves into the appearance of a wild animal, penance for three years because this is devilish (Summers, *History*, 134).

Throughout the Christian Era, the confessions of witches, the transcripts of trials, and popular writings show that certain male members of the witch cult dressed in animal skins (later in black leather) and had ritual sex with other witches at the Sabbat. The most common animal masquerades were those of bull, cat, dog, horse, and sheep (Murray, *The Witch-Cult*, 61ff).

In England, witches were associated with "familiars," which were pet animals kept for magical purposes, such as the famous black cat. Often accused of communicating with these animals, witches themselves claimed they could change themselves and others into animal forms. These stories should not be dismissed as simple fantasies, especially in view of the witches' use of hallucinogens. "There is documentary evidence of the existence over a period of *centuries* of the belief that certain women (not necessarily always old ones) could change themselves and others into animals in classical times" (Baroja, 39; original's italics).

Christianity has always taught contempt for animals, believing that animals are inferior to humans. In the old testament, humans are commanded to rule over animals: "Have dominion over the fish of the sea, the birds of the air, and all the living things that move on the earth" (*Genesis*, 1:28). In the new testament, animals play no role in God's plan for salvation, and God himself is never worshipped as an animal. Early church fathers, absorbing the traditions of Greek intellectualism, taught that humans were superior to animals because they possessed logos— the power of reasoning. The fathers viewed all non-intellectual functions (like sexuality) as "animal passions," and thus beneath the dignity of purified Christians. The word "animal" has come to connote baseness ever since.

The old religion's attitudes toward the body, hair, hallucinogens, and animals were all consistent. They were the values we'd expect to find in a culture that was practically devoid of bureaucratic institutions, existing in direct dependence on nature. Living in this way, early rural pagans and later medieval witches viewed their sensuality as the key to who they were as people, and not as some kind of low-level crud to be scraped off their souls. Their very survival depended on being in touch with their bodies and knowing how to communicate with plants and animals. As a result, theirs was an enchanted world, the world of natural feelings.

Traditional Christian attitudes were also consistent. They were the values of a culture that depended for its survival on thorough-going domination and hierarchy, a social fact that colored their view of the whole universe. In the external world, it was the domination of God over nature, humans over animals, men over women, Pope over bishops, King over knights, states and churches over people. In the internal world, it was the hierarchy of the soul: intellect over body, thoughts over passions, disciplined preparation for a future life over the anarchy of here-now sensuality. Sexual repression, self-discipline, and obedience were the means of survival in such a culture, as well as the keys to heaven. They were also the tools that enabled church and state to accumulate vast institutional control over the lives of human beings. And so Christians lived and died "within the walls," out of touch with natural feelings.

These same Christian values have found their way into the minds and laws of all highly industrialized nations. Regardless of whether they call themselves capitalist or communist, the governments of all "highly developed" nations of the world fear nudity, drugs, long hair, animals, and sex. Like medieval Christian civilization, modern industrial cultures are all institutionalized, bureaucratized societies, totally dependent on domination and hierarchy for their survival.

All of us have been institutionalized since the moment of our birth — in classrooms, prisons, offices, factories, hospitals, mad houses. We are totally dependent on great institutions for meeting our every need. There are very few of us who can do what the majority of people throughout history have always regarded as essential human activities: grow our own food, make our own clothing, build our own homes, make our own medicines, create our own gods. And there are very few of us who can guiltlessly express the full potential of our sex energies, communicate with the animals, or become transfigured by the power of the plant spirits. Instead, we have had drilled into our brains those traits that make it possible for great bureaucracies and institutions to satisfy our needs and thus dominate our lives: alienation from nature, sexual repression, self-denial, and obedience.

7 The Mass Murder of Women and Gay People

"Don't think I've come to bring peace on earth. I've come, not to bring peace, but a sword." — Jesus the Nazarene (*Matt.*, 10:34)

Christianity and the old religion, with its heretical off-shoots, could not co-exist in peace. Members of the Christian ruling class were convinced that theirs was the one true religion and that all other religions served the devil. They remembered the words of Jesus the Nazarene: "Go out into the highways and along the hedgerows and force them to come in. I want my house to be full" (*Luke*, 14:23, *New American Bible*). Taking up the sword, Christian rulers tried to annihilate those they could not convince.

The situation became critical in the late twelfth century. By 1150, the Cathars had their own culture, dialect, religion, and tradition of self-government in Languedoc (southern France) (Wakefield, 62). Cathars opposed Catholicism and were tolerant toward Gay people, Jews, and pagans. Many Cathar leaders were women, and the arts flourished free of censorship. Church leaders were alarmed at the spread of Catharism and started issuing condemnations of their practices and teachings. In 1150, Geoffrey of Auxerre published *Super Apocalypsim*, accusing the Cathars of advocating free sex (Russell, 128). In 1157, the Synod of Rheims met and formally denounced Catharism. The Synod charged that Cathars engaged in orgies and that itinerant Catharist weavers were condemning marriage and encouraging promiscuity (Runciman, 121; Russell, 128; Loos, 117; Cohn, *Millennium*, 153).

Catharist beliefs spread rapidly in the rest of Europe, becoming strong in Lombardy and in the Rhineland. Other heresies appeared. In 1173, Peter Waldo (or Waldes), a rich merchant from Lyon, France, attacked the wealth of the church and gave away all of his possessions to found the Waldensians. In 1184 Pope Lucius III condemned the Waldensians and authorized the use of the inquisition (without torture) to uncover them (Wakefield, 44 & 133).

In 1208, Pope Innocent Ill summoned the Albigensian Crusade to wipe out the Cathars of Languedoc, who were also known as Albigensians, after the city of Albi. From 1209 to 1229, Catholic troops, led by Simon de Montfort, invaded Languedoc, threw the country into a bloody civil war, and conducted a campaign of extermination. The people of Languedoc resisted with equal determination and violence, and were nearly victorious until the King of France, who had been uncommitted, joined the Catholic forces. On April 12, 1229, the Albigensians surrendered, except for a small group holding the fortress of Montsegur. They surrendered in 1243 only to be burned *en masse*. An incident reported by the Catholic writer Caesarius is indicative of the violence of the invading troops:

> From the confessions of some of these people, they [the troops] were aware that Catholics were intermingled with the heretics, so they asked the Abbot: 'Lord, what shall we do? We cannot distinguish the good from the wicked'. The abbot, as well as others, was afraid that the heretics would pretend to be Catholics only in fear of death and after the Christians' departure would return to their perfidy. He is reported to have cried: 'Kill them! The Lord knows those who are his own'. (Wakefield, 197).

At the crusade's end, both sides signed an agreement. Forfeiting one third of his land, the Count of Toulouse swore allegiance to the church and the King of France. In addition, he promised to hunt down any remaining heretics, dismiss all Jews from their jobs, and tear down the fortifications of thirty castles. He also agreed to let a university be built — the University of Toulouse — for the purpose of fighting heresy and propagating Christian values (Wakefield, 127- 130). Ironically, Augustus Caesar, twelve hundred years before, had established a university in the same town for combating the teachings of the Druids (Chadwick, *The Druids*, 78).

Despite the crusade, Catharism and other heresies continued to spread. Between 1227- 1235, Pope Gregory IX created a permanent heresy-hunting machine, the Office of the Holy Inquisition. First created by the Catholic Church, the Inquisition was later copied by courts in Protestant countries as well. Before the Inquisition was set up, heretics were tried before secular or bishops' courts acting independent of one another without any central direction. They rarely went looking for heretics, dealing only with cases that were brought to their attention. With the creation of the Inquisition, all this changed.

The Inquisition declared that heresy was a *crimen excepta* ("an exceptional crime"), which meant that prosecutions were exempt from the usual due process of law. According to the rules established by the Inquisition, a person was assumed guilty until proven innocent (see entry under "Inquisition" in Robbins, p. 266). Mere suspicion or common gossip were sufficient to bring a person before the Inquisition on such a charge. Witnesses who incriminated the accused were not publicly identified, and the accused was not given the right to cross-examine their testimony. In most cases, the accused was denied the right to counsel. In cases where counsel was allowed, a too vigorous defense of the accused could result in the counsel's being indicted for heresy.

After 1256, persons accused of heresy were almost always tortured until they "confessed." The torture was severe and could result in death. Those who did confess were generally tortured further until they named accomplices. After this, the accused was made to appear in court and swear that his or her confession was "voluntary"; refusal to swear this resulted in more torture. Once defendants confessed and swore that their confessions were "voluntary," they were given over to the secular authorities to be executed. Those who confessed were generally strangled, and their bodies burned (sometimes they were reprieved and sentenced to life imprisonment on bread and water). Those who refused to confess or who retracted a confession were burned alive. Officially, it was the secular authority, not the Inquisition, that finally executed the heretic. Throughout the entire history of the Inquisition there was never any case of simple acquittal (Robbins, 270).

The cost of running the Inquisition was paid for by the accused, whose property was seized and divided up between the accusers and the judges. Heresy hunting became a major industry of the middle ages, rewarding those who supported the Inquisition. In 1360, the Inquisitor Eymeric complained that the secular authorities in his area were no longer giving enough support to the Inquisition: "In our days there are no more rich heretics; so that princes, not seeing much money in prospect, will not put themselves to any expense; it is a pity that so salutary an institution as ours should be so uncertain of its future" (Robbins, 271).

The authorities who created the Inquisition showed an extraordinary concern with sexual matters. In 1233 Pope Gregory IX issued a bull called *Vox in Rama*, accusing heretics of practicing sex rites and calling for their annihilation:

> The whole Church weeps and groans and can find no consolation when such things are wrought in its bosom. It is the most detestable of heresies, a horror to those who hear of it, opposed to reason, contrary to piety, hateful to all hearts, inimical to earth and heaven, against which the very elements should arise. It would not be a sufficient punishment if the whole earth rose

against them, if the very stars revealed their iniquities to the whole world, so that not only men but the elements themselves should combine for their destruction and sweep them from the face of the earth, without sparing age or sex, so that they should be an eternal opprobrium to the nations (Lea, I:202).

Six years before, Gregory had issued another Bull, *Extravagantes*, which condemned sodomy (Bailey, 98). Condemnations of homosexuality among the clergy also appeared in the decrees of the Third Lateran Council in 1179, the Council of Paris in 1212, and the Council of Rouen in 1214 (Bailey, 127).

Because of the identification of homosexuality with heresy, the creation of the Inquisition seems to have spurred *secular* authorities to start harassing Lesbians and Gay men. In 1260, the legal code of the city of Orleans outlawed lesbianism and male homosexuality, calling for mutilations for the first and second offenses, and burning for the third (Bailey, 142). In 1261, the *parlement* of Amiens had to decide a dispute between the bishop and the city government as to who had the authority to try sodomites, finally deciding on behalf of the city (Bailey, 143). The fact that homosexuality came to be viewed as a form of heresy is clearly shown in the 1290 law passed by King Edward I of England. The law called for death by burning in the case of sodomites — but did so in the context of condemning *religious* criminals: 'The same sentence shall be passed upon sorcerers, sorceresses, renegades [meaning apostates), sodomists, and heretics publicly convicted" (Bailey, 145-146).

The Holy Inquisition turned homosexuality into heresy. "Heresy became a sexual rather than a doctrinal concept; to say a man was a heretic was to say that he was a homosexual, and vice versa" (Taylor, 131). Because of the methods of the Inquisition — with hearsay and the forced confession of accomplices— great numbers of Lesbians and Gay men must have lost their lives. But straight historians have not documented this aspect of the Inquisition, just as they have not documented the mass murder of Gay people in Hitler's concentration camps.

The Inquisition inevitably led to political abuse. The most famous case of this abuse involved the charge of homosexuality against the Order of the Knights Templars, a monastic military order. On Friday, October 13, 1307, Philippe the Fair, King of France, stunned Europe by having 5, 000 members of the Order arrested throughout France (Legman, 3ff). The Templars were brought before the Inquisition and charged with five counts of heresy: (1) that incoming members to the order were required to spit on the cross and reject the Christian religion; (2) that during his initiation the initiate kissed the initiator on his mouth, cock, and ass hole; (3) that sodomy was the lawful and expected practice of all Templars; and (4) that the Templars held secret religious rites where they worshipped a nonChristian deity (Lea, in Legman).

At first, Jacques de Molay, the Grand Master of the Order, and the other arrested members denied the charges. But when they were subjected to torture, many "confessed." Under an apparent plea-bargaining deal, de Molay himself agreed to plead guilty to rejecting Christ, if the charge of homosexuality was dropped

(Legman, 107-108). On November 22, Pope Clement issued the bull *Pastoralis praeeminentiae*, urging all monarchs of Europe to emulate Philippe's action (Lea, in Legman, 177). In the next few years the Templars were hunted down all over Europe. Exiled, imprisoned, or executed, they saw their property confiscated, and the order was abolished.

Most historians believe that Philippe's actions were purely mercenary. Although the Templars were founded in 1128 as a monastic, military order of poor crusaders, by the fourteenth century they had accumulated vast wealth and had become the chief bankers of the middle ages. Both Pope Clement and Philippe were in debt to them. The Templars had also gained astonishing legal privileges. They were exempt from all taxes, were above secular law, maintained their own set of confessors, and worshipped in their own chapels from which all others were barred. Legally the French Templars were not even the subjects of Philippe, but were accountable only to the Pope (Lea, in Legman, 152). Philippe was desperate for money due to his huge war debts. Previously he had debased the currency, arrested all of the Jews in his kingdom, claimed their property, and banished them (Lea, in Legman, 154). His treatment of the Templars was consistent with his ruthless policy of subsidizing, by any means possible, the emerging apparatus of the nation-state of France. Unlike the witches, no Templar advocated his supposed heresy in the face of torture, and de Molay eventually withdrew his confession, though he knew the withdrawal would cause him to be burned alive (Lea, in Legman, 163). Hence historians are probably right in seeing the Templars as the victims of a frame-up, having nothing to do with either heresy or sodomy. The real significance of their trial is that it shows the extent to which heresy had been identified with sodomy and the way in which both charges could be used for political purposes.

In 1310, King Philippe brought posthumous charges of conjuring, apostasy, murder and sodomy against Pope Boniface VIII, who had died in 1303 (Cohn, *Demons*, 185). His reasons were purely political. In 1296, he had tried to impose a tax on church property to pay for his war against England. The Pope issued a bull forbidding the tax and excommunicating those who tried to enforce it. The King had the Pope arrested, but the latter still refused to withdraw his excommunication, and soon after died. The only way to invalidate the excommunication was to have the dead Pope declared a heretic. The effort proved unnecessary, however, when the new Pope, Clement V (a stooge of the King), withdrew the excommunication, at which point the King dropped the case (Cohn, *Demons*, 182).

Despite these cases involving Popes and Kings, inquisitors spent most of their energy trying to exterminate heretics from the lower classes. In 1311, Pope Clement V issued his bull *Ad Nostrum*, which called for annihilation of the spreading heresy of the Free Spirit, popular among the very poor. The issuance of this bull marked the beginning of a crucial transition period which ended in 1484 with Pope Innocent VIII's anti-witch bull. Between these two dates, the church's entire concept of witchcraft changed. It was no longer simply viewed as the act of injuring another person through magic (bewitchment), but was regarded as a form of devil worship (demonic witchcraft). In effect, witchcraft came to be viewed as a form of *heresy*, and so fell under the jurisdiction of the inquisition.

Under paganism, witchcraft was thought of as simple bewitchment (the ability to bless or curse). Pagan laws restricted themselves to cases of actual proven injury brought about by a curse or spell. If the defendant was acquitted, the accuser was punished instead; hence the laws favored the accused. "The old pagan laws had taken cognizance of magic only in the form of *maleficium* [bewitchment], and even then had judged it solely in terms of harm done to life, health or property" (Cohn, *Demons*, 157). Under the early church, however, both good and evil magical activities— since they supposedly came from the devil— were considered evil. Furthermore, the early church viewed witchcraft as an essentially *pagan* tradition. This identification with paganism is clear from early Christian law:

> There also exist other, most pernicious, evils that are undoubtedly left over from the practice of the pagans. Such are magicians, soothsayers, sorcerers, witches, diviners, enchanters, interpreters of dreams, whom the divine law decrees to be punished unflinchingly (Lea 1:138).

Despite its contempt for magic, the early church did not organize a full-scale attack against magicians and witches because it was not yet strong enough. The Christianity of the early middle ages was largely an affair of the King and the upper class of warlords. The rest of society remained pagan. In addition, early medieval Christians were hampered by a general breakdown of centralized authority in both church and state. Anarchy favored paganism.

By the early thirteenth century, with the election of Pope Innocent III, the church was much better organized and ready to act. Its immediate target was heresy: the numerous and widespread attempts to combine traditional Christianity with elements of the old religion. To deal with this, the church launched crusades and started the Holy Inquisition. By the early fourteenth century, the church as an institution was stronger than ever, gaining the upper hand over heretics everywhere. Now it began to look at the historical sources of heresy— the surviving old religion that modern historians view as "folklore," "peasant fantasy," and "strange fertility rites." Feeling its privilege, power, and world view threatened by these sources, the fifteenth century ruling class fantasized that Satan was conspiring to overthrow the power of Christ's church on earth. Christian intellectuals fed on this fear, and they, not the lower classes, thus created the stereotype of demonic witchcraft (Kieckhefer, *passim*). In 1451, Pope Nicholas V declared that magical activities were subject to the Inquisition (Robbins, 272). And in 1484, Pope Innocent VIII gave papal backing to the intellectuals' view that witches were demon-worshipping heretics.

Two factors thus combined to produce the mass witchhunts of the 16th and 17th centuries: great power and great fear in the hands of the Christian ruling class. The combination was deadly and lead to horrible consequences. Most of continental Europe became convinced that witches were everywhere. "Every misfortune and every accident in a hamlet would be attributed to witchcraft" (Lea, III:S08).

Two companions being slain together during the Inquisition

The methods developed by the Holy Inquisition (and later adopted by the Protestant courts as well) guaranteed a steady flow of "confessions." Any person who was a non-conformist ran the risk of being brought before the court and tortured into confessing and naming accomplices. Common methods of torture used against witches included crushing their fingers in vises, pouring alcohol on their backs and setting it afire, making them sit on a red hot stove, pouring hot oil into their boots, roasting the soles of their feet over fires until the joints fell out, stretching their body on the rack until every joint became dislocated, tearing out pieces of flesh with red hot pincers, amputating parts of their body, and gouging out their eyes. Rumors of homosexuality made a person suspect of witchcraft. Typical of the attitude of the time was the book *Theologia Moralis*, published in 1625, which argued that sodomy was a crime leading to witchcraft (Lea ll:670).

Persons arrested were questioned at great length about their sex lives, and were almost always tortured into confessing an abundance of sexual "crimes." Women who showed any signs of independence or non- conformity were very suspect. Up until the fourteenth century, women and men were cited equally at the trials; after that time the majority of the victims were women (Russell, 279). There can be little doubt that Gay women suffered a great deal during this period.

Roman Catholicism had no monopoly on the terrors of the witch hunt. Some of the worst atrocities were perpetrated by the Protestants, who introduced the Inquisition to countries that had been lenient (Trevor-Roper, 138). John Calvin hunted down his religious enemies, as well as witches. He once boasted of luring the Unitarian Michael Servetus to Geneva under the guise of safety and then having him burned alive as a heretic. At Geneva, the most trivial offenses were also suppressed: dancing was illegal; a group of bridesmaids were once arrested for decorating a bride with too much color; a child was beheaded for striking its father (Taylor, 158; 163). "What the Puritans and Calvinists achieved at the Reformation was the reestablishment of the depressive, guilt-ridden attitude as the whole source of religion" (Taylor, 282).

It is impossible to determine how many people were killed by Christian witch-hunters. Estimates vary from between several hundred thousand to almost ten million. But if anything, most estimates are probably low since the great bulk of transcripts and court records still lie unseen and unanalyzed in archives and libraries throughout Europe.

The Christian oppression of women and Gay people was no accident. Their freedom and high status in the old religion made them prime targets for the new religion, which was profoundly anti-sexual. In view of these atrocities, it cannot be argued, as some still do, that the Christian religion has on the whole been humane, even though there may have been terrible injustices at certain times. Throughout its history, Christianity has been a religion of the sword. The few Christians in the past who have raised their voices against the atrocities of their co-believers have always been a tiny minority, and often they themselves have ended up being burned as heretics.

The Christians hunted down heretics and witches for fourteen hundred years, from the 3rd to the 17th centuries. Their aim, which they accomplished, was to annihilate an entire culture. For the most part, the old religion and the heresies it inspired were wiped off the face of the earth. In their place stood the grim, disciplined edifice of Christianity and the violent forces that kept Christianity in power.

Berdache dance ands Buffalo dance

8 Sex Magic in the Early Third World

Beliefs and practices similar to Europe's old religion can be found throughout the world. Cross-dressing by both men and women, masquerading in animal skins, and ritual sex are common in the oldest traditions of non-industrial societies. Here Lesbians and Gay men are often shamans (healer-priests).

The fullest account of the magical role of Gay people in nature societies was written by the German scholar Hermann Baumann, who assembled evidence from the Americas, Asia, Africa, and Europe. Concerning the American Indians, Baumann wrote that "since the days of the discovery of America, conquerors, missionaries, travelers, etc., made reports on the effeminate men and 'hermaphrodites' who, according to them, were said to be found in great numbers among the original Indian populations" (Baumann, 21). These "hermaphrodites" were not people possessing the sex organs of both sexes, but members of one sex who took on the clothes and attributes of the other sex and who had sexual relations with members of the same sex. The most famous example of this practice was the so-called *berdache*— a Gay male transvestite among the Prairie Indians— so named by the French from an Arabian word meaning slave. Actually, the *berdache* was not a slave at all, but occupied a contemptible position only in the eyes of the homophobic whites who encountered him. Among the Native Americans, before they adopted white values, the *berdache* was a magical person who played an established role in their culture.

George Catlin, who traveled across North America in the early 19th century recording Indian customs, left an eyewitness account of the *berdache* among the Sioux. They had a special joyous dance in honor of the *berdache* (whom they called *I-coo-coo-a*) and his lovers. Appalled by the high honor paid to the *I-coo-coo-a*, Catlin wrote: "This is one of the most unaccountable and disgusting customs, that I have ever met in Indian country" (Catlin, v. 2, 4th ed., 215). He urged the invading whites to suppress the custom: "I am constrained to refer the reader to the country where it is practiced, and where I should wish it might be extinguished before it be more fully recorded" (Catlin, 215). According to Baumann, the institution existed in all major linguistic and cultural groups of North America (Baumann, 21).

The widespread homosexuality of the North American Indians was given as an excuse by the invading Christian whites for their extermination. Their religious sex rites were taken as proof of their supposed racial inferiority, compared to the more sexually repressed culture of the invaders. Notes Baumann:

At the time, this was readily taken as a sign of the degeneracy of the Indian races, or at least as a reason for the quick defeat of their population. Although these often fanciful reports (which circulated from the 16th to the 19th century) were sensitively colored because of the tastes at the time of the European observers, nonetheless they are extraordinarily important, for it was precisely erotic practices that quickly disappeared in later times, suppressed by the ridicule or malicious criticism of bookish European observers (Baumann, 21).

The Indians themselves generally viewed the *berdache* with religious awe (Baumann, 21-22). For a man to dress in the clothing of a woman was not considered disgraceful in a culture (unlike our own) where women held a high status. It's only because men look down on women in our culture that effeminate-appearing men are ridiculed (they're viewed as degrading the supposedly higher status of their own sex). If women were seen as the equals of men, no man would feel threatened by a woman-appearing man. Women had a far higher status among the North American Indians than women do in modern industrial societies (Briffault, v. I, 311-328). They usually had political, religious, and sexual equality and most often formed an independent social group separate from the control of men. They even filled the role of warrior. When the ships of Admiral Colon first landed on an island near Puerto Rico in 1496, they were attacked by "a multitude of women armed with bows and arrows" (Steiner, 23).

Sometimes the *berdache* played a ritual sex role in the great religious festivals of the North American Indians. Among the Pueblo Indians of New Mexico, a man was chosen as a *mujerado* whom the other men fucked in the ass as part of the spring festival (Baumann, 24). In the buffalo dance of the Sioux, a man dressed in buffalo horns was ritually fucked by other men. In some Indian dances— as with pagan Europeans- dildos were used. "In fact, we are acquainted in the neighborhood of the Yuma peoples with numerous additional ritual acts in which men are dressed as women in order for them to function as the feminine role in a fertility rite, while the masculine role is played by men sometimes with a phallus, and both roles depict copulation as a fertility charm" (Baumann, 24). As in ancient Europe, these practices were joyous celebrations thought to make both the tribe and nature prosper.

The *berdache* could also play an important political role. In 1935, a Navaho elder said, "I believe when all the *nadle* [Lesbian and Gay-male shamans) have passed away, it will be the end of Navaho culture... They are the leaders, like President Roosevelt" (Baumann, 25). Among the Otoe Indians, becoming a *berdache* could be the climax of a man's life, even for a warrior (Irving, 94).

Many straight writers still insist that the *berdache* did not have an honored place among the North American Indians, but was at best tolerated like some kind of funny freak. They base their conclusions on the reports of some early white accounts that do sometimes give this impression. But if the accounts are read closely, the observers often contradict themselves. For example, in 1564 Jacques de Morgues reported of the *berdaches* among the Florida Indians that they "are considered odious by the Indians themselves" (Katz, 286). Yet he then goes on to say that they are the healers of the tribe! A good example of how the white observer's reaction could conflict with the Indians' practice is the account of the Jesuit Joseph Lafitau around 1711. He says concerning the *berdaches* of the Illinois and other tribes: 'They believe they are honored by debasing themselves to all of women's occupations . . . and this profession of an extraordinary life causes them to be regarded as people of a high order, and above the common man" (Katz, 288).

It's true that some accounts show that the *berdaches* were butts of jokes by other men and women. But Indians made jokes about all sorts of people. Laughter and gaiety were typical of the Indian character. The heads of the tribe themselves were often the butts of jokes. 'Those in power sometimes had to accept that they were the butts of jokes, especially of sexual jibes and jeers" (Burland, *North America*, 123). Women often ridiculed men and sometimes even had satirical rituals concerning them. The making of jokes was common to all segments of the Indian population. But no one has bothered to record the jokes the *berdaches* may have made about straight men.

North American Indian art reflects an openness to Gay sex. The oldest examples of their art (apart from arrow heads) come from the Ohio and Mississippi valleys from between 100 BC and 900 AD. The Gay themes of some of this art has scandalized white anthropologists (Burland, 121).

Although most early reports concerning the American Indians describe male *berdaches*, Gay women also played an important role in the tribes. In general, the sexist white observers tended to look down on Indian women, viewing their work as inferior to that of the men's, and giving much less attention to their rituals and practices. As a result, we have much less information concerning women. One interesting account is by the Jesuit Lafitau, who said he observed cases of "Amazons" in the tribes he visited, who were transvestite women warriors (Carpenter, *Intermediate Types*, 24). His observations came from the Illinois and the Sauk, but I suspect that the institution of the Lesbian warrior was as well established among all the North American Indians as it was in ancient Europe.

Christian missionaries denounced the North American Indian approach to religion as witchcraft, just as Catholics and Protestants had done earlier in Europe with the surviving old religion. Writing in the 17th century, Cotton Mather denounced the Indians as "the veriest ruines of mankind" (Mather, 504). He charged that they had "diabolic rites" in which "a devil" appeared to them (Mather, 506). In this context, we should note that the famous witch hunts in Salem Village in 1692 all started with accusations made by three sexually repressed young Puritans. These three young women had been present at Indian ceremonies conducted by two Carib Indians, John and his wife Tituba (Hansen, 56ff).

Sad to say, the North American Indians of today are completely out of touch with their original sexual culture, just as Europeans have lost all contact with the old religion. Nonetheless, certain myths still survive among the Indians, which tell, in symbolic language, the story of what has happened to them. A beautiful example is a myth of the Caddo Indians, which was recorded somewhere between 1903 and 1905:

> One time there lived among the people a man who always did the women's work and dressed like the women and went with them, and never went with the men. The men made fun of him, but he did not care, and continued to work and play only with the women. A war broke out with some other tribe, and all of the men went to fight but this man, who stayed behind with the women. After the war party had gone, an old man, who was too old to go with them, came to him and told him that if he would not go to fight he was going to kill him, for it was a disgrace to have such a man in the tribe. The man refused to go, saying the Great Father did not send him to earth to fight and did not want him to. The old man paid no attention to his excuse, and told him if he did not go to fight he would have the warriors kill him when they returned from battle with the enemy. The man said that they could not kill him, that he would always come to life, and would bewitch people and cause them to fight and kill one another. The old man did not believe him, and when the war party came home he told the men that they would have to kill the man because he was a coward, and they could not let a coward live in the tribe. They beat him until they thought he was dead, and were just ready to bury him when he jumped up alive. Again they beat him until he fell, then they cut off his head. He jumped up headless and ran about, frightening all of the people. They were just about to give up killing him when someone noticed a small purple spot on the little finger of his left hand. They cut that out; then he lay down and died. Soon after many people began to fight and quarrel, and even killed their own brothers and sisters and fathers and mothers. The other people tried to stop the fighting, but could not, because the people were bewitched and could not help themselves. Then the ·old man remembered

what the coward had said, and he told the people, and they were all sorry they had killed him (Dorsey, 19).

A religious attitude toward Lesbians and Gay men was not limited to the area now called the continental United States. A connection between transvestite Gay people and magical power is also found in native societies inhabiting the area around the Bering Strait. Such is the case among the Kamchadales, the Chukchi, the Aleuts, Inoits and Kodiak Islanders, where male and female Gay shamans have been reported. In these societies, Gay men grow their hair very long, wear the clothing of women, and are accorded great religious and political respect. "Homosexuality is common, and its relation to shamanship or priesthood most marked and curious" (Carpenter, 16). A similarly high position in religion and politics is reported for transvestite Gay women among peoples of the Yukon (Carpenter, 18). Here, as in other places, straight anthropologists have freaked out over what they observed. The classic account of Chuckchi shamans is by the Russian observer W. Bogoras. He describes them in a chapter with the homophobic title "Sexual Perversion and Transformed Shamans." He claims that the natives gossip about the shamans because they are "so peculiar" (Bogoras, 451). Yet he then proceeds to admit that the Gay male shaman "has all the young men he could wish for striving to obtain his favor" (Bogoras, 451). He also admits that the people have great respect for his magical powers.

In Central and South America, many reports have survived of Gay people and transvestites in native societies' religions. For example, in 1554 Cieza de Leon described religious Gay male prostitutes similar to those mentioned in the Old Testament as living in Canaan. He associated them with the Devil: "the Devil had gained such mastery in the land that, not content with causing the people to fall into mortal sin, he had actually persuaded them that the same was a species of holiness and religion" (Carpenter, 34).

In 1775, Thomas Faulkner reported that the function of male wizards among the Patagonians was performed by effeminate Gay men (Carpenter, 37). Sacred male prostitution was reported by the conquistadores in preColumbian Mexico. The sculpture of Yucatan shows that male homosexuality was "the custom of the country" (Bloch, 49). Young male religious prostitutes, whom the Spanish called *maricones*, existed among the Andes Indians (Bloch, 50).

The situation in Central and South America was complicated, however, by the rise of patriarchal civilizations like those of the Aztecs and Incas. The Aztecs were a highly militaristic society dominated by a ruling class of warriors. Like all such societies, they had a repressive attitude toward sex (Burland, *Middle America*, 147ff). For example, they feared nudity and identified sex with the witch goddess Tlazolteotl. Among the Incas of Peru, the official sex morality was also very strict (Osborne, 191). But in South American civilizations that were not patriarchal and militaristic, we find a great deal of sexual freedom, just as among the North American Indians. This is true of the Mochica people who flourished between 200

BC and 700 AD in Peru. Their art freely depicts every kind of different sex act, including Gay sex, naturalistically and without any reserve (Osborne, 193).

Rock drawings, Mashonaland, Africa

Gay shamans also existed in Africa. Such were the transvestite *omasenge* among the Ambo people of South West Africa (Baumann, 33). Among the Bantu and the Kwanyarna, all the medicine people were Gay transvestites. Gay medicine people were also reported among the following societies: the Ovimbundu and Kimbundu of Northern Angola; the Lango of Uganda; the Konso of South Abyssinia; the Cilenge-Humbi of South Quillenges; and the Barea-Kunama, Korongo and Mesakin, all of Northeast Africa (these examples from Baumann).

In certain African societies, sacred orgies occurred in which Gay people, both women and men, played an important role. People in the orgy reported that they were taken over by a divine spirit that led them to Gay sex acts. Concerning the matriarchal Bantu people, Baumann observes: "During these orgies it sometimes happens that a masculine *ondele* enters a woman, causing sexual desires that lead as an evil consequence [sic] to Lesbian acts" (Baumann, 34-35). Even in certain societies where European commentators claim that homosexuality is not accepted, such as in parts of Angola, during great religious festivals people become possessed by transvestite and homosexual spirits (Baumann, 36).

Magical Gay people were also found in Madagascar, the large island off the coast of southeast Africa. Among the Manghabei, the sacred male transvestites were called tsecats (Bloch, 45-46). The Sakalavas and Betanimenes of Madagascar knew of the same institution (Bloch, 46-47).

But an openness to Gay sex, even in a religious context, is certainly not universal in Africa. As we observed in the case of Central and South America, sexual freedom in Africa can be greatly restrained in those societies that are patriarchal and militaristic. In general, an open attitude toward sex is found most often in those nature societies that have not undertaken a program of empire-building and who are free from a rigid hierarchical class structure.

Dogon wood figure , Mali

When invading Christians encountered religious Gay practices in Africa, they attributed them to the Devil, just as Christians did in the case of the Indians of North America, and the witches of the Middle Ages. In 1492, the Christian convert Leo Africanus wrote concerning the sacred Lesbians of Morocco:

> The third kind of diviners are women-witches, which are affirmed to have familiarity with divels. Changing their voices they fain the divell to speak within them: then they which come to enquire ought with great fear and trembling aske these vile and abominable witches such questions as they mean to propound, and lastly, offering some fee unto the divell, they depart. But the wiser and honester sort of people call these women *Sahacat*, which in Latin signifieth Fricatrices [Lesbians), because they have a damnable custom to commit unlawful venerie among themselves, which I cannot express in any modester terms (Carpenter, 39).

In outlining the sacred role of Gay people in non-industrial societies, we could go on and on, and cite numerous examples outside of America and Africa. Suffice it to say that ritual transvestism and sodomy (or the worship of androgynous dieties, which is usually indicative of this) are also found in Australia, the South Sea Islands, the Middle East, Europe, and the Far East (including India, China, Japan and Vietnam).

In addition, indiscriminate sexual orgies are commonly and routinely practiced by non-industrialized societies as a form of religious devotion. Reports of these sacred orgies come from all over the world. An excellent account of their practice can be found in George Scott's book *Phallic Worship*. ("Phallic" as used in this book refers to the genitals of both sexes, and not just to cocks.) For example in the Americas, pictures surviving from ancient Yucatan show religious scenes in which men perform acts of "indescribable beastliness" (Scott, 122-123). In the Far East, the situation is the same. In Japan, many of the oldest practices of the indigenous nature religion continue under the guise of Shintoism. Ancient Shinto temples are full of orgiastic art and "were the scene of sexual orgies rivaling the Bacchanalia of ancient Rome" (229). In ancient China, one of the most celebrated goddesses was Kwan-Yin, a variant of the great mother. She was worshipped with orgies that included homosexuality (222). The most ancient religious artifacts of India are filled with depictions of orgies, and the worship of the sexual organs of both sexes (183). Jacques-Antoine Dulaure, in his classic book on sex worship, notes that "the celebrated and ancient pagoda of Jagannath, and the no less ancient one of Elephanta near Bombay, the bas-reliefs of which William Alen sketched in 1784, offer the most indecent pictures that a corrupted imagination could conceive (*The Gods of Generation*, 83).

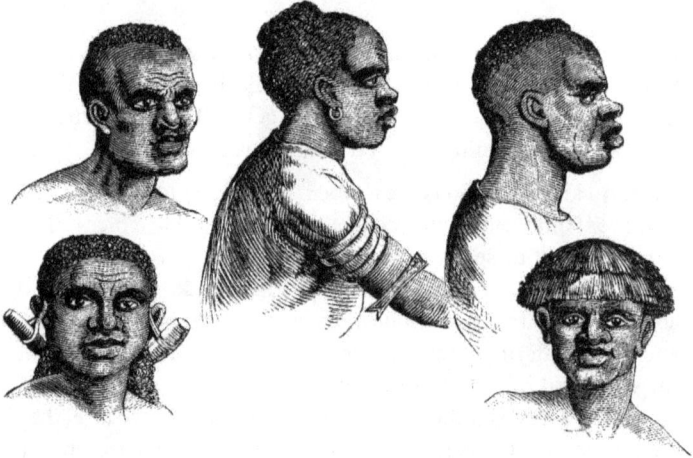

Drawings by Richard Burton

Sacred orgies regularly occurred in the religious rites of ancient peoples living around the Mediterranean Sea. Such, among others, were the worship of Isis at Bubasti in Egypt; the festivals of Baal-Peor in the Middle East; the worship of Venus at Cyprus; the worship of Adonis at Byblos; and, of course, the Dionysia, Floralia and Bacchanalia (Bloch, 95).

The purpose of these sacred orgies has been much obscured by modern commentators, who are generally straight males. The orgies were not done to increase the population as is often maintained. The notion that the purpose of sex is procreation is a modern industrial one, derived ultimately from the Judea-Christian tradition. Some of the most ancient nature societies did not even know that children are produced by fucking. Besides, most nature societies deliberately restricted population growth through the use of herbal contraceptives and abortions. Nor were their rites a secret symbolizing of some deep hidden theological meaning.

All the evidence indicates that nature people fucked for pleasure. Their purpose was to celebrate sex. Their orgies were acts of sexual worship to the power of sex they felt in themselves and in nature around them. Their religious feasts were characteristically joyous: dancing, feasting, fucking together. The Indians who have been observed in the Americas; the myths that have survived in Europe; the artifacts that exist from all over the world— all attest to the *pleasure* of what the celebrants were doing. George Scott has rightly observed "that, without exception, the worship of sex by all primitive [sic] races originated in the pleasure associated with coitus, and not in any clearly conceived notion that intercourse would produce children" (47).

Hence it is a misrepresentation for industrialized academics to call such celebrations "fertility rites," as they usually do. The orgies were not clumsy attempts to increase the gross national product by people who had a very rude understanding of economic laws. Nature people did, indeed, believe that through such acts their bodies would become stronger, the crops would grow taller, the sun would shine brighter, and the rains would come in profusion when needed. But they believed these things because they had a collective tribal *feeling* of the power of sex throbbing through the whole of nature; their experience of sex was so open, public, communal and intense that they felt it reverberate through the whole cosmos. In this, they were unlike modern industrialized people who practice sex solely for procreation — privately, in the dark, in isolation, and with guilt.

Non-industrialized societies were not in the least embarrassed to practice all sorts of sex acts in public because the notion of sexual obscenity, like the procreative ideal of sex, is a modern Christian/industrial view. "In tribes where no ideas of modesty such as are current in civilized [sic] society have arisen, there is no concept of obscenity in connexion with exposure of the genital organs or even with the performance of the sex act itself. Any taboo is concerned not with the *sight* of the reproductive parts, but with the touching of them by unauthorized persons" (Scott, 125).

Non-industrialized societies also in general treat prostitutes, both heterosexual and homosexual, much differently than Christian/industrial societies. In modern societies, as we all know, the prostitute is a purely economic being: a woman or man rents out her or his body for the sake of someone else's orgasm or phantasy. In addition, the work of prostitutes is looked down upon in industrialized societies as being somehow dirty, and prostitutes are often caught up in a web of social disrepute, legal harassment, and exploitation by pimps.

In non-industrialized societies, prostitutes are often treated with great religious respect, and their activities are considered as religious activities. For example, in the ancient Middle East, the land of Canaan, later invaded by the Israelites, was originally peopled by a society where Gay male prostitution was very prominent. These prostitutes were located in the temples. As with medieval witches, men and women who impersonated sexual deities were literally thought to become them, and having sex with these people was viewed as the highest and most tangible form of religious communion with the deity.

Drawings by Richard Burton

Payment was made to the temple as a form of religious donation after having sex with the sacred prostitute. In the original Hebrew of the Old Testament, male prostitutes were called *Kadeshim*, which literally means "consecrated ones," indicative of their high status in the eyes of their worshippers (Carpenter, 29). Most translations of this word into other languages suppress the positive meaning of the word, and mistranslate it negatively, as, for example, "effeminates" (Dulaure, 130-131). Israeli leaders denounced this sex and nature religion as witchcraft (Carpenter, *Intermediate Types*, 50).

Throughout the ancient world, both male and female prostitution was associated with religion. Such was the case in the worship of Baal-Peor, Moloch and Astarte (Syria); Osiris and Isis (Egypt); Venus (Greece and Rome); Mithra (Persia); Myllita (Assyria); Alitta (Arabia); Dilephat (Chaldea); Salambo (Babylonia); and Diana Anaitis (Armenia).

In Mediterranean civilization, the male god associated with these phenomena came in general to be called Priapus (which means "erect cock" and "dildo" in Latin). He is very reminiscent of the horned god of the witches: "In the statues raised in the temples, Priapus was represented under the form of a hairy man, with legs and horns like a goat, holding a wand in his hand and provided with a formidable virile member" (Dupouy, 503). The corresponding female deity was a great-mother figure often associated with the earth or the moon, reminiscent of the witches' Diana.

The religious prostitute seems simply to be a historical extension of the practice of having ritual sex with the shaman, either male or female. In tribal societies (where cities, temples, and money are unknown), we have seen the common practice of ritual sex with the shaman, individually or in orgies. As early Mediterranean societies fell victim to urbanism and a money economy, the function of shaman in the countryside was transformed into that of priest in the temple, and money then entered in as a form of religious donation. So we see how Gay history, the history of prostitution, and the religious history of non-industrialized societies are all tied together.

The phenomenon called "witchcraft" in Europe was by no means an isolated thing peculiar to a certain period in the history of that continent. Quite the opposite: the ritual worship of sex and nature was once the case throughout the world, and still is in the societies that industrialized academics call "primitive." In these societies, as in the case of the witches, women and Gay men generally enjoyed a high status, Gay people of both sexes were looked upon with religious awe, and sexual acts of every possible kind were associated with the most holy forms of religious expression. Admittedly, there were also great diversities and variations in the beliefs and practices of these societies, but there was one great common feature that set them off in sharp distinction to the Christian/industrial tradition: their love of sexuality. This love of sexuality was "the universal primitive religion of the world and has left its indelible impress upon our ideas, our language, and our institutions" (Howard, 7).

Slave-muster at the Casa Grande, Morro Velho

9 Sex Among the Zombies

I see
I wear
the zombie smile
of the sane
as we tiptoe past mirrors
cradling the grenades
of our truth.

Claudia Reed, "Women's Work" in *Plexus* magazine.

American civilization began in genocide.

When the early European colonists arrived in North America, they did not come upon a vacant land. Instead, they found a multitude of nature people who had lived there for ages on end. These nature people had developed some of the highest cultures in recorded history. They lived full, long, healthy lives. Their societies had little hierarchy and no government superstructure. Organized warfare, in the modern sense, was rare or unknown. Labor was free. Women generally enjoyed a high status, and Gay persons of both sexes were regarded with religious awe. They developed beautiful arts and crafts, in which nearly everyone was skilled. They managed to satisfy all the basic needs of human existence with much grace and beauty, and were able to do so without the curse of cities, police, mental institutions, or universities. Although personal violence was known among them, it paled in comparison to the level of violence in any Western society during the past two thousand years. The Indians loved nature and knew how to talk to plants and animals, whom they regarded as their equals. They were able to feel (and not just know) that everything that is, lives.

Onto this scene came the industrializing whites, burdened and propelled by over two thousand years of patriarchal institutions. The whites denounced the Indians as "primitive," "savage," and "barbarian." They accused them of worshipping devils and ridiculed their Gay shamans. They taught them how to practice organized warfare. They plied them into violence against each other, stole their land, and succeeded in killing off nearly every one of them, quarantining their survivors in concentration camps called reservations.

The whites' genocide against the Indians affected how the whites thought about sex: They came to view sex as an instrument of imperial policy. For them, the purpose of sex was to breed as large a number of people as possible in order to push aside the relatively low-density Indian population and the population of colonists from other European nations. Colonial leaders eagerly looked forward to the day when fast-breeding white Americans would force their way over the whole Western hemisphere, both north and south. In 1751, Benjamin Franklin published his *Observations Concerning the Increase of Mankind*. In it, he urged Americans to breed rapidly in order to take over new lands. He called upon the British government to forcibly displace the local Indians to make room for the growing number of rapidly breeding Americans (van Alstyne, 20-21).

One of the most outspoken advocates of the same policy was Thomas Jefferson. In 1786, when the states were under the Articles of Confederation, Jefferson stated: "Our confederacy must be viewed as the nest, from which all America, North and South, is to be peopled," (van Alstyne, 81). Later, in 1801, after the constitution was in effect, Jefferson continued along the same line: "However our present interest may restrain us within our limits, it is impossible not to look forward to distant times, when our rapid multiplication will expand it beyond these limits, and cover the whole northern if not the southern continent, with people speaking the same language, governed in similar forms, and by similar laws" (van Alstyne, 87). Jefferson continually pointed his finger at the retreating Indian tribes, whom he considered savages, and urged Americans to "press upon them" until they were pushed out of the way (Williams, 179). He even urged rich Americans to get Indian leaders in debt "because we observe that when these debts get beyond what the individuals can pay, they become willing to lop them off by a cession of lands" (Williams, 187). The early French colonists had a similar view of sex as a tool for breeding. They vied with the Americans as to who could fill up the continent first with their populations (de Riencourt, 5). Such a twisted view of sex (which must have seemed totally incomprehensible to the Indians) came easily to the colonists. It had lain ready at hand for nearly seventeen centuries in the Christian religion. The various churches of Europe (both Catholic and Protestant) had long been imperialist institutions. They had advocated the very same view of sex for similar reasons. Such a view was also found in the ancient state of Israel, which had invaded the land of Canaan, uprooted the local population, and bred as rapidly as possible to fill up the land. This attitude became so entrenched that it was projected onto the Israeli god. Accordingly, in the book of Genesis, which was accepted by both Jews and Christians, the Israeli god gives this as his very first commandment to Adam and Eve: "Be fertile and multiply; fill the earth and subdue it," (*New American Bible*; Genesis 1:28). In New England, the Puritans were infatuated with the history of the ancient Israeli state. They regarded themselves as the founders of a New Israel in the American wilderness (van Alstyne, 8). They compared the Indians to the sex-worshipping Canaanites whom the Israelis killed.

Imperialism and compulsive heterosexuality go hand in hand, as was well understood by the ancient Israeli state, the Christen churches of Europe, and the American colonial leaders. In early America, this use of sex paid off. Due to rapid breeding and the continual invasion of immigrants, the colonial population grew from 250,000 in 1700 to 1,400,000 in 1750, an increase of well over 500% in only fifty years (Williams, 103).

The British government became alarmed at the rapid growth of the colonial population and tried to stop the seizure of Indian lands west of the Alleghenies. In doing this, however, the Crown was not motivated by any humanitarian reasons. It didn't want to lose the lucrative fur trade it had forced on the Indians (de Riencourt, 6-7). These restrictions infuriated the colonial ruling class. The Declaration of Independence, which was written mostly by Jefferson, attacked the King for this policy. It listed as a justification for rebellion against the King the fact that "he has endeavored to prevent the Population of these States."

In view of the imperialist use of sex in the colonies and the dead weight of Christian tradition from Europe, it's not surprising that the colonies outlawed sodomy. Even the outbreak of the Revolution had no effect on changing these laws. The Bill of Rights spoke only of intellectual rights, such as speech, religion, and assembly. It had nothing to say about the rights of sex, the emotions, or the body. Jefferson, the originator of the Bill of Rights, helped write a law that Gay men be castrated (Katz, 24). Moreover, the right to religious freedom was (and still is) considered to apply only to patriarchal religions. Public religious orgies using hallucinogens have never been permitted in the United States.

Early America was a slave society. The first permanent English settlement in North America was Jamestown, founded in 1607. Soon thereafter, in 1619, the first boatload of Black slaves was brought to Jamestown (Hacker, 57). Throughout the 17th and 18th centuries, people from Black African cultures were kidnapped, sold to slave dealers, and shipped across the sea to America. Those who survived the wretched conditions of the journey were sold off to the colonial ruling class. Between 1686 and 1786, more than 2,000,000 Black people were forced to become slaves in the West Indies and in the American colonies (Hacker, 101).

Slaves were the basis of the economy in the *North* as well as the South. This was because of the nature of trade relations in the industrial system of early America. Ships from New England sent foodstuffs, lumber, and animals to the West Indies; they returned from there with sugar and molasses, from which they made rum; they exported the rum to the coast of Africa and with it bought slaves; the slaves were returned to the West Indies and the colonies. Hence "the slave trade made possible the expansion of the mercantile economy of the New England and middle-colony ports" (Hacker, 101). We have seen that Gay people performed the role of shamans in Black Africa, just as they did among the native American Indians. The enslavement of Blacks, like the annihilation of the Indians, is an example of how the sexually repressive American way of life built its empire on the agonies of nature peoples.

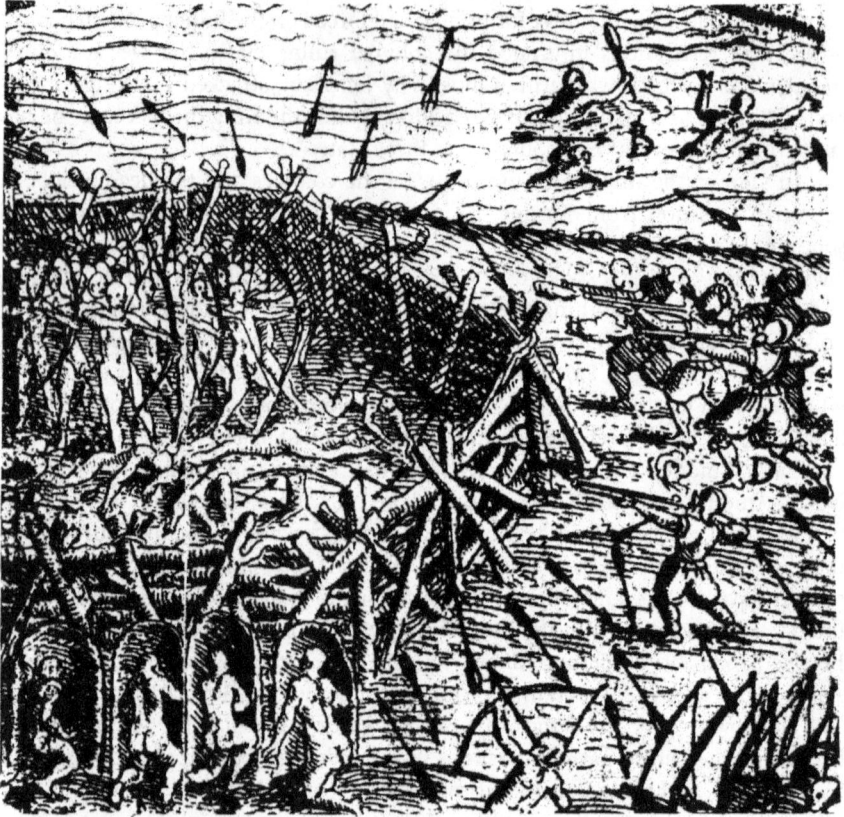

Samuel de Champlain's attack on the Iroquois (1609)

White slavery was also widespread in America. It took the form of indentured servitude. Many of the poorer people immigrating to America from Europe had to sell themselves into slavery (usually for seven years) in order to pay for the cost of crossing. Although indentured servitude did not last a life-time, indentured servants had the legal status of slaves during their service. "Colonial America was built upon the unfree labor of whites and blacks. Fully 250,000 white men, women and children and another 250,000 black persons — *constituting in all at least one half of the original immigrants to the mainland colonies by 1700* — had gone this way" (Hacker, 97; italics added). The beneficiary of this oppression was the colonial ruling class, which consisted of the landlords of huge estates, land speculators, and rich merchants. A good example of this class was George Washington, who was a plantation lord, a land speculator, a dealer in animal furs and grains, and a moneylender (Hacker, 112).

As the frontier moved westward, the first people to move in after the Indians were pushed out were not bands of pioneers, but wealthy land speculators and large real-estate companies. "The West was not opened up by the hardy frontiersman; it was opened up by the land speculator who preceded even the Daniel Boones into the wilderness" (Hacker, 131-2). Most of the pioneers who followed the land speculators were not the poor and the downtrodden. They were upwardly mobile middle-class people, since the journey was a very expensive one (Hacker, 202). These early pioneers eagerly slaughtered masses of wild animals in order to sell their furs (Hacker, 133). The images of these invaders today adorn cigarette advertisements as ideals of American masculinity.

In the earliest history of Europe, the ancient worship of sexuality originated in a matriarchal agrarian society. The people lived in close emotional communion with the land. This was the ancient economic and religious fact that lay behind the latter-day cultural forces of witchcraft and heresy. This tradition managed to survive in some form or other in Europe until the 17th century. In America— apart from the Indians, who were killed off— no such tradition of relating to nature and the land ever took root. 'The American farmer started out as a capitalist farmer from the very beginning" (Hacker, 6). American farmers were entrepreneurs, interested only in getting as much cash out of the soil as quickly as possible, and then moving on when the land was exhausted. Because of their rapid exhaustion of land, they tended to become a class of land speculators. Hence from the very beginning we find the narrowness of American rural living and the repressiveness of its small towns. Land was not viewed as a manifestation of the Great Mother to be collectively worshipped and loved. It was a mere resource to be exploited and sold on a competitive basis in the markets of big cities. In American history, there was no historical counterweight to the sexually repressive, nature-killing forces of patriarchal institutions. The absence of such a counterweight has had staggering implications for America's sexual, religious, and cultural life.

From the earliest days of independence from Britain, American leaders joyously described the new society as an empire and called for a policy of vigorous imperialism. In 1773, John Adams called for the annexation of Canada and Nova Scotia, and said, "An empire is rising in America" (Williams, 112). In 1783, George Washington described the states as a "rising empire," a phrase that had become commonplace by then (van Alstyne, 1). The ruling class of landowners and rich merchants looked with covetous eyes on the vast tracts of land still held by the Indians, the Canadians, the French, and the Spanish.

During the American Revolution, there was considerable unrest among the lower classes, and many of the poor called for an annulment of debts and a redistribution of land. In several states, poor radicals even took over the machinery of government. Some of them expressed anarchist views. But by 1780, the upper class began to re-assert itself. Upper-class leaders wanted a centralized government that would prohibit states from annulling debts. They wanted a government that would be strong enough to wage war and undertake a program of continental empire-building. Out of these upperclass interests emerged the constitution movement. Its chief spokesperson, James Madison, openly stated that the powers of the central government "ought to be so constituted as to protect the minority of the opulent against the majority" (Hacker, 187). In effect, the constitution movement became "a well organized campaign by a coalition of America's upper-class leadership to establish the institution appropriate to an American mercantilist empire" (Williams, 148). In the various elections for the new constitution, less than one-fourth of adult males were allowed to vote, and women had no vote at all (Hacker, 188). The new constitution was approved (though barely) by these select few. On April 30, 1789, George Washington was installed as President, and the world saw the birth of what was to become a terrifying new institution, the United States Government.

The single most striking fact of American history— a fact that has conditioned every aspect of the nation's life, including its sex life— is the militarism of the U. S. Government. Indeed, if the nature of an institution is determined by what it does rather than what it says, we would be close to the truth in seeing the U.S. Government as essentially a machine for making war.

In 1775, even before the government was created, the colonists were at war with Britain. They invaded Canada and tried to take it over, but were rebuffed. In 1799, the U. S. Government conducted a brief naval war against France, and in 1812 was again at war with Britain. In 1812, the U. S. Government tried to take over Canada for the second time and was again rebuffed. In 1823, the Monroe Doctrine was issued. In effect, it warned European powers that henceforth the U.S. Government was to be the only imperialist power permitted to operate in North and South America (van Alstyne, 99). Throughout this whole period, a merciless war of genocide was in progress against Indian men, women, and children. In the 1830s, President Andrew Jackson alone spent over $200 million (an enormous amount of money at the time) in wars of annihilation against the Indians (Williams, 320).

In 1847, the U. S. Government invaded Mexico. The Americans captured Mexico City, and the Mexicans were forced to give up *half of all their territory*. Out of this war booty were eventually carved the states of California, New Mexico, Texas (with the Rio Grande as border), Arizona, Utah, and Nevada (de Riencourt, 17). In 1853, the U. S. Government sent Admiral Perry to Japan to forcibly open up that country to American trading interests. From 1861 to 1865, the Americans were involved in a bloody civil war between the plantation capitalists of the South and the merchant and factory capitalists of the North.

In 1890, the last of the Indians rebels were slaughtered in the Battle of Wounded Knee. In 1891, Queen Liliuokalani ascended the throne of Hawaii and tried to eliminate American influence in the islands. In 1892, she was deposed by the U. S. Marines. In 1898, President McKinley, at the insistence of the Hearst newspaper empire, declared war on Spain and took over Cuba, Guam, Puerto Rico, and the Philippines.

Group of Gani Men (Richard Speke)

In the late 19th century, the attitude of the U.S. Government toward the rest of the world, and especially toward nature peoples, was well summed up in the words of Senator Albert Beveridge of Indiana: "We will not renounce our part in the mission of our race, trustee under God, of the civilization of the world" (van Alstyne, 187). He was later echoed by Woodrow Wilson, who in 1902 as a private citizen said it was "our peculiar duty" to teach nature peoples "order and self-control" and "to impart to them, if it be possible . . . t he drill and habit of law and obedience" (van Alstyne, 197).

In the first two decades of the 20th century, the U.S. invaded Cuba, Haiti, Nicaragua, and Santo Domingo (twice). In 1903, President Theodore Roosevelt supported a coup against the government of Colombia in order to set up a puppet government in the region of the Panama Canal. The puppet government gave the U.S. a perpetual lease over the canal, something the government of Colombia had adamantly refused to do.

In 1917, the U. S. Government declared war on Germany and Austria, and thus entered World War I, which ended in 1918. On December 7, 1941, Japan bombed Pearl Harbor, one month after Secretary of War Stimson had written in his personal diary that President Roosevelt had "raised the question of how to maneuver the Japanese into firing the first shot" (de Riencourt, 61). The U. S. Government ended World War II by dropping atomic bombs on the Japanese, thus setting the precedent for the use of nuclear arms in war.

In 1947, the U.S. Government created the Central Intelligence Agency. In the 1950s the U.S. Government got involved in a cold war with the U.S. S.R. and a hot war with Korea. In 1953, the CIA overthrew the government of Iran and installed a fascist Shah; in 1954, it overthrew the government of Guatemala. In 1960, it overthrew the government of Laos, and since that time has been so active no one can keep up with it. By the 1950s, the U.S. Government established a military protectorate over more than 40 nations covering 15,000,000 square miles and more than 600 million human beings (de Riencourt, 96). In the late 1960s, the U.S. Government brought out of the closet a secret war in Indo-China, which became the longest war in American history.

The entrenched militarism of the U.S. Government throughout its history has had a profound influence on American values. It has affected the way Americans think about nature, other people, their own bodies, and sex roles. One notable effect has been on the American concept of sanity, reflected in the American psychiatric movement. The father of American psychiatry was Benjamin Rush, who lived from 1746 to 1813. *Benjamin Rush was the Physician General of the Continental Army.* He was a stern disciplinarian who believed in using violence against mental patients. He condemned both masturbation and sodomy. He believed that being Black was a disease. He locked up his own rebellious son in a mental hospital for 27 years (Szasz, 137ff.). Today he is highly regarded by many American psychiatrists.

The American Psychiatric Association currently publishes an official list of mental disorders, which, as most readers know, recently listed homosexuality (the A.P.A. was forced into an about face on the issue due to action by Gay activists). This list, which is comparable to the Vatican's index (except that it applies to behavior instead of books), is of *military* origin. It was first developed by Brigadier General William C. Menninger, who was head of the psychiatric division of the Surgeon General's office in the U. S. Government during World War II (Szasz, 38). Before the A.P.A. adopted the list, it was put into use by all the branches of the armed forces. Its purpose was to weed out men who are not fit for military slaughtering. Today, at least one-half of all American psychiatrists are employed by institutions (Szasz, 235). The institutional nature of the A.P.A. itself goes back to its beginning. Its original name was the Association of Medical Superintendents of American Institutions. The first proposition publicly approved by this group was a justification for the use of violence in "treating" the insane (Szasz, 306). Most mental institutions in America are governed on a military model (with lines of command, central control, the threat of forcible confinement, etc.). In 1964, more people were in mental institutions than in prisons (Szasz, 65).

In the U. S. S.R., psychiatry has a similar militaristic coloring and is also used to suppress dissent. In Nazi Germany, the leading role in the development and use of gas chambers was played by psychiatrists, and their first victims were mental patients (Szasz, 214). An untold number of Gay people were exterminated in these chambers.

American militarism has affected the way Americans view masculinity, just as Roman militarism affected Roman views. All American men have been conditioned throughout their lives to think of disciplined aggressiveness as masculine; to look down on effeminacy, playfulness, passivity, and open emotionalism; to admire hardness in other men; to dread above all things being called a sissy; to enjoy relations of domination and obedience; to get a thrill out of seeing pain inflicted on others; to get turned on by uniforms; and to be able to accommodate themselves to functioning in large, impersonal, hierarchical institutions. Men who internalize these values are considered admirably sane by American society. But this is a concept of sanity that supports war. When the orders come, such sane men are ready to kill other men on command. They are totally unprepared to deal with other men in an openly loving, warm, sexual manner. To them, that's insane. Until just recently, most psychiatrists would have agreed.

In 1960, with the election of President John Kennedy, a revolutionary change took place in the nature of American militarism. This change was to have stunning repercussions in every aspect of American life. President Kennedy centralized control over all the purchasing activities of the Pentagon within the office of the Secretary of Defense (then Robert McNamara). Stringent requirements were written into contracts for firms doing business with the Pentagon, giving the Pentagon the right to decide all important management decisions of these firms, determine their budgets, and oversee the hiring and firing of employees. In effect, the firms doing business with the Pentagon were made into subsidiaries of one giant corporation with the Pentagon as the central office. Kennedy and McNamara deliberately made these changes on the model of the business empire of the Ford Motor Company, with the Pentagon patterned after Ford's central office (Melman, *Pentagon Capitalism*, 2ff.).

The effect of these changes was to create the largest single business monopoly in the history of the United States, and possibly in the world. By these actions, the President and other top officers of the U.S. Government got control over the 15,000 to 20,000 firms that are prime contractors with the Pentagon and over the 45,000 to 60,000 firms that are sub-contractors. The total number of employees working for all these firms is unknown, but the Department of Defense itself employs 10% of the nation's entire labor force (Melman, *Pentagon Capitalism*, 83). More than two-thirds of the spending by the U.S. Government each year is for current or past military operations, despite the fact that such spending is often disguised by such phrases as "payments to individuals" or "interest on the national debt" (Melman,

Pentagon Capitalism, 174). From 1946 to 1969, the U.S. Government spent more than one trillion dollars on the military; *half of this entire amount was spent under the administrations of John Kennedy and Lyndon Johnson*. In 1968, the Pentagon business empire produced $44 billion worth of goods and services. This exceeded by far the sales of America's leading civilian businesses (AT&T, duPont, GE, GM). In its post-exchange operations, the Pentagon business empire ranks as the third largest retail distributor in the United States, exceeded only by Sears and A&P (Melman, *Pentagon Capitalism*, 24, 73).

The product manufactured by this giant business empire is war. Recent examples are the genocidal wars against Vietnam, Laos, and Cambodia. These wars happened, not because they were in the interests of the American people, but because war-making is the job, the specialty, the unique product of the nation's largest business monopoly. A government that spends two-thirds of its national budget on a war factory is a government that will manufacture wars.

One effect of this new kind of militarism is the co-option of science and technology. More than two-thirds of America's technical researchers now work for the Pentagon business empire (Melman, *Our Depleted Society*, 4). Another effect is Pentagon influence over universities. During 1963-1966, research in chemical and biological warfare was carried on at 38 universities under contract with the Pentagon (Melman, *Pentagon Capitalism*, 99).

A third effect is Pentagon control over the electoral process. Both the management and the unions of Pentagon subsidiaries make huge campaign contributions to political candidates. They also spend a lot of money on political propaganda. In 1963, Secretary McNamara publicly praised the leadership of the AFL-CIO for "utilizing extensive communications media to promote greater understanding among its millions of members and the public of the vital objective of defense programs" (Dibble, 182). A notorious example of this control over the electoral process is the buying and selling of the Presidency. 'The readiest source of campaign funds and political support for nomination and election as President lies in the military-industrial complex. It is also the most skillfully hidden source" (Stone, 25).

In 1969, the Pentagon maintained an army of 339 lobbyists on Capitol Hill, or one lobbyist for every two members of Congress (Melman, *Pentagon Capitalism*, 175). In cases where Congress votes against the Pentagon's wishes, the Pentagon often goes ahead and does what it wants anyway. For example, in December of 1966 it was revealed that in the previous year, the Pentagon had spent $20 billion on the war in Vietnam exactly twice what had been authorized by Congress (Melman, *Pentagon Capitalism*, 182). This overspending was a violation of the U. S. Constitution and of U. S. law. The matter was never investigated, and no one was ever indicted. Soon everyone forgot about it. Similar examples could be cited involving directives of Presidents.

Through the CIA and the FBI, the top government officials who control the Pentagon business empire also exercise a reign of propaganda and terror over the lives of the American people. In 1967, it was revealed that CIA money was being channeled to Billy Graham's Spanish-American Crusade; the National Council of Churches; the Harvard Law School; the National Student Association; the Institute of International Labor founded by Norman Thomas; and hundreds of universities, churches, unions, and legal organizations (de Riencourt, 110). In the mid-1970s it was revealed that the FBI and the CIA had for a long time been reading people's mail, burglarizing offices, planting infiltrators and disrupters in radical groups, infiltrating or buying dissident news media, censoring established news media, training and equipping local police forces, and possibly assassinating protest leaders.

King of Uganda (Richard Speke)

In 1976, a Congressional committee investigating the FBI and the CIA stated that an ex-FBI informer (Robert Merritt) helped the FBI keep tabs on Gay people, especially when they were involved in radical politics. "Merritt told the Committee that his FBI handling agents instructed him to conduct break-ins, deliver unopened mail acquired illegally, and solicit and provide information to the FBI regarding homosexual proclivities of politically prominent people and individuals of the New Left" *(Report of the House Select Committee on Intelligence*, 43). Gay political groups, like the rest of the New Left, continue to be either disrupted or co-opted by government informers and agents.

The United States is a garrison society. The extension of Pentagon and secret-police control over American life has been the material equivalent of a military coup d'état. As when Augustus Caesar took control in Rome in 27 B.C., so it is today: the Senate continues to meet, the tribunes of the people are elected, the courts hand down decisions, new Presidents take office, and all the proper outward forms are observed. But behind the show of the visible government there looms the overwhelming institutional power of the military and the secret police. True, there still remains a degree of freedom of speech and thought, especially for the middle class and the privileged professional classes. But if any group becomes an effective threat to the establishment — as the Black movement did in the 1960s — it will soon find its organizations infiltrated, its offices bombed, and its leaders shot. As I write these very words, I hear reports that American Indian activists are regularly being killed by the FBI. Such news is not likely to be reported in the middle-class press.

The Pentagon business empire has cast its shadow over the lives of Gay people. For one thing, neither the Pentagon nor any of its vast array of subsidiaries will willingly or knowingly hire a Gay person as an employee. This makes the Pentagon business empire the largest single discriminator against Gay people in the United States. It also encourages Gay people to mimic straight appearances and lifestyles in order to get work. But even more important, this shadow of militarism brings into the lives of millions of American working people the specter of masculinism. The following two facts are not unrelated: 1) most Gay men in American society in the mid-1970s are masculine-identified wearers of denim and leather; 2) the single most powerful employer in the United States is the Pentagon war machine. Consider Castro Street, a major Gay hangout in San Francisco and the center of one of the largest Gay ghettos in the country. On any given day, Castro Street is filled with a conformist mob of male impersonators meticulously decked out in denim, leather, and even Nazi-like uniforms. One of the most popular Gay baths in San Francisco was until recently called The Barracks. A popular bar is The Folsom Prison. Another is The Bootcamp. These facts of Gay life take on added significance when we realize that one-third of all jobs in the San Francisco Bay area are tied to the Department of Defense (Gellen, 190). Historically, the superstructure of sexual style is determined by the substructure of economic power. Our society will never be rid of masculinism until we are rid of militarism.

Steam bath of the Mandans (George Catlin)

The history of militarism in the United States with its culmination in the Pentagon business empire is not an isolated social fact. Militarism is related to industrialism. Furthermore, militarism and industrialism are not unique in the United States. Similar phenomena can be seen in all "highly developed" societies, regardless of whether they are capitalist or communist. Industrialism, like militarism, has had a devastating impact on our sensual and sexual lives. Since the end of the Christian era, it has been the single most pervasive force in mutilating Gay culture. No understanding of the oppression of Gay people in modern times is even half adequate without an understanding of the nature of industrialism.

Industrialism is the process by which people cease producing things directly for their own immediate needs. Instead, things are produced through specialized and centralized institutions. The producing institutions can be quite varied (for example, factories, universities, governments) depending upon the things produced (automobiles, knowledge, law and order). In any given society, there are degrees to which such specialized and centralized institutions control production. Among the American Indians, for example, there were practically no such institutions. In modern America, on the other hand, nearly every aspect of life has been industrialized. When most of a society's production (of whatever nature) is controlled by specialized institutions, I call that society industrialized.

There is no recorded instance in history where a highly industrialized system of life was voluntarily chosen by a non-industrial society. In every case, industrialism has been imposed on the people by the violence of the institutions themselves. In Europe, industrialism was an edifice built on the blood and gore of centuries of Christian violence. In America, it came to power through the annihilation of the Indians and the enslavement of the Blacks. In Russia, it was the fruit of Stalin's grim war of terror against the peasants. In the modern Third World, it is everywhere coming to power through the conflicting imperial ambitions of America, Russia, and China. In every case, militarism has been the means by which industrialism has triumphed. Industrialism, therefore, is not just a system of production. *It is also a system of power.*

Why do nature people everywhere resist industrialism? For one thing, industrialism is not necessary for a nature culture to survive (as long as it's left alone by "higher" civilizations). The classic example is the North America Indians, who managed to meet all basic human needs with a minimum of centralized institutions and without destroying their environment.

There is a second reason for this resistance to being industrialized. Industrialism, by its very nature, destroys the magic of human existence. Consider the way we, as industrialized people, relate to our environment. Everywhere we see huge cities, highways, factories, universities, airports. Everywhere the trees, the plants, the animals have been slaughtered. In 1969, the Atmospheric Sciences Research Center reported that there was no longer any uncontaminated air anywhere in North America (Roszak, 16). In 1970, Thor Heyerdahl crossed the Atlantic in a handmade boat. He reported that he could not find one oil-free stretch of water during the entire crossing (Roszak, *loc. cit.*). What kind of people are we that we do this to the environment? "Only those who have broken off their silent inner dialogue with man and nature, only those who experience the world as dead, stupid, or alien and therefore without a claim to reverence, could ever turn upon their environment and their fellows with the cool and meticulously calculated rapacity of industrial society" (Roszak, 168).

We have seen in past chapters how the triumph of Christianity and the emergence of the industrial system resulted in the objectification of nature. What we must now realize is that this objectifying has resulted in the deadening of our feelings. Nature people everywhere believe that the earth, the trees, the moon are living personalities who talk to us and with whom we can communicate. We laugh at them and call them savages. Could they be right, after all? If so, when they talk to us about these things they must feel like people with vision trying to explain color to someone who is blind.

Another loss of the industrial system is art. There are very few of us left with any artistic skills at all. Artists are considered rare birds, slightly bizarre, and not at all normal like everyone else. The artistic skill that remains has been co-opted by industrial institutions, either for selling toothpaste (as in the West) or socialism (as in the East). So rare indeed is art in our lives that art objects are kept locked up in special institutions (museums) which we go to view on special occasions. No doubt in a few more generations there will also be tree museums.

But how could the situation be otherwise with art? In an industrial society, we no longer make things for ourselves. We buy them as consumers. *Art is part of the process of making.* In nature societies, people make everything for themselves. As a result, every inch of their environment is filled with art. Museums are unknown. Wherever industrialism has triumphed, art has disappeared from the life of the people, and museums have taken its place.

Industrialism has killed the animal within us. We become indoor people, surrounded by concrete and plastic, working hours on hours as factory workers, bureaucrats, academics, living in our skulls and dead to our bodies. "Man was created to have room to move about in, to gaze into far distances, to live in rooms which, even when they were tiny, opened out on fields. See him now, enclosed by the rules and architectural necessities imposed by over-population in a twelve-by-twelve closet opening out on an anonymous world of city streets" (Ellul, 321).

Industrialism continues to teach that humans are superior to animals and that "civilization" consists in getting as far away as possible from our animal nature. Wilhelm Reich correctly believed that the rise of fascism in industrialized countries was dependent on the repression of our animal nature within the bourgeois family. "The theory of the German superman has its origins in man's efforts to dissassociate himself from the animal" (Reich, 334). When alienated from their animal nature, people come to view it as evil, and then look for an outside authority-figure to keep it repressed. "The Leader," whether political or religious, suppresses from without what is feared from within. The Nazis associated homosexuality with animal behavior (which, like all sexuality, it is). They violently purged their own party of known Gay people, destroyed the early antecedents of the Gay Liberation Movement, and sent masses of Gay people to the gas chambers (Lauritsen). Similar attitudes could be found among Russian Stalinists (whose overriding obsession was to industrialize Russia as fast as possible).

The industrial system has made us forget how to live. Nature people know how to make their own houses, food, medicine, clothes, religious rites, humor, and entertainment. These skills keep them from becoming enslaved by money. Since people always retain the skills of survival, it's very difficult for an aristocracy of money to get control of their lives. The people don't need money to survive. In an industrial society, however, we are never taught the skills of how to live. We become totally dependent on money for meeting our every need. If the money runs out, we have nothing to eat, nothing to wear, nowhere to sleep. As a result, we become totally dependent on those who control money. In capitalist countries, these are the huge business monopolies. In communist countries, it is the state.

Industrialism has degraded both labor and leisure. Most people in industrial societies are in fact wage slaves, working forty hours a week or more at monotonous, hateful "jobs" for the sole purpose of making enough money to live and enjoy life. When they come home debilitated from such alienated labor, they have nothing left to their souls except alienated leisure: television, movies, newspapers, all of which indoctrinate with industrial values. Like schools and universities, these media are part of the general anesthesia.

Workers in industrial societies tend to work longer hours than people in nature cultures. And industrial work is far less interesting. Industrial workers are kept at their jobs through their dependence on money and through constant indoctrination by institutions. 'The natural tendency of man, as manifested in primitive [sic] societies, is almost certainly to work until a given consumption is achieved. Then he relaxes, engages in sport, hunting, orgiastic or propitiating ceremonies or other forms of physical enjoyment or spiritual betterment. This tendency for primitive man to achieve-contentment has been the despair of those who regard themselves as agents of civilization and remains so to this day. What is called economic development consists in no small part in devising strategies to overcome the tendency of men to place limits on their objectives as regards income and thus on their efforts" (Galbraith, 279).

Industrialism has devastated our sexual lives. We complain that we treat each other's bodies unfeelingly, as so many objects, to use and dispose of. Yet we fail to realize that we treat everything (including ourselves) as so many objects to use and dispose of. We fail to see that the total objectification of our environment and of nature is a direct effect of the power system of industrialism. If we have been conditioned throughout our lives to objectify everything, how can we fail to objectify those who excite us sexually?

Making Beer (Richard Speke)

The industrial system has reduced sex to a productive activity, just as it reduces all human functions to productive activities. Under industrialism, the purpose of sex has become purely economic: to breed consumers, workers, and soldiers for their proper roles in industrial and military hierarchies. Sexual relations have been reduced to productive relations. The basic unit of people-production is the monogamous heterosexual family.

Sex itself is locked up in secrecy, privacy, darkness, embarrassment, and guilt. That's how the industrial system manages to keep it under control. Among nature peoples, as we have seen, sex is part of the public religion and education of the tribes. It becomes a collective celebration of the powers that hold the universe together. Its purpose is its own pleasure. Any group of people with such practices and values can never be dominated by industrial institutions. That's why the first thing industrial societies do on contact with "primitives" is make them feel guilty about sex and their bodies. The historical tools for doing this have been patriarchal religions.

The whole industrial system is like one great night of the living dead where the entire populace has been reduced emotionally to the level of zombies. It has deadened us to our environment, deprived us of art, sterilized our animal nature, robbed us of the skills of survival, degraded our labor and leisure, and decimated our sexual lives. And so it has made us like the living dead — dead to nature, dead to each other, dead to ourselves.

Some people may say: "Even if this is true, industrialism has also generated its own antibody, a thing that will ultimately transform it. This is technology, which in itself is neither good nor bad. We can transform the world for the better if we only use technology in the right way. Technology will save us!" Unfortunately, the historical evidence does not support this view. For example, it used to be said that computerization would eliminate idiotic, repetitive jobs, thus giving people more leisure and also giving birth to new kinds of jobs that allow for more creativity. In fact, however, the exact opposite has happened. As a study of the actual evidence shows, "the largest single occupation created by computerization is that of the key punch operator" (Braverman, 83). Being a key punch operator is one of the most deadening jobs in modern society. It involves dealing with machines in the most mechanical, mind-and-body killing way.

One of the most important areas in which computers have had a mass impact is that of clerical work. Since 1900, there has been a disastrous fall in the status of clerical workers, in their pay, and in the avenues for creativity in their work (Braverman, 51). Coincidentally since 1900, the mechanical working-class segment of the general labor force has *increased* from 50% to between 67% and 75% (Braverman, 113). "It takes but a moment's reflection to see that the new mass of working-class occupations tend to grow, not in contradiction to the speedy mechanization and 'automation' of industry, but in harmony with it" (Braverman, 114). The actual effect of technology has been to create a vast surplus of workers available for deadening work at low wages (Braverman, 114).

The economist Harry Braverman notes that corresponding to the disastrous fall in the status of clerical workers has been a change in their sex. In 1900, three-fourths of all clerical workers were male. In 1960, two-thirds were women (Braverman, SO). As all of us who have been clerical wage-slaves know, a very large number of the men who remain in clerical occupations are Gay. Hence the largest growing segment of the work force in industrial America— the one that is among the lowest paid and is most due to the growth of technology— is based on the exploited labor of women and Gay men.

This situation brings to mind the earliest days of industrial technology in England. The first workers in factories were women and children, not men. Because of this situation, large families were encouraged. Large families meant having more workers who could be put to work for wages. "With the rise of the factory, the practice of hiring low-wage child and female labour in preference to male labour in some areas and industries might confront the man with the economic necessity of marrying early, reproducing quickly and abundantly" (Lazonick, 40; original's italics). Historically, industrial technology has been the cause of overpopulation, not vice-versa.

Technology has not produced more leisure, either. Between 1941 and 1965, a period of great technological innovation and application, the average work week actually *increased* (Galbraith, 370, note 1). During roughly the same period, the economic power of workers declined. From 1940 to 1950, wholesale prices doubled (Burns, 113). From 1964 to 1970 alone, the purchasing power of the dollar dropped 20% (Melman, "From Private to Pentagon Capitalism," 4). With every passing year, goods are produced with increasingly inferior quality.

Historically, technology has been associated with militarism. As we have seen, more than two-thirds of the nation's technical researchers are now employed by the Pentagon business empire. The greatest technological innovations have always occurred during times of war. The modern factory system, itself a crucial technological innovation, was derived from 17th century businesses that manufactured war material (Gilbert, 51). It's true that machines and technical skills are not in themselves evil, but only become so when controlled by powerful institutions beyond the will of the people. But the essence of industrial technology is that very fusion of technical skill with institutional power. *Industrial technology, like industrialism itself, is a system of power.*

To be effective, it requires the quantification of needs, which means that personal needs are debased and reduced to mass needs. Once applied, it creates problems that can only be solved by more technology. Hence arises the inevitable elite of experts. To be most efficient, it needs the greatest amount. of centralized control. Hence arises monopoly. In the Soviet Union, all major industry is controlled by one institution, the state. In the U. S., as early as 1944, 62% of all workers were employed by 2% of all enterprises (Ellul, 154). Today, the concentration is certainly much higher.

All the highly industrialized nations of the earth, regardless of whether they are communist or capitalist, show the same effects of the impact of technology: concentration of political and economic power in the hands of a few; increasing regimentation of every aspect of life, including thoughts, emotions, and even fantasies; and devastation of the environment. "In spite of all the men of good will, all the optimists, all the doers of history, the civilizations of the world are being ringed about with a band of steel" (Ellul, 127).

Of course, it's possible to divorce technical skill from institutional control, but then we no longer have industrial technology. Such a change would mean a *new type of technology*, something far different from any productive system that now prevails on the planet.

"But," someone may finally say, "look at all the progress brought about by technology. What about progress?" And, indeed, technology has brought about breath-taking progress — *for the privileged classes of industrial societies.* But what of the cost? What of the annihilation of the old cultures of Europe and the cultures of the American Indians? What of the enslavement and exploitation of the Blacks? The exploited labor of the modern Third World? The destruction of nature? The twisting of sexuality? What of the millions upon millions of people killed in wars made possible only by technology? Yes, the survivors (some of them) have it very good. But when we take into consideration the *entire* historical cost, "we cannot say with assurance that there has been progress from 1250 to 1 950" (Ellul, 192).

The industrial wasteland has come upon u s from our past. It is the gestation of over 2, 000 years of patriarchal rule, the last offspring of Christian/ industrial institutions. It is vast. It is powerful. It has respected neither culture nor ideology. It has spread like a cancer over the whole face of the earth. It has ruined our work, our art, our environment, and our emotional and sexual lives. It has cost us the magic sense of life.

If we are ever to rise up from the dead and regain our rightful place in nature, we will have to do more than put our faith in the state, the party, or technology — all of which are mere props of industrialism. We will have to tap the saving energies that now lie buried in ourselves and in nature. And that means we will have to summon forth powers that have not been known since the days of the shamans.

Photo by Bernie Boyle   (front, second from right, Hal Offen)

10 Magic and Revolution

What is revolution?

Many of us answer this question by rote. As if somebody pushed a button, we feed back the "right line" we've been taught in our particular school of thought.

The rote response is bad because it makes us overlook many things we take for granted. For example, almost all of us are locked into the habit of seeing everything through patriarchal eyes. We carry this tunnel vision around with us even when we allow ourselves flights of revolutionary fantasy.

In the past, many revolutionaries, on coming to power, falsely believed they were starting a new order. Often all they really did was re-establish the old patriarchal order under a more efficient or humane management. In my opinion, this has been the fate of the two most important progressive forces of the past few hundred years: liberalism and industrial socialism. In what follows, we will take a look at each of these two movements in view of what we've found out about Gay history. In doing so, I believe we will see the need for transcending both.

Historically, liberalism has been associated with the bourgeoisie. It was originally the ideology of European merchants and business owners in their revolt against the landed aristocracy and the monarchy. Today it is preeminently the ideology of educated members of the middle class and of reform-minded members of the privileged professional classes. Spokespeople for modern liberalism are often connected to schools and universities. Their great hope is for reform through education and peaceful compromise.

Liberalism has had a good record in ending some forms of oppression. It has been of great benefit for those oppressed members of society who have been able to adjust to middle-class lifestyles. In this respect, it has especially helped upwardly-mobile people from a lower middle-class background.

But for those who cannot or will not adjust to a middle-class lifestyle, liberalism has had little to offer. The United States has seen two hundred years of basically liberal institutions and a great host of liberal leaders and programs (recent examples being the New Deal, the New Frontier, and the Great Society). Yet despite this liberal tradition, the United States today is a corrupt garrison society, living off the exploited labor of non-white people throughout the world and violently repressive within its own borders of Gay people, women, Blacks, poor people, Indians, and Mother Earth.

The great flaw of liberalism is that it accepts the basic values of Western culture as that culture has been handed down from generation to generation through schools and universities. As we have seen, this cultural tradition everywhere represents the values of the patriarchal ruling classes. For example, the most cultured leaders of medieval Europe were the very ones who called loudest for the annihilation of witches and heretics and the lifestyles they were practicing. "The more learned a man was in the traditional scholarship of the time, the more likely he was to support the witchdoctors [that is, the witch-hunters]. The most ferocious of witchburning princes, we often find, are the most cultured patrons of contemporary learning" (Trevor-Roper, 154). This cultural savagery did not stop with the end of the Middle Ages. "It was forwarded by the cultural popes of the Renaissance, by the great Protestant reformers, by the saints of the Counter-Reformation, by the scholars, lawyers and churchmen" (Trevor-Roper, 91).

Within modern times, schools and universities have become servants of the military-industrial complex. Most of their money comes from the government, the military, or private industry. Their regents most often come from the ruling class (the Hearst family's influence over the University of California being a notorious example). Modern schools and universities push students into habits of depersonalized learning, alienation from nature and sexuality, obedience to hierarchy, fear of authority, self-objectification, and chilling competitiveness. These character traits are the essence of the twisted personality-type of modern industrialism. They are precisely the character traits needed to maintain a social system that is utterly out of touch with nature, sexuality, and real human needs. The degrees issued by modern schools and universities have become little more than tickets of admission to the privileged professional classes. Despite this dismal situation, modern liberals such as John Kenneth Galbraith continue to place their hope for the nation's salvation in "the educational and scientific estate" (Galbraith *passim*).

Liberalism fails to recognize that schools and universities have been major vehicles through which prejudice has been spread against Gay people, women, and Third World people. What is today called "common prejudice" was only yesterday taught in the schools as the refined thinking of learned teachers. Schools, not common people, have "proved" by the most exacting scholarly methods that Gay people are sick; that women are inferior to men; that Third World cultures are primitive, barbaric, and savage. Just as schools today continue to teach that reason is better than emotion; that animals are inferior to humans; that rocks, hills, and stars are inanimate objects; that the most important thing in life is to get a good job; and that education consists in reading books.

Liberals worship professionalism. They urge us to turn to professional historians to find out about history; to sociologists, to find out how social groups work; to psychologists, to find out about the soul. They fail to realize that the more "educated" a person is the more she or he is likely to embody the twisted personality-type of modern industrialism and thus to see reality through the dead eyes of the industrial mentality. They fail to see a horrible irony in the fact that many professional institutions now do the very opposite of what they claim. And so we find state departments of ecology functioning as agencies for licensing the rape of the earth; nursing homes and hospitals as places where most people die; newspapers as means for distorting and censoring the news; schools as graveyards of all personal learning and growth; and departments of defense as machines for planning and carrying out aggressive warfare. Liberals are blind to the fact that the privileged professional classes of modern industrial society are utterly bankrupt, having been bought and paid for by the rotten system that feeds them their money and their values.

Photo by Bernie Boyle

Liberals are also blind to the class struggle. They overlook the fact that what is called Western "civilization" has been made possible only by wave after wave of patriarchal domination. As we have seen, this domination has grown in leaps, beginning in the Bronze Age and increasing through the period of the Greco-Roman patriarchy, the Christian Era, and finally the Dark Age of Industrialism. In each period, the patterns of domination have been passed on in sequence from one ruling class to the next. To liberals, this sequence is rarely even acknowledged, let alone resisted.

Within the context of the Gay movement, liberals have been very effective in changing laws and in changing attitudes on the part of some professionals.

But Gay liberalism has had little relevance for those of us who reject a middle-class lifestyle. At its worst, Gay liberalism has encouraged Gay men to mimic the behavior of upwardly-mobile straight professional types. This is the line pushed by David Goodstein, the millionaire owner of *The Advocate*, the leading organ of Gay liberalism in the U.S.; Goodstein, who is proud of his hobby as a horse breeder, urges Gay men to get "respectable" and to push on with the job of being assimilated into the American dream. In effect, he would have all of us become Straight-Identified-Faggots (or STIFFS, for short).

A more subtle emphasis on professionalism and middle-class values is found in the National Gay Task Force, the nation's leading Gay liberal political group. NGTF greatly admires the ideal of the highly educated, middle-class professional Gay person. It emphasizes the importance of a "professional approach" to Gay liberation. NGTF runs itself internally on the model of a professional business organization. Interestingly, the phrase "Task Force" is a military-bureaucratic term, first being used by the U.S. Navy to denote a particular group of differing specialists under the leadership of one commander (see entry under "task force" in *The Random House Dictionary*). The founder and co-boss of NGTF is Dr. Bruce Voeller, an ex-geneticist for Rockefeller University, a prominent center of independent research financed by the military-industrial-scientific establishment.

Gay liberals have been indifferent to the way the Gay movement has been co-opted by the owners of Gay bars, baths, and businesses. These owners have capitalized on the new tolerance toward Gay people by creating a network of businesses designed to swallow as much Gay money as possible. Having gotten rich from this take, they now control the largest single source of money in the Gay community. Hence they set the tone and atmosphere of such publications as *The Advocate*.

Gay capitalists are prepared to spend a bundle for Gay "civil rights" (by which they mean the right to run Gay businesses free of harassment). But they raise bloody hell if the Gay movement brings up class issues. Two examples of this type of Gay-bar liberalism are Dale Bentley and Emerson Propps, the Reno-affiliated duo who own the western branch of the Club Baths chain (not to be confused with the eastern branch). These two capitalists boast that they have put a lot of money into making things looser for Gay people in Denver and Idaho. Yet early in 1976, they began a policy of refusing admittance to their San Francisco baths to anyone wearing the T-shirt of Bay Area Gay Liberation (BAGL). In their opinion, BAGL members were "troublemakers" and "communists." The troublemaking they were referring to was BAGL's recent protest against racism and sexism at a local Gay bar, the Mindshaft. Bentley and Propps were also accused of discriminating against Gay men who were effeminate, old, or Third World (which they denied). They were sued in court over the BAGL incident and lost. A suit over the other forms of discrimination is still pending. To Bentley and Propps, Gay liberation seems to mean making the world safe for the owners of Gay bars and businesses. People like them are now footing the bill— and, therefore, calling the tune— for many liberal Gay activist organizations.

Gay liberal organizations tend to seek out "respectable" (that is, bourgeois) Gay men as their spokespeople. These, unfortunately, have been known to oppress Gay people who can't or won't fit into the mainstream. We have all seen the late Dr. Howard Brown, health bureaucrat from New York, running around on behalf of the National Gay Task Force. *He was put into that position solely because of his middle-class credentials and connections.* Soon after coming out on the front pages of the New York Times, he appeared before a mid-west Gay group and proceeded to tell them that cross-dressing should be discouraged because it offends middle America!

So, on the whole, Gay liberalism has all the advantages and disadvantages of any middle-class movement: On the positive side, it has accessibility to the media, to establishment politicians, and to opinion makers in the privileged professional classes. On the negative side, it is insensitive to the struggles of non-middle-class people and is generally oblivious to penetrating questions about lifestyles. Since it takes bourgeois industrialism for granted, it is never revolutionary. In effect, it is nothing more than a movement on behalf of white, middle-class, masculine-identified men.

The second great progressive force of modern times has been industrial socialism. Historically, industrial socialism has been associated with the urban proletariat and those who claim to be its leaders. It reached its classic expression in the 19th century in the writings of Karl Marx. In general, it advocates the overthrow of the power of the bourgeoisie and the collective seizing of the means of production by a highly disciplined party. Industrial socialism has been the single most important force for human liberation in the 20th century. In nearly every case where it has come to power and managed to hold on to power, it has driven out foreign exploiters (usually American business interests), ended mass hunger, and provided the necessary means of survival for its people. Such has been the case, for example, in Russia, China, and Cuba.

Unfortunately, industrial socialism has had some disastrous blind spots, especially concerning sex, the family, nature, science, the state, and industrialism itself. These weaknesses are all interconnected.

One of the first things the Bolsheviks in Russia did after seizing power in 1917 was to repeal the old Czarist laws, including the laws against homosexuality. For a time, the regime seemed to encourage a freer status for women and a more humane atmosphere for Gay people. Within seventeen years, all this had changed. In January 1934, Joseph Stalin carried out a mass arrest of Gay people in Moscow, Leningrad, Kharkov, and Odessa (Lauritsen, 68). In March 1934, Russia again outlawed homosexuality (Lauritsen, 69).

Corresponding to this drastic reversal were other outrages. In 1929, Stalin had undertaken a war against the peasants, who at the time constituted 80% of the population. Peasant families were deported, their land was confiscated, and many were sent to concentration camps. Those who weren't imprisoned were sent to large-scale industrialized farming units. Stalin compared his war against the peasants to Russia's war against the Germans (Nove, 160-177).

Stalin's goal was to industrialize Russia at any cost, and that's what he did. The industrialization of Russia was made possible through the blood of its peasants, just as the industrialization of Western Europe was made possible through the annihilation of the old religion and its cultures, and the industrialization of the North American continent was made possible by the enslavement of Blacks and the seizure of Indian lands.

Although Stalin was the most extreme example of industrial violence in Russia, the roots of his actions go back to both Lenin and Marx, both of whom never questioned the inevitability or desirability of industrialism and science. Lenin in particular believed there was a necessary link between industrialism and the need for a powerful centralized state. In 1917, shortly after the Bolsheviks came to power, he said: "Neither railways nor transport, nor large-scale machinery and enterprise in general can function correctly without a single will linking the entire working personnel into an economic organ operating with the precision of clock-work. Socialism owes its origin to large-scale machine industry" (Nove, 57). From the earliest days of the revolution, Lenin was accused of taking Russia in the direction of state capitalism, a criticism he rejected as "left-wing childishness" (Nove, 58).

Karl Marx had argued that industrial civilization was the last and highest stage in the progressive dialectic of human civilization. All other forms he viewed as outdated, primitive, or savage. Marx had faith in science and called his theory *scientific* socialism. He ridiculed socialists who questioned the nature of industrialism itself as "utopian."

Many modern Marxists continue to view nature societies with contempt. An example is George Thomas, a well known Marxist historian who has written about matriarchy in early Greece. He says concerning nature people in general that "the primitive [sic) cultures still surviving in other parts of the world are products of retarded or arrested development" (Thomas, 35). This type of thinking comes straight out of Marx's theory of dialectical materialism. According to this theory, nature societies are rather low in the scale of social evolution. Sooner or later, as a result of internal class struggle, they develop in the direction of white industrial civilization, which is viewed as high in the scale. The development in this direction is considered inevitable, desirable, and progressive. Such a theory, apart from being false, is inherently racist.

Neither Marx nor Engels had a very good record in dealing with Gay rights. They never lifted a finger to help the Gay struggle in their time, even though both were aware of it (Kennedy, 6). In fact, they were even homophobic. Engels believed that male homosexuality was historically linked to contempt for women, as when he said concerning ancient Athens: "this degradation of women was avenged on the men and degraded them also till they fell into the abominable practice of sodomy and degraded alike their gods and themselves with the myth of Ganymede" (Engels, 128). Marx, like Engels, usually referred to Gay men with derogatory words. He called Karl Boruttau, an early advocate of sexual freedom, "cock-queer" Kennedy, 6).

Industrial socialism in Russia has turned into state capitalism. Russian society is now greatly industrialized and urbanized like the U. S., but the means of production are owned by the state instead of corporate business people. The state itself is the chief capitalist in Russia, and the Russian state competes with other states (both capitalist and socialist) just as corporate capitalists compete with each other in the West. Industrial technology has had the same impact in Russia that it is having everywhere: repression of sexuality, regimentation of every aspect of life, and reduction of the populace to emotional zombies.

Photo by Bernie Boyle

As long as socialists do not raise questions about the nature of industrialism itself, I believe that socialism will always end up by becoming state capitalism. This will happen because there are certain features of industrialism that are in and of themselves capitalist. To understand this point, we recall that industrialism is the system where people stop making things for their own immediate needs. Instead things are produced by specialized and centralized institutions (such as factories). Whether these institutions are called socialist or not makes no difference with respect to one point: they cannot exist at all unless the workers' labor creates a surplus value above what is needed for the workers to survive. All of this surplus value cannot be returned to the workers themselves; otherwise, there would then be no means of paying for the factory or its expansion. So there arises a need to manage and plan the use of this excess capital. If these factories are to be integrated into one huge complex economic system, a special group of experts is necessary to do this managing and planning. Hence, in a socialist society, arise the planners who become agents of the state (if they aren't state agents, there's the risk of the return of corporate capitalism). And so the state itself emerges as the director of all important capital decisions and thus becomes the chief capitalist.

Whenever any socialist society deliberately undertakes to industrialize itself, it immediately comes under tremendous pressure toward state capitalism. The classic example in our time is the People's Republic of China. Under Chairman Mao, China approached closer to the ideal of a true socialist society than any other country. Academics and other professional types spent part of each year working in factories or on the land. Wage differentials were narrowed. Most important of all, Mao emphasized the great importance of the peasants, whom Stalin annihilated in Russia and whom Marx at times considered little better than a sack of potatoes.

But this socialist thrust has been maintained only at the cost of great internal upheaval after the revolution and in the face of stiff opposition. From 1966 to 1969, Mao pushed the Great Proletarian Cultural Revolution. This was in fact a civil war in China whose purpose was to stop the rising power of the privileged professional classes. These privileged classes were getting stronger as China moved along the road to industrialism. In the end, the forces unleashed by the cultural revolution seem to have become a threat to the Chinese state itself. They were finally suppressed by the army on orders from Mao (Macciocchi, 59).

No one can say what will happen in China now that Mao is dead, but the forces working toward state capitalism still exist. This threat is actually intensified by the structure of the Chinese Communist Party, which is heavily indebted to the ideal of organization and discipline that it borrowed wholesale from earlier Christian missionaries and monastic orders (Fitzgerald, 133). It is conceivable that communism in China could end up becoming just another patriarchal religion, as it already has in the U.S. S.R. Or perhaps China will continue to raise penetrating questions about industrialism and so take socialism on to a new and unprecedented path.

Industrial socialism of all stripes has been very uptight about sex. As we have seen, homosexuality is now illegal in Russia. In China, Gay people are said not to exist and the subject is not publicly mentioned. In Cuba, homosexuality was declared a "social pathology" in 1971 and many Gay people were sent to concentration camps. The nuclear family — which is the life blood of patriarchal civilization — has never been questioned in any industrializing socialist society, and in fact has been greatly re-enforced. In addition, industrial socialism eagerly embraces science, views industrialism as desirable and inevitable, and ridicules the old animistic religions that have existed in each country in which it has come to power (which is ironic, since these old religions, if anything, represent the basic values of the peasant masses over the centuries). The leaders of industrial socialism have generally been masculine-identified males who owe their initial success and power to organized armies.

In the context of the Gay movement, industrial socialists often have weak feelings of Gay identity and a shallow concept of Gay culture and Gay spirituality. Typically, they view Gay revolution as meaning nothing more than supporting the programs of the New Left, while also having Gay sex on the side. Too often, they believe that Gay men have nothing more in common than sex (which is actually a lot!).

Just like liberals, Gay industrial socialists also have been insensitive to the true depth of corruption in Western civilization. This insensitivity comes out through such slogans as, "Socialism is the answer!" This implies that all we have to do is get worker control over the factories and all other means of production. As we have seen, however, the problem is not only who controls the means of production, but the means of production themselves. Industrial socialists step back from the conclusion that what we need is not a new administration in Washington or a new economic policy, but a new civilization.

In making these criticism, I am not saying that industrial socialism has not helped people. It certainly has, far more than bourgeois liberalism ever did or could. But what I *am* saying is that industrial socialism is not necessarily the highest or only form of revolutionary socialism. Even in cases where it has been absolutely necessary (as in China), we can view it as something to begin with, to build on, rather than as the absolute and final end of all human struggle toward liberation. The revolution shouldn't end when the revolutionaries take power.

I believe it is necessary to develop a *new* socialism, one that takes into account the failures of industrial socialism and that makes room for the special contributions of Gay people, women, and ancient Third World cultures. In the remaining part of this chapter, I will try to outline the main features, as I see them, of this new socialism.

Photo by Bernie Boyle   *(right, Jacob Schraeter, Arthur's partner)*

To begin with, I believe we must bring about a massive withdrawal of allegiance from the dominant institutions of industrialism. We have all been assaulted with incessant industrial propaganda and lies from newspapers, magazines, television, schools, and universities. As a result, most of us still feel some sense of allegiance to such things as formal education, industrial medicine, and the professions. Nearly every American still has some faith in the U.S. government, the Christian religion, and the American way of life. But as we have seen from this entire book, the dominant institutions of industrialism arose from an oppressive patriarchal culture and continue to function as oppressors to this day. As new socialists, we should never fail to expose the inherent fraud of lawyers, doctors, academics, police, politicians, priests, psychiatrists, generals, and business people. We should miss no opportunity in denouncing their privileges and power and in undermining all vestiges of their moral authority. And we must demystify *ourselves* to overcome the belief instilled in us that we can't heal ourselves, educate ourselves, create our own religion, or wage warfare on our own behalf. We can do all these things — and more! We must work to regain confidence in ourselves as the makers of our own culture and satisfiers of our own needs and to throw off the yoke of the professional parasites who now live off our life energies.

The way to do these things is through collective work. I mean *real* collective work, not the forced collectivity of industrial socialism (which is often nothing more than state control masquerading as collectivity). For example, we can form small collectives to start getting food for ourselves in the cities (such as the many non-profit food co-ops on the West Coast). We can join together to publish our own magazines and books. We can study herbs and people's medicine to heal ourselves. We can form collectives to work on satisfying practically any of our needs— and we can do it better than the privileged professionals can (I've seen it happen).

In this way we begin replacing industrial technology with people's technology. In place of large corporations controlled by profiteers and staffed by an elite of experts, we create decentralized productive units that are integrated into the neighborhoods they serve. We rediscover the joys of learning and sharing craft mysteries and feeling love toward the products of our labor. We encourage technical methods that are humane and democratic (like solar energy and wind power) and reject methods that encourage central control and regimentation (like nuclear power). Of course, some may object that such methods are totally inappropriate to "modern" society. But that's the whole point! Non-alienated labor will always be irrelevant as long as society is based on class domination,exploitation of nature, and overpopulation.

Photo by Bernie Boyle

The most favorable spot for such collective work is the countryside. There we can remove ourselves as much as possible from industrializing influences and begin struggling collectively with the earth, learning again how to become peasants. If such collective groups are cemented together by magic (which we'll discuss in a moment), we can start building the cells of a new society within the old. We Gay people (like industrialized Third World people) have been locked up in the cities for too long. We have a right to the countryside! But if we can't or won't leave the inner cities, we can still organize there, too. The inner cities of today are comparable to the ancient countryside in the sense that that's where the most oppressed part of the population now lives.

The new work collectives that we form must be more than loose functional groups. Experience shows that such loose groups are usually short-lived and weak. If we are ever to overthrow the industrial patriarchy, I believe we must tap into deeper energies, energies that the ruling classes of Christianity and industrialism have always desperately tried to deny and repress. These are the energies of magic.

Magic is the art of communicating with the spiritual powers in nature and in ourselves. Nature societies throughout history have known that trees, stars, rocks, the sun and the moon are not dead objects or mere resources but living beings who communicate with us. They have also known that there are mysterious non-rational powers within ourselves. The Christian power system, on the other hand, has taught that spirit and matter are two utterly separate categories and that spirit emanates from one being who exists above and beyond nature. Industrialism has continued this same distinction between matter and spirit, but modified it by viewing spirit as either an illusion or as a quality of certain subjective (and therefore suspect) mental states. Accordingly, we have all been told from childbirth to repress, deny, hide, and kill our natural abilities to communicate with nature spirits and our own inner spiritual energies (just as we have been told to deny and repress our sexuality). This suppression has been aided by forcing people to live in huge urban wastelands, where we scarcely even encounter nature, let alone communicate with it. Urban wastelands also atomize us, keeping us in conflict with one another, and out of touch with our collective power centers.

This suppression has been very useful to the ruling classes in the industrial power system. The moon, for example, ceases to be the fateful goddess whom we worship with rituals in the silence of night and becomes instead a piece of real estate on which to plant an American or Soviet flag. Since we are kept out of touch with our real collective power centers, we have n6 collective entities to identify with except large, impersonal, industrial, false ones, such as the state.

Magic is inherently a collective activity, depending for its practice on group song, dance, sex, and ecstasy. It is through magic that so-called "primitive" societies are able to hold themselves together and function in perfect order without prisons, mental hospitals, universities, or the institution of the state. Until very recently in history, magic was the birth right of every human being. It is only within the last few hundred years that whole societies have come into being where people live magicless lives.

Magic is one of our most powerful allies in the struggle against patriarchal industrialism. One reason, as we've just seen, is that magic holds our work collectives together and gives us great inner power. But there is a second reason. Patriarchal industrialism has come to power not only by suppressing and killing great numbers of people, but also by violating nature. No one has ever fully recorded (or could record) the atrocities of industrialism against the animal people or the plant people. From the annihilation of animals for their furs in early colonial America to the widespread and grotesque experimentation on animals in the present, industrialism in America has utterly decimated the animal kingdoms. In addition, industrial society in general, in all times and places, has blackened the whole environment and viewed nature as something to conquer. Indeed, throughout its range in time and space, the entire Christian/industrial system has been one great crime against nature.

By tapping into magic, we tap into nature's own power of defending herself, her corrective for "civilization." We give avenues of expression to a natural force for correction and balance that otherwise would never even be acknowledged. We are in league with the memories of the forest and our own forgotten faery selves, now banished to the underworld. Let us invoke our friends, the banished and forbidden spirits of nature and self, as well as the ghosts of Indian, wise-woman, faggot, Black sorcerer, and witch. They will hear our deepest call and come. Through us the spirits will speak again.

A genuine counterculture that fully affirms the magic of human life is an ominous threat to the entire industrial order. Once we begin creating such a counterculture, we can expect to encounter a vast barrage of resistance from the establishment. Industrial authorities will try to take our children away and send them to the wasteland's schools. They will try to suppress our medicine people and force us to go to the licensed practitioners of industrial medicine (who cure through violence and chemical drugs). If we live in the country, they will try to force our shelters to follow industrial building codes. If we organize in the cities, they will find a thousand ways to harass us. If we try to openly celebrate our magic and sexuality, they will send in the police. Even if all we ask for are simple human rights, Christian/ industrial forces will organize against us. Look at the coalition of churches and corporations behind Anita Bryant in Florida or John Briggs in California.

Hence there arises the need for political resistance. For the sake of our survival, we will need allies. Our natural allies-people who have been victimized by industrialism just like us-are women, Third World people, the poor, the unemployed, the unemployable, and the insane.

Photos by Bernie Boyle

Although America is controlled by straight-identified, upper-class people, these classes do not control the rest of the world, and the rest of the world is now on the verge of revolt. It is in our interest to give support to (and demand support from) victims of industrialism throughout the world. And it is in the interest of the international movement against imperialism to get our energy, criticisms, and input, especially concerning matters of sex and the family. A difficult struggle lies ahead in forming these alliances. Many Left leaders are men who come from a hard, masculine tradition within industrial socialism. But what is the alternative to cooperation with other oppressed people?

The industrial patriarchy has maintained itself in power by means of the most incredible violence, as we have seen in previous chapters. Witchhunts, torture, and genocide have been regular features of the patriarchy's arsenal from the age of Constantine to the age of Richard Nixon. *These tactics have been effective.* I personally doubt, therefore, that mere good intentions, education, and above-ground organizing will ever be enough on our part. Do we really think that such things can stop a civilization that wiped out the witches? Or murdered the Indians? Or sent Jews and Gay people to the ovens? Or bombed Vietnam into the Stone Age? Or infiltrated domestic protest groups and assassinated their leaders? I doubt it. I doubt that we will ever stop the patriarchy until we fan out like viruses in the body politic, when the time is right, carrying our secret weapons, and striking without warning against ruling institutions, and the politicians, industrialists, warlords, and academics that run them. Many will undoubtedly disagree, but without a revolutionary underground, I fear we will again perish like burning faggots.

I admit that violence against other human beings is a terrible desecration of life. But what are we to do in the face of the atrocities of the patriarchy, when our backs are up against the wall. Trust in liberalism? Pray? Give up? *Every important above-ground movement for reform in the U.S. during the past decade has either been annihilated or co-opted.* When we read *The Pentagon Papers* or follow the Watergate scandal, it's not hard to understand why.

Violence among humans seems to be worst when it is institutionalized (as in a standing army). Then it becomes the basis of the society's economy. It becomes self-perpetuating and self-justifying. In addition to the death and destruction it causes, it re-enforces a masculinist character among the people. This is not the violence I am talking about, but rather the hit-and-run spontaneous violence of autonomous anarchist collectives. Not against the general populace, but against those in control. Anarchist violence still kills, but it is quite a different thing from the massive, scientifically planned objective violence of institutions like the Pentagon. It is more like the violence of a cornered animal defending itself. Still, those who kill defile themselves, and they must be prepared to accept the consequences of that defilement. But at this stage in the crisis in international industrialism, I see no effective alternate to revolutionary violence. And revolutionary violence is effective — that's why the U.S. government is so uptight about it. Despite the great newspaper publicity that erupts when members of the underground are caught, very few terrorists are in fact ever tracked down and arrested.

Photo by Bernie Boyle

I'm not saying that revolutionary violence is the only form of resistance or even the most important form at all times. But it does play a part, depending on circumstances. Revolution is an act of both creation and destruction.

For those who detest the very thought of violence, let them consider for a moment the powder keg the U.S. ruling class is already sitting on. The U.S. today is a country whose economy is based on ghastly exploitation of peoples throughout the world. Not only do U.S. corporations exploit these peoples' labor, but they take the better part of their natural resources, churn them into commodities, and sell them in the U.S. and other countries, where they are quickly converted into garbage. As a result of this imperialism, mass starvation now stalks the Third World. Within the borders of the U.S. itself, the ruling class and the privileged, professional classes live as zombies, utterly alienated from their sexuality, from nature, and from themselves. The great American middle class lives in a plastic bubble, surrounded by suburbs and television, totally oblivious to the dragon whose tail it is treading on. At the bottom, the lower classes burn with resentment. With each passing year, the skies grow darker with pollution, and the earth is ever more gorged with refuse. The privileged classes grow old, filled with fat and cancer.

These outrages cannot last forever! Sooner or later, something is going to give, and when it does, the debate over violence will be academic indeed. The justification for all these struggles is the new society we look forward to. How can we describe it? What does it look like? In many ways, it is practically the opposite of the one we now live in.

We look forward to the passing away of the state, the church, the university, the large corporation, the prison, the mental hospital, and all other institutions that rob people of the meaning of life. These institutions are only necessary within the basic assumptions of industrial patriarchy. For example, industrialism has spread compulsive heterosexuality and repressed homosexuality, thus giving rise to disastrous overpopulation and hideous urban wastelands. Industrialism has kept us from learning the skills of how to survive, thus making us dependent on money and productive institutions. Industrialism has been fostered by an elite ruling class, thus making necessary the existence of prisons, schools, and other coercive institutions for keeping people in their "proper place". There is no reason in the nature of things why these practices and institutions should be part of human experience. There have been many societies in which they were absent.

What is to take the place of the state-and all these institutions? We look forward to the rebirth of the tribe and tribal communism. We look forward to a myriad number of autonomous tribes, small in population, growing like plants from the earth. We look forward to a society in which everyone spends some time working the earth with his or her own hands to provide the food necessary for survival. We look forward to a gradual decrease in the importance of books, and the revival of the oral tradition, where each tribal collective passes on its cumulative wisdom through poetry, song, and dance. We look forward to the revival of personal and sexual learning, as it was once practiced by Sappho and Socrates and the Native American Indians. We look forward to freeing technical skill from institutional control and to the days when local tribal collectives forge their own metals and make machines that serve people rather than dominate them. We look forward to freeing the spirit of art, to the day when we all become artists because we all participate in creating our environment. We look forward to re-establishing our communication with nature and the Great Mother, to feeling the essential link between sex and the forces that hold the universe together. In so doing, we remember the prophecy of Edward Carpenter, the Gay historian and prophet. In 1889, surveying the industrial wasteland around him, he said this concerning man (and, we might add, women too):

"The meaning of the old religions will come back to him. On the high tops once more gathering he will celebrate with naked dances the glory of the human form and the great processions of the stars, or greet the bright horn of the young moon which now after a hundred centuries comes back laden with such wondrous associations-all the yearnings and the dreams and the wonderment of the generations of mankind-the worship of Astarte and of Diana, of Isis or the Virgin Mary; once more in sacred groves will he reunite the passion and the delight of human love with his deepest feelings of the sanctity and beauty of Nature; or in the open, standing uncovered to the Sun, will adore the emblem of the everlasting splendour which shines within" (Carpenter, *Civilisation: Its Cause and Cure*, 57).

We look forward to creating a genuine Gay culture, one that is free from exploitation by bars, baths, and Gay business owners. We look forward to re-establishing women's mysteries and men's mysteries as the highest expression of collective Gay culture and sexuality. We look forward to regaining our ancient historical roles as medicine people, healers, prophets, shamans, and sorcerers. We look forward to an endless and fathomless process of *corning out* — as Gay people, as animals, as humans, as mysterious and powerful spirits that move through the life cycle of the cosmos.

So we see that the new socialism is a movement that is not just political, but also magical and sexual. It rejects the dominant traditions of the West's ruling classes, including mass industrialism and urbanism. Instead, it calls for these features: creation of tribal collectives that are held together through shared work, sex, and magic; liberation of technical skill from institutional control; release of the captive powers of art; assertive cooperation between all groups oppressed by industrialism; revolutionary violence; and creation of a post-industrial communist nature-society where Gay culture can flourish free from repression and exploitation.

We are casting aside the shackles of the industrial patriarchy. Like butterflies, we are emerging from the shells of our past restricted existence.

We are re-discovering the ancient magic that was once the birth right of all human beings. We are re-learning how to talk to the worms and the stars. We are taking flight on the wings of self-determination.

Come, blessed Lady of the Flowers, Queen of Heaven, creator and destroyer, Kali — we are dancing the great dance of your coming.

Appendix:
CALENDAR OF SOME
INTERESTING EVENTS IN THE
HISTORY OF HERESY AND
WITCHCRAFT

399 BC   The Athenian philosopher Socrates is condemned to death for corrupting young men and believing in gods the state doesn't believe in (Plato, 248).

186 BC   The Senate of Rome outlaws the Bacchanalia, responding to charges that the rites undermine militarism and make men effeminate (Partridge, 54).

169 BC   The Senate of Rome outlaws male homosexuality among Roman citizens (Meier, 179).

122 BC   The City of Rome begins a conquest of Celtic civilization (Hatt, 305 ff).

58 BC   Julius Caesar conquers the Celts of Gaul (Hatt, 305 ff).

28 BC   The Emperor Augustus Caesar orders all temples of the goddess Isis removed from the inner city of Rome (Angus, 38).

13 BC   The Emperor Augustus assumes the title *Pontifex Maximus* (Supreme Priest), a title assumed by all subsequent emperors and later by the Popes (Angus, 37)

12 BC — The Emperor Augustus begins a campaign to suppress Celtic religion (Chadwick, *Druids*, 71 ff)

0-100 AD — Gnosticism, an underground religion combining elements of Christianity and paganism, arises in Asia Minor (Obolensky, 3).

19 AD — The Emperor Tiberius dismantles the remaining temple of Isis (Angus, 38).

100 - 200 AD — Gnosticism spreads rapidly throughout the Roman Empire (Runciman, 6).

190 AD — Clement of Alexandria, prominent Christian theologian, condemns the pagan practice of worshipping images of human sex organs, as well as ritual sexual promiscuity among certain Gnostic sects (Benko, 113, Summers, *History*, 99).

242- 276 AD — Mani, a Persian Christian Gnostic, founds Manicheism as a powerful rival to Christianity (Runciman, 12-26; Loos, 23).

296 AD — Arnobius, Christian propagandist, condemns the use of dildos in the pagan worship of Cybele, the Great Mother of the Gods (Summers, *History*, 99).

300 AD — The Council of Elvira decrees that the last rites of the church should be denied anyone guilty of pederasty (Vanggaard, 139). From this date onward and for the next several hundred years, numerous church synods repeatedly condemn the continued practice of pagan rites and the survival of nature worship (Russell, 55, n. 12; 58, n. 19 & n. 20; Cohn, *Demons*, 157).

312 AD — Constantine, supported by the Christian party, becomes sole emperor of the West after a period of civil war, marking the beginning of the Christian Era in Western history.

313 AD — Constantine declares Christianity to be a legal religion, appoints Christians to high level government jobs, and lays the groundwork for making Christianity the state religion of the Roman Empire.

342 AD — The law code of the emperors Constantius and Constans condemns male homosexuality and urges that sodomites be subjected to "exquisite punishments" (Bailey, 70).

350 AD — Bishop Epiphanius publishes his *Panarion*, condemning certain Gnostics for practicing ritual sexual promiscuity (Benko, *passim*).

350 - 400 AD — The Massalians, a group of Christian Gnostics prominent in Syria and Asia Minor, absorb pagan traditions and teach mystical revelation through sensual experience (Obolensky, 49-50; Loos, 72).

382 AD Augustine of Hippo converts from Manicheism to traditional Christianity (Runciman, 16).

390 AD The Emperor Theodosius I declares Christianity to be the state religion of the Roman Empire and bans all other religions. He also passes a law making sodomy a capital offence (Barnett, 82, n. 45).

414 AD Nicetas repeats the condemnation of worshipping sex images (Summers, *History*, 99)

430 AD Augustine attacks the Manichees as libertines (Cohn, *Demons*, 17; Summers, History, 99).

431 AD The Virgin Mary is declared to be the Mother of God by the Council of Ephesus, in the same city noted for its previous pagan worship of the Mother of the Gods (Branston, 197).

438 AD The Emperor Theodosius II publishes the Theodosian Code, in which the penalty for sodomy, as for heresy, is declared to be burning (Barnett, 80).

447 AD The Council of Toledo establishes the doctrine of the Devil, who is subsequently identified with the Celtic horned god.

450 - 600 AD Western European writers condemn the survlvmg worship of the goddess Diana (Cohn, *Demons*, 212; Russell, 57 & 58, n. 21).

527 AD Justinian becomes emperor in the East and briefly re-establishes the Roman Empire. He conducts a pogrom against Gay men, whom he tortures and castrates (Bury, 412, n. 5).

550 AD Visigothic Christian law condemns those who offer sacrifices at night to "demons" (Cohn, Demons, 157).

650- 700 AD Pagan Bulgars move into the slavic Balkans and set up the pagan kingdom of Bulgaria (Runciman, 4 & Obolensky, 63). Paulicianism, a movement hostile to the church hierarchy and infavor of a return to early Christianity, breaks out in nearby Armenia (Obolensky, 28).

689 AD The Christian missionary Kilian is killed for trying to convert the East Franks away from the worship of Diana (Grimm, 237; Russell, 61, n. 25; Cohn, *Demons*, 212).

690 AD A penitential of the Archbishop of Canterbury is the first to mention lesbianism (Hyde, 31).

693 AD The Council of Toledo condemns male homosexuality (Bailey, 63).

7?? AD Armenian Massalians are accused of holding orgies and worshipping Satan (Cohn, Demons, 18).

744 AD A note attached to the regulations of the Synod of Septinnes condemns the practice of men dressing as women on the occasion of pagan feasts (Russell, 67).

787 AD Charlemagne decrees that anyone making sacrifices to "the Devil" should be put to death (Cohn, Demons, 157); later he outlaws sodomy (Hyde, 31).

864 AD Boris, the King of Bulgaria, is forced to convert to Christianity after a Christian invasion of Bulgaria (Obolensky, 71). He tries to force Christianity on the rest of the country. Pauli cianism enters Bulgaria and begins to spread (Obolensky, 82; Loos, 42).

866 AD Pope Nicholas I writes to King Boris of Bulgaria, complaining that many Bulgarians continue to practice paganism (Obolensky, 85; Loos, 242; Runciman, 5).

889 AD Boris retires as King of Bulgaria in favor of his son Vladimir, who tries to restore paganism as the official religion. Boris returns from retirement, defeats and blinds his son, and restores Christianity (Loos, 42; Obolensky, 87).

906 AD Regino of Prum publishes a lost ordinance of the 9th century, the canon episcopi. It derides the widespread belief of women who "profess themselves in the hours of the night to ride upon certain beasts with Diana, the goddess of the pagans" (Russell, 75-76).

950 AD Theophylact, Patriarch of Constantinople, writes to Tsar Peter of Bulgaria mentioning a new heresy there, which he defines as Manicheism mixed with Paulicianism (Runciman, 67; Loos, 47; Obolensky, 112 & 112, n. 7).

969-972 AD The priest Cosmas condemns a new Bulgarian heresy called Bogomilism, which he says recognizes two gods and rejects the church and its sacraments (Loos, 50-59; Runciman, 68-69; Obolensky, 117-122).

1000 AD Burchard of Worms calls the goddess of the night-riders "the witch Holda" (Russell, 81).

1071 AD Adam of Bremen reports that a large dildo figure is still being worshipped under the name of Fricco in the city of Upsala (Wright, 26).

1022 AD Heretics are uncovered at Orleans and are said to practice ritual sex orgies, worship the Devil, and have visions of traveling after eating a "heavenly food." They are called "Manichaeans" (Wakefield and Evans, 75-81; Lerner, 33-34; Cohn, Demons, 20-21; Russell, 86-87).

1050 AD The Byzantine theologian Michael Psellus claims that the Massalians practice ritual sex orgies and worship the Devil as the brother of Christ (Obolensky, 185-187). Catharism, a Manichaean heresy derived from Bogomilism, spreads throughout Western Europe (Loos, 115).

1054 AD Peter Damiani writes his *Liber Gomorrhianus*, claiming that homosexuality is spreading at an alarming rate among the clergy (Bailey, 111-114).

1091 AD Ordericus Vitalis tells of popular beliefs in ghostly night riders following "Harlechin" (Lea, v. I, 171).

1100 AD Euthymius Zigabenus reports that the Bogomilism of Constantinople is a mixture of Paulicianism and Massalianism, and that it regards the Devil as the brother of Christ (Obolensky, 206-214; Loos, 67-70; Runciman, 73-78).

1112-
1220 AD Peter of Bruys, a priest influenced by heresies from the Balkans, criticizes the 1163 AD need for an organized church or sacraments (Wakefield, 23).

1114 AD Peasant heretics are uncovered at Bucy-le-long and accused of practicing ritual lesbianism and male homosexuality. From this date on, charges of ritual samesex acts become commonplace in heresy trials (Russell, 94-95 & 95, note; Wakefield and Evans, 102- 104; Runciman, 120).

1150 AD Catharism becomes entrenched in Languedoc (southern France) and constitutes itself as an organ-1173 AD ized rival to traditional Christianity (Wakefield, 30- 31). Geoffrey of Auxerre accuses the Cathars of preaching free sex (Russell, 128).

1150-
1170 AD Heretics in Germany are accused of holding orgies and of eating cum as a holy food (Russell, 129).

1156-
1179 AD Philosopher John of Salisbury ridicules women who claim they ride out at night with a goddess (Grimm, 235; Cohn, *Demons*, 218- 219).

1157 AD The Synod of Rheims condemns spreading Catharism, accusing the Cathars of holding sex orgies. It also complains that Manicheism is being spread throughout the diocese by itinerant 1182 AD weavers who condemn the sacrament of marriage and encourage sexual promiscuity (Runciman, 121; Russell, 128; Loos, 117; Cohn, *Millennium*, 153).

1163 AD Hildegard of Bingen reports that there are heretics who reject the sacrament of marriage, advocate sexual freedom, and say that their god is not invisible (Cohn, *Millenium*, 155). Eleven heretical weavers are burned at Cologne for advocating sexual freedom (Cohn, *Millennium*, 153-154).

1167 AD The Cathars hold a large meeting at St. Felix de Caraman, near Toulouse, with representatives from France, Italy, and Constantinople (Loos, 127 & Runciman, 72).

1173 AD Peter Waldo (or Waldes) forms the Poor of Lyon (Waldensians). He advocates a return to early Christianity and opposes both traditional Christianity and Catharism (Cohn, *Demons*, 32).

1175 AD Heretics at Verona are accused of holding orgies in an underground hall (Russell, 126).

1179 AD The Third Lateran Council condemns the spread of homosexuality among the clergy (Bailey, 127). Alan de Lille says of certain heretics that in order to rid themselves of concern for the body they practice random sexual intercourse (Russell, 129; Cohn, *Demons*, 22 ff).

1182 AD Walter Map accuses heretics of holding orgies and of kissing the genitals and ass hole of "a black cat of marvelous size" (Russell, 131; Cohn, *Demons*, 22

1184 AD Pope Lucius III condemns the Waldensians and authorizes the use of inquisitorial methods by bishops in trying heretics (Wakefield, 44 & 133).

1190 AD Joachim of Flora preaches that there is no need for law, government, or churches (RussellL 138).

1198 AD Lothar of Segni, a Roman aristocrat and a bitter foe of heresy, becomes Pope Innocent III, the strongest Pope in the history of the church (Wakefield, 86)

1200-1300 AD A new movement arises in which women and men form sexually separate begging groups that are independent of church control. They are called beguines and beghards (Lerner, *passim*).

1206 AD Death of Amaury of Bene, leader of the Amaurians, a group of heretics who have trances, claim miraculous powers, and say that everything that is, is God (Cohn, *Millennium*, 157-161, 166). They are popularly called by names that are usually applied only to women (Cohn, *Millennium*, 166; Lerner, 13).

1208 AD Pope Innocent III, fearful of the Cathars of southern France (Albigensians), calls for a crusade to wipe them out (Wakefield, 68).

1209-1229 AD A crusade is waged against the Cathars of southern France leading to a bloody civil war and ending in the overthrow of Cathar civilization (Wakefield, 97).

1211 AD The Synod of Tirnovo repeats the definition of Bogomilism as a combination of Massalianism and Paulicianism (Obolensky, 238).

1212 AD The Council of Paris condemns the occurrence of homosexuality among the clergy (Bailey, 127).

1214 AD The Council of Rouen condemns the occurrence of homosexuality among the clergy (Bailey, 127).

1221 AD Pope Gregory IX calls for a crusade against rebelling peasants in Germany (Wakefield, 134).

1222-1224 AD Gautier de Coincy publishes a poem claiming that homosexuality is common among the beghards (Lerner, 39).

1227 AD   Pope Gregory IX issues his bull *Extravagantes*, reproducing condemnations of early church councils against sodomy (Bailey, 98).

1227-1235 AD   Pope Gregory IX passes legislation creating the Office of the Holy Inquisition, a special body of professional heresy-hunters centrally controlled by the Vatican (Russell, 158).

1231 AD   William of Paris accuses heretics of worshipping the Devil in the form of an animal and holding orgies (Cohn, *Demons*, 22).

1233 AD   Pope Gregory IX issues his bull *Vox in Rama*, accusing certain heretics of holding bisexual orgies (Russell, 161). He also sends Dominican inquisitors to southern France to hunt down any lingering Cathars in the wake of the crusade there (Wakefield, 140).

1235 AD   Stephen of Bourbon, an inquisitor in France, tells of male night-time wanderers who dress up as women and who are popularly called "the good women" (Russell, 157).

1240 AD   Caesarius of Heisterbach says demons collect all the cum that is ejaculated "contrary to nature" (Lea, v. I, 152).

1245 AD   The Inquisition at Toulouse uncovers many Cathar followers who claim that homosexuality is not a sin (Borst, 182 & 182, n. 7).

1249 AD   William of Paris mentions popular beliefs in a goddess — Abundia or Satia — who travels at night with a band of followers (Ginzburg, 49).

1256 AD   Pope Alexander IV allows inquisitors the use of torture to extract confessions (Wakefield, 179, n. 7).

1259 AD   Bishop Bruno of Olmutz condemns beguine women for refusing to obey the orders of men (Cohn, *Millennium*, 167).

1260 AD   The legal code of Orleans outlaws male homosexuality and lesbianism, calling for bodily mutilations for the first and second offences and burning for the third (Bailey, 142).

1261 AD   The Bishop of Amiens and the town government of Amiens quarrel over who has the proper authority to try sodomites (Bailey, 143).

1268 AD   *The Chronicle of Lanercost* reports that some priests in the Scottish district of Lothian urged peasants to raise up a phallic image in order to save their cattle from a rampant disease (Wright, 31).

1270 AD   Jean de Meung, author of the second part of *Roman de la Rose*, ridicules the popular belief that large numbers of people roam about at night with Lady Habonde (Russell, 135).

1272 AD   The laws of Orleans, Anjou, and Marne call for the burning of anyone convicted of *bourgerie* (Bailey, 141-142).

1279 AD   An episcopal statute of Auger de Montfaucon condemns women who claim to ride at night with Diana, Herodias, or Bensozia (Alford, 355).

1282 AD A Scottish priest, John of Inverkeithing, leads an Easter dance around a dildo figure, and, when challenged by his bishop, says it is the ancient custom of the country (Wright, 31-32).

1290 AD Beguines and beghards increase in number. Among some of them a new heresy appears, the Free Spirit movement. Free Spirits are accused of attacking all existing institutions and saying that there is no sin "under the belt." The first beghards are arrested for heresy (Lerner, 16-20 & 44; Cohn, *Millennium*, 164).

1290 AD King Edward I of England decrees the death penalty for anyone convicted of sorcery, apostasy, heresy, or sodomy (Bailey, 145-146).

1292 AD A homosexual scandal erupts at the University of Paris, and many professors are banished (Lea, *Templars*, 155).

1296 AD Pope Boniface VIII issues a bull condemning a sect whose members are said to pray in the nude (Lerner, 79).

1300 AD An accused Cathar named Lepzet confesses before a secular court that ritual lesbianism and male homosexuality are practiced at the meetings of his religious group (Russell, 162).

1307 AD King Philippe of France arrests all the French Templars and accuses them of heresy and sodomy (Lea, *Templars*, 158).

1307-
1314 AD Through a conspiracy of King Philippe of France and Pope Clement V, the Templars are hunted down all over Europe, and the order is abolished (Russell, 195).

1307 AD Archbishop Henry of Virneburg condemns beguines and beghards for rejecting the concept of sin and saying that simple fornication is not sinful (Lerner, 66-67).

1310 AD Marguerite Porete is executed by the Provost of the University of Paris for practicing heretical mysticism (Lerner, 71-72). The Franciscan Nicholas of Lyra writes that new heretics have appeared who say that people should not obey the prophets but live freely after the flesh (Lerner, 79). Again through a conspiracy of King Philippe, Pope Boniface VIII is accused posthumously of ritual magic, sodomy, and murder (Cohn, *Demons*,180-185).

1310-
1315 AD Heretics are accused of worshipping Lucifer and practicing orgies in Austria, Brandenburg, Bohemia, Prague, and Krems (Russell, 177-179; Lerner, 28).

1311 AD Pope Clement V, acting through the Council of Vienne, issues the bull Ad Nostrum. It condemns the heresy of the Free Spirit, accusing its advocates of rejecting the concept of sin and of believing that no sex act in itself is sinful (Lerner, 81-84).

1317 AD The Bishop of Strassbourg organizes an inquisitorial persecution against the Free Spirit in his diocese (Cohn, *Millennium*, 170; Loos, 85-87).

1320 AD The inquisitor Bernard Gui mentions women who are called "the good people" and who ride out at night (Russell, 175). Pope John XXII empowers inquisitors to act against practitioners of ritual magic as heretics, thereby broadening the concept of heresy (Cohn, *Demons*, 176).

1323-1328 AD The peasants of Flanders revolt (Cohn, *Millennium*, 216).

1324 AD Lady Alice Kyteler of Kilkenny, Ireland, is accused of sorcery, having sex with a demon, and holding orgies (Cohn, *Demons*, 198-201; Russell, 189-192).

1325 AD Heretics of the Free Spirit are spied on at one of their meetings in Colgone and are arrested and burned for holding a communal sex orgy (Cohn, *Millennium*, 190-191).

1327 AD The Austrian Abbot John of Viktring reports that heretics are holding orgies in caves (Lerner, 25-26 & 30-31).

1332 AD Beguines of Silesia in Bohemia confess that lesbianism is accepted in their community (Lerner, 117-119).

1338 AD Heretics at Brandenburg are burned for holding nightly meetings under a "leader of boys" (Russell, 181, n. 25). The Franciscan John of Winterthur claims Swiss heretics are holding homosexual orgies (Cohn, Demons, 35; Lerner, 25).

1339 AD The people of southern Bohemia revolt against the Inquisition. The Pope sends in troops and suppresses the revolt (Lerner, 107). Two ex-heretics in Czechoslovakia, John and Albert of Brunn, say that while they were heretics they believed that any passion of the flesh was permissible, including homosexuality (Lerner, 109-110).

1350 AD Daniel of Thaurizio reports that there are Armenian-speaking heretics in Tondray near Manzikert; that they are neither Christians nor Jews; that they worship the sun; and that they practice indiscriminate sex (Russell, 93, n. 49).

1353 AD Boccaccio's *Decameron* mentions a secret society that meets twice a month for feasting and orgies (Russell, 193). Pope Innocent VI appoints the first papal inquisitor in Germany; his purpose is to suppress the Free Spirit (Cohn, *Millennium*, 171).

1355 AD Lazarus, a Bulgarian Bogomil, refuses to recant his advocacy of nudism and free sex and is branded on the face and exiled (Runciman, 97).

1358 AD Peasant revolts occur in France (Cohn, *Millennium*, 216).

1365 AD Pope Urban V orders the French Inquisition to be on the lookout for heretical beguines and beghards (Lerner, 52).

1367 AD John Hartman of Ossmann-stedt confesses enthusiastically and without torture to the Inquisition of Germany that he believes no sex act is sinful in itself and that God is to be found in pleasure (Lerner, 135-139).

1370 AD The Inquisition in Milan indicts a woman for being a member of the "society of Diana" (Russell, 210).

1375 AD An old woman named Gabrina Albetti is convicted by a secular court at Reggio of teaching other women how to pray to the stars. She is branded, and her tongue is cut out (Russell, 210).

1381 AD Peasant revolts occur in England (Cohn, *Millennium*, 216). A German beggar is accused of being "a perverter of young boys" and then executed for heresy, though no doctrinal dispute is involved (Lerner, 145).

1384 AD A woman named Sibillia admits to a secular court at Milan and to the Inquisition that she and other women are accustomed to travel at night with Signora Oriente, whom they pay homage to; she insists that there is nothing sinful in this. She is sentenced to a relatively light penance and released (Russell, 211-212; Kieckhefer, 21-22; Cohn, *Demons*, 217-218).

1387 AD The Inquisition at Turin accuses heretics of practicing orgies. Followers of Catharism are uncovered who say that homosexuality is not a sin (Russell, 220-223; Borst, 182 & 182, n. 7).

1390 AD Sibillia is again tried at Milan, saying her practices go back to her childhood. Another woman, Pierina de Bugatis, also admits to traveling with Signora Oriente and to robbing the houses of the rich. She says Signora Oriente rules their society as Christ rules the world (Russell, 212-213).

1396 AD John Wasmod, an Inquisitor at Homburg and later rector of the University of Heidelberg, writes a book accusing beghards of practicing homosexuality (Lerner, 57-58). The Synod of Tours repeats the condemnation of those who worship sex images (Summers, *History*, 99).

1400 AD Groups of heretics called Fraticelli appear and are accused of practicing orgies (Cohn, *Demons*, 43-48).

1411 AD A group of Free Spirits called Men of Intelligence are condemned at Cambrai, after being accused of preaching nudism and free love (Russell, 224; Lerner, 158-161).

1421 AD The chronicle of Laurence of Brezova reports that heretics in Bohemia are accused of practicing nudity, dancing around fires, and sodomy. They are exterminated by the Christian John Zizka (Lerner, 123; Russell, 224-225).

1428 AD The earliest trials for witchcraft proper by inquisitorial methods are instigated against Swiss peasants. In these trials, the figure of Diana is replaced by the Devil (Cohn, *Demons*, 225-226).

1431 AD Joan of Arc is burned alive at the stake for practicing transvestism as a religious duty and for believing that her personal visions are more important than the institutional authority of the church.

1435 AD A woman of Cologne is excommunicated for wearing men's clothing in imitation of Joan of Arc (Kieckhefer, appendix under 1435).

1435-1437 AD Johann Nider tells of peasant women who anoint themselves and believe they fly with the goddess Diana. Similar stories are later told by Alfonso Tostato, Bartolommeo Spina, and Johann Weyer (Cohn, *Demons*, 219-220).

1438 AD Pierre Vallin of la Tour du Pin is tried for witchcraft. Under torture, he confesses to giving himself body and soul to a male demon (Cohn, *Demons*, 230).

1439 AD Thomas Ebendorfer, in his *De Decem Praeceptis*, condemns the practice of leaving food out at night for Perchta or Habundie (Ginzburg, 51).

1440 AD Gilles de Rais, a dose personal friend and bodyguard of Joan of Arc, is executed, after having been charged with sodomy, heresy, and child murder and molestation.

1450-1460 AD Witch hunts make their first appearance in Northern Italy (Cohn, *Demons*, 145). .

1451 AD Pope Nicholas V declares that sorcery as such is subject to the Inquisition, even where heresy as previously understood is not involved (Robbins, 272)

1455 AD Pope Calixtus III condemns the practice of holding religious rites in caves decorated with pictures of horses (Rawson, 10).

1460 AD A popular tract appears accusing the witches of Arras with lesbianism and male homosexuality (Robbins, 468).

1475 AD For the first time, reference is made in a trial document to the witches' "sabbat" (Russell, 249).

1484 AD Pope Innocent VIII issues his bull *Summis desiderantes*. He accuses witches of having sex with both male and female demons and gives full backing to a mass witch hunt in Germany. This is a major turning point in the history of witchcraft, since it establishes the view that witchcraft in and of itself is heresy and thus subject to the Inquisition.

1487 AD Pope Innocent VIII organizes a crusade against the Waldensians of Dauphine and Savoy (Lea, v. I. 204).

1500 AD Tomas de Torquemada, the Grand Inquisitor of Spain, declares, "Diana is the Devil" (Russell, 235, note). A reign of mass terror against supposed witches builds up and lasts for about 200 years. The terror is supported by both Catholics and Protestants and is backed by most intellectuals and members of the privileged professional classes.

1514 AD John Panter of England is accused of consulting demons near the location of Bronze-Age burial mounds (Grinsell, 73).

1532 AD Domenica Barbarelli of Novi, Italy, admits to traveling with Diana, whom she calls Lady of Play (Ginzburg, 36, n. 3).

1533 AD King Henry VIII of England outlaws sodomy (Barnett, 80).

1539 AD The Protestant leader John Calvin condemns members of the Free Spirit as "spiritual libertines" (Cohn, Millennium, 178).

1542 AD King Henry VIII of England passes a law making witchcraft a capital offence (Summers, *Popular History*, 216).

1562 AD A large wood and leather dildo, worshipped at the Catholic church of St. Eutropius at Orange, is seized and burned by Protestants (Wright, 51).

1566 AD John Walsh of Netherburg in England says he gets the power of witchcraft from fairies who reside in prehistoric burial mounds (Grinsell, 73-74).

1573 AD A Swiss woman nicknamed *Seelenmutter* ("Mother of Souls") is arrested and tried by a secular court for "non-Christian fancifulness" and burned as a witch (Ginzburg, 59).

1575 AD Members of a remnant of the cult of the goddess Diana are uncovered in Friuli, Italy. They are tortured into confessing that they are witches who worship the Devil (Ginzburg, xv).

1576 AD The inquisitor Bartolommeo Spina says the nightriding goddess of the chase is worshipped by "witches" (Lea, v. I, 178).

1582 AD Witches in Avignon are condemned by the Inquisition for having committed "actual sodomy and the most unmentionable crime" (Lea, v. II, 485).

1589 AD King Henry III of France is accused by an anonymous pamphlet of being a homosexual and a witch (Summers, A Popular History, 164-165).

1600 AD From this date on, numerous witch trials in Guernsey mention that sabbats occur in the vicinity of Stone-Age burial sites (Grinsell, 77, n. 18).

1612 AD Conflict arises in Lisbon between secular and religious authorities over the proper method of executing sodomites (Lea, v. II, 485).

1615 AD The reputed witch Gentien le Clerc of Orleans confesses to ritual lesbianism and male homosexuality among his co-religionists (Murray, Witch-Cult, 249).

1619 AD Henry Bouget, a judge involved in a large number of witchcraft trials, says sodomy is commonly practiced at witches' rituals (Summers, History, 157).

1620 AD Manual do Valle de Moura, a Portuguese inquisitor, condemns the connection between sodomy and witchcraft (Lea, v. II, 485).

1625 AD Paul Laymann, a Jesuit, publishes his Theologia Mora/is, in which he says that sodomy and adultery are crimes that lead to witchcraft (Lea, v. II, 680).

1630 AD Diel Breull of Assia claims that he has traveled to the Mound of Venus and seen Frau Holt (Ginzburg, 64).

1650 AD Numerous Ranters appear in England. They are a remnant of the Free Spirit and advocate sexual freedom and economic communism. (Cohn, *Millennium*, 317; 319-320). Parliament passes a law to suppress them, calling them "obscene, licentious, and impious heretics" (Cohn, *Millennium*, 325).

1660 AD Pagan celebrations are still being reported outside of Edinburgh, Scotland (Hope, 118-120).

1661 AD Florence Newton of Ireland is charged with kissing and bewitching a young servant women (Robbins, 352-353).

1670 AD Thomas Weir, a 70-year-old bachelor, stuns public opinion by confessing, on his own initiative, to witchcraft, fornication, and sodomy (Robbins, 534).

1694 AD A group of men called the Brotherhood of John are tried at Leopoli, Italy, and claim they have visited the souls of the dead on the Mound of Venus and have the power to evoke them (Ginzburg, 64).

1780 AD An ancient dildo is still being worshipped under the name of St. Cosmus in Isernia, Naples (Hamilton, 18-21).

1794 AD Pagan celebrations are reported as still being held in Pertshire, Scotland (Hope, 73).

1801 AD The goddess Demeter is still being worshipped under her own name in the form of a statue in Eleusis, Greece. Two Englishmen, Clarke and Cripps, accompanied by an armed guard, forcibly remove the statue. The peasants riot (Briffault, v. III, 182).

ACKNOWLEDGEMENTS

Although my name appears on the title page, this book has actually been a collective effort. I give my love, blessing, and thanks to those who put their insight and labor into it. Among the many who did so are:

* Leo Martello, friend and witch, who first suggested to me in 1970 that there was a link between witchcraft and the history of feminism.

* Ernest Cohen and the staff of Out magazine, who carried the first and second installments of the magazine version of the manuscript, beginning in December 1973.

*Charley Shively, Paul McPhail, Ken Sanchez, Larry Anderson, John Mitzel, and others of the Fag Rag collective for making possible, in December 1974, the continuation of the magazine version when Out folded.

* Larry Mitchel for putting up a generous loan in order to publish the material in book form.

* Michael Bronski and Charley Shively, for editing the book-version of the manuscript, giving me good critical feedback and moral support, tracking down illustrations, doing layout, and overseeing production.

* Michael Capizzi, for helping with the index.

* David Stryker of Xanadu Graphics, for his careful typesetting.

* Faygela ben Miriam, for providing me with a typewriter.

* Randy Alfred, for scholarly leads, moral support, and vision.

*Bernie Boyle, Michael Heppard, Paul Stewart, Michael Johnson, Michael Ferri, Steve O'Neil, Dan Smith, Earl Galvin, and Margot Schulter, for helping produce, in the spring of 1976, the San Francisco slide show based on this research. A special thanks to Bernie for his hundreds of slides.

* Jacob Schraeter, for bringing goddess energy to both the magazine series and the slide show.

* Murray Edelman, for enlightening dialogues and a loan to help defray printing costs.

* The Faery Circle of San Francisco for revelation/revolution.

* Tede, Jamal, Sylvana, Soula, Harley, Jonathan Schwarz, Aaron Shurin, and Assunta Femia, for supportive energy when I wondered whether it was all worth it (which was often).

* Mitch Walker for informed, precise, and caring criticism.

* Hal Offen, for being my best friend.

* The spirits that bring visions to us all.

BIBLIOGRAPHY

Alford, Violet and Rodney Gallop, "Traces of a Dianic Cult from Catalonia to Portugal," *Folk-Lore*, v. 46, 1935, 350-361.

Angus, Samuel, *The Mystery-Religions and Christianity*, University Books, New Hyde Park, NY, 1966.

Apuleius, *The Golden Ass*, Loeb Ed., G. F. Putnam's Sons, NY, 1928.

Aristotle, *The Politics*, Loeb Ed., G. F. Putnam's Sons, NY, 1932.

Augustine, *Concerning the City of God*, Penguin, Baltimore, 1972.

Aurand, A. Monroe, Jr., *Witches in Our Hair,* Aurand Press, Harrisburg, Pa., n.d.

Bachofen, Johann, *Myth, Religion and Mother Right*, reprinted by Routledge & Kegan Paul, London, 1967.

Bailey, Derrick, *Homosexuality and the Western Christian Tradition*, Anchor, 1975.

Barnett, Walter, *Sexual Freedom and the Constitution*, U. of New Mexico, Albuquerque, 1973.

Baroja, Caro, *The World of the Witches*, U. of Chicago, Chicago, 1961.

Baumann, Hermann, *Das Doppelte Geschlecht*, Dietrich Reimer, Berlin, 1955.

Benko, Stephen, "The Libertine Gnostic Sect of the Phibionites According to Epiphanius," *Vigiliae Christianae*, v. 21, 1967, 103-119.

Bethe, E. , "Die Korische Knabenliebe," *Rheinisches Museum fur Philologie*, v. 62, 1907.

Bloch, Iwan, *Anthropological Studies*, Falstaff, NY, 1933.

Bober, Phyllis, "Cemunnos: Origin and Transformation of a Celtic Divinity," *American Journal of Archaeology*, v. 55, 1951, 13-51.

Bogoras, W. , "The Chuckchee," Part 2, *Memoirs of the American Museum of Natural History*, v. 11, G. E. Steckert, NY, 1907.

Borst, Amo, "Die Katharer," *Schriften der Monumenta Germaniae Historica*, v. 12, Stuttgart, 1953.

Branston, Brian, *The Lost Gods of England*, Oxford, NY & London, 1974.

Braverman, Harry, "Labor and Monopoly Capital," *Monthly Review*, Special Ed. , Summer, 1974.

Briffault, Robert, *The Mothers*, 3 volumes, unabridged, reprinted by Johnson Reprint Corp., NY, 1969.

Brown, Sanger, *The Sex Worship and Symbolism of Primitive Races*, Richard Badgen, Boston, 1916.

Burland, Cottie, "Middle America," *Primitive Erotic Art*, ed. by Philip Rawson, G. P. Putnam's Sons, NY, 1973.

Burland, Cottie, "North America," *Primitive Erotic Art*, as above.

Burns, Arthur, "The Defense Sector," *The War Economy of the United States*, ed. by Seymour Melman, St. Martin's, NY, 1971.

Burr, George, *Narratives of the Witchcraft Cases*, Charles Scribner's Sons, NY, 1914.

Bury, John, *History of the Later Roman Empire*, v. 2, Macmillan, London, 1923.

Butterworth, E.A.S., *Some Traces of the Pre-Olympian World*, Walter de Gruyter & Co. , Berlin, 1966.

Campbell, Joseph, *The Masks of God: Occidental Mythology*, Vol. 3 of 4 vols. Viking Press, NY, 1969.

Carpenter, Edward, *Civilisation: Its Cause and Cure*, reprinted by Tao Books, Boston, 1971.

Carpenter, Edward, *Intermediate Types Among Primitive Folk*, George Allen & Co., London, 1914.

Castenada, Carlos, *The Teachings of Don Juan*, Ballantine, NY, 1968.

Catlin, George, *Letters and Notes on the Manners, Customs, and Condition of the North American Indians*, v. 2, 4th ed., Wiley & Putnam, NY, 1842.

Chadwick, Nora, *The Celts*, Penguin, Baltimore, 1970.

Chadwick, Nora, *The Druids*, U. of Wales, Cardiff, 1966.

Cipolla, Carlo, ed., *Fontana Economic History of Europe*, vols. 1 & 2, Collins-Fontana Books, London, 1972.

Cles-Reden, Sibylle von, *The Realm of the Great Goddess*, Prentice-Hall, Englewood Cliffs, NJ, 1962.

Cohn, Norman, *Europe's Inner Demons*, Sussex U., London, 1975.

Cohn, Norman, *The Pursuit of the Millennium*, Essential Books, Fairlawn, NJ, 1957.

Comnena, Anna, *Alexiad*, Barnes and Noble, NY, 1967.

Czaplicka, M.A., *Aboriginal Siberia*, Clarendon, Oxford, 1914.

Davis, Elizath, *The First Sex*, Penguin, Baltimore, 1971.

Dawson, Christopher, *The Age of the Gods*, Howard Fertig, NY, 1970.

De Riencourt, Amoury, *The American Empire*, Delta, NY, 1968.

Dibble, Vernon, "The Garrison Society," *The War Economy of the United States*, ed. by Seymour Melman, St. Martin's, NY, 1971.

Dillon, Myles and Nora Chadwick, *The Celtic Realms*, Weidenfeld & Nicolson, London, 1967.

Diodorus Siculus, *Library of History*, v. 3, Loeb Ed., Harvard, Cambridge, Mass. , 1961.

Dodds, E.R., *Euripides' Bacchae*, Oxford, NY, 1960.

Dorsey, George, *Traditions of the Caddo*, Carnegie Inst. of Washington, 1905.

Driver, Harold, *Indians of North America*, U. of Chicago, Chicago, 1961.

Dulaure, Jacques-Antoine, *The Gods of Generation*, reprinted by Panurge Press, NY, 1933.

Dupouy, Edmund, "Prostitution in Antiquity" in *The Story of Phallicism*, v. I, ed. by Alexander Stone; Pascal Covici, Chicago, 1927.

Ellul, Jacques, *The Technological Society*, Vintage, NY, 1964.

Engels, Friedrich, *The Origin of the Family, Private Property, and the State*, International Publishers, NY, 1972.

Finley, M.I., *The Ancient Economy*, U. of California, Berkeley, 1973.

Fitzgerald, C.P., *The Birth of Communist China*, Penguin, Baltimore, 1964.

Fontana Economic History of Europe — see Cipolla, Carlo.

Ford, Clellan and Frank Beach, *Patterns of Sexual Behavior*, Harper, NY, 1951.

Galbraith, John, *The New Industrial State*, Signet, NY, 1967.

Gellen, Martin, "Whither California," *The War Economy of the United States*, ed. by Seymour Melman, St. Martin's, NY, 1971.

Gibbon, Edward, *The Decline and Fall of the Roman Empire*, 3 volumes, Modern Library ed., NY.

Gilbert, Felix and others, *The Norton History of Modern Europe*, Norton, NY, 1971.

Ginzburg, Carlo, *I Benandanti*, Guilio Einaudi Editore, Turin, 1966.

Graves, Robert, *The Greek Myths*, 2 volumes, Penguin, Baltimore, 1955.

Greek-English Lexicon, ed. by Liddell & Scott, Oxford, NY & London, 1966.

Grimm, Jakob, *Deutsche Mythologie*, v. I, 4th ed., reprinted by Wissentschaftliche Buchgesellschaft, Darmstadt, 1965.

Grinsell, L.V., "Witchcraft at Some Prehistoric Sites," *The Witch Figure*, ed. by Venetia Newall, Routledge and Kegan Paul, Boston, 1973.

Hacker, Louis, *The Triumph of American Capitalism*, McGraw-Hill, NY, 1947.

Halliday, W.R., *The Pagan Background of Early Christianity*, Hodden and Stoughton, London, 1925.

Hamilton, William, "An Account of the Remains of the Worship of Priapus," reprinted in *Sexual Symbolism*, Julian Press, NY, 1957.

Hammer-Purgstall, Joseph von, "Die Schuld der Templer," *Denkschriften der Kaiserlichen Akademie der Wissenschaften*, Philosophisch-Historische Classe, v. 6, Vienna, 1885.

Hammond, N.G.L., *A History of Greece*, Clarendon, Oxford, 1967.

Hansen, Chadwick, Witchcraft at Salem, Signet, NY, 1969.

Harner, Michael, *Hallucinogens and Shamanism*, Oxford, NY & London, 1973.

Harrison, Tom, "Equatorial Islands of the Pacific Basin," *Primitive Erotic Art*, ed. by Philip Rawson, G. P. Putnam's Sons, NY, 1973.

Hatt, Jean-Jacques, *Celts and Galla-Romans*, Nagel, Geneva, 1970.

Hawkes, Jacquetta, "Prehistory," *History of Mankind*, v. I, ed. by Hawkes and Leonard Woolley; Harper and Row, NY, 1963.

Herbig, Reingard, *Pan, der Griechische Bockgott*, Vittorio Klostermann, Frankfurtam- Main, 1949.

Hope, A.D., *A Midsummer Eve's Dream*, Viking, NY, 1970.

Howard, Clifford, *Sex Worship*, published by the author, Washington, DC, 1897.

Hughes, Pennethorne, *Witchcraft*, Penguin, Baltimore, 1965.

Hyde, Montgomery, *The Love That Dared Not Speak Its Name*, Little, Brown and Co., Boston, 1970.

Irving, John, *Indian Sketches*, U. of Oklahoma, Norman, 1955.

Jacobus [pseudonym], *Untrodden Fields of Anthropology*, Falstaff, NY, n.d.

James, Grace, *Joan of Arc*, Methuen, London, 1910.

Karlen, Arno, *Sexuality and Homosexuality*, Norton, NY, 1971.

Katz, Johnathan, *Gay American History*, T.Y. Crowell, NY, 1976.

Kennedy, Hubert, "J. B. Schweitzer," *Fag Rag*, No. 19, Boston, Mass. , Spring, 1977.

Kieckhefer, Richard, *European Witch Trials*, U. of California, Berkeley, 1976.

Kinsella,Thomas, *Tain Bo Cuailnge*, Oxford, NY & London, 1969.

Kittredge, George, *Witchcraft in Old and New England*, Harvard, Cambridge, Mass., 1929.

Kors, Alan and Edward Peters, *Witchcraft in Europe*, U. of Pennsylvania, 1972.

Kott, Jan, *Shakespeare Our Contemporary*, Doubleday, NY, 1966.

Latin Dictionary, ed. by Lewis Short, Oxford, NY & London, 1966.

Lauritsen, John and David Thorstad, *The Early Homosexual Rights Movement*, Times Change Press, 1974.

Lazonick, William, "Karl Marx and Enclosures in England," *The Review of Radical Political Economics*, vol. 5, no. 2, 1974.

Lea, Henry, *A History of the Inquisition of the Middle Ages*, v. 3, Harbor Press, NY, 1955.

Lea, Henry, *Materials Toward a History of Witchcraft*, v. I, U. of Pennsylvania, Philadelphia, 1939.

Lea, Henry, *Materials Toward a History of Witchcraft*, v. 2, T. Yoseloff, NY, 1957.

Lea, Henry, "The Innocence of the Templars," The Guilt of the Templars by G. Legman, Basic Books, NY, 1966.

Legman, G., *The Guilt of the Templars*, Basic Books, NY, 1966.

Lerner, Robert, *The Heresy of the Free Spirit*, U. of California, Berkeley, 1972.

Lethbridge, T.C., *Witches*, Citadel, Seacaucus, NJ, 1968.

Levy, Jean-Philippe, *The Economic Life of the Ancient World*, U. Chicago, Chicago, 1964.

Licht, Hans, *Sexual Life in Ancient Greece*, Barnes and Noble, ' NY, 1952.

Lightbody, Charles, *The Judgments of Joan*, Harvard, Cambridge, Mass., 1961.

Loos, Milan, *Dualist Heresy in the Middle Ages*, Martinus Nijhoff, The Hague, 1974.

Macciocchi, Maria, *Daily Life in Revolutionary China*, Monthly Review Press, NY, 1972.

Malleus Maleficarum, Pushkin Press, London, 1951.

Markale, Jean, *Women of the Celts*, Gordon Cremonesi, London, 1975.

Mather, Cotton, *Magnalia Christi Americana*, Silas Andrus, Hartford, 1820.

Meier, M.H.E., *Histoire de l'Amour Grec*, Stendhal, Paris, 1930.

Melman, Seymour, "From Private to Pentagon Capitalism," *The War Economy of the United States*, ed. by Melman; St. Martin's, NY, 1971.

Melman, Seymour, *Our Depleted Society*, Delta, NY, 1965.

Melman, Seymour, *Pentagon Capitalism*, McGraw-Hill, NY, 1970.

Michelet, Jules, *Satanism and Witchcraft*, Citadel, NY, 1949.

Mueller, C.O., *The History and Antiquities of the Doric Race*, John Murray, London, 1839.

Murray, Margaret, *The God of the Witches*, Oxford, NY & London, 1931.

Murray, Margaret, *The Witch-Cult in Western Europe*, Oxford, NY & London, 1921.

Murray, T. Douglas, Jeanne d'Arc, McClure, Phillips, and Co., NY, 1902.

New American Bible, P.]. Kennedy & Sons, NY, 1970.

Notestein, Wallace, *A History of Witchcraft in England*, T. Y. Crowell, NY, 1968.

Nove, Alec, *An Economic History of the U.S.S.R.*, Penguin, Baltimore, 1969.

Obolensky, Dmitri, *The Bogomils*, Cambridge U. Press, Cambridge, 1948.

Osborne, Harold, "Central Andean Region," *Primitive Erotic Art*, ed. by Philip Rawson, G. P. Putnam's Sons, NY, 1973.

Oxford English Dictionary, unabridged, Oxford, NY & London.

Parker, Thomas, *The Knights Templars in England*, U. of Arizona Press, Tucson, 1963.

Partridge, Burgo, *A History of Orgies*, Crown, NY, 1960.

Piggott, Stuart, Ancient Europe, Aldine, Chicago, 1965.

Piggott, Stuart, *The Druids*, Praeger, NY, 1975.

Plato, *Apologia*, Loeb Ed., Harvard, Cambridge, Mass., 1960.

Plutarch, *Lives*, v. I, Loeb ed. , Harvard, Cambridge, Mass., 1967.

Quispel, G. , "Gnosticism and the New Testament," *Vigiliae Christianae*, n. 19, 1965, 65-85.

Random House Dictionary, Random House, NY, 1967.

Rawson, Philip, "Early History of Sexual Art," *Primitive Erotic Art*, ed. by Rawson; G. P. Putnam's Sons, NY, 1973.

Reich, Charles, *The Greening of America*, Bantam, NY, 1971.

Reich, Wilhelm, *The Mass Psychology of Fascism*, Farrar, Strauss and Giroux, NY, 1964.

"Report of the House Select Committee on Intelligence," *Village Voice*, v. 21, no. 7, NY.

Robbins, Rossell, *Encyclopedia of Witchcraft and Demonology*, Crown, NY, 1959.

Ross, Anne, "Celtic and Northern Art," *Primitive Erotic Art*, ed. by Philip Rawson, G. P. Putnam's Sons, NY, 1973.

Ross, Anne, *Everyday Life of the Pagan Celts*, Putnam, NY, 1970.

Ross, Anne, *Pagan Celtic Britain*, Columbia U. Press, NY, 1967.

Rostovtzeff, M., *The Social and Economic History of the Roman Empire*, Clarendon, Oxford, 1926.

Roszak, Theodore, *Where the Wasteland Ends*, Doubleday, NY, 1972.

Runciman, Steven, *The Medieval Manichee*, Cambridge U. Press, Cambridge, 1947.

Runeberg, Arne, "Witches, Demons, and Fertility Magic," *Societas Scientiarum Fennica, Commentationes Humanarum Litterarum*, V 14, No. 4, Helsingfors, 1947.

Russell, Jeffrey, *Witchcraft in the Middle Ages*, Cornell U. , Ithaca, NY, 1972.

Schoff, Wilfred, "Tammuz, Pan and Christ," *The Open Court Magazine*, v. 26, no. 9, 1912.

Scott, George, *Phallic Worship*, Mental Health Press, Westport, Conn., n.d.

Scott, W.S., *The Trial of Joan of Arc*, The Folio Society, London, 1956.

Showerman, Grant, 'The Great Mother of the Gods," *Bulletin of the University of Wisconsin, Philology and Literature Series*, v. 1, No. 3, 1898-1901.

Steiner, Stan, *The Islands*, Harper, NY, 1974.

Stone, l.F., "The War Machine Under Nixon," *The War Economy of the United States*, ed. by Seymour Melman; St. Martin's Press, NY, 1971.

Strabo, *Geography*, v. 2, Loeb ed., Harvard U, Cambridge, Mass., 1960.

Summers, Montague, *The Geography of Witchcraft*, Citadel, Secaucus, NJ, 1965.

Summers, Montague, *The History of Witchcraft*, Citadel, Secaucus, NJ, 1971.

Summers, Montague, *A Popular History of Witchcraft*, E. P. Dutton, NY, 1937.

Symonds, John, *A Problem in Greek Ethics*, Areopagitica Society, London, 1908.

Szasz, Thomas, *The Manufacture of Madness*, Delta, NY, 1970.

Taylor, G. Rattray, *Sex in History*, Vanguard, NY, 1954.

Thomas, George, *Studies in Ancient Greek Society*, Citadel, NY, 1965.

Thompson, James, *An Economic and Social History of the Middle Ages*, The Century Co. , NY, 1928.

Trevor-Roper, H.R., *The European Witch-Craze*, Harper and Row, NY, 1956.

Turcan, Robert, "Les Religions de l'Asie dans Ia Vallee du Rhone," *Etudes Preliminaires aux Religions Orientales dans l'Empire Romain*, v. 30, E. J. Brill, Leyden, 1972.

Van Alstyne, R.W., *The Rising American Empire*, Quadrangle, Chicago, 1960.

Van Gennep, Arnold, *The Rites of Passage*, U. of Chicago, Chicago, 1960.

Vanggaard, Thorkil, *Phallos*, International Universities Press, NY, 1972.

Von Cles-Reden, Sibylle — see Cles-Reden, Sibylle von.

Wakefield, Walter, *Heresy, Crusade and Inquisition in Southern France*, U. of California, Berkeley, 1974.

Wakefield, Walter and Austin Evans, *Heresies of the High Middle Ages*, Columbia U. , NY, 1969.

Wason, Margaret, *Class Struggle in Ancient Greece*, Victor Gollancz, London, 1947.

Williams, William A., *The Contours of American History*, New Viewpoints, NY, 1973.

Winthuis, J. , "Das Zweigeschlechterwesen bei den Zentral australiern und andern Volkem," *Forschungen zur Volkerpsychologie und Soziologie*, v. 5, 1928.

Woolley, Leonard, "The Beginnings of Civilization," *History of Mankind*, v. I, ed. by Jacquetta Hawkes and Woolley; Harper and Row, NY, 1963.

Wright, Thomas, 'The Worship of the Generative Powers During the Middle Ages of Europe," reprinted in *Sexual Symbolism*, Julian Press, NY, 1957.

Book Two

Moon Lady Rising

The Eclipse and Return of the Magic of Life

By Arthur Evans

White Crane Institute
22 County Route 27 • Granville NY 12832
www.gaywisdom.org • editor@gaywisdom.org

Jim Gilson, Bob Barzan, and Arthur Evans
Mask of Dionysos by John Soares
December 1997

Introduction to
Moon Lady Rising

Bob Barzan

One of my favorite memories of Arthur was a Halloween night when we were walking on Castro Street in San Francisco. The street was not yet closed to vehicle traffic but the sidewalks were thick with people, so much so that it was difficult to walk and many people, include Arthur and I, were walking in the street just beyond the parked cars. Suddenly, Arthur ran out dancing into the middle of the street stopping the traffic. I followed with many other people and we all danced together effectively closing the street for the evening. It was a wonderful moment and Arthur was beaming, full of energy and joy. This was the kind of magic that Arthur wanted us all to experience. It was what gave his life meaning.

Most Saturday mornings through the 1990s, Arthur and I met in the Castro District to check out garage sales, have coffee or hot chocolate, and talk. We discussed many things over the years, but the primary topic was often meaning. What is meaning? How do we make our lives meaningful? Are some meanings better than others? Meaning was a major part of Arthur's life - creating it for himself and helping others to create it for themselves.

All of his writings, *Witchcraft and the Gay Counterculture* in 1978, *The God of Ecstasy* in 1988, *Critique of Patriarchal Reason* in 1997, and his many essays in *White Crane Newsletter* and other publications were either implicitly or explicitly about living a meaningful life.

So were his lectures and talks that began in the 1970s and that continued for more than thirty-five years. One of his last public talks was to the PFLAG chapter in Modesto, California, a few years before his death. Arthur was amazingly gifted in his ability to inspire people by the spoken word, I think even more so than through his writings. Still, his writings reflect much of his enthusiasm for life and his desire to encourage others to live a full passionate life. Now with Moon Lady Rising, his most explicit work on meaning, Arthur encourages us all to create meaningful lives that include the magic that comes through nature and sex.

The first section of Moon Lady Rising repeats some of what he wrote decades ago in *Witchcraft and the Gay Counterculture*. It is in the last chapter that Arthur begins to share some of what he learned from his life experience of how to create a meaningful life. Unfortunately, Arthur died before he could complete the last portion of the manuscript. Besides what he wrote here, we can get some insight of what he might have included in his directives by the way he lived his life and his own efforts with finding meaning.

Arthur's excursions into meaning were not all academic as in his writings and lectures. In 1974 he formed the Fairy Circle, a group of men who explored gay identity and meaning through art, play, and ritual. His production of *The Bacchae* in 1984 was another artistic excursion into meaning, as was his insistence that art be included in his philosophically rich *Critique of Patriarchal Reason*. Even the flyers he posted around the Castro District as the Red Queen were about finding meaning in life. Through his witty and poignant flyers, Arthur encouraged the "Castro Clones" to find a deeper meaning than what was encouraged by mainstream Gay society.

In creating meaning for himself, Arthur was not afraid to try different things, and when something was no longer meaningful to him, he dropped it and changed his life. He changed majors in college, he changed colleges, he moved to new cities, he left Manhattan and moved across the continent to live in the isolated forest of northeastern Washington State next to the Canadian border. Then for more than thirty years he lived at the intersection of Haight and Ashbury, the epicenter of 20th century counter-culture. He was a fierce crusader for Gay Liberation and then for the human rights and for the health care rights of those with HIV.

Through the whole time I knew Arthur, there were several values that seemed to guide his life and his quest for meaning. Arthur was dedicated to the truth and he used his amazing intellect and skills in scholarship to expose the lies told about oppressed people especially Gay men and Lesbians and to uncover the suppressed and forgotten stories that give us a deeper sense of our own history, identity, and meaning.

Underpinning his scholarship was a devotion to social justice for the oppressed. His devotion was not just theoretical and scholarly. He embodied his commitment by his actions in the Gay Liberation Front, the Gay Activist Alliance, through demonstrations, arrests, and work to improve the quality of life in his neighborhood.

Though I never participated in or witnessed one of his zaps, I heard him tell the stories about them many times. I am still taken aback by his ability to create a situation that confronted, amused, and garnered media attention in such a creative and often fun way. This was art, this was magic. I think, though, that the magic worked for Arthur, not because of his devotion to justice and truth or because of his intellect and scholarship, essential as these were, but because underpinning all he did was a deep love for his friends and for the human community. He wanted to see us all thrive, to live joyful meaningful magical lives.

Chapter 1.

Whatever Happened to Meaning?

A SPECTER is haunting modern life, the specter of the loss of meaning. All the powers of modernity have entered into an unholy alliance to exorcise the specter: pope and Prozac, scientists and gurus, presidents and terrorists. All have failed. The ghostly emptiness at the heart of modernity persists and grows.

Workers in offices and factories, clerks behind counters, salespeople, teachers, public employees—how few find meaning in their work! And who would expect otherwise? The top ranks of big business, big labor, big government, and big education feed on the energies of those below. Husks remain at the bottom, drained of time, energy, and meaning.

"Does your work express who you are, develop your best potentials, or contribute to a higher social good?" Most working people would laugh if asked this question. They know "the job" has little to do with meaning. Its purpose is to pay "the bills." They get through the day by deadening their feelings, or going a little crazy, or getting stoned, or taking anti-depressants, or all of the above. Even the well paid often feel a hollowness at the center of their work.

Meaning has also been banished from art. Or rather, it is art that has been banished. Art is part of the process of making. But people are consumers now, not makers. The few makers who are left, independent artists, have been banished to the periphery. They amuse each other and a small following with their creations, and sometimes scandalize the larger public. But artists no longer have any serious impact on the way society sees things.

Ugliness by design prevails. Works of art are consigned to special institutions called "museums," to be admired on special occasions, like animals at the zoo. When the moderns stumble on tribes living in the rain forest, filling every inch of their world with art, with every tribal member an artist, they call them "primitive."

Religion? It too lost meaning a long time ago, now mostly consisting of lip-service and formal gestures. They appear perfunctorily one day a week, or at special occasions like weddings and funerals, religion's last great hold-outs. The small minority who parade their religiosity in public are mostly scoundrels, or else merely pathetic.

Science, the last great religion of modernity, is no exception. Scientists now rarely strike out adventurously on their own, in quest of the sublime mysteries of the universe, like Galileo, Kepler, and Newton. Instead, they are among the most expensive hirelings of the military-industrial complex, almost as expensive as lawyers, and with as little vision.

The gods that scientists now worship are the power of the military and the state, and the profitability of the business corporation. The few scientists who genuinely adore nature would be embarrassed to say so publicly. It might jeopardize their security-clearance or their hope of landing grants.

Nature, too, has lost meaning. Or as with art, we should say that nature has been lost. Food comes contained in cans and Cellophane. Lives come contained in institutions. Scant emotional connection remains with plants, animals, or the silent processions of the stars. The moon, if visible at all through the smog, is a mere pea-point of light, paling next to the street lamps. Or else, in the fantasies of generals and developers, it is a promising piece of real estate on which to plant the national flag and, some day perhaps, tract housing.

Even sex, the electric soul of nature, has lost meaning. In place of meaningful sex, people now settle for objectification, forcing their bodies into stereotypes, like the figures in porno movies or comic books. Breast implants and liposuction for women. Men on steroids, pumping up in gyms. The investment pays off. Other people want to use their bodies as toys. But eventually the scene becomes mechanical, boring, and sad.

How could it be otherwise? As if people who are disconnected from art, meaningful work, their own inner selves, and each other would know how to have sex! As if sex had nothing to do with the planting of crops or the phases of the moon! As if the boundaries of our bodies were our skin, and not the stars!

Once Upon a Time

Throughout history, most human beings have had hard lives, but rarely have entire societies felt that life was meaningless. Until just a few hundred years ago, most people in most societies, despite their hardships, felt a sense of connectedness—to their own inner spiritual powers, to each other, to the majesty of nature. Evidence for this connectedness is the richness of their art and culture. The cultural and artistic accomplishments of modernity pale by comparison, despite greater resources and larger populations.

Only people who experience meaning in their lives are capable of great cultural accomplishments. When the soil of meaning dries up, the branches of art and culture wither. Contrast, then, the cultural legacy of ancient Athens to that of modern Gary, Indiana, a city of roughly the same number of inhabitants.

Even in regard to material wealth, modernity's achievements are dubious when the whole picture is taken into account. The middle and upper classes of North America, Western Europe, and Australia today enjoy the greatest material comforts of any classes in history. Even the richest lacked such comforts two thousand years ago. But this coin has another side. Two thousand years ago, the poorest classes in the Americas, Africa, Australia, China, and India were better off than their modern equivalents. And the world was not on the verge of ecological collapse.

The privileged moderns are learning a hard lesson: material comfort is no guarantor of meaning. Behold the modern e-trading, coke-sniffing, Lexus-driving, TV-watching, cell-phone-using Yuppie. Is he or she better off than the barefoot pottery maker in ancient Athens who had dialogues with Socrates, and whose vase paintings have enchanted people for more than two millennia? A people can be poor in physical comforts yet lead lives rich in meaning, just as the most affluent classes in history can become dependent on anti-depressants.

Meaning

What, then, is meaning? It is not something found but created. It is not a thing, but a process, *the process of creating contexts*. But what are contexts? They are the ways in which we connect things, the ways in which we make *many* become *one*.

Example: I walk down Castro Street in San Francisco on a crisp, crystalline day in early March. I look up and see the Court of Heaven, with Sun beaming gloriously from his throne on high, surrounded by his retainers, a host of white and purple clouds, billowing in glory. A stranger nods on the street below, smiles, and passes on. In my mind's ear I hear the strains of Satie's *Gymnopédies*. I sense that I am part of a great natural commonwealth stretching from Earth to Heaven, where everything is right and well-ordered.

The sunlight, the clouds in the sky, and the people on the street are many separate things, the natural givens. My senses and mind combine these givens into a coherent physical whole. To this physical whole, I add the memory of Satie's music, which I often hear in my mind as I walk, and the metaphor of the heavenly bodies as persons, fresh in my memory from reading Virgil and Ovid. Finally, I add my love for the majesty and beauty of nature.

The result is an encompassing context, partly generated by objects in nature, and partly created by me from personal feelings and cultural expectations. My connecting things in just this way, my creating just this context, is the meaning for me of this particular experience of walking down Castro Street in San Francisco on an early day in March.

Others walking down the same street at the same time may give it an entirely different meaning. In fact, they will likely laugh at my dreamy musings. To them, this is a fast-paced scene of gyms, dildo stores, and bars, a place to pass through when you want to pump up your biceps or find this afternoon's sexual partner. For yet others, it's a collection of old neighborhood stores, where you buy pasta for tonight's dinner or a condolence card for a bereaved friend.

The underlying physical realities of Castro Street—quarks and quanta—are the same for us all. But they are not the only realities. Each of our meanings is also real because each makes a difference, in the same way that any human purpose makes a difference. Meaning is subjective, variable, and culturally influenced. But it is not a nothing, just as Blake's image of the brightly burning tiger is not a nothing, either.

The Magic of Life

The art of synthesizing meaning from personal, cultural, and natural experiences, and of responding to the meanings of others, is magic. When a magician synthesizes meaning with props and practiced gestures in a small, closely controlled area, the result is stage magic. A wider kind of magic occurs when people synthesize meaning on the open, shifting turns of their life paths.

Like any art, magic must be learned and developed through practice, and so it is partly a cultural construct. But magic also builds on natural capacities, and brings natural forces into focus, and so it is rooted in nature as well.

The richer our personal experiences are, and the more skillful we are in synthesizing contexts from them on our life path, the more meaning our lives will have. The sum total of meaning in our lives, created through the artful synthesizing of the full range of our life experiences, is the magic of life insofar as we experience it.

Sometimes a metaphor is better than a definition. Consider the last scene in Federico Fellini's movie 8½. All the characters in the hero's previously disjointed life, both living and dead, both real and fantasized, join hands with him in a climactic circle-dance in the dusk. They rotate with a celebratory air around an empty space in the center, illuminated with a spotlight from on high. Into this spotlight the hero himself finally steps, but as a child, playing circus music on a flute, as the dance continues around him.

Nearly 1,700 years before 8½, the pagan philosopher Plotinus used a similar image. He compared the many individual things in the world to objects rotating around an invisible One, located in the center of reality.

Fellini's subject was biographical wholeness, and Plotinus's was the unity of the universe. But the works of both can serve as metaphors for understanding the synthesis of the magic of life.

Techniques of Wholeness

Most human societies in the past devoted much attention to synthesizing the magic of life. Elaborate techniques were developed and studied in order to integrate sexual feelings, the harvesting of crops, the hunting of animals, and the changing of the seasons into encompassing experiential contexts. Typical techniques used to create this synthesis were singing, dancing, praying, body-painting, playing musical instruments, reciting poetry, dressing up as animals or in the clothes of the opposite sex, and participating in orgies.

Modern industrial society is unique in human history in the degree to which it neglects, and even scorns, the art of synthesizing the magic of life. It is also unique in the degree to which a sense of meaninglessness pervades all social classes. These two uniquenesses are not unconnected.

Tꞁe Eꞓlipse

The catastrophic eclipse of the magic of life in modern industrial society is no accident. To the contrary, a vast loss of meaning is exactly what we would expect to find from the divisive history of Western power-politics that created modern society.

This book will focus on a crucial link that connects the divisive history of Western power-politics to the modern loss of meaning. That link is *collective self-definition through the demonization of others.* I am who I am, this mentality says, because I am not like *them,* for *they* are possessed by the *Devil.*

We will see that the elite of both Christianity and modern European civilization came to define who they were through the demonization of women, gay people, sex, nature worship, and indigenous cultures around the world. This demonization manifested itself in three great waves: the hunt for "heretics" from the 13th to the 15th centuries; the hunt for "witches" from the 16th to the 17th centuries; and the European conquest and exploitation of "the filthy heathen" in the Americas, Africa, and elsewhere.

In all three waves, the underlying enemy confronting the European elite was the ancient paganism of the people. So-called "heretics" were often groups that drew on both pagan and Christian elements in their religious practices. Their hybrid ways fell outside the elite's definition of Christianity and were demonized as forms of Devil-worship.

After making heresy-hunting into an industry, European authorities created the stereotype of the Devil-worshipping witch. This they applied *en masse* to rural folk—especially women—who continued to draw on the old pagan traditions.

Likewise, when the European conquerors encountered the pagan religions then flourishing in the Americas and Africa, they scorned the natives as Devil-worshippers. They forcibly converted the natives to Christianity, or reduced them to slavery, or killed them, or seized their land, or some combination of the above.

The immediate purpose of the demonization was to increase the power and wealth of the demonizers—priests, popes, academics, inquisitors, kings, lords, land-holders, business owners, and conquistadors. The cultural goal was to establish cultural definitions, to let the world know what was "Christian" and what was not, what was "civilized," and what was not.

But lo, a great historical irony appeared. Centuries of divisively castigating sex, women, nature-worship, and native cultures had an unintended side effect. It corroded people's synthesizing abilities for creating meaning in life. As a result, a spiritual trap-door fell open beneath the gilded throne of European high culture. Below lay a deep pit of meaninglessness that European institutions had been diligently digging for centuries. The European privileged classes tumbled in, followed later by all societies influenced by modern European culture.

Tɧe Retur?

What is repressed from above returns from below—one of the great principles of the ancient Chinese *Book of Changes* (*I Ching*). This principle is also manifest in the quest for meaning in Western civilization. Despite repeated historical assaults, the quest for meaning in Europe was able to stage a number of comebacks.

The reason for these comebacks is that pagan traditions did not die out, after all. In fact, a vigorous pagan-inspired counterculture long continued in various forms in Europe, holding alternative views about women, sex, and nature. This counterculture influenced the great mass of unlettered country-dwellers, but has largely been overlooked by modern bourgeois academics. They typically identify "European civilization" with the values of the tiny literate elite, just as the elite themselves did.

Renaissance Humanism

A significant comeback in the quest to reclaim meaning in European life occurred in the 15th and 16th centuries, with the appearance of the Renaissance. Many independent thinkers started embracing pagan sensibilities, albeit in an intellectualized form. For a time, the basic sensibilities of the peasants and of some intellectuals actually ran in parallel.

The cause of the intellectuals' new parallelism was the recovery of many manuscripts of the ancient pagan philosophers, historians, and poets. This recovery triggered Renaissance humanism, a development as momentous in modern Western cultural history as was the birth of theater in ancient Greece.

Renaissance humanism differed greatly from what today goes by the name of humanism, whether religious humanism or secular humanism. The uniqueness of Renaissance humanism comes out clearly in the classic *Speech on Human Dignity*, written in 1486 by the humanist Giovanni Pico della Mirandola.

Contrary to typical 21st century humanists, Pico associated human dignity, love of nature, and the new learning with what he called "beneficent magic." In using this term, Pico acknowledged a spiritual dimension in the forces of nature, as well as the restraints of morality in the human use of them.

Pico's enthusiasm for beneficent magic rested on a belief that he shared with many other Renaissance humanists, the peasants of his time, and ancient pagan philosophers. This is the belief that the universe is a gigantic living being, permeated by bonds of common feeling. Pico regarded beneficent magic as a celebration and use of these bonds. He spoke of "that harmony of the universe which the Greeks with greater aptness of terms called *sympatheia* [inter-affectedness]."[1]

1   Pico, trans. by Caponigri, 57.

Alas, the Renaissance humanists did not carry their new open-mindedness to its logical conclusion. Instead, they dragged their feet, perpetuating old narrow biases about women and non-European people. Nonetheless, they had stepped onto a path that could lead to wider horizons if one walked far enough.

Although not all Renaissance humanists shared Pico's beliefs about the harmony of the universe, they were generally critical of Christian dogmatism. As a result, they briefly succeeded in putting a brake on the burgeoning witch hunts of the time. Unfortunately, though, the brake was soon released because of the Protestant Reformation, the Catholic Counter-Reformation, and the great religious wars between Catholics and Protestants.

These new developments all pumped fresh energy into the familiar Christian practice of self-definition through the demonization of others. The Renaissance humanist ideal of cosmic harmony receded. As the 17th century progressed, the witch-hunts rebounded with a vengeance, vigorously supported by both Catholic and Protestant zealots.

Eventually, however, true believers on both sides of the religious wars reluctantly came to the same conclusion: they would never succeed in killing off all the Christians on the other side, however much they might pray to the God of Love to achieve this worthy goal.

At the same time, the nation-state roared into its own, asserting secular goals as ends in themselves. Finally, thanks to the lasting influence of the Renaissance humanists, the universities started turning out a new breed of educated elite, thinkers who gave less credence to Christian dogmatism.

The Enlightenment followed, along with the spread of science, the age of revolution, and the rise of democracy. The upshot of all these developments was that Christian totalitarianism lost its hold on Europe.

DIVERSITY & MEANING

The pluralism of post-Christian Europe has been a friend to the quest for meaning. New developments in the arts and in self-governance appeared that would have been unthinkable when authorities ruled according to Christian dogma.

But new obstacles also appeared. Most notable were the subsequent rise of industrialism, and the co-option of science by military-industrial complexes around the globe. These developments represented as much of a retrenchment in the 19th and 20th centuries as did the Reformation and Counter-Reformation in the 16th and 17th centuries.

Despite these obstacles, recent decades have witnessed a new impetus in the quest for meaning. People who have long been demonized in the West are finding their voices and speaking out with strength—women, people of color, gay people, transgender people, and members of indigenous societies.

The return of the demonized to the center stage of history represents not only a righting of old wrongs, but also a broadened opportunity to create meaning. By embracing the rich diversity of human experience, we strengthen our capacity to synthesize richer contexts of what it means to be human. That leads to expanding the circle of magic in our own lives. We become like the youthful flute player in the last scene of *8½*. Only now the great dancing circle is expanded to the circumference of the globe. Thus do we extend the cultural miracle begun haltingly 500 years ago by the Renaissance humanists, who drew on the humanist values of Greco-Roman civilization 1,500 years before that.

The Historian as Artist

This book is an outgrowth, and redirection, of my *Witchcraft and the Gay Counterculture*, first published 25 years ago by Fag Rag Books, a small radical collective in Boston. Like the previous work, this one too reflects my own personal values, emotions, and life experiences. But it is not exceptional in doing so. *All* historical works do the same.

The reason: history is not the same as the past. Rather, history is the art of making an argument about the past. There is no way that the past in all its complexity and richness can ever be retrieved by any finite document in the present. Even for the tiny part of the past that is accessible to the present, the historian always makes a host of decisions as to what is important or not, what is interesting or not. These decisions partly depend on who the historian is.

There are objective standards by which to judge a work of history, regardless of the author's personal circumstances. These are fairness, completeness, logical coherence, discerning use of sources, etc. But even so, if you remove the historian, you diminish the history, just as you diminish the painting if you remove the painter.

My own values are those of a 61-year-old white, gay man, born and raised in a working-class family, formally educated in the humanities, and energized by the progressive political activism that has blossomed in the U.S. since the 1960s. They are also the values of someone who feels the pulse of life in all of nature's forces and still has faith in the redemptive value of the humanist tradition.

That said, let us now proceed to enter a historical path along which we will witness the eclipse and then the return of the magic of life. We will take our first steps in Milan, in northern Italy. There we will encounter two obscure peasant women who had a special connection to the moon. We will embrace that connection as a metaphor for larger themes yet to come, looking to the rising moon as the very image of the magic of life recovered.

Chapter 2.

The Yellow Brick Road from Milan

The roots of the loss of meaning in modern Western society go back to at least 1000 A.D. From that date on, two Europes faced each other across a widening cultural gulf. One—the Europe of state, church, and university—increasingly consolidated its institutional power. The other—the Europe of rural village, forest, and heath—increasingly found itself on the defensive. Ancient pagan religious practices and sexual customs of the countryside, overlooked for hundreds of years because the machinery of power had been too clunky to expunge them, were overlooked no more.

Thus began a protracted culture war between the two Europes that lasted for hundreds of years. Its most notable manifestation would be a systematic hunt for heretics, first emerging in the 11th century, and culminating in the ghastly witch hunts of the 16th and 17th centuries. These struggles would help create and define what today is called "modern Europe."

Nowhere was the division between the two Europes more evident than in attitudes toward meaning. Unlike the peasants, the literate elite did not look for meaning in the sounds of brooks, the flights of birds, or the desires of the flesh. Instead, they regarded meaning as an institutional thing, encased within heaped-up walls of stone, topped by gnarly spires and crosses. Hierarchies of priests, speaking a learned language incomprehensible to the people, became the official keepers of meaning. It could be glimpsed only through the institutional shutters that they themselves opened and closed.

The Road from Milan

Milan—timeless city of Lombardy, in northern Italy—has provided us with an unforgettable example of the struggle between the two Europes over meaning. It was here in the 14th century that two peasant women—representing popular rural culture, resonating with the lore of the ages—clashed with the literate ruling culture's staunchest defender, the Holy Inquisition.

The story that these two women told the Inquisition of Milan provides the fulcrum on which the rest of this book turns. Beginning with their little drama, a mere footnote in the Munchkinland of history, we will step onto a small path that eventually becomes a widening spiral, carrying us to our own Emerald City, historical understanding.

The yellow brick road that unfolds ahead will sometimes lead us to great, palpable events that changed the course of history. For now, though, we begin with a more ethereal scene—a sighting of the Lady in the Moon.

Signora Oriente

On April 30, 1384, two peasant women of Lombardy, one known simply as Sibillia, the other as Pierina de' Bugatis, were summoned before the Inquisition, then sitting at a local church in Milan. They confessed, apparently without torture, to things that have flummoxed many later historians, but which make sense in the context of the struggle over meaning.

Sibillia claimed that every Thursday night she traveled with a certain Signora Oriente and "her society," giving Oriente homage. Sibillia claimed that all sorts of animals also went to the assembly, except the donkey, because the lines of dark fur on its back formed a cross. Sibillia believed that at least two people had to show up at the rites, or else the world would be destroyed.

Sibillia said their mistress, Signora Oriente, predicted the future and revealed secret things, a knowledge that Sibillia passed on to other people. Signora Oriente could take the animals slaughtered and eaten by the society and revive them from the dead. Sibillia said she had never confessed these things before because she didn't believe they were sinful.

Pierina de' Bugatis confirmed Sibillia's account and amplified it. She said Signora Oriente was also called "Horiens." Pierina claimed that both the living and the dead participated in these rites. After the celebrants ate the animals they had slaughtered, they put their bones into their hides. Signora Oriente struck the bags of bones with her staff, bringing them back to life.

Pierina said the celebrants traveled to the houses of the rich, where they ate and drank. When they found the houses well ordered, they blessed them.

Signora Oriente taught the women the power of herbs, answered their inquiriwiop[es about diseases, told them where to find stolen things, and instructed them on how to remove curses. She bade them never tell anyone about their assemblies.

The name of God was never mentioned at the rites. Pierina added that she "believes Oriente is mistress of her 'society' as Christ is master of the world."

Under pressure from the Inquisition, Sibillia and Pierina abjured these practices. The inquisitor (Beltramino da Cernuscullo) imposed a light sentence. The women had to wear red crosses sewn onto their garments as penance, and on certain days stand in the doorways of churches during mass and the homily. These punishments would guarantee that Sibillia and Pierina would be marginalized by their neighbors, but they would not be imprisoned, tortured, or killed. At least not yet.

Six years later, in 1390, Sibillia and Pierina were again hauled before the Inquisition of Milan for the same practices. Sibillia's testimony was similar to what she had said six years before. She confirmed Pierina's comment made before in 1384 that no one dared mention the name of God in the presence of Signora Oriente, whom Sibillia also called "Madona [*sic*] Horiente."

When it came Pierina's turn, the inquisitor's interest had changed. He was no longer preoccupied with Signora Oriente. Now what he wanted to hear about was "the Devil." Did the women make a pact with him at these rites? Did they have sex with him? Prodded repeatedly, probably tortured, Pierina finally confessed that she had done so, having made a pact with the Devil in her own blood.

Pierina said that since she gave herself to the Devil she had not been able to confess, and begged the Inquisitor to save her soul. Because this was their second offense, however, they were now relapsed heretics in the eyes of the church. Our worthy Christian inquisitor turned both women over to the secular authority, which executed them.

SILLY OLD WOMEN?

What are we to make of the reports of Sibillia and Pierina? Many Anglo-American historians have made light of them. Let's examine some of their reactions. We'll see how their bias against peasant culture, as an unworthy superstition when compared to the literate culture of the elite, has blinded them to an underlying struggle over meaning.

An example is the historian Norman Cohn. Commenting on the church's growing interest in suppressing women like Sibillia and Pierina, Cohn says:

> Something that hitherto has happened only in the minds of silly
> old women has taken on an objective, material existence.

Cohn jumps to the conclusion Sibillia and Pierina were old. But all that can be inferred from clues in their testimony is that Pierina was at least 24 years old during the first trial in 1384. And although it's true that Sibillia and Pierina probably recounted visions experienced in trances, and not actual events, Cohn's disparaging use of the phrase "silly old women" clearly reveals a misogynist and ageist bias.

Another historian, Richard Russell, is more generous. He doesn't disparage Sibillia and Pierina for being female or old; however, he balks at the notion that what they experienced could be called by the honorable name of "religion." Instead, they were involved in "strange fertility rites" or "old folk tradition."

Another historian, Richard Kieckhefer, concedes that these practices had a religious ring. Nonetheless he argues:

It would be misleading to speak of them as conscious or deliberate pagan survivals, since the participants seem to have viewed themselves as Christians, despite the reservations that churchmen evidently held.

Here Kieckhefer simply disregards the evidence. The women testified that they paid homage to Signora Oriente, that she ruled their society as Christ rules the world, and that they were careful never to mention the name of God at the rites. If this isn't a pagan survival, then what is? And their inquisitor-judge didn't just have "reservations." He condemned these women as heretics and had them put to death.

Our three distinguished historians overlook an important question: Even if these peasant women viewed themselves as good Christians, as they may have, could their version of Christianity have been so influenced by ancient pagan practices and beliefs that the church hierarchy regarded it as a form of Devil-worship? In fact, as we will see later, that's often exactly what the church meant when it invoked the dread words "heresy" and "witchcraft."

Moon Lady Rising

Let us take Sibillia and Pierina more seriously than these historians. If we do so, we will understand that the two women were not historical freaks. Rather, we will see that they were part of a widespread and ancient cultural tradition that created meaning through the celebration of natural objects and forces.

Our first clue is a linguistic one, overlooked by all previous commentators. The name of the female figure followed by the two women was Oriente or Horiens. Historians have overlooked the fact that the Italian *Oriente* is derived from the Latin participle *oriens* (*oriente*, in the ablative case). The name *Signora Oriente* is the Italian equivalent of the Latin *Domina Oriens*. This name literally means "Lady Rising," or more fully, "The Lady Who Rises in the East." Latin literary usage shows that this phrase-name is not a meaningless jumble. It refers to the moon.

The defendants' terminology isn't the only clue concerning Oriente's identity. A comment inserted by the author of the trial report (preserved in a summary in the Milan archives) explicitly associates the female figure worshipped by Sibillia and Pierina with Diana, the ancient Roman goddess of the moon.

The report's mention of Diana is significant. It brings to mind a well known series of reports, dating back hundreds of years. They tell of people (mostly women) who claim to have visions of traveling through the night sky with Diana, the pagan goddess of the moon.

The most famous of these reports is an anonymous tract dating from the early 10th century known as *The Bishop's Rule* (*Canon Episcopi*). The author of *The Bishop's Rule* is worried about the survival of paganism among the people, which he sees as the Devil's work. He warns bishops and priests to uproot "the pernicious art of sorcery," which the Devil has inspired. He continues:

> Some wicked women, perverted by the Devil, seduced by illusions and phantasms of demons, believe and profess themselves, in the hours of night, to ride upon certain beasts with Diana, the goddess of pagans, and an innumerable multitude of women, and in the silence of the dead of night to traverse great spaces of earth, and to obey her commands as of their mistress, and to be summoned to her service on certain nights. ... An innumerable multitude, deceived by this false opinion, believe this to be true, and so believing, wander from the right faith.

Although the author regards these reported experiences as "illusions," he was not a tolerant skeptic, as some historians today claim. The illusions come from the Devil, he says, and they promote the worship of the Devil:

> It is therefore to be proclaimed publicly to all that whoever believes such things or similar to these loses the faith, and he who has not the right faith in God is not of God but of him in whom he believes, that is, of the Devil.

Tꜧe Good Tꞧavelers of Fꞧiuli

Thanks largely to the work of Italian scholars, we now know that Sibillia and Pierina were not alone, but part of a larger pattern of meaning creation. Many European peasants reported similar visions, spanning a wide range of both geography and time.

One of the most striking examples is a group called the *benandanti*, or Good Travelers, uncovered by Carlo Ginzburg in the vicinity of Friuli, Italy, near the Austrian Alps. As their name suggests in Italian, the *benandanti* were thought to make the community *fare well* because they *traveled about well*. Good fortune thanks to good traveling!

It was in the 1570s, almost 200 years after the trial of Sibillia and Pierina at Milan, that the Inquisition of Friuli first uncovered the Good Travelers. Without torture, they confessed that at certain times of the year (especially the beginning days of the four seasons) they went into trances. In this state, they had the experience of leaving their bodies and doing things that reveal a fascinating mix of pagan and Christian beliefs.

When in their trances, the Good Travelers moved about in company with animals and carried large fennel stalks, which they used as weapons against another group of spirits, who were evil and carried stalks of sorghum. They called these evil spirits "witches" and said that they themselves were fighting for the faith of Christ.

These practices had deep roots. Ginzburg has shown that the Good Travelers were remnants of a widespread shamanistic tradition that existed continuously among segments of the peasant population since classical antiquity. Originally they worshipped a Diana-type goddess who was mistress of animals and vegetation, and queen of the dead, similar to Signora Oriente. During the change of seasons, her followers celebrated the changes as a ritual conflict between different nature spirits.

In the course of time, the Good Travelers started absorbing Christian beliefs. Eventually, they came to the conclusion that what they were fighting for at the seasonal feasts was the faith of Christ. By the 16th century, these rituals were no longer acted out but were experienced only when the believers went into trances. Nonetheless, the Good Travelers insisted that their experiences were *real*.

In addition to having visions, the Good Travelers were healers. In fact, the Inquisition first got wind of them because they were healing people. On March 21, 1575, a priest spoke to the Inquisition at Friuli, saying he had come upon a certain Paolo Gasparutto. He claimed he could heal bewitched people through the power of vagabond healers who traveled at night on animals carrying fennel stalks.

Once the Inquisition realized how widespread the practices of the Good Travelers were, they launched a broad attack against them. Members of the cult were arrested. Although the Inquisition did not apply torture to the Good Travelers, they were subjected to continual harassment and psychological coercion until they confessed to what the inquisitors wanted to hear. And what the inquisitors were interested in was not Diana, but the Devil, since they viewed Diana as a demon. The upshot was that by 1618, many of the Good Travelers, constantly badgered by the Inquisition, came to view themselves through the eyes of their oppressors. They now said they were Devil-worshipping witches.

Religion By Any Other Name

Consider: Women in the early 10th century said they traveled through the night sky with Diana, the pagan moon goddess. Women in 14th-century Milan said they traveled through the night sky with Signora Oriente (the Lady Who Rises in the East). People in 16th-century Friuli said they traveled through the night fighting witches, a practice similar to an old local form of worshipping of Diana.

Are these cases evidence of late-surviving pagan religion in the very heart of Western Christendom? It would certainly seem so. The traits of the later Signora Oriente are similar to those of the earlier Diana. Like Signora Oriente, Diana traveled through wild places at night, accompanied by a throng of spirits.

A beautiful example of the ancient view of the traveling Diana appears in Virgil's poem *Aeneid* (first century B.C.). The scene is set in ancient Carthage, years before the founding of Rome. Dido, the city's queen, is about to make her grand entrance into a temple. Virgil compares Dido's stirring movements as she approaches the temple, thronged by her retainers, to an epiphany in the wilderness of the traveling goddess Diana, thronged by her band of spirits:

> The queen in procession approached the temple, Dido the beautiful,
> Thronged by a great crowd of troops.

Just as Diana on Eurota's banks or the peaks of Cynthus
Brings out and drills her bands—and a thousand mountain
    nymphs
Follow, swarming now here, now there—
And she, advancing with a quiver of arrows on her shoulder,
Stands out above all her spirits,
While their rapture excites her placid heart,
Even so now in the midst of all did joyous Dido approach.

The tradition goes back even farther. Centuries before Virgil, Greek poets had used the title "Moon Lady" to refer to a goddess invoked by women when casting spells. An example is a poem by Theocritus (third century B.C.). It describes Simaetha, a Sicilian woman whose husband had jilted her. In the middle of the night, Simaetha prepares an altar on which she burns grains and bay leaves, calling on the full moon to bring her husband back to her. As part of the spell, Simaetha recounts the history of her relationship with her husband, beginning each episode with this simple refrain—

Take note of my love and how it came to be, Moon Lady.

Believe it or not, such similarities between the ancient Greco-Roman moon goddess and the female figure celebrated in later Europe are not enough for many Anglo-American historians. They continue to deny the possibility that pagan religion long persisted in European culture.

These denying historians are under a spell—their own ethnocentric biases. Why is it "fantasy" when a peasant woman imagines she has traveled through the night sky with the moon, but "religion" when a male Catholic priest imagines he has converted a wafer into the body of Christ? Who is to say that the former belief is silly or strange, while the latter is profound and familiar?

Historians who deny the word "religion" to the practices discussed above can't see beyond their own Judeo-Christian upbringing. They're not much better than their intellectual forebears in medieval universities, who labeled these practices "Devil worship."

The Superstition of the Intellectuals

Right up until the dawn of modernity, European peasants participated in a system of meaning creation that was independent of church control and grounded in ancient pagan nature worship. The biggest obstacle to acknowledging this fact is a superstition found among many modern Western intellectuals—the belief that paganism died out in Europe by 1000 A.D. Although that's largely true for the urban literate classes, it's a different story for the non-lettered peasants, who long constituted the overwhelming majority of Europe's population.

The intellectuals' superstition arose because medieval Western universities were originally outgrowths of the church. So Western intellectuals commonly regard Christianity, in its academically refined form, as the great civilizing force in the Middle Ages. The culture of the peasants, which was alien to the universities, falls below the intellectuals' threshold of vision. But there is more to civilization than universities.

Even after the violent Christianization of rural Europe from the 13th to the 17th centuries, pockets of pagan practices persisted. Intellectuals who insist otherwise ignore a large body of evidence collected by travelers and folklorists from the 18th to the 20th centuries. Their first-hand reports tell of striking pagan practices that continued in the European hinterland.

The refusal to acknowledge the evidence from folklore feeds into Christianity's presumption to define meaning for everybody. Once we appreciate paganism's long hold on rural Europe, we'll see how much of human experience was excised from meaning by Christian authorities. This cutting was especially deep in the area of sex. Christian authorities were horrified by the degree to which frank sexuality was meaningful in paganism. A modern legacy of this Christian bias is the pervasiveness of sex without spirit.

Religion & Dildos

A good example of late pagan survivals with a sexual coloring appears in the reports of Julien Sacaze and Édouard Piette, two travelers who visited peasants in the French Pyrenees in the 1870s. Their eye-popping accounts were published in French anthropological journals, although ignored later. Let us pause and consider what many historians say does not exit.

While visiting Poubeau in the Pyrenees, Piette and Sacaze found a megalith above a steep slope near the local church. The peasants held rituals there that shocked the authors:

> Till not long ago, on the night of Mardi Gras, the young men of this village used to go out in a procession in order to build a big straw fire on the rock. They marched in single file, each one holding the backside of the one in front of him, advancing with postures and gestures that were both burlesque and obscene. After the fire was lit, they danced around the rock, *penem manu proferentes* [holding the penis out with the hand]. The rites of this nocturnal feast, which people still celebrated some thirty years ago, calling it the feast of the *gagnolis*, offend decency too much for me to describe them in complete detail.

Although the authors say they're embarrassed to go into detail, they do point out that one of the rocks at Poubeau was phallic-shaped. They can't bring themselves to use the word itself, but indicate that the rock was used as a dildo. The peasants believed that contact with it would increase their fertility:

> The phallic rock of Poubeau is positioned near the large block in such a way that one can sit astride it, or bend over immediately next to it on a slab placed near it, right below it. In making this statement, we intend a meaning that is not hard to discern. Certain kinds of physical contact with the rock have been reported to us, particularly by Mr. S___, and several people have confided to us that the rock shaped into a point is, it seems, a thing which we may not mention.

GIVE ME THAT OLD-TIME RELIGION

Academics often dismiss peasant practices like those at Poubeau as weird flukes having no relation to religious history. But that dismissive attitude won't wash here because Piette and Sacaze found local folks who insisted that these rites were part of an ancient religious tradition.

The most impressive of these locals was the elderly Augustin Germès, former mayor of the nearby village of Jurvielle. He took the authors to a megalith near Jurvielle where he said lived a type of spirit called *incantade* ("spell-caster"):

> With religious fervor and obvious feeling, he showed us the semicircle which serves as a passage way for the *incantade*, the place where one must put his lips or ears in order to converse with the spirit.

Germès said the spirits of the stones were angels that had remained neutral in the primordial battle between good and evil. After his victory, God exiled these angels to earth, where they had to purify themselves. They would continue to live in the stones until purified, which would allow them to return to heaven.

To some, this belief may sound like nothing more than one individual's eccentric fantasies. But as we will see in chapter four, Germès's angels bring to mind the beliefs of a well known medieval French heresy, Catharism. This heresy, which absorbed many pagan beliefs and practices, was the original stimulus for creation of the Holy Inquisition.

Germès insisted that these beliefs and practices were ancient and well established. In the presence of the authors and the local parish priest, he lamented the fact that they were now dying out, saying:

> In the old days, when people were upright, everybody had a great faith in these stones. Everybody worshipped them and addressed their prayers to them. As for myself, I've always believed in them. I'll die believing in them.

After the parish priest chided him for his comments, Germès confronted him forcefully:

> If you don't believe in these stones, my dear sir, I believe. I believe, like all my ancestors. But two men today are not worth one from the old days.

The authors mention that Germès was not alone, either in his belief in the stones or in his hostility to the priest. They point to the case of a large phallic stone which the local parish priest ordered smashed. Afterwards, the priest directed a handyman to plant a cross in its place. Alas for the priest, the locals secretly removed the cross later. They also gathered the debris from the rock and returned it to its former place. The priest again scattered the fragments of the stone and again had a cross erected. By chance, however, the handyman who erected the cross fell ill afterwards and died. The locals viewed his death as a divine retribution for putting up the cross.

I Sing the Body Electric

The story of pagan survivals among European peasantry doesn't end in the 19th century. Pagan rituals with sexual overtones, and even a historical connection to the ancient goddess Diana, survived into 20th-century Romania. A fascinating account can be found in anthropologist Gail Kligman's book *Calus*.

In 1975-76, Kligman went to live in the southern part of Romania, then under Communist rule. There she encountered the Calusari, bands of costumed dancing men who roam about the countryside performing skits and dances during the feast of Rusalii. This feast corresponds to the Christian celebration of Whitsunday, occurring fifty days after Orthodox Easter, and commemorating the descent of the Holy Spirit.

During this period, Romanian peasants believe the spirits of the dead roam the countryside, and they first prepare the fields for planting. Through their skits and counterclockwise dancing, the Calusari are thought to placate these spirits, strengthen people's health, and promote the fertility of the soil.

The head of a band of dancing Calusari is called the *vataf*, which means "leader." Another major participant is the *mut*, or "mute." He's a comical figure, dressed partly as a man and partly as a woman, who usually communicates through mime, although sometimes through speech. Under his dress, he carries a large red sword that looks like a phallus.

In one skit performed by the Calusari, a dancer falls over and pretends to be dead. The *mut* (mime) takes out his red phallic-looking sword from under his dress. He caresses various parts of the body of the fallen dancer with the sword and then inserts it into his mouth, which brings him back from the dead. This act, notes Kligman, elicits "screams of delight" from the spectators.

In one dance in the Dolj region, one of the Calusari crouches on all fours, picking up coins with his teeth out of a hole dug in the ground filled with water. The villagers crowd around watching intently. While he is bent over picking up the coins—

> The vataf [leader] feigns intercourse with him from the rear, much to the enjoyment of the crowd.

To Romanian peasants, skits and dances like these celebrate the exuberance of sex and nature. Through their dancing and singing, the Calusari become a kind of collective lens, magnifying and focusing that exuberance. The villagers believe the amplified energy promotes bountifulness in their crops and strength in their bodies. Even from a purely naturalistic view, the rites build morale in the community and energize people for their shared labors in the fields.

This is the vibrant religious and sexual experience—expressed through communal art and passion, uniting sex, meaning, and labor—that lies behind the wooden academic phrase "fertility rites." Walt Whitman, who used a better language, called it "the body electric."

The Queen of the Faeries

The skits and dances of the Calusari have a long history. Kligman found that in some areas in the 19th century the Calusari used to dress as women and speak in falsetto. Going back further, she found that in 1230 the Archbishop of Ohrid denounced a celebration "in Bulgarian territory" where young men gathered on the 50th day after Easter, dancing and performing "obscene" theater.

The rites of the Calusari are also tied to ancient peasant beliefs in *rusalii, iele,* and *zine*—female faeries. Peasants view the Calusari as mediators between the community and the *iele*, whom the Calusari impersonate in their rites. In addition, the Calusari in the past prayed to the queen of the fairies, Irodeasa. She functioned as the Romanian equivalent of Diana.

The appearance of the name Irodeasa in Romanian folk history is significant. Many ancient sources in Western Europe refer to the goddess of the night-wanderers not only as Diana, as we have seen, but also as Herodias, similar in sound to the Romanian Irodeasa. Both likely represent a garbling of the names of various pagan goddesses.

Abundant evidence from both Western and Eastern Europe points to the longstanding practice of worshipping a Diana-type goddess who had absorbed other pagan goddesses. Four of the documented names that we've seen so far for this syncretistic goddess are Signora Oriente, Diana, Herodias, and Irodeasa. Some others that appear in Medieval and Renaissance sources are the following: Abundia, Arada, Befana, Bensoria, Domina Ludi, Epona, Faste, Habonde, Hera, Herodiana, Holda, Holle, Holt, Mére Folle, Noctiluca, Perchta (or Berchta), Pharaildis, Queen of the May, Selga, Sibyl, and Venus.

Tђe Hoꝛꝝeꝺ Goꝺ

In addition to a Diana-type goddess, European paganism also survived in the person of a male deity associated with wild animals, and often wearing horns. He was the patron of the hunt, male sexuality, and public masquerading. Among his many names were these: Berchtold, Harlequin (derived from Herla the King), Herne the Hunter, King of the May, Kwaternik, Lord of Misrule, Quatembermann, Robin Goodfellow or Robin Artisson, Scrat, and Wild Man.

Harlequin survived in the Latin literary tradition as the figure of the Fool. In late-Renaissance Italian comedy, he usually appeared on the stage in bright clothes, sporting a cap with horn-like appendages.

Harlequin's appearance as the Fool is rooted in the medieval holiday called the Feast of Fools, a survival from paganism. It usually took place around January 1, the festival of Janus (Dianus, the sun god, who was the brother of Diana, the moon goddess). It was characterized by drinking, feasting, orgies, and transvestism.

The word "Fool" as applied to Harlequin didn't mean silly or stupid, but rather frenzied or ecstatic, akin to the French word *folie*, which means madness of lunacy. This latter meaning is in line with the ecstatic nature of the Feast of Fools.

The rites of Harlequin were originally celebrated in the countryside and the forest, and impressed early Christian authorities with their wildness. Participants were variously known as *sauvages*, *silvatici*, and *selvaggi*, meaning "wild men," from the Latin root *silvus*, meaning "forest."

Throughout the Middle Ages, we find numerous reports of troops of men following Harlequin at night. An early example is from the historian-monk Ordericus Vitalis. In his 11th-century *Church History*, he described beliefs in Bonneville, France, concerning the night-riding Harlequin. A priest claimed to have witnessed a large, nocturnal crowd on horse and on foot, including the recently dead (similar to the visions of the *benandanti*). On seeing the entourage, the priest remarked:

> This is doubtless the troop of Harlechin, of which I have heard
> but never believed.

In the early Middle Ages, Christian intellectuals regarded Harlequin and his equivalents as manifestation of the Devil's power, just as they did Diana and her equivalents. Centuries later, this demonization of peasant practices provided a precedent for something more sinister—the full-blown witch stereotypes created in the High Middle Ages and the Renaissance.

Tђe Hisꜩoꝛy oꝼ Meꜹꝺiꜹg

In this chapter, we've explored the importance of ancient peasant culture, with its surviving spirits and rites. Drawing on this culture, people in the countryside created meaning in their lives through practices and myths that were nature-focused and sex-positive. Their creations were not well received by the learned elite, who saw meaning in institutional terms and wanted everybody else to do the same.

We've also seen how Anglo-American historians have trivialized the importance of these developments for the history of meaning. An example is their superficial treatment of Sibillia and Pierina de' Bugatis of Lombardy. These women were not crazy flukes, as many maintain. Rather, they embraced pagan beliefs and practices that were widespread in European peasant culture. They used them as vehicles for both survival and celebration.

In later chapters, we'll see that the 14th-century trials of Sibillia and Pierina de' Bugatis were a presage of greater horrors to come. If we fast-forward the tape of history to the end of the Renaissance, we find a sobering spectacle: the mass burnings of the practitioners of the old peasant rites (mostly women), now denounced as "witches."

The historical road leading to the witch hunts of the 16th and 17th centuries crossed over an important historical bridge along the way—the great war on heretics from the 13th to the 15th centuries. Sibillia and Pierina de' Bugatis, naively celebrating old pagan rites in Lombardy, were two travelers who got caught on this bridge.

In the next chapter, we'll find another victim: a young, 15th-century French woman who drew on pagan traditions in her village to create her own special vision of Christianity. In the end, she, too, was executed. Her story in France rings with unexpected echoes of Sibillia and Pierina de' Bugatis in Italy and provides additional evidence for the shared history of heresy, paganism, sex, and meaning.

Chapter 3.

Joan of Arc, Transvestite and Heretic

On May 30, 1431, in the town of Rouen, France, a peasant woman named Joan of Arc, age nineteen, was burned alive at the stake. Today she is known as Saint Joan, having been canonized 500 years later by the same Holy Mother Church that originally had her barbecued.

Joan's life and death are connected to those of Sibillia and Pierina de' Bugatis of Lombardy, discussed in the last chapter. The connection lies in the wellspring of Europe's ancient pagan traditions. All three women drew on this wellspring to create meaning in their lives. All three also suffered repression from the church hierarchy, which insisted that the creation of meaning was an institutional monopoly of its own.

The church prevailed against Joan, Sibillia, and Pierina, just as it would against hundreds of thousands of others. This victory meant that the quest for meaning in Europe became an institutional monopoly. But that eventually led to an unintended irony. When the victorious institutions themselves later tottered, their canned meaning fell with them. What remained was the soullessness of modernity.

In this chapter, we'll see that the real Joan of Arc was quite different from the religious image that the church later foisted on her when it made her a saint. Certain facts about sex roles and paganism were left out. We're going to put them back in. By reclaiming the omitted aspects of Joan's life, we will gain a fuller understanding of the battle over controlling the creation of meaning.

A Transvestite Saint

Because Joan of Arc today bears the title of saint, many people think she was executed for devotion to established Christian dogma, like many past martyrs. But the actual reason for Joan's death was something else: her persistence in wearing men's clothing.

From 1425 on, when she first rallied French troops against the English invaders of France, Joan of Arc was an adamant transvestite. At a battle against the English on May 23, 1430, she was captured by a sell-out French-speaking faction. They called her *homasse*, a derogatory word in Old French meaning masculine woman, and sold her to the English for a huge fee.

The English charged Joan with heresy and in 1431 turned her over to the Holy Inquisition for trial. Her judges made much of her transvestism. Article 12 of her indictment read:

> Jeanne, rejecting and abandoning women's clothing, her hair cut around like a young coxcomb, took shirt, breeches, doublet ... tight-fitting boots or buskins, long spurs, sword, dagger, breast-plate, lance and other arms in fashion of a man of war.

When brought before the inquisitors, Joan refused to promise to wear women's clothing, even though her refusal meant she couldn't received the Eucharist. What's more, she insisted that her transvestism was a religious duty:

> For nothing in the world will I swear not to arm myself and put on a man's dress; I must obey the orders of Our Lord.

To the judges, it was bad enough that Joan had been wearing men's clothing. But to say this was a religious duty was heresy! They fumed:

> Jeanne attributes to God, His Angels, and His Saints, orders which are against the modesty of the feminine sex, and which are prohibited by the Divine Law ... such as dressing herself in the garments of a man, short, tight, dissolute, those underneath as well as above.

The English repeatedly drew attention to Joan's transvestism and urged the Inquisition to condemn her for heresy for that reason. The king of England, Henry VI, even got involved on this point. In a letter he wrote about Joan, he said:

> It is sufficiently notorious and well-known that for some time past a woman calling herself Jeanne the Pucelle [the Maid], leaving off the dress and clothing of the feminine sex, a thing contrary to divine law and abominable before God, and forbidden by all laws, wore clothing and armour such as is worn by men.

Not only did Joan wear men's clothing as a religious duty, but in the eyes of her judges she did something else just as bad—she acted with male assertiveness. Article 63 of the original indictment condemns her for "allowing herself a tone of mockery and derision such as no woman in a state of holiness would allow."

The judges were also upset that Joan had abandoned "feminine work," devoting herself to work that was traditionally done by men. She laughed in their faces, saying:

> As to the women's work of which you speak, there are plenty of other women to do it.

Other Women & Sex

Joan's judges took a special interest in her relationship with other women and her sex life. One of her women friends was nicknamed "La Rousse" ("the Red," from the color of her hair). She operated an inn in Neufchâteau, Lorraine, which was popular with soldiers. The judges claimed that Joan went to work for La Rousse without the permission of her parents. Inns in the Middle Ages were often brothels, and the judges said that Joan stayed with prostitutes while working at La Rousse's inn.

The judges were also interested in Joan's relationship with another woman, Catherine de la Rochelle. Joan admitted to the judges that she had slept in the same bed with Catherine on two successive nights, but that her reason for doing so was religious. She said that Catherine had told her that she had visions of "a Lady" at night, and Joan said she wanted to see this lady, too. But Joan saw no such thing while staying in Catherine's bed.

The two women, who seemed to view each other as rival prophets, eventually had a falling out. Catherine later collaborated with the English, claiming that Joan was in league with the Devil.

After her death, Joan inspired other women to imitate her. An example is Claude des Armoises, a woman who used a man's name, dressed as a man, and fought in battle. In 1440 Joan's two mercenary brothers took Claude on tour as part of a road show, falsely claiming that she was Joan, saying Joan had escaped from execution.

Joan's judges wanted to know if she was a virgin and had her examined by a panel of women. They reported that she was. Although she had spent time with prostitutes, she herself had never had sex with a man. After her death, rumors spread that she was a lesbian. An example is a reference to her as "a creature in the form of a woman, whom they called the Maid—what it was, God only knows."

Armed Lady Rising

The plot thickens. Joan's behavior at her trial was hardly that of a traditional Christian saint. When she was asked to swear to tell the truth on the gospels, she repeatedly refused. Usually, after much haggling back and forth, she would partially give in, by swearing on the missal. In addition, she refused to recite either the Pater Noster or the creed, although she was asked to do so many times.

These facts were red flags to Joan's judges. There had been notable heretics in the last 200 years who rejected the taking of oaths. Also, Joan seemed to be poorly versed in Christian dogma, although she was obviously very bright. Church authorities were becoming increasingly suspicious of peasants who could think for themselves and who continued to adhere to rural pagan customs. The authorities viewed this situation as fertile soil for the growth of heresy.

Joan's judges claimed that she had not been raised as a Christian, but as a pagan:

In her childhood, she was not instructed in the beliefs and principles of our Faith, but by certain old women she was initiated in the science of witchcraft, superstitious doings, and magical acts. Many inhabitants of these villages have been known for all time as using these kinds of witchcraft.

The mystery of Joan deepens when we look at other aspects of her life. Before her capture, when she appeared in public, peasants often prayed to her, a practice she never discouraged. They believed she had the power to heal, and many would flock around her to touch her body or her men's clothing, in hopes of a cure. Subsequently her moon-white armor was put on display at the Church of St. Denis, where it was worshipped.

The area of Lorraine, where Joan grew up, was notorious for the lingering paganism of its people. In the century before Joan's trial, the Synod of Trèves had condemned the peasants of Lorraine for practicing rites associated with the moon goddess Diana:

All kinds of magic, sorcery, witchcraft, auguries, superstitious writings ... the illusions of women who boast that they ride at night with Diana or Herodias and a multitude of other women.

This description brings to mind the practices of Sibillia and Pierina de' Bugatis of Lombardy, discussed in the last chapter. In addition, the peasants who lived in Joan's neighborhood retained memories of prophecies from the old Celtic religion that existed there before the introduction of Christianity. One of these concerned a wooded area called Bois Chesnu that was near Joan's house. The prophecy, which was well known and attributed to the sorcerer Merlin, said that a maid would come forth from Bois Chesnu, perform many marvels, and unite the French people.

In certain parts of Europe where Celtic beliefs survived, the word "Maid" or "Maiden" was a religious title, signifying a type of divine being who had the power to cure people.

The old French word for this title was *la Pucelle*, which was also applied by French Christians to the Virgin Mary. When Joan was asked by what title she called herself, her standard reply was "Joan *la Pucelle*, Daughter of God."

The Fairy Connection

The judges spent a lot of time questioning Joan about her supposed relations with "fairies"—a fact that has puzzled many modern commentators. Near Joan's home was an old beech tree (*fagus* tree, in Latin). Rumor had it that the fairies sometimes came and danced around this tree at night. They were not conceived then as fairies are today, as small, toy-like creatures with wings, but as protective spirits with significant powers.

By Joan's time, the tree was considered sacred to Our Lady of Domrémy, but suspicion remained that it had once been a holy spot in the old pagan religion. Near this tree was a spring where the peasants often went to be cured of diseases.

Joan denied ever seeing fairies at the tree, but she did admit to participating in celebrations around it as a child, decorating it with garlands. She added that when she decided to take up her mission to liberate France she gave up "these games and distractions."

Tɧє Dᴀᴜgɧᴛєʀ ᴏғ Gᴏᴅ

Historians have paid scant attention to the judges' interest in the surviving paganism of Joan's village and in her possible association with fairies. They have also undervalued Joan's encouragement of peasant adulation of herself and her white armor, her use of the title "*la Pucelle*, Daughter of God," and her religious-based transvestism.

Let us, however, take these things seriously. In the last chapter, we saw that the rites associated with a Diana-type goddess had long survived throughout rural Europe. And we noted above that the church had previously condemned the survival of these rites in the area where Joan herself was raised. When Joan's peculiarities are viewed in the context of these survivals, they no longer seem so peculiar.

From the viewpoint of the peasants of the time, Joan's practices had a certain consistency and logic. To understand this point, imagine that you yourself were a peasant then. You would be unlettered, with no formal education. But through the ancient oral tradition, you would be familiar with the image of the silvery female moon spirit, armed with bow and arrow, riding in strength across the night sky, followed by a throng of spirits and faeries, driving out evil spirits. That image would be part of your culture. It would seem as natural and familiar to you as was the beech tree in the town-square decked out with garlands to Our Lady.

Now suppose a woman appeared—a maiden, or virgin, just like the goddess Diana. Suppose she called herself the Daughter of God, just as Diana was the daughter of Jupiter. Suppose she bore arms, as did Diana, and wore moon-white armor. Suppose she rode into battle, followed by a throng of soldiers, driving out the foreign invaders just as Diana and her followers drove out evil spirits.

If you were a peasant familiar with the motif of the armed moon lady, Joan's dramatic appearance in her likeness would likely send shivers down your spine. You would view her as an angel in the flesh, pray to her, seek to be cured by her, and reverently touch her gleaming armor.

Suppose, on the other hand, that you were a pious, university-educated inquisitor. The image of the night-flying moon goddess would also be familiar to you, but not in the way it was to the peasants. To you as an inquisitor, it would be another manifestation of the Devil, part of a long series of devilish manifestations going back centuries, all aiming at one thing—corrupting the faith of the peasantry.

The woman in white armor deliberately evoking these images, rousing the people to adoration, would be a heretic to you. And you would want her killed.

Whose Christianity?

Was Joan of Arc a pagan? No. Her testimony, even as recorded by her enemies, is filled with expressions of devotion to God, Jesus, Mary, the angels, and the saints. And she was truly disheartened when the church withheld the sacrament of the Eucharist from her.

Was Joan of Arc a Christian in the way her educated judges were Christians? No. And this difference is the crux of the matter.

We need to remember that Western Christianity today is much different from what it was in the days of Joan of Arc. Before the Reformation and the Counter-Reformation, many priests were poorly trained, even illiterate. Manuscripts were rare and costly. Formal schooling for the very poor was unknown.

The knowledge that medieval peasants had of church dogma was fragmentary. Attendance at mass was spotty. The peasant faithful, and even priests, commonly offered prayers and sacrifices to spirits and celebrated old pagan feasts, all the while insisting that they were good Christians. In the eyes of the university-trained elite, however, those who persisted in such hybrid practices were heretics.

In incorporating pagan motifs into her religion and still regarding herself as a good Christian, Joan of Arc was a typical peasant of her times. However, she was untypical in becoming a noted actor on the stage of history. Because of this notoriety, and the political enemies she made, Joan's heresies would not be overlooked as they would be for peasants who didn't count in the eyes of the elite.

Joan's execution was a sign of things to come. As the machinery for social control expanded in the High Middle Ages and the Renaissance, the educated Christian elite were willing to overlook less and less. The dragnet for heretics was lowered ever deeper into the sea of the faithful. Eventually, the net snared a great mass of ordinary peasant women who had no historical notoriety at all. The ensuing slaughter helped to define both modern Christianity and modern European identity. And that, in turn, helped define the quest for meaning in the West.

To The Stake!

Joan was originally charged with a long list of offenses. Most fell under two categories—heresy and witchcraft. Although Anne Barstow has recently disputed the matter, the formal charges for witchcraft were probably dropped, as prior historians maintained.

Informally, though, Joan's detractors continued to stigmatize her as a witch. Nonetheless, the Inquisition was careful to observe legal niceties in its formal sittings with her. Witchcraft as such would not come under the Inquisition's purview until decades later.

The remaining charges against Joan were for heresy. The two principal ones were these: practicing transvestism as a religious duty; and regarding her "voices" as more authoritative than the pronouncements of the institutional church.

Joan's captors did everything they could, short of torture, to break her. Just after her arrest, she had tried to commit suicide by jumping out of a tower window. Although badly injuring herself, she eventually regained her strength. Later, during her trial, she was subjected to unending psychological abuse, imprisoned in foul quarters, and repeatedly threatened with being burned alive.

On May 24, 1431, as the sentence of death was about to be pronounced against her, Joan suddenly recanted and abjured her previous practices and beliefs. The court showed her mercy as Christians understand it: she was sentenced to life imprisonment on bread and water.

Soon thereafter, Joan resumed the wearing of men's clothing in her tiny prison cell. It's not clear from the record whether she did so deliberately or was tricked into it by her guards. In any event, as Margaret Murray observes—

> The extraordinary fact remains that the mere resuming of male garments was the signal for her death without further delay. On the Sunday she wore the [male] dress, on the Tuesday the sentence was communicated to her, on the Wednesday she was burned as an "idolater, apostate, heretic, relapsed."

This fact is extraordinary because the laws that regulated the wearing of clothing never made transvestism as such a capital offense. Apparently, in the eyes of her judges, Joan's resumption of male clothing was a sign of relapse into "heresy." By again dressing as a man, she had guaranteed her own martyrdom.

In the eyes of the peasants, Joan's execution probably had the aura of a religious sacrifice. She was a virgin. She applied to herself the title *la Pucelle*, an epithet of the Virgin Mary. And she was burned in May, the month of the Virgin. Although these facts are coincidences, the peasants likely saw a magical connection among them.

Divine Drag

Why did Joan's judges equate her transvestism with heresy? A clue comes from a recommendation of the faculty of the University of Paris, then under English influence. On May 14, 1431, the faculty condemned Joan and urged that she be burned as a heretic. (Medieval academics, like their modern counterparts, were often mouthpieces for establishment values.) The *reason* for the faculty's condemnation of Joan's transvestism is striking. They said that by cross-dressing she was "following the custom of the Gentiles and the Heathen."

This remark is a wake-up call that should make us ask, What custom? What heathen? Answer: The "custom" was religiously-validated transvestism. The "heathen" were most human beings then living on the planet (that is, people who did not live under monotheistic regimes).

Many animistic and polytheistic societies around the world have something in common: they practice transvestism as a form of religious devotion. Even in ostensibly monotheistic Europe, church authorities repeatedly denounced surviving transvestite practices, which often occurred at new-year's festivals. These condemnations show that Joan was tapping into an old pagan European tradition in insisting that her cross-dressing was a religious duty.

As an example of the entrenched tradition of religious transvestism, consider Servian, writing in the fourth century:

> Look, the holidays are coming, the Kalends of January. Public processions for the devils are everywhere. ... People dress up as cattle, and men become women. ... These are not amusements, they are crimes.2

In the 10th century, Regino of Prüm asked:

> Have you done anything that the pagans do on the Kalends of January? Like dressing up as a little stag or an old woman? Three years penance.3

In the 13th century, Stephen of Bourbon, an inquisitor in southern France, denounced female worshippers of Diana and male transvestites in the same breath. In the 19th century, May Day celebrations in the British Isles commonly included transvestism, as did the Hogmanay celebration in Scotland. The Feast of Fools, a remnant of the old pagan religion where men dress as women, has survived into modern times.

Today many gay people throughout Europe and America celebrate Halloween as a gay holiday, with lots of cross-dressing. Halloween was originally the old pagan Celtic holiday of Samhain (pronounced "Sawin"), when faeries and the spirits of the dead were thought to travel through the night.

Joan's learned judges had read the chronicles of earlier generations, condemning the persistent transvestism that had been part of Europe's old pagan religion. And they could see with their own eyes similar practices in the popular religion of their rural contemporaries.

When Joan of Arc stepped forward onto the stage of history and proclaimed that her transvestism was a religious duty, her judges understood immediately that she was drawing on this ancient pagan tradition. In Joan's eyes, doing so was part of being a good Christian, because she had integrated much of the old paganism into her own Christian piety. But in the eyes of her judges, her practices smelled of the Devil and deserved the punishment for heresy.

Due to the relentless hunts for heretics and witches, the authorities' definition of Christianity, not Joan's, was the one that would come to prevail in the modern West.

---

2   Servian, 4th Century
3   Regino of Prüm, 10th Century

Cross-dressing would be disconnected from the spiritual life of the community and consigned to the realm of the Devil, part of the larger process of disconnecting sex from meaning.

A Midsummer Night's Dream

What about the fairies? Why were Joan's judges interested in her possible association with them? For the same reason they were interested in her transvestism: the judges smelled the presence of the Devil.

Before the Christian elite demonized them, the faeries were well established in peasant belief as local spirits who could help or hinder human efforts. They also often wandered through wild places at night, attendants of a Diana-like goddess, and of a male god in the style of Harlequin.

A classic 16th-century literary depiction of the faeries is William Shakespeare's play *A Midsummer Night's Dream*. When the bard introduces them, the faeries come streaming across the forest at night in two companies. One is lead by their queen, Titania, the other by their king, Oberon.

Shakespeare's choice of names is revealing. "Titania" is a Latin word, literally meaning "descended from the Titans," and is commonly used as an epithet of the goddess Diana. Shakespeare's Titania is thus a version of the familiar night-riding moon goddess whom we encountered in the last chapter.

Shakespeare's name for the king of the faeries is Oberon. Scholars have quibbled over its derivation. My own view is that the name comes from the Latin verb *oberrare*, meaning "to wander about." The participle form of this verb, when used as a name, is *Oberrans*, meaning "he who wanders about." This derivation is consistent with Oberon's behavior in the play, swooping about over the forest floor, followed by his train of traveling fairies.

Shakespeare's Oberon brings to mind the night-riding god Herne the Hunter, or Harlequin. Oberon is also reminiscent of the Good Travelers of Friuli (*benandanti*), discussed in the last chapter.

The Outdoor Ladies

Although Shakespeare cooked up some delicious escapades in his play, the main ingredients—Titania, Oberon, and their fairy followers—were not just figments of his imagination. There is plenty of evidence for a widespread belief in the faeries among European peasants even into modern times. This evidence throws light on why Joan's judges were so upset by her association with fairies.

The island of Sicily provides one example, among many, for the pervasive belief in fairies in Europe. During the age of Shakespeare, Sicily was part of the Spanish Empire, and so fell victim to the Spanish Inquisition. The historian Gustav Henningsen has come across records of the Spanish Inquisition dealing with

Sicilian peasants who believed in "the outdoor ladies" (*donni di fuora* in Sicilian; in Spanish, *donas de fuera*).

This term referred both to fairy-like beings and to popular healers (mostly women) who believed they embodied the fairies. The healers said they had trances or dreams where they traveled together in companies, led by a queen. She was variously known as "the Queen of the Faeries," "the Greek Lady," "the Mistress," and "the Wise Sibyl."

The Inquisition called these healers "witches." They arrested a number of them, but were restrained in their use of torture and punishment. Most of the victims were not executed, but sentenced to banishment or prison.

Despite persecution, the Sicilian tradition of night-flying folk-healers continued into the 20th century. In 1958, Gustav Henningsen personally interviewed one such healer named Marta in the village of Milocca, Sicily. She made no mention of "fairies," but related that on special days of the year she would leave her body and fly over the world in spirit, thereby increasing her healing powers.

Shakespeare from Renaissance England would have recognized Marta from modern Sicily as a familiar type. And so would Joan of Arc, Sibillia, and Pierina de' Bugatis.

The Outdoor Ladies of Sicily also bring to mind the Calusari of Romania and the Good Travelers of Friuli (discussed in the last chapter). Also the *jnun*-healers of Morocco. These have visions of the goddess *'A'isha Qandisha*, who is black, with pendulous breasts and long nipples, like the famed statue of Diana in Ephesus. And there are fairies known as *Faggen* in the Austrian Tyrol, among many others.

Joan's judges knew about the widespread peasant belief in fairies, whom they regarded as demons. They also knew that Joan claimed to hear "voices" at a spring where the locals went to be cured by fairies. Joan said her voices belonged to three saints, Catherine, Margaret, and Michael, not fairies. But because Joan believed her voices were more authoritative than the institutional church, her inquisitors discounted them as fairy-demons. For Joan to continue to heed them was heresy.

Joan's openness to the fairy tradition and religious transvestism was not inconsistent in her mind with being a good Christian. That's because the European peasant culture of her time had not yet succumbed to the dogmatism of the university-educated elite. The peasants still saw nature and sexual variation as domains of meaning.

MΛGICΛL CHRISTIΛNITY

This, then, is Joan of Arc's importance to the history of meaning: her life got caught up in the struggle between the two Europes of the High Middle Ages— the Europe of peasants (the vast majority); and the Europe of lords, bishops, and academics. Joan's religion was a form of *magical Christianity*, the religion of the peasants, as opposed to the *institutional Christianity* of the educated elite.

In many ways, Joan was like the polytheists and animists of yore. They heeded spirits who appeared at fountains, springs, and groves, not just in churches. If convinced by the message of the spirits, those who heard, acted. Otherwise, not. No additional approval was expected from institutional authorities.

The Roman Catholic Church, on the other hand, had become a bureaucratic juggernaut by Joan's time. The pope in Rome had made good on his pretensions, sidestepped in earlier centuries, of controlling bishops throughout Europe. The Office of the Holy Inquisition had made good on its scheme of imposing a uniformity of dogma on the educated, and was now moving to accost the uneducated as well.

In the decades after Joan's death, magical Christianity would crumble under the burgeoning onslaught of institutional Christianity. Protestantism, the surviving dissenter of later centuries, would come through with even less of the old rural magic than its Catholic adversary. Thus would be laid the groundwork for the disconnection from sex and nature that characterizes modern industrial society. And that has impoverished the lives of us all.

Joan's Gay Buddy

There was an unconventional, pagan ring not only to Joan's beliefs but also to her associates. During her military career, Joan's closest friend, personal bodyguard, and most devoted follower was a rich French knight named Gilles de Rais (1404-1440). He was commonly reputed to be gay, just as Joan had been rumored to be a lesbian.

In 1440, nine years after Joan's execution, the bishop of Nantes publicly charged Gilles de Rais with violating the ecclesiastical immunities of a certain priest, conjuring demons, and sodomy. At the time such crimes were tried by church tribunals.

At the insistence of the bishop, a concurrent civil trial was also begun. In the civil court, Gilles was accused of molesting and murdering large numbers of children, mostly boys. At first, Gilles vehemently denied everything and spoke contemptuously to his judges, like Joan of Arc at her trial years before. Unlike Joan, however, Gilles was tortured, along with some of his closest friends and his servants.

Medieval tortures were ghastly, and could result in horrible pain, crippling mutilation, and death, not unlike the methods used by the American CIA and Soviet KGB during the Cold War. During the heresy hunts and the great witch hunts, torture victims would commonly confess to anything in order to stop their horrible suffering.

Under torture, Gilles eventually confessed to everything his judges wanted to hear. Accordingly, he was condemned to death and was publicly strangled on October 26, 1440, at age 36.

Rush to Judgment

Historians have been quick to take the charges against Gilles de Rais at face value. Jeffrey Russell, for example, calls Gilles "a vicious sexual pervert." Likewise, Anne Barstow concludes that Gilles "procured, sexually abused, and murdered over one hundred children."

The eagerness of these two historians to believe the charges against Gilles contrasts with their caution in evaluating the charges leveled against other alleged heretics and witches. In the other cases, they rightly note that evidence procured through torture is always suspect. And they point to the arbitrary methods used by inquisitorial courts. These functioned as prosecutor, judge, and jury, all in one, which usually guaranteed a guilty verdict.

There is another reason to pause in the rush to condemn Gilles: his case arose because of a conflict over money with his relatives. Although Gilles was one of the richest nobles in Europe, he had gone deeply into debt. His relatives feared that he would sell off too much of the family estate in order to settle his accounts, leaving little for them to inherit.

Things came to a head in 1436, when the relatives got Charles VII, king of France, to issue a decree forbidding Gilles to sell off any more family land. In September 1440, a priest tried to repossess one of the estates that Gilles owned outside the king's jurisdiction and had sold off. Gilles arrested the priest and had him roughed up. The priest then collaborated with Gilles' relatives and with the bishop of Nantes, who stepped forward and made his sensational charges.

Even his enemies admitted that Gilles had been deeply devoted to Joan of Arc during her life. After her death, he traveled around France staging plays about her suffering and execution, hoping to rehabilitate her reputation against the calumnies of the Inquisition. And on the day of his execution, there was a large demonstration by the people on his behalf.

Could a person as shrewd and perceptive as Joan of Arc have been taken in by a mass murderer? Yes, but her faith in Gilles should raise a doubt in our minds about the truth of the charges. If the courts had credible evidence against Gilles, could there have been a public demonstration on his behalf on the day of his death? Possibly, but the demonstration proves that many people were not convinced by the charges.

Gilles was a practitioner of magical Christianity, like his heroine, Joan of Arc. Thus he was open to charges of heresy and sorcery. And he was also probably gay, perhaps having sex with young men. Thus he was open to charges of sodomy. Finally, he was anti-clerical, haughty, and wasteful of money. Thus he easily made enemies.

The known circumstances of Gilles' life would have been hook enough for holding meatier charges, if people with the right connections and sufficient motivation decided to act. His relatives had both the connections and the motivation. In any case, once the inquisitorial machinery was set in motion, the result was a foregone conclusion.

Gilles de Rais may have been guilty as charged. The important point is that the question of his guilt is not so easily settled as most historians pretend. Could their haste in racing past this question reflect a discomfort with things gay?

Witches and Fairies and Buggers, Oh My!

A discomfort with things gay perhaps explains why most historians have overlooked a number of curious coincidences associated with heresy in general and Joan of Arc in particular. For one thing, as noted earlier, Joan was suspected of being a lesbian, and Gilles de Rais was probably gay. For another, words in contemporary European languages that now refer to gay people keep popping up in the history of heresy. Some examples we've seen above are *fairies*, *Faggen*, and *fagus* tree. In addition, the 13th-century Cathar heresy (to be discussed in chapter four) gave rise to a number of words in medieval vernaculars that meant both "heretic" and "homosexual."

Also, unrepentant heretics and witches were burned on bundles of sticks called "faggots." Heretics were sometimes obliged to wear an embroidered emblem of a faggot on their sleeves. Expressions popped up in the popular speech like "to fry a faggot," suggesting that the victims themselves may have been called "faggots."

Finally, we've seen that transvestism played an important role in the old pagan religion of Europe. Joan of Arc's judges saw her as drawing on this tradition when she insisted on the religious importance of her own transvestism.

What does all this mean? That all heretics were gay or lesbian? No. That all gays or lesbians were heretics? No. What then? Only this: if heresy drew on the old paganism, and if the old paganism viewed all sexuality as sacred, then women and gay people might have played roles in paganism and heresy that the Christian elite regarded as the work of the Devil.

Subsequent chapters will show that there were in fact deep connections among sexual diversity, heresy, and paganism. In demonizing heresy, the church also demonized sexual diversity and nature-worship. The result was to banish sexual diversity and nature worship to the realm of the Devil. That banishment laid the groundwork for a fixture of modernity—downplaying the importance of sex and nature in framing the meaning of life.

Language & History

Because part of the story ahead deals with homosexuality, we should note here that some historians object to the use of the words "homosexual" or "gay" when referring to people living before the 19th century. The word "homosexuality," they argue, wasn't coined until the 19th century. Therefore, there was no reality corresponding to this word before that. This view is popular among cultural constructionists influenced by the French theoretician Michel Foucault.

Space doesn't permit a comprehensive response here to Foucault and company. Instead, let's just note that just because a certain word didn't exist in the past doesn't mean that the reality it names didn't exist either. Also, although the modern English word "homosexual" didn't exist in the ancient world, Greeks and Romans had plenty of names to apply to people who had sex with members of their own gender. Finally, the phrase "culturally constructed" has conflicting meanings, a fact often overlooked by the people who use it.

Strict adherents of cultural constructionism can be very dogmatic. But if we rely on evidence instead of dogma, we may be in for some surprises. For example, the word "homophilia," close in meaning to our modern "homosexuality," was applied by the 14th-century Inquisition to heretics in the French Pyrenees. So something close to what we now mean by "homosexuality" existed in Europe before 1800, after all, despite the dogma of the strict cultural constructionists.

The chapters ahead will acknowledge the roles of *both* culture *and* nature in history. In particular, they will use the words "gay" and "lesbian" in describing certain people in earlier societies. This usage doesn't mean that people who had sex with members of their own gender in the past looked at themselves the way gay men and lesbians do today. It does mean, though, that in every human society a minority of people preferred to have sex with their own gender, just as a minority preferred to have sex with the opposite gender, while the majority were to some degree bisexual.

The important point is this: some societies saw in sexual diversity a form of spiritual power, while others demonized it. From this difference, great consequences flowed for the history of meaning.

Another Silly Old Woman?

The chapters ahead will draw out the implications for the history of meaning of the things we've discovered about Joan of Arc and Gilles de Rais. Some of the ideas expressed will be indebted to the controversial work of Margaret Murray.

In 1921, Murray, then a professor of Egyptology at University College in London, unsettled conventional historians with the publication of *The Witch-Cult in Western Europe*. Murray approached the subject of the European witchcraft as an anthropologist. She collected transcripts from witch trials (mostly from Britain, where torture was rare), went through the evidence for common themes, and compared the results with existing mythological and archaeological knowledge of western Europe. She concluded that "witchcraft" was a lingering pre-Christian religion ("the old religion," as she called it) and that various pagan cults continued to exist underground until recent times.

In the decades following the publication of her books, Murray was subjected to a furious academic assault. Her most trenchant critic was the influential American scholar Norman Cohn. He insisted that European folklore was irrelevant to the history of the witch hunts, which he sought to explain in psychological terms. He derided Murray because she was nearly 60 years old when she turned her attention to the subject (she lived to be 101), just as he had derided female victims of the Inquisition as "silly old women."

Murray was wrong in many details. But for all that, her work drew attention to certain elements that had been overlooked in the history of witchcraft: anthropological evidence, sexuality, and transvestism.

Thanks to the rise of new feminist scholarship, beginning in the 1970s, Margaret Murray is finally getting the credit she deserves. Anne Barstow, a contemporary feminist historian of witchcraft, puts matters right when she says:

> Murray erred by forcing her evidence too far, by re-creating late medieval witchcraft as an "alternative church" instead of a loose collection of magical practices, a decision that pushed her into many anachronisms. Still, her attention to *what people were doing*, to folk ritual and belief, was on the right track.

In the next chapter, we'll take a closer look at what some people were doing as they combined pagan and Christian motifs to form their own brands of magical Christianity. They will differ from Joan, Gilles, Sibillia, and Pierina in being more ideologically oriented. Their struggle against institutional Christianity will provide us with a new passageway on our journey to the Emerald City of historical understanding.

Chapter 4.

Heretics, Women, and Buggers

Today when people hear the word "Christianity," they think of the big three—Roman Catholicism, Eastern Orthodoxy, and Protestantism. They don't realize that these traditions are but the remaining threads in a fabric that was once far more richly woven.

In the Middle Ages, before the Reformation and the Counter-Reformation, Europe was home to an amazing tapestry of belief-systems, especially among the lower classes in the countryside. A major strand in this tapestry was institutional Christianity. This was Christianity as defined by church councils and papal pronouncements, and perpetuated by the learned elite.

But institutional Christianity wasn't the only strand in medieval religion. The people of the time commonly wove many others that contained fibers from institutional Christianity but dyed with pagan colors, creating varieties of what could be called magical Christianity. These Christian/pagan hybrids would shock many Christians today. Nonetheless, their practitioners usually thought of themselves as good Christians.

In the previous two chapters, we saw magical Christianity at work in the lives of Sibillia and Pierina de' Bugatis of Italy, and Joan of Arc and Gilles de Rais of France. They all found themselves in conflict with the official doctrines of the power structure. But even so, they did not seek to create new institutional forms for perpetuating their beliefs against the power structure.

Others did. The most noteworthy example was Catharism, the medieval West's best-organized hybrid of Christian tradition and pagan polytheism. Catharism eventually became so powerful that it created a European counterculture, challenging established notions about divinity, nature, sex, and women.

In response, institutional Christianity demonized Catharism. The effect was to pump new energy into the old Christian habit of viewing nature worship, sex, and women's experience as tainted by the Devil.

This chapter will show how Catharism arose, and the next, how it was destroyed. Both chapters will disclose a highly organized quest for meaning that might have changed the subsequent course of Christianity and Western society, had it been allowed to survive. In reflecting on what was, and what might have been, we will gain insight into the status of meaning in society today.

Tꜧe Persistence of Erotic Religion

Where did Catharism come from? It roots ran deep, reaching all the way back to the first century A.D. In that age, a new religious movement known as Gnosticism emerged in the Eastern regions of the Roman Empire. The Gnostics believed that knowledge (*gnosis* in Greek) from personal mystical experience was more important than dogma (*pistis*). Because the tree of medieval Catharism would later grow from Gnostic roots, we'll briefly explore Gnostic beliefs and history.

The Gnostics were polytheists who drew on many different religious traditions, including stories that circulated about Jesus. You could find Gnostics who worshipped Jesus while at the same time believing in a great-goddess figure and acknowledging the god of the Old Testament. This last god they generally regarded as evil. Consequently they sympathized with people who had suffered from his wrath, including the ancient Sodomites.

In classical antiquity, religious rites often included sexual activity, even orgies. The ancients did not draw a dividing line between religion and sex, like monotheistic religions. Some Gnostic Christian groups continued this ancient pagan tradition, which scandalized non-Gnostic Christians.

For example, Irenaeus, the 2nd-century Christian missionary to the Celts, condemned a group of Gnostics for their promiscuity. Clement, the 3rd-century bishop of Alexandria, denounced Gnostics for holding orgies. The same condemnation appears in the 4th-century historian Eusebius.

Epiphanius, a fourth-century monk and former Gnostic, claimed that Gnostic Christians had sex in common and worshipped semen and menstrual blood as the body and blood of Christ. He said the Gnostics believed in sexual pleasure but not in procreation, because giving birth divided up the world-soul. Salvation consisted in gathering themselves together and returning to Barbelo, the great-mother goddess, by means of communal sex rites.

Mani

In the middle of the third century A.D., a potent new form of Gnosticism appeared in the eastern Roman province of Mesopotamia, led by a charismatic teacher named Mani. Mesopotamia was the land of the old Zoroastrian religion, which viewed the world as a scene of conflict between two great gods, one good, the other evil. Mani concocted his own special brew of Christianity, Zoroastrianism, and Gnosticism. His menu later inspired Catharism in Western Europe.

Mani divided believers into two separate categories, the leaders (or the elect) and the followers (or the hearers). Both women and men could be leaders in Mani's religion, as was generally the case with the Gnostics. In addition, leaders were forbidden to accumulate personal wealth. These practices contrasted to those of institutional Christianity, which forbade women to be priests and saw nothing wrong with wealthy priests and bishops.

Like other Gnostics, Mani believed in reincarnation and polytheism. But he put a special stress on the idea of two great gods in conflict, which he borrowed from Zoroastrianism. Mani identified the evil god with the god of the Old Testament. Salvation for the elect (or the leaders) consisted in escaping from the control of this evil god, which meant renouncing all material possessions and earthly power. Insofar as the elect were concerned, Mani's religion was severely ascetic.

The mass of followers, on the other hand, were exempt from puritanical injunctions, although Mani hoped they would adopt the strict life of the leaders sometime before they died. Most waited until they were on their death beds to make this conversion. If they failed to do so, they would continue to reincarnate, and so remain subject to the rule of the evil god of the Old Testament.

Mani's brand of Gnosticism was known as Manichaeeism or Manichaeanism. From the third to the fifth centuries, Manichaeism swept westward across the Roman Empire and became a major opponent of institutional Christianity. Augustine, the 5th-century bishop of Hippo, was a Manichee for nine years before converting to institutional Christianity. He accused the Manichees of loose sexual behavior, giving this as a reason for his conversion to institutional Christianity.

Manichaean Melodies

As it spread, Manichaeism mutated into many different varieties. In the latter part of the 4th century, a new variety bubbled to the surface in Syria and Asia Minor. These Manichees were known as Massalians (or Messalians). As with other Manichaean sects, their leaders included both men and women.

The Massalians introduced a novelty. Some of them believed that after a period of strict self-denial, they could engage in any kind of sexual activity without sin. In fact, they regarded sensual experience as a window into mystical visions.

In the 10th century, a turning point occurred when Massalian beliefs entered Bulgaria, a land rocking from political upheaval. In Bulgaria, Messalian beliefs fused with a local variety of Manichaeism known Bogomilism. This variation on Mani's theme was named after the priest who created it, Bogomil ("Beloved of God"). The fusion was significant because the followers of Bogomil had a political awareness. They rejected the hierarchy of the institutional church and preached passive resistance to governmental authority.

In their religious beliefs, the Bogomils at first had a reputation for puritanism, but their contact with incoming Massalian beliefs changed that. They soon became associated in the minds of their critics with "the most extreme forms of sexual indulgence," as one commentator, Dmitri Obolensky, puts it.

Another factor contributed to this shift. Under the heat of persecution from Bulgarian authorities, the Bogomils allied themselves with the peasant masses, among whom paganism was still very strong. In fact, Boris, the king of Bulgaria, hadn't converted to Christianity until 864. His attempt to impose Christianity on the people resulted in a civil war in which he eventually defeated and blinded his own pagan son.

The pagan masses of Bulgaria remained hostile to Boris and his successors, while the Bogomils became increasing politicized, siding with the serfs in their battles against aristocratic land-owners. The other side of this coin is that the peasants' pagan sensibilities, reinforced by Massalian practices, reshaped Bogomilism at the very moment it was becoming more political.

Under these Massalian and pagan influences, the religion of Bogomil moved farther and farther away from the practices of institutional Christianity. An example is an incident that occurred in the early 14th century. A Bogomil monk named Lazarus appeared in Tirnovo, the capital of Bulgaria. He advocated nudism and sexual freedom as ways to salvation. Arrested, but refusing to recant, he was branded on the face and exiled. Another Bogomil named Theodosius advocated orgiastic sex, but his fate is not recorded. Most Bogomils did not share these views, but they were examples of where pagan and Massalian influences could lead. Institutional Christians were horrified.

Beware of Greeks Bearing Heresy

Although the city of Rome fell in 476 A.D., creative theological ferment continued in the former eastern provinces of the Roman Empire (the Balkans and what is today called Turkey). The reason is that political fragmentation did not occur in the East to the same degree as in the West.

Western Europe had become deeply fragmented after the fall of Rome— socially, politically, and geographically. Despite some notable exceptions (like the brief empire of Charlemagne), the fragmentation continued until the 11th century. At that time, the state and the church begin to reassemble themselves in Western Europe on a grand scale. During the earlier period, political fragmentation hampered the spread of new ideas.

During the Middle Ages, Western Europeans knew the residents of the Eastern realm simply as "the Greeks." That was because the literary language of the area remained Greek. As trade and travel gradually revived, "the Greeks" occasionally introduced daring new theologies into Western Europe.

These Greek gifts often found eager takers among the peasants, who sensed in them a kinship to their own ancient pagan sensibilities. The most substantial bloom to grow from this revived East-West insemination was Catharism. Roman Christianity viewed it as a latter-day Trojan horse, sent by the Devil from the land of the Greeks to infiltrate and destroy the City of God.

Enter the Cathars

The big breakthrough occurred in the 11th century. The Bogomil religion, which by then was a composite of Massalianism and Manichaeism, started infiltrating the West. The practitioners of this infiltrating religion were known in the West as Cathars, from the Greek word *Katharoi*, meaning "Purified Ones." Within a hundred years or so, the Cathars managed to organize a rival church, create a counterculture in southern France and elsewhere, and raise armies on their behalf.

Catharism was deeply imprinted with Gnostic and Manichaean traditions. The result was a bifurcated religion, being extremely ascetic for leaders on the top, but exactly the opposite, in practice, for the mass of believers on the bottom. This mentality shocked and confused institutional Christians. They were the just opposite, preaching ascetic values to the masses, but condoning earthly indulgences and a wealthy lifestyle for members of the upper hierarchy.

As might be expected, matters came to a head over sex. From their very first appearance in the West, the Cathars were associated by their critics with ritual sex and homosexuality, like many Gnostics before them.

Heretics at Orleans

An early example is a group of heretics uncovered in Orléans, France, in 1022. Although there is some debate on the question, these heretics were probably early adherents of Catharism.

The following mishmash of charges were leveled against the Orléans heretics: they worshipped the Devil in the form of a black man or an animal; they rejected the idea that Christ suffered in the flesh; they repudiated the sacraments; they consumed a "heavenly food" that gave them angelic visions; and they claimed to enjoy the "consolation" of angels.

In one of the few passages where they were quoted in their own words, the Orléans heretics rejected the virgin birth of Jesus, saying "What nature denies is always out of harmony with the Creator."

One report claimed the heretics participated in orgies. If a child was born from the sexual acts, it was killed, then burned, and its ashes used for making the "heavenly food."

What are we to make of all these charges? Historians offer conflicting answers. Some dismiss the charges in their entirety as the delusional fantasies of persecuting authorities. Other historians caution that they may contain grains of truth.

The accusers' accounts undoubtedly exaggerated and demonized the heretics' practices. Nonetheless, they alluded to a tell-tale Cathar feature, the sacrament of "consolation" (*consolamentum*). This was a distinctive rite of Catharism, but was not yet widely known as such in the West. Also, the accusers called the heretics "Manichaeans." This was as close a description of Catharism as one could get before the word "Cathars" itself became widely known. Accordingly, the Orléans heretics were probably early Cathars, combining features of local paganism with newly arrived Cathar thinking.

We know from Joan of Arc, the Maid of Orléans, that pagan traditions long continued in this area. As with Joan later, so with these early Orléans heretics: Christian authorities viewed hybrids of Christianity and paganism as plots by the Devil.

But what about the charge of murdering newborn infants? We should remember that Catholic authorities have often stigmatized the practice of birth-control and abortion as child-murder. Also, many dominant religions have made such charges against dissenting sects in the past. The ancient Romans made similar charges against early Christians.

The charge may also have been connected to the Cathars' rejection of the sacrament of baptism. A refusal to baptize could be seen as the equivalent of infanticide if the child died after childbirth. According to some 16th-century laws, a woman was legally guilty of infanticide if she gave birth to a child out of wedlock and concealed it, and the infant died before it could be baptized.

The Orléans heretics were arrested and tried for heresy, although apparently not tortured. Except for two who recanted, they were locked into a small cottage. On December 28, 1022, Christian authorities—moved no doubt by the spirit of Christmas—burned the cottage to the ground, with the heretics locked inside.

This was the first execution for heresy in the West since the 4th century. The political fragmentation of the early Middle Ages did not lend itself to systematic heresy-hunting. Local bishops were often isolated from Rome, a centralized heresy-hunting bureaucracy did not exist, and Christians were greatly outnumbered by pagans. Burnings increased in the later Middle Ages, as church, state, and university—all controlled by men— consolidated their institutional powers over the rest of society.

Heresy and Homosexuality

Another early case that probably involved Cathars occurred in 1114 in Bucy-le-long, France, near Soissons. The French abbot Guibert of Nogent wrote about two brothers, Clement and Evrard, whom he knew personally. He said they were heretics who had a following among the peasants.

These heretics, claimed Guibert, denied that Christ had suffered in the flesh, and rejected any sexual intercourse that led to birth. Instead, they practiced homosexuality:

> You may see them living with women but not under the name of
> husband and wife ... but men are known to be with men, women
> with women.

As with the heretics at Orléans, authorities accused Clement and Evrard of holding orgies in cellars and killing any children that might be born from such unions. This charge is inconsistent with the claim that the heretics preferred to have sex with members of their own sex. It's probably an exaggeration of some erotic peasant rite, as well as a demonization of birth control and abortion.

On trial before the bishop of Soissons, one brother confessed but refused to repent. The other brother denied the accusations. Both were burned to death by an angry mob, incited by the clergy.

The charge that these heretics avoided any kind of sex that led to procreation is a tip-off that they were probably Cathars. That's because the Cathars believed that giving birth ensnared the soul of an angel in the newborn's body and so extended the power of the evil god who ruled the material world. If you have to have sex, the Cathars believed, do it in a way that doesn't lead to birth—the direct opposite of the view of institutional Christianity.

Beginning with Bucy-le-long, charges of lesbianism and male homosexuality became routine against the Cathars:

> This, the first explicit allegation of homosexuality, also became a commonplace in later trials. Variations on the phrases *vir cum viris* [the men with men] and *femina cum feminis* [the woman with women] appear again and again.

The word for "Cathar" quickly became the word for "homosexual" in many European vernaculars of the time. Examples are German *Ketzer*, French *hérite*, Italian *gazarro* and *Bulgaro*, French *Bougre*, and English *Bugger*. The last three words originally meant "Bulgarian," because Catharism grew out of Bulgarian Bogomilism, as we saw above.

Cathar heresy and homosexuality became so interchangeable that those accused of heresy attempted to prove their innocence by proclaiming their heterosexuality. A 13th-century weaver accused of heresy replied:

> Gentlemen, listen to me! I am not a heretic, for I have a wife and I sleep with her. I have sons.

When the people of Toulouse rebelled against the heresy-hunting Dominicans, they cried out to their persecutors that "they were unjustly accusing decent married men of heresy."

Mere suspicion of homosexuality was enough to condemn a person for heresy, even though the person was not known to have believed in any heretical doctrine. In 1381 an epileptic German beggar named Brother Hans was thought to have magical powers. He was arrested and tortured into confessing that he was a "perverter of young boys." He was consequently burned at the stake for *heresy*, even though no doctrinal dispute was involved.

Because the same words often meant both heresy and homosexuality, we sometimes have trouble deciphering what was meant by legal codes of the times. In 1272 the laws of Orléans, Anjou, and Marne called for death by burning of anyone guilty of "bougerie." It's unclear whether this term refers to homosexuality, heresy, or both.

As a result of this confusion, a person's sexual orientation became a test of religious orthodoxy and political loyalty:

> Heresy became a sexual rather than a doctrinal concept; to say a man was a heretic was to say that he was a homosexual, and vice versa.

The Cathar World-View

The Cathars' tolerant attitude toward homosexuality was an integral part of their theology. Unlike institutional Christians, Cathars didn't believe in Hell, Purgatory, or damnation. But they did believe in reincarnation.

In Cathar theology, souls continued to be reborn as animals or humans until they escaped from the life-death cycle. Eventually all souls would escape. None would be damned.

The one great sin in Cathar eyes occurred when certain angels, led by the evil god of the Old Testament, rebelled against the good god and were thrown out of Heaven. These angels became human souls, weighed down with matter, and so were continually reborn. Only when they regained their original angelic state, brought about by a complete renunciation of this world, would they escape from the cycle of rebirths and return to the good god in Heaven.

How does this view lead to a tolerant attitude toward homosexuality? Because of a catch in Cathar thought, mentioned above: they believed that at any given time only a tiny minority of people could attain this angelic state. The rest, the great majority, lived by worldly standards influenced by pagan traditions.

The few who attained the angelic state were called the "Purified Ones" (*Katharoi* in Greek; in Latin, *Cathari*). They led completely ascetic lives and were worshipped by ordinary Cathars as angels in human form.

The way to become a Purified One was to be initiated by a sacrament, a kind of laying-on-of-hands, called the consolation (*consolamentum*). Once receiving the consolation, the Purified Ones were expected to live in strict self-denial, sometimes even starving themselves to death.

The Purified Ones who didn't starve themselves to death were strict vegetarians, refusing to eat meat, eggs, or any dairy products. Because animals were viewed as reincarnated souls, killing an animal was akin to killing a human being. All procreation, even in the animal world, was the work of the evil god.

Because of the severity involved, the great majority of Cathars put off receiving the consolation until they were on their death beds. In the meantime, they lived by a code much looser than that of the Purified Ones. Its moral values were close to those of the old rural paganism, and its religious practices included animism and polytheism. Unlike institutional Christians, Cathar leaders did not feel threatened by surviving pagan traditions of the countryside.

One thing that the Purified Ones did inveigh against, though, was procreation, since the birth of a baby would ensnare yet another angelic soul in matter. Sex must not lead to birth. If the mass of the ordinary faithful must engage in sex, then the best forms were masturbation, heterosexual sex that did not lead to conception, and homosexuality. The most immoral form of sex was heterosexual intercourse undertaken for the sake of producing offspring.

Consequently, many of the Cathar faithful believed that until they received the consolation, non-procreative forms of sex were permissible and even desirable. When arrested and questioned by the Holy Inquisition at Toulouse and Turin, many said they didn't regard homosexuality as a sin, which shocked institutional Christians. The Cathar faithful, especially among the peasantry, displayed a frank and casual attitude toward sex in general.

Cathar Women

When it came to the role of women, Catharism continued its divergence from institutional Christianity. A woman as well as a man could become a Purified One, who was viewed as a combination of priest and angel. Accordingly, women also administered the Cathar sacrament of consolation. Women were the principal proselytizers for Catharism in the countryside. Cathar peasant women often left their husbands in order to live in houses reserved exclusively for female Purified Ones.

Institutional Christianity, on the other hand, forbade women to be priests. It continues to do so to this day. In fact, Pope John Paul II forbids Catholic theologians even to discuss the idea of women priests.

The prejudices are based squarely on the New Testament, which reeks of male chauvinism. Jesus had no women apostles, always used male pronouns when speaking of God, and treated his mother and other women peremptorily. No book of the New Testament was written by a woman. Paul of Tarsus forbade women to be teachers and repeatedly expressed a condescending attitude toward women.

The Old Testament is just as offensive, with its raging testosterone god, Yahweh. Modern Christians and Jews who call themselves feminists would be more consistent if they followed the example of the Cathars and junked most of the Bible.

Again, contrary to Catholic values, Cathar women participated in war. A woman catapultist killed Simon de Montfort, the leader of the Catholic army that attacked the Cathars of southern France. Like Joan of Arc, the Cathars probably drew on the ancient Celtic tradition of strong, independent women, including women warriors.

The high status of Cathar women, compared to institutional Christians, was connected to the Cathar attitude toward marriage. Historically, the ideal of "the sanctity of marriage" has been used to validate the power of husbands over wives in the household. Catharism scorned marriage, viewing it as on the same level as prostitution, and was one of the few religions in history that had no marriage rites.

Because being a good Cathar had nothing to do with conforming to sex roles, it made no sense to tell a Cathar wife that she should obey her husband as a good Cathar woman ought.

Will the Real Christians Please Stand Up?

Despite all these differences with institutional Christians, the Cathars regarded themselves as the real Christians. Their preferred name for themselves, in addition to "the Purified Ones," was *boni homines*, "the Good People." They regarded their opponents (the pope and his hierarchies of bishops and priests) as the bad people who had strayed from the true spirit of Christianity. In the eyes of the Cathars, the pope's church was in love with the material world, ruled by the evil god.

Just as institutional Christians appealed to an ancient tradition that included the Bible and other writings, so the Cathars also had an ancient tradition of their own. As noted above, this tradition reached back through a rich legacy of Bogomil, Manichean, and Gnostic writings.

The parts of the New Testament that the Cathars did accept could easily be given a Gnostic or Manichean reading. The most noteworthy example is the Lord's Prayer (*Pater Noster*), which played a prominent part in Cathar ritual.

Most Christians today recite the Lord's Prayer by rote, mumbling through it without much thought. If they reflected on its contents, though, they would see that it contradicts the Old Testament's view of God. The Old Testament insists that there is one God Almighty whose control extends seamlessly from the depths of Earth to the heights of Heaven. The Lord's Prayer, by contrast, rings with familiar Gnostic and Manichean themes: the sharp division between the earthly realm below and the heavenly realm above; the yearning for the Father in the Heavens to manifest his power below as he does above; and the desire to escape from the power of the Evil One who rules the realm below.

For those who have forgotten, here is the New Testament prayer that so inspired the medieval Cathars:

> Our Father in the Heavens,
> May your name be held holy.
> May your Kingdom come.
> As your will is done in Heaven,
> So may it be done on Earth.
> Give us today the bread that is needed for today.
> Forgive us our failings as we forgive those who fail us.
> Do not lead us into temptation,
> But deliver us from the Evil One.

Institutional Christians scorned the ancient tradition that the Cathars drew on as "heresy," while promoting themselves as "the one true Catholic and Apostolic

Church." But if the Cathars had won the religious wars launched against them by the pope, and had become as intolerant in victory as their enemies did, the word "heresy" would today denote what we call "Roman Catholicism." The word "Christianity," at least as used in the West, would refer to a religion that recognized two gods, had a tolerant attitude toward homosexuality, and respected the religious power of women.

Tῆε Goɒ of Tῆis Woṛłɒ Gṛọus Stṛọngεṛ

Although Cathar leaders formed a hierarchy, they did not become institutionally rigid in matters of belief. This doctrinal fluidity reflected their historical descent from Gnosticism. As noted above, Gnosticism valued personal experience (*gnosis*) over formal profession of belief (*pistis*).

This doctrinal fluidity encouraged tolerance toward the pagan sensibilities of the peasants. In effect, Catharism became a two-tiered religion. On the bottom, the polytheistic and animistic practices of the peasant masses flourished as never before in a Christian regime. On the top, the Purified Ones, always relatively few, led lives of extreme asceticism, but without seeking to suppress the old ways of the peasants.

At the same time that paganism was flourishing among peasants in Cathar areas, the leadership of the Roman Church decided to clamp down on it in Catholic areas. The reigning pope, Innocent III, viewed the pagan resurgence in Cathar areas as evidence of a conspiracy by the Devil to overthrow Christendom.

The Cathar belief in two gods easily encouraged a this-worldly attitude among Cathar peasants, even though it had an other-worldly force among the Purified Ones themselves. Some peasants came to the conclusion that maybe the evil god of this world wasn't so evil, after all. Or even if he was, he should be placated anyway, in view of his great power over material things, like crops, the weather, and cattle.

Pagan sensibilities also affected the Cathar concept of the good god. Many Cathar peasants identified the good god with the sun. This was an understandable identification in view of the preferred titles used by the Purified Ones for the good god—"Our Father in the Heavens" and "Lord of the Heavenly Hosts."

An example comes from late 12th-century Milan. A man named Bonacursus, having converted from Catharism to Catholicism, said the Cathars of Milan worshipped the sun and the moon. This is the same area in which Sibillia and Pierina de' Bugatis were arrested for worshipping the moon in the 14th century (chapter two). In 1350, Cathars in Armenia were accused of worshipping the sun.

Εntεṛ Łucifεṛ

The worship by Cathar peasants of the sun and the moon opened the door for the grand entrance of Lucifer onto the stage of European history. In the 14th century, heretics were uncovered in Austria, Brandenburg, and Bohemia. Their Roman Catholic detractors accused them of worshipping "Lucifer" and called them

"Luciferans." They were also accused of the usual crimes of murdering children and holding orgies.

Who were these Luciferans, and what were they up to? Some of their beliefs, as described by their accusers, ring with Cathar echoes. Most likely, they were a remnant group of peasants who worshipped the sun, identifying him with the good god of the Cathars.

The uncovering of sun-worship or moon-worship would naturally lead Catholic authorities to invoke the word "Lucifer." That's because of the peculiar history of this word.

Catholic literary tradition had long used "Lucifer" as a personal name for the Devil. This usage stemmed from a misinterpretation of a passage in Isaiah, as it appeared in the Vulgate (the Latin translation of the Bible).

The passage in Isaiah reads thus:

> How have you fallen from the heavens, O morning star, son of the dawn!

This passage is a mocking reference to the king of Babylon, comparing him, before his fall, to the morning star. In the Vulgate, the word for "morning star" is translated by the Latin word "Lucifer," understood as a personal name.

This translation is correct, inasmuch as "Lucifer" literally means "light-bringer," and is the standard Latin name for the morning star. However, the early church fathers misinterpreted the translation. They thought Isaiah was talking about the expulsion of the Devil from Heaven, which was far from Isaiah's mind. So they regarded the word "Lucifer" as a name of the Devil.

In pagan antiquity, as noted, writers commonly used the word "Lucifer" as a name for the morning star. They also used the word to refer to the light of day, the moon, and the goddess Diana (in the feminine form, "Lucifera").

These pagan uses of the word "Lucifer" are all logical, whereas applying the word to the Prince of Darkness is not. A more logical choice for this gloomy character would be "Umbrifer" ("shade-bringer"). But as just noted, the early church fathers misinterpreted the passage in Isaiah.

Because of this literary and religious history, the word "Lucifer" came to have two meanings for Catholic authorities: "the Devil" and "the light-bringer." So when authorities encountered Cathar peasants worshipping the sun or the moon, they found it easy to regard the offenders as worshipers of the Devil under the name of Lucifer. Thus did linguistic confusion, heretical dissent, and institutional paranoia all contribute to the demonization of peasant practices.

In time, some remnant Cathars, constantly accused of worshipping Lucifer, came to view themselves as doing so, just as some remnant *benandanti* eventually did (see chapter two). These developments all worked to inflate the importance of Lucifer in the consciousness of Europe, which in turn helped pave the way for the great witch hunts of later centuries.

A Medieval San Francisco

In the 11th & 12th centuries, various strains of Catharism spread in waves from Eastern into Western Europe. These Cathar strains established strongholds in the Netherlands, Germany, Italy, France, and Languedoc (southern France, then separate from the kingdom of France).

By 1150, the Cathars of Languedoc had succeeded in creating a counterculture in the heart of Western Europe. The region, nominally headed by the Count of Toulouse, was politically independent from the king of France. Residents spoke their own dialect of French. The area even had its own climate-system, bathed by mild breezes from the Mediterranean.

A form of Christianity prevailed in Languedoc that diverged greatly from the institutional variety pushed by Rome. Although the Purified One themselves were morbidly ascetic, the peasants enjoyed unprecedented freedom in creating meaning for themselves. They could find religious validation for their own personal experiences and ancient peasant culture in a way that was becoming increasingly difficult under institutional Christianity.

The arts flourished free of censorship. Troubadour poetry took its rise. Jews fled there because of the atmosphere of tolerance. Albi, a major city of Languedoc, became like San Francisco in the 1960s and 1970s—an easy-going, colorful oasis of cultural diversity and mild climate, but attached to a continent that had rigid institutions and less appealing weather.

The zealots of institutional Christianity in the rest of Europe were outraged at this diversity and tolerance, which they saw as a great offense to the God of love. They denounced Albi with the same fury as modern-day Christian zealots denounce San Francisco, also on behalf of the God of love.

There was a big difference, however, between the two cases. Thirteenth-century Europe had a poor appreciation of the separation of church and state. Imagine the Christian zealots of our own time in total control of the government and the army, and you'll understand what happened to the Cathars of Languedoc.

In the next chapter, we'll watch as institutional Christians forced their own beliefs about God and Heaven onto the Cathars. In the process, institutional Christianity inadvertently cut off meaning in the West from its last connections to the realms of nature, sex, and women's experience.

Chapter 5.
Onward, Christian Soldiers!

Jn 1208, Pope Innocent III, the strongest pope in the history of Christendom, called for a holy war to wipe out the Cathars of Languedoc, discussed in the last chapter. Thus was created the famous Albigensian Crusade, named after the residents of the city of Albi in Languedoc.

The Albigensian Crusade eventually crushed the Cathars on the battlefield. The Holy Inquisition, created in the crusade's wake, hunted down surviving Cathars all over Europe. Both the crusade and the Inquisition were devastating blows to religious diversity in the West. They uprooted the creation of meaning from the control of ordinary men and women interpreting their everyday life experiences in the countryside. The creation of meaning became the institutional monopoly of high-placed male bureaucrats. This chapter tells the story of that uprooting.

Christian Logic

From 1209 to 1229, Catholic troops, summoned by Innocent III and led initially by Simon de Montfort, conducted a war of extermination against the Cathars of Languedoc. During 20 years of battle, the prospects of each side rose and fell, but the Catholic forces eventually prevailed. After the war, two Cathar strongholds—Montségur and Quéribus—held out until 1244 and 1255, respectively. Montségur was reputed to be an old temple to the sun.

An example of the logic of the Catholic invaders comes from the siege of Béziers in July 1209, at the beginning of the crusade. After Catholic troops took the town, they were in a dither as to who was Catholic and who Cathar, because there was no obvious way to distinguish between the two.

The troops asked the local Catholic abbot for advice. He must have studied formal logic, which was then coming into vogue at the universities. God would surely know, he reasoned, which were the true Christians, to save them, and then damn the rest. Therefore, it was only logical that the troops should kill all the townspeople, every man, woman, and child. Convinced by this exemplary logic, the troops dispatched each resident to his or her deserved abode in the hereafter.

The capitulation of the Cathars undid the counterculture that had been thriving in Languedoc. Raimond VII, the count of Toulouse and the chief secular authority in Languedoc, swore fidelity to the Roman Church. He also forfeited one-third of his holdings to the French regent, Blanche of Castile, the recently widowed wife of King Louis VIII of France. In addition, Raimond agreed to hunt down any remaining heretics, dismiss all Jews from their jobs, and tear down the fortifications of 30 castles. Finally, he consented to let a university be built, the University of Toulouse. Its purpose was to propagate the values of institutional Christianity against Catharism.

Although the Albigensian Crusade overthrew Cathar civilization in Languedoc, it did not succeed in extirpating all the Cathars. The survivors fled to back-water areas throughout Europe. To pursue and neutralize them, the papacy created a new, centrally-controlled bureaucratic machine, the Office of the Holy Inquisition. It survives to this day, but under the name of the Congregation for the Doctrine of the Faith, currently headed by Cardinal Joseph Ratzinger. He takes a dim view of a woman's right to have an abortion, and of civil rights for gays and lesbians. We're about to see where he got his ideas from.

Burn the Faggots!

The Holy Inquisition and its later Protestant imitations were destined to cast a long shadow over European life. Although it did not appear until the High Middle Ages, the Inquisition was rooted in a concept as old as the New Testament itself— heresy. Let us take a moment to examine this seminal concept.

In ancient Greek, the word "heresy" (*hairesis*) literally means "choice." Among pagan Greeks, *hairesis* had positive associations. In the plural, the word referred to the various philosophical schools of the day, such as Platonism, Aristotelianism, and Stoicism.

For Christians, however, *hairesis* usually had negative associations. Christians were open to the idea of choice, up to the point where people made a commitment to Christian dogma. After this point, however, to deviate from the teachings of priestly authority was to insult God.

This hostility to choice dates back to the religion's founder. In an ominous remark that was to have horrifying historical repercussions later, Jesus said:

> If somebody doesn't stay with me, he'll be thrown away like field trimmings, and dry up. People gather them together and throw them into the fire, and they're burned.

The term "field trimmings" translates the Greek *klema*. This word is derived from farm life, and refers to twigs or sticks that are trimmed from bushes and trees in vineyards and orchards, gathered together into a bundle, and burned.

Jesus' use of field trimmings as a metaphor probably came from his upbringing in Nazareth, a tiny village of a few dozen families in Galilee that specialized in wine making. The metaphor conveys a fierce message: stay with me, or expect to be burned like the useless trimmings from the vineyard.

The word *klema* is close in meaning to another Greek term, *phakelos*, meaning a bundle of sticks. *Phakelos*, as a bundle of sticks to be burned, is the original source of the words "faggot" or "fagot" in various Western European languages.

Following Jesus' precedent, later Christian leaders expressed visceral hostility toward those who diverged from their teachings. Paul of Tarsus called such people perverts, saying they should be shunned:

> After one or two warnings, break off with the heretic, knowing
> that such a person is a perverted, self-convicted sinner.

Significantly, Paul condemned one group of Christians of his time because they rejected marriage and the eating of meat. Against their views, Paul insisted that the material world is the creation of a good God. Paul's criticism of these heretics is proof that a Christian tradition congenial to what would later be called "Manicheeism" was as old as the New Testament itself, as the Cathars maintained.

Jesus' metaphor about the burning of trimmings enjoyed a long life. In the Middle Ages, the Holy Inquisition appealed to it when burning unrepentant heretics alive on piles of faggots. Sometimes the Inquisition required heretics who had repented to wear an embroidered image of a faggot on their clothing, as a warning of what they deserved if they should relapse. The image made its way into popular speech, as well. Burning a heretic was called "frying a faggot," implying that the heretics themselves were sometimes called "faggots."

The association of heretics with faggots takes on added significance in view of the special history of the Cathars. They were the very heretics that the Holy Inquisition, with its zeal for burning, was created to destroy. As we saw in the last chapter, the Cathars were also associated in the minds of the Inquisition with homosexuality, so much so that the words for "Cathar" and "homosexual" became interchangeable.

These facts imply that the modern use of the word "faggot" as a slur against homosexuals, viewed as perverts fit for killing, is not a 19th-century innovation, as many maintain. In fact, use of the term in this sense can be traced back to the demonization of the Cathars in the 13th and 14th centuries. This demonization was in turn inspired by a metaphor coined by Jesus himself in the first century.

These facts also show something else: doctrinal blood-letting is not something peripheral to the true spirit of Christianity. The condemnation of heretics as perverts and their association with faggots that should be burned is solidly grounded in the sentiments of Jesus, Paul, and many church fathers and theologians. Murderous heresy-hunting is as essentially Christian as anything could be.

Sacrifices to God

Invoking Jesus' metaphor of burning the field trimmings, the Inquisition declared that heresy was "an exceptional crime" requiring exceptional methods. That meant disregarding the usual legal protections for defendants. The accused was assumed guilty until proven innocent. Mere suspicion or common gossip were enough to bring a person before the Inquisition on a charge of heresy. Witnesses who incriminated the accused were not publicly identified, and the accused was not given the right to cross-examine their testimony. The accused was also usually denied the right to counsel. In cases where counsel was allowed, a too vigorous defense of the accused could result in the counsel's being indicted for heresy.

Although the Inquisition was always coercive, in its early period it often sought reconciliation with the heretic rather than the heretic's torture, mutilation, or death. In later periods, however, when the inquisitorial machine was up and running at full steam, scenes of great horror repeatedly occurred.

Inspired by the Inquisition, secular courts in both Catholic and Protestant countries later embraced inquisitorial methods and jumped into the heresy-hunting business. In the 16th and 17th centuries, these courts were responsible for killing many people (largely women) as "witches."

During the worst episodes of the Inquisition, persons accused of heresy were tortured until they confessed their crimes and named accomplices. The tortures were horrible and could result in crippling mutilations and death. Examples: pouring alcohol over areas of the body and setting it on fire; pulling out finger nails; crushing arms and legs in vices; dislocating arm and leg joints; tearing off tongues, noses, ears, and other body parts with red-hot irons; gauging out eyes. After being tortured, the accused was forced to appear in court and swear that his or her confession was "voluntary."

Those who confessed, with or without torture, were spared the horror of being burned alive. They might be required to wear the sign of the heretic (an embroidered faggot, or some other emblem), perform acts of public penance, or be imprisoned for life on bread and water. They could also be handed over the secular authority to be publicly strangled or decapitated, and their dead bodies burned. The persons they named as accomplices were then arrested and given the same treatment.

Those who refused to confess, or who confessed but later returned to heresy, were handed over to the secular authority to be burned alive on heaps of faggots. These burnings were conducted as great public spectacles designed to cleanse and strengthen the community in the eyes of its fiercely ruling deity. These spectacles were in fact, if not in theory, human sacrifices, similar in spirit to the human sacrifices of the Indians of Meso-America. The difference is that the Indian gods were less sadistic. They just wanted blood. The victim was drugged, and his or her heart was cut out so quickly that it would still beat in the priest's hands. The Christian God of love wanted his victims not only to die but to die as horribly as possible.

Officially, it was the secular authority, not the Inquisition, that executed heretics. But secular officials almost always fell in line. Otherwise, they too could end up on a pile of faggots.

A Window Into Another World

An example of the Inquisition at work in its early period, following the Albigensian Crusade, comes from the tiny village of Montaillou in the French Pyrenees, near Albi. The village was the last place in Languedoc where people continued to actively practice Catharism.

In 1318, the Inquisition had the entire population of Montaillou arrested, except for young children, about 200 people. Their story provides a window into the rural world of the late Middle Ages. Peering through, we can see the Inquisition's real goal. It wasn't just to suppress a system of erroneous dogma. Much more was at stake—sterilizing the cultural soil that had allowed heresy to flourish. That soil was an ancient way of rural living, resistant to the power-structure of institutional Christianity. It had to be ploughed up and made receptive to the institutional seeds of the new Europe. The plough was the Holy Inquisition.

Powerful Old Widows

An important issue that divided the peasant culture of Montaillou from institutional Christianity was the status of women. Although the father was head of the Montaillou household, an old matrilineal tradition persisted in many families: husbands came to live in the houses of their wives, and children took their mother's last name. Large extended families were the norm, in which women developed their own support networks.

If the husband died before the wife, which was common, the widow became the head of the extended family and ruled it as a matriarch. These powerful old widows, at the center of female networks that ran through several families, were a principal avenue through which Catharism spread. Whereas institutional Christianity was male-dominated and church-oriented, Catharism included both male and female priests, and was practiced at home, not in a church.

In Montaillou, as in most rural areas of medieval Europe, men were not better educated than women. Each sex learned the skills that were necessary to carry out its special functions in rural life. The skills of both sexes were equally important to the community's survival.

A gender imbalance in education developed later in Europe, when education in rural areas was taken over by parish schools. These were run mostly for boys. Girls were left behind. Above the parish schools were the new universities, which developed from monasteries and cathedral schools. They were attended exclusively by men. From their ranks came the bureaucrats who ran the increasingly powerful institutions of church and state.

In Montaillou, as elsewhere in rural Europe, what today is called "folk magic" was especially the province of women. This was a system of ancient lore that dealt with the healing of people, the vitality of crops and animals, and the evocation of the spiritual powers of nature. As the educational process hardened into a system of male-dominated, church-oriented scholasticism, the lore that rural women knew became increasingly suspect as the work of the Devil. Thus did academic misogyny promote the disenchantment of the world, and with it, the loss of meaning.

The Birds & the Bees & the Goats

The status of women wasn't the only source of conflict between the people of Montaillou and institutional Christianity. They also clashed over sex itself. As noted in the last chapter, the Purified Ones of Catharism, although strictly ascetic themselves, were tolerant of the worldly practices of the mass of believers. Part of this tolerance was due to theology, since only the few who received the Cathar sacrament of consolation were required to be ascetic. But part was also due to practical politics. Catharism in the West, like Bogomilism in the East, survived by finding refuge in rural areas beyond the writ of pope and king. The country dwellers who shielded the Cathars, being heirs to millennia of pagan traditions, had a casual attitude toward sex.

For example, the peasants of Montaillou believed that extra-marital sex, even with prostitutes, was not a sin, provided it was consensual and enjoyable for both parties. Couples made no bones about living together without being married. Herbal contraceptives were used.

For theological reasons, the Purified Ones regarded homosexuality as preferable to heterosexuality. This theological loophole for homosexuality horrified institutional Christians. However, it didn't rankle the peasants of Montaillou because their culture provided ample opportunities for gay sex. Peasants of the same sex often slept together nude in the same bed. The area's shepherds, nearly all men, had their own tribal-like subculture. Spending much of their lives wandering the hills, they held most of their possessions in common, developed deep emotional bonds with each other, and rarely had social contacts with women.

Some contemporary academic theoreticians, influenced by the French philosopher Michel Foucault, insist that homosexuality as we know it today didn't exist before the 19th century. The reason: the word "homosexuality" and similar words didn't exist then.

However, the records of the Inquisition that operated around Montaillou in the early 14th century prove otherwise. The Inquisition arrested a certain Arnaud de Verniolles, an ex-Franciscan monk from nearby Pamiers. He admitted that as youth he was initiated into what he called "homophilia" by a fellow-student, who later became a priest. Afterwards, Arnaud joined a monastic order that was said to practice sodomy. Despite our worthy academic theoreticians, this situation sounds just like the Catholic Church today.

Moon Lady Rising

The Cathars of Montaillou weren't the only ones who caught the eye of the Inquisition. Montaillou Catholics themselves tended to be nature-loving and pantheistic, contrasting sharply with the other-worldly line that Rome was then pushing. An example is Raymond de Laburat, a Catholic peasant from nearby Sabarthès. Like many of his rural Catholic contemporaries, he regarded "the body of Christ" as the natural world. Excommunicated for this belief, he said he wanted to see all the churches destroyed and the mass celebrated in the open air, where it belonged.

Many of the numerous saints worshipped by Catholic peasants were actually old pagan deities with a Christian veneer. The most important was the Virgin Mary. She appears but rarely in the New Testament, where Jesus sometimes treats her peremptorily. But by the Middle Ages, institutional Christianity had turned Mary into the Queen of Heaven, standing on a crescent moon, with stars around her head. Many of the Catholic peasants of Montaillou viewed this figure as an image of the moon, or the earth, or mother nature. Some viewed her as a redeemer in her own right.

In the guise of Mary, the Queen of Heaven has continued to the present day, a crumpled encapsulation within patriarchal Catholic dogma of the last vestiges of woman-focused nature worship. One of the goals of this book is to come to her aid, helping her break free of the institutional capsule that continues to contain and co-opt her. Mary is too important to be left a hostage of the institutional Church.

Bleaching the Peasant Culture

During the High Middle Ages, the universities started turning out a new breed of rigorously trained theologian. After polishing their shiny dogmas in the lecture hall, they sought to impose them on the rough pantheistic beliefs of the peasants working in the fields. The result in many cases was to drive the peasants into the arms of the Cathars, who were polytheistic and tolerant of beliefs with rough edges.

In addition, the peasants were deeply impressed with the simplicity and sincerity of the Purified Ones who led Catharism. The Purified Ones actually practiced the simplicity they preached, without trying to impose it on others. They presented a marked contrast to the comfortable, highly educated agents of Rome. These wanted to bleach the color out of everyone else's life while keeping a whole spectrum of institutional privileges for themselves.

Authority and Meaning

The peasants of Montaillou were lucky in their dealings with the Inquisition, because its ferocity had not yet come into full force. Most were allowed to return to their homes. Only twenty-five were tried and convicted.

Their punishments were varied: obligatory wearing of a yellow cross as a sign of heresy, pilgrimages, confiscation of goods, and imprisonment. Only one man from Montaillou, Guillaume Fort, was burned at the stake as a relapsed Cathar.

Though mild by later standards, the methods of the Inquisition at Montaillou taught the peasants a lesson: religion was not a matter of personal experience and choice, or of participating in their age-old rural culture. Religion was a matter of submitting to institutional authority. To directly invoke spiritual powers without the mediation of sanctifying bureaucracy was an invitation to the Devil. Grace could come only through institutional validation. This was the same stern message given to Sibillia, Pierina de' Bugatis, and Joan of Arc.

The Inquisition triumphed in 14th-century Montaillou, just as would later triumph throughout much of Europe and parts of the Americas. But the victors overlooked certain larger questions, ones that are the subject of this book: if people's spiritual lives are channeled through bureaucratic institutions, what happens to the meaning of life when the institutions start to totter? And what will become of sex and the love of nature when meaning is allowed to flow only through bureaucratic conduits? Finally, what would happen to the quest for meaning if human institutions were made to serve human needs, rather than the other way around?

Power, Wealth & Real Estate

The Inquisition did not just extend institutional control over belief, or sterilize rural culture. It also increased the power and wealth of those who ran it.

The cost of running the process was paid for by the accused, whose property was seized and divided up among the accusers and the inquisitors. In some areas, heresy-hunting became a major industry. In 1360, the Inquisitor Nicolas Eymeric of Aragon complained that the secular authorities were no longer giving enough support to the Inquisition:

> In our days there are no more rich heretics; so that princes, not seeing much money in prospect, will not put themselves to any expense; it is a pity that so salutary an institution as ours should be so uncertain of its future.

When ambitious political leaders coveted the wealth, or resented the influence, of certain segments of society, the envied could always be accused of heresy, and their assets seized. The great precedent for this abuse was the Albigensian Crusade. By supporting the pope's war against the Cathars, King Louis VIII of France hoped to annex Languedoc into his realm. Although Louis died before the defeat of the Cathars in 1229, the war weakened Languedoc, which fell more and more under French influence in succeeding years. In 1271, King Philip III of France brought the entire region under his rule.

Knightly Sodomy

The most famous case of heresy-hunting for the sake of money and power involved the Knights Templars, a monastic military order that had fought in the crusades in Palestine. In a sudden sweep on Friday the 13th, October 1307, Philippe the Fair, King of France, had 5,000 members of the order arrested throughout France. He hauled them before the Inquisition, charging them with four counts of heresy: (1) that initiates were required to spit on the cross and reject Christianity; (2) that they kissed the initiator on the mouth, cock, and ass hole; (3) that sodomy was expected of all Templars; and (4) that members participated in secret rites where they worshipped a non-Christian deity.

At first, Jacques de Molay, the Grand Master of the Order, and the other defendants denied all charges. But when they were tortured, many "confessed." Under a plea-bargaining deal, de Molay himself agreed to plead guilty to rejecting Christ if the charge of homosexuality was dropped. Later, he retracted the confession, even though he knew the withdrawal would cause him to be burned alive.

On November 22, Pope Clement V, a stooge of King Philippe who would soon move the papacy from Rome to Avignon, issued a bull urging all monarchs of Europe to emulate the king's action. In the next few years, the Templars were hunted down through much of Europe. Exiled, imprisoned, or executed, they saw their property confiscated, and the order was abolished.

At the time of their arrest, the Templars were the chief bankers of Europe, having accumulated great wealth from their plunder of Palestine. Both pope and king were among their debtors. They were also exempt from many taxes and much secular law, and worshipped in their own chapels from which non-Templars were excluded. Legally, they were not even subjects of Philippe, but were accountable only to the pope.

Philippe was hungry for money due to his large war debts. Previously he had debased the currency, arrested all the Jews in his kingdom, seized their property, and banished them. His treatment of the Templars was consistent with his ruthless policy of subsidizing, by an means possible, the emerging nation-state of France.

Although some Templars may have practiced sodomy, the charges against them were probably just a frame-up for the sake of grabbing their money. Still, their story has significant implications for sexual history and the history of meaning. It shows the extent to which heresy and homosexuality had become associated in the minds of institutional Christians. It also shows how the newly emerging nation-state could exploit both these charges to aggrandize itself.

The Demonization of Jews

Cathars and Templars weren't the only victims of the Inquisition. As noted in the last chapter, Cathar-controlled Languedoc provided a haven for Jews. As in other aspects of life, Cathar tolerance toward Jews was a holdover of earlier customs. These began to crumble in the 11th century, as the church, the state, and the university consolidated their powers over the rest of the population. Although Christian theology was anti-Semitic in the early Middle Ages, Jews faced only periodic harassment in this period. The social machinery necessary to carry out large-scale persecutions did not emerge until the late Middle Ages.

The Cathar tolerance of Jews had been a bone in the throat of institutional Christians. As noted above, after the defeat of the Cathars in the Albigensian Crusade, the Count of Toulouse was forced to dismiss all Jews from their jobs. The Inquisition, which was the spirit of the Albigensian Crusade in a new guise, started giving Jews close scrutiny. Secular authorities, seeing the Inquisition put Jews on the defensive, had fewer scruples in plundering them.

The situation for Jews became especially bad in Spain. In 1478, the Spanish Inquisition was created. Its first task was to question and test *Maranos* and *Moriscos* (Jews and Moslems who had recently converted to Christianity). In 1492, their Most Catholic Majesties, Ferdinand and Isabella, expelled the Jews from Spain, seized their property, and used the profits to pay for Christopher Columbus's voyage to the New World. Thanks to this plundering of the Jews, European Christians were able to bring war, disease, and Inquisition to the American Indians. But more of this story later, in chapter eight.

Institutional Machinery

All the horrors mentioned in this chapter converged to a common effect: the uprooting of the quest for meaning from the control of ordinary people and its transfer to powerful institutions. The demonization of Cathars, Templars, and Jews lubricated the gears of the institutional machines that were creating modern Europe. At the same time, this demonization consigned whole ranges of human experience to the realm of the Devil. Sex, women's experience, religious diversity, and the natural world were slipping into eclipse. The state, the church, and the university loomed ever larger, extending their shadows across the landscape of European life. Eventually they replaced both personal choice and ancient peasant culture as the arbiters of both meaning and power.

A Shocking Discovery

As inquisitorial eyes looked ever deeper into private lives in the back-country, institutional Christians made a shocking discovery. Great numbers of peasants, and not just isolated groups of heretics, held to beliefs and practices that were clearly unchristian, at least by the standards of the higher clergy and the new universities. How could this great affront to God have arisen? Was there a conspiracy afoot by the Devil to overthrow Christian civilization?

Yes, said many of the best and brightest minds in the Christian establishment. We must organize, they insisted, to purge Europe of this hellish conspiracy.

And so they did, as the next chapter will show.

Chapter 6.

Witches

J n order to combat the spread of the Cathar heresy in the 13th century, the church created the Holy Inquisition, which later took on a life of its own. In earlier chapters, we have watched the heresy hunters at work against the Cathars, as well as Sibillia, Pierina de' Bugatis, Joan of Arc, the Good Travelers, the Knights Templars, and Jews.

In this chapter and the next, we will turn to the historical culmination of heresy hunting, the great witch hunts of the 16th and 17th centuries. Two forces led to this culmination—the continual expansion of the notion of heresy, and the growing machinery for suppressing heretics.

As the machinery of heresy-hunting grew, so did the preoccupation with witchcraft. Eventually witchcraft became the heresy of heresies. Invoking the name of Jesus, witch hunters all across Europe associated women's experience, sex, and nature-worship with the Devil.

Thus marginalized, these realms of experience fell off the horizon when Christian thinkers reflected on what it meant to be human. Although Christian theology eventually lost control over European thought, its diminished understanding of human nature persisted. It helped create the modern Western notion of the person as a man, and one alienated from women, sex, and nature. This long diminishment of humanity, begun under Christianity and continued into modernity, has crippled the magic of life in both eras.

The Great Fault-line of Europe

The historical force that most resisted the Christian diminishment of meaning was ancient peasant culture. For that reason, it became the ultimate target in both the early persecution of Cathars and the later persecution of witches.

The Inquisition's persecution of the Cathars led it to take a hard, new look at peasant culture. That's because the peasants often gave the Cathars refuge, and because Catharism soaked up rural pagan practices. The Inquisition, as it poked around in the countryside, was unnerved to discover Cathar peasants worshipping the sun or the moon. In the paranoid eyes of the Inquisition, these rural folk were worshipping "Lucifer." The Kingdom of the Devil was at hand!

The new universities empowered the Inquisition's paranoia by cranking out an elite of intolerant ideologues. To them, Christianity was defined by authoritative pronouncements in Greek and Latin, not by personal religious experience or rural custom. The new academic elite wanted to purify Christianity of the accretions it had picked up from illiterate peasant culture. At the same time, both the church and the state were consolidating their organizational powers over the countryside.

A fault-line developed across the terrain of the late medieval world. On one side was a small minority of university-educated ideologues, all men, who staffed the growing bureaucracies of church, state, and university. Empowered with new machines of social control, and flush with victory over the Cathar heresy, they wanted to impose religious uniformity everywhere. On the other side was a great mass of unlettered peasants. Their religion was a multi-colored mosaic of institutional Christianity and rural paganism which they created based on their own life experiences.

When this fault-line slipped, the great witch hunts rippled across the High Middle Ages and the Renaissance. They would sever Europe's last connections of meaning with women's experience, sex, and nature worship. And that would change the West forever, including our lives today.

Bewitchment vs. Demonic Witchcraft

Sometimes we can get an insight into historical upheavals by looking at shifts in the meanings of words. So it is with the words "witchcraft" and "witch." In pre-Christian Europe (and many other pagan cultures as well), "witchcraft" meant the inflicting of harm on people through curses, charms, or the invocation of spirits and gods. This view differed from the Christian one. To avoid misunderstanding, let's call the pre-Christian notion of witchcraft *bewitchment*.

People in pre-Christian Europe took bewitchment seriously, especially in times of great social stress, like war or crop failure. Nonetheless, the procedures of pagan law made it difficult to prove that a bewitcher had actually harmed someone through bewitchment. And if the accuser failed to make good on the charge, he or she could be punished in place of the accused.

The focus in prosecuting cases of bewitchment was on the actual sufferings of the victim, such as the onset of disease, or injury from accident, or the withering of crops. It was not on whether the accused invoked a certain god or spirit. By their very nature, polytheistic or animistic religions are loath to offend any god or spirit, even nasty ones. All the gods must get their due.

Christianity, like other monotheistic religions, changed the meaning of witchcraft from *bewitchment* to something more sinister, which we'll call *demonic witchcraft*. This is bewitchment with something extra—help from the Devil. In the Christian view, the horror of demonic witchcraft lies not only in the harm done to others, but also in calling on the Devil to do the harm.

Pacts with the Devil

The notion of demonic witchcraft, as opposed to simple bewitchment, is a natural byproduct of monotheism. That's because monotheists acknowledge only one true God, theirs. All other gods are false. If monotheistic clergy do not channel (or at least condone) some alleged spiritual power, then it can't be from the one true God. That leaves just one alternative, the Devil (contrary to polytheism, which offers many alternatives).

Christian clergy have diligently cultivated this mentality throughout the ages. When they encounter people who summon spiritual powers on their own, apart from church channels, they often conclude that the summoners are worshiping false gods. But false gods are just so many masks worn by the Devil. Therefore, to worship false gods in the hope of getting something is to make a pact with the Devil. And that is *heresy*, or treason against God. What do we call people who specialize in this sort of heresy, if not witches? And what sort of people are most qualified to hunt down and kill witches, if not professional inquisitors?

Christian clerics haven't always drawn out the full implications of this line of reasoning. And even when they have, they often lacked the power to impose their beliefs on everybody else. In the High Middle Ages and Renaissance, the conclusions were drawn, and the power was available. From this lethal combination came the great European witch hunts.

The Heresy Balloon

The Christian notion of demonic witchcraft fostered the development of a fearsome stereotype of the witch. This stereotype did not reach its apogee until rather late, in the 17th century. Nonetheless, it drew on doctrinal motifs about heretics that went back to the 13th century.

After the Albigensian Crusade, the papacy pumped more and more energy into the doctrinal balloon dealing with heretics. A papal preoccupation with sex remained a notable part of the inflation. As the heresy balloon swelled over the years, it took on various frightening shapes, as if in a big Macy's Day Parade in Hell. In the end, it blimped out into the figure of the demonic witch, scaring decent folk all over Europe.

The ballooning began in 1233, when Pope Gregory IX issued his bull *Vox in Rama*. It accused certain heretics (probably Cathars) of engaging in bisexual orgies and worshiping Lucifer as the creator of the heavenly bodies. After issuing it, Gregory sent Dominican inquisitors into southern France to hunt down any lingering Cathars.

In 1256, Pope Alexander IV permitted inquisitors to use torture to extract confessions from accused heretics. In 1312, Pope Clement V issued his bull *Ad Nostrum*. It accused certain heretics of claiming that sex was not sinful when demanded by nature. In 1326, Pope John XXII issued *Super Illius Specula*, denouncing heretics who sacrificed to demons and who made pacts with the Devil. In 1451, Pope Nicholas V declared that sorcery as such was subject to the Inquisition, even when heresy as previously understood was not involved.

The last big puff into the heresy balloon came in 1484, when Pope Innocent VIII issued his epochal bull *Summis desiderantes affectibus*. It accused witches in Germany of having sex with demons that united with either sex at will. Innocent believed that this practice resulted in a loss of fertility in the fields and among women and farm animals. The bull also marked the beginning of a reign of terror against supposed witches that lasted for about 200 years. Eventually the terror engulfed both Catholic and Protestant lands, and was pushed by both religious and secular courts.

The Stereotype Polished

According to the witch stereotype in its most developed form, in the 17th century, a witch was a person (commonly a woman) who had bound herself or himself to the Devil in order to possess supernatural powers. She or he also flew through the air at night, attended nocturnal assemblies that included wild sex rites ("sabbats"), killed infants and ate their flesh, and conspired to overthrow Christian civilization.

This stereotype takes paranoia about women and sex and combines it with monotheistic hatred for alternative gods, especially nature gods. Add to this concoction the unlimited institutional power to coerce others, and you get the equivalent of putting a match to a pile of faggots. Not surprisingly, most of those who went up in flames were women, people who practiced alternative forms of sexuality, and people who invoked the spiritual powers of nature.

Witches Old & New

Because the Christian stereotype of the demonic witch is so familiar to us today, we may not fully appreciate the extent of its difference from earlier pagan views. So let's take a moment to compare the Christian stereotype to a classic pagan depiction.

Perhaps the most awesome portrayal of a witch in pagan classical literature is that of Medea in Euripides' play of the same name. Written in the 5th century B.C., Euripides' electrifying work has burned the character of Medea into the consciousness of generations. Yet what is often overlooked is how much she differs from the later Christian stereotype of the witch.

Medea is a cunning woman, or a wise woman, learned in charms, potions, and incantations. She is also the granddaughter of the sun, possessing from him magical implements. Through her craft, she has the power for both good and evil. Using her power for good, she promises to help the king of Athens make his barren wife conceive.

The evil use of Medea's power is the subject of Euripides' play. In the first scene, Medea's husband, Jason, spurns her for the young daughter of the king of Corinth. After initial protests, Medea feigns agreement to the new marriage. She gives her youthful rival a golden crown and robe once owned by the sun. When the new bride dons the gleaming gifts, she breaks into flames and burns to death. When her father, the king, embraces his daughter's corpse, he too catches fire and is killed. In the meantime, Medea slays the two young sons she had borne to Jason in their halcyon days.

When Jason returns to punish Medea, he finds her standing invulnerable in a dragon-drawn chariot given her by the sun. Departing in triumph with the bodies of her dead children, she snarls at her helpless husband "Go home and bury your new bride."

Euripides pulls out all the stops in developing the fearsome character of Medea, slyly playing on patriarchal fears about women's witchy powers. The effect is devastating, and must have knocked the Athenian audience out of their seats. Even so, however, Euripides does *not* demonize the gods associated with Medea. That is the key point for us.

Medea's descent from the sun is presented as something positive. The evil lies in the bad use of a good lineage, not the lineage itself. A similar situation exists with Hecate, the goddess of the old moon and the dead. Euripides has Medea invoke Hecate in making threats against her enemies. Nonetheless, the playwright does not impugn the goddess herself:

> I swear by Hecate, my mistress—
> Whom I adore above all the gods,
> Whom I have made my partner,
> Who dwells in my house's deep recesses—
> None of them shall grieve my heart and thrive.

If this play had been written by a medieval Christian cleric rather than an ancient pagan playwright, much would be different. The gods invoked by Medea would come off as manifestations of the Devil, understood as the cosmic source of evil. Medea's sins would not only be her murders but also the pact she made with the Devil to get her powers. The implicit moral of the play would not be "Live in balance and moderation, giving all the gods their due." Instead it would be "Beware of the Devil, who is everywhere, especially in sex and women, and above all in witches."

FOR THE GREATER GLORY OF GOD

As the powers of church, state, and university grew in Europe, the stereotype of the demonic witch ballooned. Taking advantage of these parallel developments,

Christian authorities steadily expanded their war against those they believed had made a pact with the Devil.

The most fearsome examples of the witch hunts occurred on the continent, less so in England. Defendants were arrested and tortured until they confessed to embodying some or all of the stereotype of the demonic witch. If they were quick to confess, they would receive mercy—being strangled, hanged, or beheaded, and their dead bodies burned on large bundles of faggots. Otherwise, they would be burned alive. In either case, they met the fate recommended by Jesus in his metaphor of the field trimmings. These were Bible-believing times.

An example from the earlier period of the witch hunts, following the Cathar persecution, is the 14th-century case of Gabrina degli Albeti, a citizen of Reggio Emilia, Italy. In the summer of 1375, at the insistence of the town vicar, Gabrina was brought to trial before a secular court and accused of being "a witch woman" (*mulier malefica*). Her accusers said she taught people the use of herbs and had them pray to the stars. "Herbs" was often a code word, implying that the accused taught people about contraception and abortion.

Gabrina was convicted. As punishment, her tongue was cut out, and she was branded on her face. Her case shows that secular courts, increasingly resorting to inquisitorial methods in imitation of the Inquisition, could be just as ferocious as their religious models.

Gabrina's judges wanted to make a lasting impression with her case, and they succeeded. As a result of the trial, the word "Gabrina" came to mean "witch" in the local dialect. It occurs with this meaning in the famous 16th-century poem *Orlando Furioso* by Ludovico Ariosto, who came from Gabrina's hometown.

An example of the later witch hunts is the 17th-century case of Anna Ebeler of Augsburg, Germany. Ebeler, age 67, was a lying-in-maid. That is, she was a midwife who attended mother and infant in the six to eight weeks following birth, known as the lying-in period.

In early 1669, Ebeler was accused of debilitating some of her clients rather than helping them. In ordinary times, there would have been an inquest concerning her competence. But because of the prevailing witch-hunt mentality, she was arrested and threatened with torture unless she confessed to having had sex with the Devil.

Knowing that the tortures were horrible and that a woman in her position had no hope of escape, Ebeler confessed. She tearfully pleaded with her judges for a merciful execution (public decapitation, instead of being burned alive). Her judges granted her request.

Ebeler breathed a sigh of relief. On March 12, 1669, she was placed on a horse-drawn cart, to be taken to the place of execution. However, Ebeler didn't realize that her most-Christian judges were not yet through with her. When she was on the cart, the blouse of this 67-year-old woman was ripped off, and both her breasts were squeezed with red-hot tongs. After being carried thus to the public square, humiliated and sobbing in pain, Ebeler was beheaded, and her body was burned.

Accused witches could be tortured until they named accomplices, who were tortured until they too named accomplices, and so on. An example is Johannes Junius, the mayor of Bamberg, Germany. He was arrested and tortured in the summer of 1628. After confessing and naming accomplices, he was executed.

Before his death, Junius managed to sneak out a letter to his daughter Veronica. The letter says his confession was a complete fabrication to stop the tortures. His tormentors told him what to confess and whom to implicate. At first he refused. But he was tortured, first with the thumb-screws, then with the strappado. This device consisted of a rope attached to the hands of the prisoner, tied behind the back. The prisoner was lifted by the rope, with weights attached to the feet, and then suddenly jerked up and let drop, to dislocate the shoulders:

> And then came also—God in highest heaven have mercy—the executioner, and put the thumb-screws on me, both hands bound together, so that the blood ran out at the nails, and everywhere, so that for four weeks I could not use my hands, as you can see from the writing. ... Then I thought heaven and earth were at an end; eight times did they draw me up and let me fall again [in the strappado], so that I suffered terrible agony.

Piety vs. Humanity

Innocent VIII's bull of 1484 opened the gates to a new level of carnage in Europe. But the new witch-hunting frenzy was not one great explosion. It was more like a thick, bubbling stew in a cauldron. Clusters of local trials would rise to the surface, break, dissipate, and then bubble up again. Some areas, like England, where torture was rare, saw only sporadic outbreaks of cruelty. Other parts of Europe, especially Germany, saw periods of sustained bloodshed. Despite local variability, however, the overall pattern was clear. A great upwelling of torture and killing appeared in much of Europe in the 16th & 17th centuries, justified by appeals to the Bible, and stirred and heated by the learned and powerful.

For a while, one phenomenon managed to put a damper on the witch hunts, Renaissance humanism. It was much different from what today goes by the name of humanism, being originally a literary reaction against the scholasticism of the universities. The Renaissance humanists disliked the scholastics' emphasis on theology, logic, and science. Instead, the humanists pushed for poetry, grammar, rhetoric, moral philosophy, history, and research in Greek and Latin literature.

But then something remarkable happened. Through the recovery of ancient pagan manuscripts, especially the writings of Plato, some Renaissance humanists became practitioners of a learned form of beneficent magic. They associated this magic with the notion of human dignity and the "inter-affectedness" (*sympatheia*) of the cosmos, which they viewed as a great living being. Giovanni Pico della Mirandola gave classic expression to these ideas in his *Speech on Human Dignity*.

Thinkers with these views felt a sense of kinship with the rural folk healers and wizards whom the church was demonizing, and were skeptical of the theologians' stereotype of the demonic witch. As a result of humanist influences, the witch hunts leveled off a bit in the first half of the 16th century.

Even so, not everyone influenced by Renaissance humanism was critical of the witch hunts. Jean Bodin, the 16th-century French political philosopher, made a plea for religious tolerance for Jews, Muslims, Protestants, and Catholics. However, he was an enthusiastic backer of the witch hunts and bitterly denounced those who criticized them.

Unfortunately, a powerful force was at work against the new humanist values—the growing piety of the Reformation and the Counter-Reformation. Catholics proved how pious they were by demonizing Protestants, and Protestants did the same in regard to Catholics. Despite their many differences, both sides concurred in defining who they were by demonizing those who differed from themselves. This penchant for the demonization of people who were different served to re-inflame the witch-hunt mentality in both Catholic and Protestant lands, and in both religious and secular courts.

A Mighty Fortress is Our God

Martin Luther was originally somewhat indifferent to witches, not out of a spirit of toleration, but because of his preoccupation with fighting the papacy. Later, though, he said:

> I should have no compassion on these witches; I would burn all of them.

After abolishing the priesthood, Lutherans found themselves in the embarrassing position of lacking the necessary priestly tools (such as exorcism) to fight the Devil. So they brandished their vernacular copies of the Bible to ward off the Devil, just as Catholics brandished their crucifixes.

John Calvin of Geneva is an example of how ferocious Protestant divines could be. Under the guise of providing safety from Catholic persecution, Calvin lured the Unitarian Michael Servetus to Geneva, burned him as a heretic, and then boasted of the feat. At Geneva, the most trivial offenses were suppressed. Dancing was illegal. A group of bridesmaids were arrested for decorating a bride with too much color. A child was beheaded for striking his father. G. Rattray Taylor rightly observes:

> What the Puritans and Calvinists achieved at the Reformation was the reestablishment of the depressive, guilt-ridden attitude as the whole source of religion.

Holocaust

How many people perished at the hands of the witch hunters? A few decades ago, estimates ranged as high as 9,000,000. Today, many researchers believe the number was as low as 100,000.

Both estimates are shots in the dark. Alleged witches were tried before the Inquisition, other religious courts, and secular courts. Only a fraction of the trial records have survived. Of these, some of the most important remain concealed. The Vatican, for example, has never opened its archives on the matter. Many courthouses and libraries throughout Europe do not even know what records they contain, to say nothing of archives destroyed by flood, fire, earthquake, and warfare. We will never know how many died.

One thing is certain, though: the witch hunts were frequent enough, and lasted long enough, to make a deep impression on the consciousness of Europe. Evidence for this impact is the prominent role played by the Devil and witches in the decrees of popes, bishops, and councils; in the treatises of the learned; and in the works of poets, dramatists, painters, and sculptors. Egged on by the educated elite, European authorities made a frightening example of many people they believed were in league with the Devil. Nobody forgot the lesson.

The word "holocaust" comes from a Greek term meaning "whole burnt-offering." In ancient pagan times, the offered-up victims were animals. The Christian age gave the concept a more generous embrace. The great witch hunts of the 16th & 17th centuries can justifiably be called a holocaust because large numbers of people were systematically burned as sacrifices in order to purify the community of devilish influences and appease the ruling deity.

The key word here is "systematically." The best-educated minds of the times developed and promulgated a demonizing ideology. Religious and secular authorities created specialized bureaucracies to implement the demonization. Exterminating bureaucrats diligently perfected techniques of torture and execution.

Imagine what the witch hunters could have done, had they possessed the technological resources of the 20th century. Alas, we know. The holocausting of Jews by Nazi Germany can be seen as the witch-hunt mentality taken to its technological limits. For the 20th century, that is. We have yet to see what possibilities will be brought to us by 21st-century technology.

Women

Until the 14th century, victims of the witch trials were about evenly divided between women and men. In later centuries, the peak period, women became the great majority of victims, although there was some local variation. Older women who had never married, or who were widows, were especially at risk for being accused of witchcraft, as were rebellious women of any age.

Because women did not constitute a majority of victims in all times and places, some scholars have questioned the importance of gender to the witch hunts. However, they overlook the other side of the coin of persecution. *All* the persecutors—popes, inquisitors, priests, academics, jurists, marshals, torturers, and the presiding deity himself—were male. In the worst period, after 1484, the witch hunts were a systematic and sadistic male assault on women, especially women who lived outside the immediate control of men.

The witch hunters' focus on women was no accident. Witch hunting evolved from heresy hunting. Among the Cathars, women performed the role of priest and prophet, as we saw in chapter four. In the countryside, elderly Cathar widows often became matriarchs of extended clans, and were major proselytizers for their religion. Catharism encouraged wives to leave their husbands and live in all-female houses independent of male control. The Inquisition, created in the wake of the Albigensian Crusade, sought to force Cathar women back into the narrow religious roles of institutional Christianity.

When the inquisitors turned their attention to rural peasant culture, which had nurtured Catharism, they discovered that peasant women played important religious and cultural roles. They were healers, herbalists, and midwives. They gave advice on contraception and abortion. They invoked the spirits of hearth and heath. Most viewed themselves as good Christians, but their practices drew heavily on surviving pagan traditions, including the worship of old pagan spirits and gods. Their brand of Christianity—magical, rural, and experiential—was alien to the religion of the male, university-educated elite, which was doctrinal, urban, and institutional.

The new universities, which vigorously pushed dogmatic conformity, were attended by men only and had evolved from all-male monasteries or all-male cathedral schools. As education in Europe increasingly became a matter of university study, the knowledge possessed by rural women fell in status. To be learned and rational was to think like a man, a God-like activity. Women's mysteries were an invitation to the Devil.

Womeᴎ & тhe Devil

Monastic ideals continued to dominate the church and the university throughout the Middle Ages and into the Renaissance. In all three institutions—monastery, church, and university—piety meant putting aside the joys of this world, especially sex. The important thing was to prepare for eternal life with God in the world to come. To be a professor, a priest, or a monk was to be celibate, or at least to profess to be so.

Heterosexual men who lived in this world viewed their sexual attraction to women as a stumbling block put in their paths by the Devil. It was only a small step to viewing women themselves as devilish. Homosexual men became conflicted and hypocritical. They had furtive sexual relations with other men in the institution, while publicly preaching that such behavior was sinful.

Regardless of their sexual orientation, the men who ran the church, the university, and the monastery were often neurotic, erotically crippled, and estranged from women's realities. When they did cast their eyes on women, what they saw was the other, the unknown, the temptation, the threat, the Devil.

The witch hunters, who carried out in practice what the universities taught in theory, were university-educated or members of monastic orders, or both. Two classic examples were the Dominicans Heinrich Kramer and Jakob Sprenger, active in Germany. It was to endorse their efforts that Pope Innocent VIII issued his infamous bull of 1484, inaugurating the worst phase of the witch hunts.

Kramer and Sprenger wrote a classic manual on how to identify and hunt down witches, *Witch Hammer* (*Malleus Maleficarum*). The book repeatedly associates the Devil with women and sex, as in these memorable words:

> A woman is beautiful to look upon, contaminating to the touch,
> and deadly to keep. ... All witchcraft comes from carnal lust,
> which is in women insatiable.

Witch Hammer is filled with paranoid fears about sex: Witches make men lose the ability to ejaculate. Bisexual demons have sex with men, collect their semen, and then deposit it in women, who give birth to witches. Midwives consecrate newborn infants to Lucifer.

In 16th- and 17th-century Europe, the men who ran the church, the university, and the monastery were fearful of women, sex, nature, and religious diversity. Drawing on the old connection between heresy and women, they concocted the stereotype of the demonic witch. Invoking this stereotype from the pinnacles of institutional power, they launched a massacre of women and called it piety.

The Father-&-Son Act

The misogyny of the witch hunts was part of a larger trend—the increasing masculinization of an already-patriarchal Christianity. Other examples of this trend were the rise of Bible-driven Protestantism and changes in the status of Mary among Catholics.

Protestant divines, looking for a replacement to hierarchical tradition as the bedrock of faith, settled on the Bible, with special emphasis on the misogynistic writings of Paul of Tarsus. At the same time, they took an ax to the worship of Mary, the saints, and the angels. As a result, most Protestant sects lost all female images of the divine. God the Father from the Old Testament and God the Son from the New Testament hogged the Protestant stage, and with a vengeance.

The Puritans were the worst of all. They invaded existing churches, smashed the statuary of Mary and the saints, and white-washed murals. John Knox published a pamphlet entitled *The First Blast of the Trumpet Against the Monstrous Regiment of Women.* Thomas Hall published *The Loathsomeness of Long Hair.* The Puritans wanted to make men more masculine, and women, invisible.

Finger Puppets

To counteract Protestantism, the Catholic hierarchy launched the Counter-Reformation. But in its efforts to reform and modernize, the Catholic hierarchy was unwilling to let go of Mary, the saints, and the angels. To the contrary, they were emphasized even more, to distinguish Catholicism from its Protestant rivals. Nonetheless, a big change occurred that is often overlooked by church historians. Mary and company were reduced to so many finger puppets, fitted to the hands of the institutional church. They lost their rootedness in the experiential life of the peasantry and women.

When peasants in the early Middle Ages had turned their thoughts to the Queen of Heaven, their principal concerns were their bodies, their crops, their animals, and the weather. Although priests interjected a call for penance when they could, they couldn't smother the rural magic.

After the Albigensian Crusade in the 13th century, the hierarchy worked steadily to rein in the magical, feminine, and anarchic elements that had circulated in early medieval Christianity. With the Counter-Reformation, the clergy finally got control of Marian chemistry. Whatever experience the faithful might have of Mary, priests precipitated from it a single message: do penance, and submit to the authority of the church. Otherwise, the vision was discounted.

Today the Catholic faithful still have experiences of Mary that don't fit into the institutional mold. To that extent, a vestige of the old Mary still moves in the world. But as filtered and proclaimed by the modern hierarchy, Mary has lost all her old connections to Moon Lady Rising and become a mere mouthpiece for papal bulls.

A good example is provided by the famous "three secrets of Fatima," delivered by Mary at Fatima, Portugal, in 1917. According to the Vatican, the three secrets are about penance, international politics, and the well-being of the pope. They have nothing to do with the day-to-day experiences of women or peasants. The official Mary of today's Roman Catholic Church is little more than the pope in drag.

In the next chapter, we'll take the witch hunters' attitudes toward women and put them into a larger of context of beliefs about sex. These beliefs created a model of human experience that outlived its creators and has continued to affect the quest for meaning today.

Chapter 7.
Demonic Sex

Jn the last chapter, we explored the role of misogyny in the great witch hunts of the 16th and 17th centuries. We saw that the witch hunts were an example of the increasing masculinization of an already-patriarchal Christianity. Other examples were the rise of Bible-driven Protestantism and the co-option of Mary by the Catholic hierarchy. These developments all worked together to rob women's experience of meaning.

In this chapter we'll see how the witch hunters strove to demean sex, pushing it ever farther into the realm of the Devil. Their principal weapon was the notion of "the witches' sabbat," which they used to discredit surviving pagan traditions that celebrated sex as part of religion. Their efforts paid off. The West became ever more alienated from sex, a development that lessened the magic of life.

Bisexual Demons

The witch hunters' obsession with sex, like their assault on women, evolved from heresy hunting. As noted in chapter four, the Inquisition had so identified Cathars with homosexuals that the same vernacular words came to mean both. As the educated elite in later centuries inflated the stereotype of the demonic witch, they projected all sorts of sexual fantasies onto both demons and witches.

The elite were especially vexed at the thought that the same demon could have sex with a man, and then with a woman. When having sex with a man, the demon was called a "succubus" ("lying on the bottom"). When having sex with a woman, the demon was called an "incubus" ("lying on the top"). Pope Innocent VIII's bull of 1484, which launched the worst phase of the witch hunts, explicitly mentions these demons:

> Many persons of both sexes, heedless of their own salvation and
> deviating from the Catholic faith, abuse themselves with incubus
> and succubus demons.

In making this pronouncement, Innocent VIII drew on a long-standing academic tradition about demons and sex. One of the knottier questions addressed by this learned tradition was this: How can demons, which are beings without bodies, have sex? Caesarius of Heisterbach, a 13th-century monk and historian, offered a memorable answer. Demons collect all the semen that is ejaculated "contrary to nature" and use it to make bodies for themselves! However demons got their bodies, sex with them was considered the moral equivalent of "buggery" (meaning both "heresy" and "homosexuality").

Although some witch hunters felt that homosexuality was so base as to be below even the Devil, most associated it with witch practices. For example, the Inquisition at Avignon in 1582 delivered this judgment against a group of male and female witches:

> You men have fornicated with succubi and you women with incubi. You have wretchedly committed genuine sodomy and the most unmentionable of crimes.

In Lisbon in 1612, homosexuality and witchcraft had become so intermixed as to confuse those who carried out executions. They didn't know whether sodomites should be executed under the civil procedures for criminals or under the religious procedures for witches.

During the peak of the terror, judges, theologians, and intellectuals combined charges of witchcraft with lesbianism and male homosexuality. An example is Henri Bouguet, who personally tried a great many cases. In 1619, he wrote:

> You may well suppose that every kind of obscenity is practiced there, yea, even those abominations for which Heaven poured down fire and brimstone on Sodom and Gomorrah are quite common in these assemblies.

Homosexuality wasn't the only sexual obsession of the witch hunters. Defendants were tortured until they confessed to all sorts of sexual behavior, with each other, and with demons. Because of these confessions, the judges found themselves stuck in the bind that usually constrains sexual censors. By noisily condemning various sex acts, they endowed them in the public mind with the allure of the forbidden. So the judges forced accused witches to confess that the sex they had with demons wasn't pleasurable, after all.

The Witches' Sabbat

The witch hunters' demonizing fantasies about sex culminated in the notion of the witches' sabbat (or sabbath). As noted in the last chapter, this was thought to be a nocturnal assembly attended by both witches and demons (often the Devil himself) that included wild sex rites.

As applied to witches, "sabbat" was a buzz word. It brought to mind, with a malicious twist, the Jewish sabbath. It also suggested the ancient pagan rites of the god Sabadzios (another name for Dionysos). Because of these associations, the word "sabbat" insinuated that the rituals of the witches combined the perfidy of the Jews with the salaciousness of the pagans.

A memorable description of the sabbat is provided by the 17th-century witch hunter Pierre de Lancre. A highly learned man educated by the Jesuits, de Lancre was active in Bayonne, a Basque region near the Pyrenees, in southwestern France. There he tortured and burned 600 people, mostly women.

In 1613, de Lancre published a detailed account of his experiences as a witch hunter, overflowing with personal observations and scholarly citations. The book devoted 200 hundred pages to descriptions of the sabbat.

De Lancre said that the Devil often appeared at the sabbat in the form of a goat or other animal, with huge balls and cock. Celebrants kissed the Devil's ass hole, had sex with him, made ointments from the fat of children they had killed, and participated in naked dances and orgies that lasted until morning.

De Lancre derived great pleasure from expressing his horror at the sabbat, as is evident from the throbbing cadence of his prose:

> Indecently dancing, passionately carousing, abominably sodomizing, scandalously blaspheming, insidiously plotting vengeance; pursuing every horrible, foul, and perverted desire; gingerly handling toads, vipers, lizards, and every kind of poison; passionately loving a stinking goat, amorously fondling him, and horribly, shamelessly becoming intimate with him, and coupling with him.

Just a Myth?

Most Anglo-American academics dismiss the notion of the witches' sabbat as nothing but mythological garbage. The witch hunters, they say, were a repressed lot. They just projected their own inner demons onto the witches. Or else they took the positive values of society, inverted them into their opposites, and smeared the witches with the result. Remove the inner demons and the inverted values of the witch hunters, and what sort people do we find the witches to be? Not much different from folks today. So it's unlikely that they gave themselves over to orgiastic sex and animal worship. Ordinary people simply don't behave like that. In the words of Robin Briggs:

> The whole myth of the sabbat was a fabrication from beginning to end.

But the matter isn't so simple. Although the witch hunters did project their fantasies onto witches, the question of what is humanly normal is a stickier matter. We can't just assume that the ordinary white Euro-American of today is the default for human nature. Even less can we assume that bourgeois academics are the default, and least of all where sex is at issue. (Have you ever met a bourgeois academic—and especially a historian—who was sexually vibrant? Okay, maybe one or two.)

Before we dismiss the whole idea of the witches' sabbat as humanly improbable, we should look at the anthropological evidence. We need to see how humans have in fact behaved in regard to sex, animals, and the worship of nature. We will do so in chapter nine. It will show that the sexual norms of modern patriarchal-industrial society are hardly universal.

Christian Self-Definition

Although they overstate their case, those who dismiss the witches' sabbat are right on one point: the sabbat was part of a larger stereotype, that of the demonic witch. So malicious fantasizing was indeed a part of the sabbat. However, something else was also involved that should not be overlooked.

The key to understanding the something else is historical context. The stereotype of the demonic witch, of which the sabbat was a part, didn't just pop out of the air. It was developed by particular institutions acting in particular historical contexts.

One of the great historical contexts in Europe from 1100 to 1700 A.D. was the process of defining Christianity. Some of the questions at issue were these: What does it mean to be a Christian? Who has the right to decide this question? What methods shall be used in enforcing definitions?

From 1100 to 1700, the principal method used by European authorities to define Christianity was the demonization of heretics. Religious authorities stigmatized those who dissented from their teachings as deviants in league with the Devil. Academics and theologians developed the stereotype of the heretic, which they eventually inflated into the stereotype of the demonic witch. Church, state, and university colluded in hunting down heretics and, after that, witches.

The Reformation and the Counter-Reformation took the process of defining Christianity to a new level of violence. Catholics and Protestants enlisted entire nation-states in their drive to exterminate each other. Thus ensued Europe's great religious wars and the great witch hunts. This massive institutional violence, inflicted in the name of ideology, occurred just as modern Europe was coming to birth. As a result, it helped form the character of the modern age.

The Reality Behind the Fantasy

Throughout their long-standing efforts to define Christianity through demonization, European authorities repeatedly encountered a stumbling block—rural paganism. Peasants celebrated age-old pagan rites that included sexual activities. At first they did so openly. Later, they used the names of Christian saints and holidays as a veneer. In time, many came to regard themselves as good Christians. But even so, Christianity was defined for them by personal experience and rural custom, not by bureaucratic authority.

In the 13th century, Catharism endowed this ancient, magical form of Christianity with a new potency in both organization and ideology. The changes transformed the magical Christianity that existed in southern France and elsewhere into an organized counterculture. That's when institutional Christianity struck back with a holy war and the Inquisition. No longer would Christian self-definition be a matter of mere decrees. Henceforth it would be enforced by systematic institutional violence.

After crushing the Cathars, Christian authorities continued to view reality through demonizing lenses. When they held them up to ancient peasant traditions that celebrated sex and nature, a distorted image emerged. Their name for this distortion was "the witches' sabbat." But behind the fantasy of the witches' sabbat lay a reality that the fantasy distorted and sought to obliterate—recalcitrant pagan tradition. Ignore this reality, and you render the fantasy historically unintelligible.

Flying on Drugs

The ancient rites that the authorities distorted into the witches' sabbat reflected both the practical needs of country-dwellers and their efforts to create meaning. They celebrated their rites in order to increase the abundance of game and the fertility of the soil, placate the dead, invigorate the living, mark the changing of the seasons, and invoke the powers of sun, moon, and stars.

The rites sometimes included shamanic elements. Celebrants might anoint their skins with hallucinogenic salves, go into trances, and have visions of flying through the air or of turning into animals. These traditions extended far back into the past, long before the introduction of Christianity into Europe.

Modern people often misinterpret the shamanic use of drugs. An example is historian Norman Cohn. He scoffs at the claim that witches used drugs, like shamans, viewing the idea as an anachronistic fantasy of the modern drug culture. Other moderns see a parallel between shamanic and modern drug use but draw a different conclusion. They view shamanic practices as precedents for their own personal use of recreational drugs.

Both approaches miss the point. Shamanic drug use is sacramental. That is, it is limited to ritual occasions that are regarded as sacrosanct. It is also intensely practical, with specific survival goals, like identifying with an animal in order to be a better hunter. Shamanic drug use is *not* a personal predilection, as is the case with most drug use in modern industrialized societies.

People accused of witchcraft did sometimes use hallucinogens in the shamanic manner. But their use was part of an entire way of life that was rooted in practical necessities and created meaning through myth and ritual. These practices are not comparable to modern recreational drug use as it usually occurs. A cigarette butt in the gutter is not the same as an Indian peace pipe, even though both contain tobacco.

The Lady of the Journey

When celebrated at night, the ancient peasant rites gave particular attention to the moon. That was understandable because the moon's light made nocturnal rites possible. As discussed in chapter two, many European peasants, especially women, believed in a great nocturnal journey of the living and the dead, along with animals and fairies. These travelers traversed the night sky, following the moon goddess in her orbit. Among the ancient Greeks and Romans, the goddess had been known as Artemis and Diana. In the Christian era, she had many names in various languages, commonly including variants of the word "Lady" (*domina, signora, Frau*).

The witch hunters seized on the motif of the moon goddess and her women devotees. Authorities kneaded this motif like putty, fashioning it into the witches' sabbat, and turning the moon goddess herself into the Devil.

A clear example of this transformation comes from the 16th-century Italian witch-hunter Bartolomeo Spina, who said:

> As we learn from the confession of witches, before anointing themselves, they hear in the night the manifold din of their mistress approaching with a multitude of leaping feet. And not until then do they anoint themselves, so that they may be carried away and follow her through the air, until they all come together at the spot fixed by the will of the Lady of the Journey [*domina cursus*].

I've translated *cursus* in this passage as "journey," but it also means "orbit," as in the orbit of the heavenly bodies. So there is a play on words here. "The Lady of the Journey" is also "the Lady of the Orbit," that is, the Moon Lady.

Tomas de Torquemada, the 16th-century Grand Inquisitor of Spain, was more succinct:

> Diana is the Devil.

Old Horny

In creating the fantasy of the sabbat, the witch hunters also seized on old rural traditions that were male-oriented. As discussed in chapter two, the most notable was the nightly procession of hunters and spirits called the Wild Hunt (*die wilde Jagd*), led by a horned-god figure. He was related to the ancient horned god Dionysos (or Bakkhos), who bounded over mountains like a wild goat. In the Christian era, this figure took on many different names, such as Herne the Hunter, Harlequin, Harlechin, and Robin Goodfellow.

Christian authorities drew on the horned god's physical features—horns, goat legs, fur, erect cock—to portray the Devil. The assimilation began as early as the fifth century, when Christian law began denouncing the old Teutonic nature gods as "devils."

Authorities also turned the minor nature spirits worshipped by peasants into succubus and incubus demons, discussed above. Felix Hemmerlin, speaking of the trolls of Denmark and Norway in the 15th century, said:

> And because of familiarity, they are not feared by people, but people make use of their services. They are also called "incubi" and "succubi," and in human form they mingle with [that is, have sex with] people's sons and daughters.

A Certain Consistency

Reviewing the last few chapters, we can see that the witch hunters' assault on nature spirits, sex, and women was consistent with the heresy hunters' earlier assault on Cathars. Both assaults had a common target—the ancient pagan-inspired culture of the countryside.

This consistency was no accident. We've seen that many peasants in the early Middle Ages were pagans, or else they practiced various forms of magical Christianity. These were hybrids, combining elements of institutional Christianity with surviving pagan motifs. Magical Christianity defined itself through personal choice and ancient rural culture, not bureaucratic authority.

Beginning in the 11th century, Catharism turned the magical Christianity of certain areas of Western Europe into a powerful counterculture. At the same time, the agents of institutional Christianity—the state, the church, and the university— began asserting greater control over European society. In the 13th century, institutional Christianity resorted to war and Inquisition to annihilate Catharism.

After the defeat of Catharism, educated Christian authorities (all men) saw surviving pagan practices in a new light. Now they seemed ominous because of their previous role in energizing Catharism. Authorities genuinely believed they were part of a conspiracy by the Devil to overthrow Western Christendom. They took umbrage at the sacramental role of women in ancient rural traditions, as well as the celebratory attitude toward sex.

The Reformation, Counter-Reformation, and great religious wars aggravated the situation. Princes proved how pious they were by demonizing other states whose religion differed from their own. And they put troops into the field to prove their point. The great motto of the age became *cuius regio, eius religio*—"rule the region, rule the religion."

Eventually, Catholic and Protestant princes depleted themselves militarily, as the state became leery of religious conflict. In addition, the function of the universities changed. They had originally been founded to crank out clerics, but eventually they started teaching people how to think for themselves. When witch hunting lost both the allegiance of the princes and the zeal of the intellectuals, it imploded.

Any historical account that loses sight of these facts about peasant culture and heresy cannot explain the witch hunts. They were not some kind of fluke or aberration, but the logical outcome of long-standing efforts to demonize rural paganism and pagan-Christian hybrids. The goal was to define, perpetuate, and empower forms of Christianity that would be serviceable to ruling institutions. The goal was achieved.

Sex & Meaning

As noted above, a prominent feature of the quest for institutional power in the name of religion was the witch hunters' fierce assault on sex. This assault represented a complete reversal of the religious sentiments of classical antiquity. Many people today don't realize how profound the change was. Its effects have continued into the present, driving a wedge in many modern people's minds between sex and meaning, and between sex and religion. To highlight the change, we'll conclude this chapter with a few examples showing how the ancients linked sexual passion and the divine.

An early example is Mimnermos of Kolophon, writing about 600 years before Christ. He acknowledges that the goddess Aphrodite is the patron of sexual pleasure, without which life is empty:

What life is there, what joy, without golden Aphrodite?
Let me die when I care no more for these—
Secret love, sweet gifts, and a bed.

In marked contrast to the Christians, the ancients also attributed same-sex desires to the gods and called on the gods to help them fulfill their own gay and lesbian desires. An example is a famous prayer of Sappho of Lesbos to Aphrodite, asking the goddess to appear and help her win the love of another woman. The prayer, written in the 7th century B.C., begins thus:

Immortal and wily Aphrodite,
Zeus's crafty daughter, I pray you, hear my prayer.
Don't let my heart break, goddess, with grievous longings,
But come and help me here ...

Another example is a 5th-century-B.C. prayer by Anakreon of Teos to Dionysos. He calls on the god to help him win the heart of a young man named Kleobulos:

Lord Dionysos, playmate of seductive Eros,
Playmate of the dark-eyed Nymphs
And of shimmering Aphrodite,
You who travel the high mountain peaks,
To you I pray.

Be gracious, come to me,
Hear, and grant my prayer.
Give Kleobulos some good advice,
To accept my love, O Dionysos!

Imagine if modern Christian books of prayer contained pleas to help parishioners find sexual partners of either sex. Inconceivable, of course. That shows how far religion and meaning have receded from sex during the Christian era. But it wasn't always so.

The Great Goddess Sex

The ancients' fusion of sex and meaning went beyond personal love affairs. They also saw sex as a power that energized and held together the entire universe, and made human history meaningful. Even the ancient atomists, who sought to explain all things in terms of atoms and the void, prayed to Aphrodite (Venus). They saw the goddess as endowing the atoms with motion, coherence, beauty, historical meaning, and life.

An example is Lucretius, the great Roman poet of atomism, writing in the first century B.C. He invokes Venus as the mother of Roman history and as the energizer of Fire, Earth, Water, and Air, whom he regards as alive:

Mother of the Roman people, desire of gods and men,
Bountiful Venus,
Beneath the gliding stars of Heaven, you make the ship-bearing Sea
And the fruitful expanse of Earth to teem with life.
Through you every kind of creature is conceived,
Brought forth, and made to see the light of day.
For you, goddess, and at your approach, the winds flee and the clouds.
For you, artist Earth sends up sweet flowers,
Sea's smooth surface smiles,
And calm Sky shines, resplendent in light.

A Shift in Metaphors

The ancient atomists would have been dumbfounded by the modern atomists' notion of the universe as a big dead machine. Such an idea ran counter to the feelings that the ancients had of a personal connection with nature (*sympatheia*). The moderns accuse the ancients of animism (belief that the universe is alive). But the ancients could equally well accuse the moderns of mortism (belief that the universe is dead).

The roots of the shift from animism to mortism lay in the High Middle Ages and the Renaissance. As the West was losing its emotional connection with nature, it was also demonizing women and sex. This demonization occurred in two great waves: the heresy hunts from the 13th to the 15th centuries, and the witch hunts of the 16th and 17th centuries. The cumulative effect was to undermine nature goddesses like Diana and Venus in their roles as metaphors for the meaning of life. Later, in the modern era, they were supplanted by the metaphor of the big dead machine.

Tђe Legacy of Demonization

Centuries of demonizing people as heretics and witches left a harmful legacy. Sexual exuberance, women's experience, and nature worship all fell under a long shadow. When modernity later constructed a new model of what it means to be human, it overlooked what had fallen into eclipse during the Christian era. Women receded into the shadows. The modern person turned out to be a man, and one who was disconnected from sex, women, nature, and his own femininity. Then he wondered why his life was meaningless.

But how could it be otherwise? The demise of the metaphor of the old nature goddesses during the Christian era had paved the way for the triumph of the metaphor of the big dead machine in the modern era. Women had no place in the big dead machine. Men still did, but only as cogs. What meaning is there in being a cog?

Later chapters will examine in more detail the triumph of the metaphor of the big dead machine. First, though, we need to step back from Europe and take a broader view of the world. Due to the development of new technologies in travel and warfare, Christian Europe was able to export its demonization of sex, women, and nature worship to other societies around the globe. The next chapter will look at this early instance of "the global economy." We'll see how it built on the heresy hunts and witch-hunts to crush the cultures of the invaded and to cripple the magic of our lives today.

Chapter 8.

Native Magic

In the late 15th century, just as the worst of the European witch hunts got underway, another cataclysm of even wider extent began. European men—inspired by religious zeal, hungry for profits, and empowered by technological breakthroughs in travel and weaponry—undertook to conquer and Christianize the rest of the world.

Their efforts unleashed a tsunami of institutionalized male violence. It surged forth from Europe and rolled across the planet for hundreds of years, leaving a swath so destructive that it can be rightly called the Great Devastation. It reached its greatest extent in the early 20th century, by which time nearly eighty percent of the globe had become subject to European hegemony.

The Great Devastation didn't involve only the material conditions of life of subject peoples, but also their capacity to create meaning. Cultures around the globe were systematically and relentlessly bled of the meaning of life. In the end, ironically, the invading culture itself succumbed to the blood-letting.

The invaders' destruction of meaning came about through their attack on the traditional values and practices of the invaded. That's another irony, since the invaders' spiritual descendants today pose as defenders of traditional values (as in the Traditional Values Coalition). But their values violently supplanted others that were in place for much longer.

When Europeans reached the shores of the Americas and elsewhere, they encountered ancient pagan practices that called to mind rites in pre-Christian Europe. In the new lands, as in Europe before, the invaders branded these practices as Devil-worship and witchcraft. The demonization had the effect of poisoning the process of autonomous meaning-creation from below and replacing it with canned, institutionally imposed meaning from above. This chapter will look at the New World variations on this familiar Old World theme.

Native Fullness

The Europeans did not find vacant lands in the Americas, but rather a multitude of societies who had lived there time out of mind. By the end of the 15th century, when the European onslaught began, about 65 to 70 million Indians lived in the

Americas, roughly equal to the population of Europe west of Russia. The largest concentrations were in central Mexico and the coastal Andes. About five million lived in the present-day United States. These populations were far less dense than those of today. Nonetheless, the Americas were not a vacuous wilderness waiting to be occupied by European fullness.

Both the cultural richness and the historical longevity of these societies were astounding. Moderns often lose sight of these facts. One reason is that, until recently, most archeologists believed the American Indians all descended from a few related groups in Siberia. They started migrating into the Americas across the Bering Strait around 9000 B.C., at the end of the last Ice Age (so the argument went). They pursued the mastodon and other big game farther and farther south. Eventually, their descendants evolved into the various societies encountered by Columbus and his successors.

Recently, however, archeologists have come to view the Siberian influx as just one current in a fuller flow. New linguistic, genetic, and archeological discoveries all point to the same conclusion: The human settlement of the Americas came from various sources (including Europe and Japan), at different times, and starting as early as 20,000 to 30,000 years ago.

Some archeologists claim there was sporadic trade between the Americas and the Old World many centuries before Columbus. Artifacts found at American Indian settlements, they say, point to repeated contacts with ancient Mediterranean and European societies.

Most archeologists discount this claim. However, the moderns typically underestimate the seafaring skills of the ancients, especially the Phoenicians and the Greeks. Archeologists used to believe that ancient Mediterranean mariners were primitive travelers, hugging the shoreline in their sorry little boats. That's because ancient shipwrecks were usually discovered near port cities. Recently, though, new technologies have disclosed ancient shipwrecks in the middle of the Mediterranean, implying more ambitious routes for their owners.

The moderns also underestimate the scientific knowledge of the ancients. Aristarchus of Samos (third century B.C.) taught that the earth was round and orbited the sun. Democritus (4th century B.C.) said that all matter was composed of atoms. Other Greek thinkers said humans had evolved from animals.

Ancient sailor-merchants who shared Aristarchus' view would naturally think of reaching India by sailing westward, just as Columbus did much later. Given their seafaring skills and scientific knowledge, ancient mariners could have repeatedly bumped into the American shoreline, mistakenly thinking they had landed in India, and calling the natives *Indoi* and *Indi* (Greek and Latin for "Indians").

Whatever the extent of pre-Columbian contact, one big difference remained between the older and the later visitors. The older visitors lacked the motivation and means to expropriate, enslave, or kill everybody they met. Such accomplishments had to wait upon two later developments: the triumph of institutional Christianity in Europe, and the technical insemination of institutional Christianity by the newly emerging sciences.

That lethal copulation first began in the late 15th century, just as the techniques of witch-hunting were also perfected. Thus began a long period of horrific violence for both Europe and much of the world. From the womb of that bloody era there eventually emerged, like Nero from Agrippina, the offspring named "Modernity."

Emerging from the Earth

The native peoples of the Americas, like the ancient peasants of Europe, drew on cultural continuities that were tens of thousands of years old. Many Indian societies lived in the same regions so long they had forgotten their earlier migrations. This long connection to place gave rise to a common motif in Indian mythology, that their people had originally emerged from inside the earth.

For example, the Zuni of the American Southwest believe they originally existed with animal-like features deep in the earth. Two guiding spirits led their ancestors to the surface, near the Grand Canyon or the Mohave Desert. After the ancestors emerged, the spirits cut off their tails and sliced the webs on their hands and feet, giving them fingers and toes.

Similar motifs can be found in Europe, again due to long association with place. According to ancient Greek myth, the earliest Athenians were called Kekropidai, after their first king, Kekrops. He was said to have emerged from the earth at Athens (then called Kekropia) with a snake's tail.

Myths like these reflect a strong and lasting sense of connection to place, nature, and tradition. Admittedly, Indian societies showed much diversity—from the roaming Buffalo hunters of the plains, to the semisedentary agriculturalists of the eastern woodlands, to the urban dwellers of Mexico. Some were peaceful, egalitarian, and balanced in relations between the sexes; others were militaristic, hierarchical, and patriarchal. However, Indians of all stripes felt personally connected to the places where they lived, and also to animals, sex, the seasons, the weather, and the heavenly bodies. They likewise felt a sense of family kinship toward other members of their own tribe, however fierce they might be to outsiders. And they were devoted to their own ancient traditions.

Indian myths, rites, and art throughout the Americas all testify to this powerful sense of personal connection to place, nature, tribe, and history. Without these connections, the Indians' world would have lacked meaning. When the invading Europeans broke the connections, they also shattered the meaning, just as ruling institutions in Europe were doing at that time to peasant life there.

Here Comes Civilization!

On October 12, 1492, Christopher Columbus stumbled onto an island in the Bahamas, mistakenly believing he had reached India. Following Columbus came

Hernando Cortés, who destroyed Aztec civilization in Mexico in 1521. Following Cortés came Francisco Pizarro, who destroyed Inca civilization in Peru in 1532. Following Pizarro came others who subjugated and forcibly converted millions of Indians in Central and South America. Descendants of the conquistadors eventually married many Indians survivors.

In North America, Europeans were less interested in converting and assimilating the Indians than in pushing them aside and grabbing their lands. The United States Government, created in 1789, pushed both Indians and Europeans aside. In their place, the U.S. Government undertook a century-long program of pushing the Indians ever farther westward, killing those who resisted, seizing their lands, and confining survivors to reservations. Whether through assimilation or displacement, the European newcomers uprooted and shattered ancient Indian cultures throughout the Americas, both north and south. Many Indians were killed outright. Even more perished from strange new diseases.

Even Europeans who were not overtly hostile caused many deaths. In 1602, Bartholomew Gosnold explored what is now known as Martha's Vineyard in New England. He admiringly described the Indians he met as "people of perfect constitution of body, active, strong, healthful, and very witty." Within a few years of Gosnold's visit, more than 90% of the Indians of the area had died from diseases contracted from their congenial visitors.

Most Europeans were not as admiring of the Indians as Gosnold. Typically, they reacted to Indian customs with horror, especially where sex, women, and nature worship were at issue. They accused the Indians of worshiping the Devil and tried to force them to change their ways. The behavior of the Spanish in what is now the Southwest United States provides a telling example.

Sexual Exuberance in New Mexico

In the mid-16th century, Spanish conquistadors entered what is now the American Southwest. The area had been occupied for thousands of years by various Indian groups known collectively today as "the Pueblo," named from their distinctive adobe houses. Although linguistically diverse, the various Pueblo groups shared many cultural traits.

The Anasazi, the oldest Pueblo group, began building a civilization in the American Southwest around 9000 B.C. In 1250 A.D., they abandoned many of their villages, apparently because of climate changes or soil exhaustion. Other Indian groups later moved into the region and intermingled with an Anasazi remnant. In 1300 A.D., a Pueblo group founded the settlement of Acoma, 70 miles west of modern Albuquerque. It survives to this day, the oldest continually occupied human settlement in the United States.

Unlike the invading Christians, the Pueblo Indians did not regard sex as a tool to be cranked guiltily in hidden places for the sole purpose of generating offspring. Like the ancient Greeks and other pagan peoples, the Pueblo saw sex as a divine power holding together both the cosmos and their society. Their sexual practices were characterized by exuberance, openness, and variety.

When visitors (usually men) came to the Pueblo, the residents—both men and women—would openly offer to have sex with them, in order to partake of their powers. When Pueblo warriors brought back slain animals or the scalps of enemies, the women would speak bawdily to the objects and mimic having sex with them, to welcome them into the community.

Sex also occurred at public rites. In one dance, aimed at stimulating the clouds to yield their precious fluids, male dancers handled snakes and then performed fellatio on the rain chief. The solstice rites, the two greatest celebrations of the year, ended in an orgy.

Like many American Indians, the Pueblo acknowledged the existence of a third gender—men (sometimes women) who dressed in clothes of the opposite sex, performed work traditionally associated with the opposite sex, and had sex with members of the same sex.

The Zuni called such a third-gender person *lhamana*; the Tewa, *kwidó*; the Hopi, *hova*; and the Keres, *kokwimu*. They were viewed as embodiments of the male and female energies that held the cosmos together and sometimes functioned as healers and shamans.

Europeans have left written accounts of third-gender figures for 130 North American tribes. The Europeans called such a person, especially when male, *berdache*, a derogatory French term derived from the Persian *bardaj*, meaning male prostitute. Throughout the Americas, the Europeans demonized and persecuted third-gender people. They were one of the first aspects of Indian culture to crumble before the Christian onslaught.

Womeɲ & Meɲ

As in early pagan Europe, Pueblo women enjoyed important prerogatives. They built and owned their own homes and ruled within the household. Houses were handed down from mother to daughter (matrilineal inheritance). When men married, they left their mother's household and lived in the wife's household (matrilocal habitation).

Most people had one spouse, and either the wife or husband could divorce at will (serial monogamy). However, the most prosperous of elder males were polygamous. The average Pueblo household consisted of a large extended family defined by the grandmother and her daughters. Women presided over the religious rites pertaining to domestic functions—household maintenance, food preparation, and giving birth.

While women stayed put, men moved about, depending on their age. In childhood, they stayed with their mothers. On reaching adolescence, they moved into a kiva, which was an all-male subterranean chamber, entered through a hole in the top. There they were subjected to sadistic blood-letting rites, to steel them as warriors. When they married, they moved into the homes of their new wives. If the couples later divorced, the men went back to live with their mothers.

While the home was women's space, men and women had complementary roles and powers in the settlement's public life. But outside the settlement, men were in charge, and above all in warfare. As with many Indians, the Pueblo sadistically tortured prisoners of war to death. However, they did not engage in the massive spectacles of human sacrifice typical of the Aztecs of Mexico.

Jesus Loves You

Acting with great cruelty, Spanish conquistadors began the conquest of the Pueblo Indians in the 1540s. On capturing Acoma in 1599, they condemned all adults to 20 years of slavery, cut off one foot of all adult men, and harvested the young as their personal servants.

In the wake of the conquistadors came the fanatical disciples of St. Francis, who imposed a grim theocracy on the Pueblo. The Franciscans were to New Mexico in the 16th and 17th centuries what the Taliban were to modern Afghanistan. They recruited compliant natives and formed them into a "spiritual police" (*policía espiritual*) to spy on their neighbors. They raided Pueblo homes, seized religious articles, and burned them. Indians who persisted in worshipping "idols" were beaten until bloody, covered with turpentine, and set on fire.

The followers of St. Francis condemned all forms of sex except heterosexual intercourse in the missionary position. They regarded the *hlamana* and other third-gender people as the work of the Devil. They deprived women of their prerogatives in land use, home ownership, food production, and the rearing of children. As in Europe, the friars used the cult of the Virgin Mary to co-opt the worship of indigenous goddesses.

However, the friars looked with favor on one Pueblo religious practice, ritual blood-letting, because it appealed to traditional Catholic sadomasochism. But the friars redirected blood letting toward penance and mortification of the flesh, not toward steeling men for battle.

The Franciscans of New Mexico were as fanatical in suppressing Indian religion as their Old World confreres were in exterminating heretics and witches in Europe. But there was a big difference from Europe. Arid New Mexico was far removed from Spain's fountains of power, which flowed fitfully in the reigns of Philips II, III, and IV. Although the imported plants of church and state grew big thorns in New Mexico, their roots lacked institutional replenishment and eventually dried up. In 1680 the Pueblo revolted and drove the weakened Spaniards out, along with Jesus, Mary, and St. Francis. Christian authorities did not again succeed in stifling Pueblo culture until the U.S. government consolidated control over the area in the 1890s.

Although it eventually faltered, the Spanish conquest of the American Southwest revealed the ruthless intentions of the Christian invaders. In the name of God's love, they demonized any aspect of life that did not fit into their narrow institutional paradigms. They sought to lower the status of women and third-gender people, associate sex with the Devil, and weaken people's connections to place, nature, and their own history. The effect of this onslaught was to uproot the quest for meaning from the personal experience of natural and cultural diversity, and to constrain it within the institutional definitions and decrees of church and monastery.

New Jerusalem (a.k.a. Salem)

At the other end of the American continent, in what is today called New England, the invading Christians were mostly Protestants. They admired the Old Testament's account of how the ancient Hebrews conquered the Canaanites and suppressed their pagan traditions. They saw themselves as creating their own New Jerusalem by pushing aside the heathen of a New Canaan.

Archeologists no longer put much faith in Old Testament accounts of the ancient Hebrews' conquest and occupation of Canaan. The artifacts found at digs are inconsistent with those accounts. Nonetheless, both Jews and Christians have long taken the old stories at face value and accepted them as admirable role models for their own behavior.

The Old Testament's demonization of Canaanite beliefs, combined with the precedent of recent European witch hunts, inspired the famous 17th-century witch trials at Salem, Massachusetts. The name "Salem" itself is a truncated form of "Jerusalem." In 1628, the Puritans changed the original Indian name for their settlement, Nahum Keake (or Naumkeag), to Salem. The new name accorded with the Puritans' view of themselves as latter-day Hebrews, and of the Indians and black slaves as idol-worshipping heathen.

In 1689, the influential Boston clergyman Cotton Mather, inspired by European precedents, started railing against the dangers of witchcraft in the area. Quoting the Old Testament injunction "Thou shalt not suffer a Witch to live," he thundered:

> Such an Hellish thing there is as *Witchcraft* in the World. ...
> There is confined unto the *Atmosphere* of our *Air* a vast *Power*,
> or *Army* of *Evil Spirits*, under the Government of a Prince who
> employs them in a continual Opposition to the Designs of GOD.

Three years later, in 1692, two Puritan girls at Salem began suffering some sort of seizure. In most non-European societies of the time, the problem would have been dealt with by a healer or shaman. But Puritan fantasies of themselves as latter-day Hebrews, reinforced by the precedent of the raging witch hunts in Europe, produced different results at Salem.

The authorities zeroed in on Tituba, a Carib Indian slave in one of the Puritan households. Tituba said she had performed rituals to see if the girls were possessed by a spirit. In the classic style of European witch hunts, Tituba was coerced into "confessing" that she was a witch who had invoked the Devil.

Things spiraled out of control after that, as the authorities turned neighbor against neighbor. The justification for doing so was provided by Cotton Mather. Commenting on the events of 1692 in his book *Wonders of the Invisible World*, he depicted the Salem witches as part of a wider conspiracy by the Devil to undermine Christian civilization in New England.

The Salem witch hunt was thus another example of the familiar Christian practice of self-definition through the demonization of otherness, which we have traced in previous chapters. In the words of Itala Vivan:

> As the Puritans saw it, the healing and propitiatory rites of the Indians and Black slaves seem to confirm that everything different from the Puritans themselves was connected to Satan, and that the non-Christian world was implicated in a Satanic conspiracy.

By embracing the European witchcraft model, and demonizing Indian practices, early Massachusetts leaders distanced themselves from an indigenous culture that had developed in that area for thousands of years. At the same time, they expropriated the indigenous people themselves of their lands.

These developments bore cultural fruit in later years, when New England became the intellectual leader of the newly independent United States of America. The ideas that came forth from that region had lost nearly all contact with the accumulated wisdom of the peoples who had lived there long before. As a result, the quest to create meaning in early America perpetuated European precedents of alienation from sex, women, and nature. Indian precedents—which afforded a fuller and more balanced view of humanity, sex, and nature—were lost.

Sex, Empire & Meaning

As the British colonies grew in North America, local colonial leaders stressed the reproductive function of sex, regarding it as a useful tool for imperialist expansion. For example, Benjamin Franklin, in his 1751 essay *Observations Concerning the Increase of Mankind*, said the white colonists should breed rapidly, squeezing out the low-density Indian populations, and filling up their lands.

For a time, the British Crown tried to stop the colonists' seizure of Indians lands west of the Alleghenies, fearing it would disrupt the lucrative fur trade the Crown had forced on the Indians. These restrictions infuriated the colonial ruling class. The Declaration of Independence (1776) rebuked the king because "he has endeavored to prevent the Population of these States."

In 1786, when the newly independent states were under the Articles of Confederation, Thomas Jefferson expressed the hope that rapidly breeding white Americans would fill up the entire Western hemisphere. Later, in 1801, after the new U.S. Constitution had gone into effect, Jefferson reiterated the idea:

However our present interest may restrain us within our limits, it is impossible not to look forward to distant times, when our rapid multiplication will expand it beyond these limits, and cover the whole northern if not the southern continent, with people speaking the same language, governed in similar forms, and by similar laws.

Early French colonists likewise viewed sex as a tool for breeding in the quest for empire building. They vied with British colonists, and later U.S. citizens, as to who could fill up the continent first with their rapidly breeding populations.

The early colonies also encouraged massive immigration from Europe. The emphasis on breeding and immigration paid off. From 1700 to 1750, the colonial population grew from 250,000 to 1,400,000, an increase of well over 500% in just fifty years.

The tendency to reduce sex to breeding, and to see it as a tool in the service of imperialism, was incomprehensible to the Indians. They valued sexual pleasure for its own sake and as a force for holding the cosmos together. They integrated sex into their spiritual practices, regarding it as a vehicle for creating meaning.

The view of sex as a tool for group expansion came easy to the early American colonists. It had lain ready at hand for centuries in European Christendom. The major churches of Europe, both Catholic and Protestant, were aggressive, expansionist institutions, seeking to increase their membership at the expense of their competitors. Prolific breeding was a way to do that.

The churches found sanction for this view in the Bible. As noted, the Old Testament depicts the ancient Hebrews as swarming into the land of Canaan, uprooting the indigenous peoples, and breeding rapidly to fill up the land—all with the blessing of their ferocious god, Yahweh. In fact, the very first commandment that the Old Testament mentions as given by this god to the Hebrews is this:

Be fertile and multiply; fill the earth and subdue it.

The high regard for sex as a breeding tool in the service of nationalist expansion was consistent with the disdain for Indian traditions about sex. Both attitudes drew on the monotheistic tradition's longstanding hostility to the enjoyment of sexual pleasure for its own sake.

All three views produced the same effect. They peeled sexual pleasure away from the life experiences that people drew on when creating meaning. As the field of experiences available to people for meaning-creation narrowed, meaning itself diminished. Sex in particular fell along the wayside, having become meaningless except as a tool for breeding.

Slavery & Racism

In addition to seizing Indian lands and mangling Indian cultures, the European invaders and their descendants spread the institution of slavery, based on race. The slaves were uprooted from their ancestral homes and shipped off to a distant continent. There they were allowed to participate only subordinately in the prevailing culture. Their own traditions withered. At the same time, their masters viewed them as subhuman, scorning their myths and art, just as they had done to the Indians.

Because of this racism, both masters and slaves lost ground in the realm of meaning. The former closed themselves off from an entire continent of cultural richness. Their understanding of what it meant to be human narrowed to a tight little fortress of white values. The latter lost the rich ancestral earth that had nourished the roots of their culture. Increasingly, the quality most shared by both was a lessened sense of the meaning of life.

What was to become the United States was a slave society from the outset.

Chapter 9.

Creating Meaning

Rarely in history do we find an entire civilization that feels life has no meaning, although pockets of disenchantment are common in many societies. Today, however, patriarchal-industrial civilization is orbiting on the edge of a massive black hole of meaninglessness.

People in all social classes feel disconnected from their own lives, each other, and nature. They sense a hollowness at the core of themselves and the surrounding society. To fill the void, many have turned to alcohol and drugs. Others have joined religious or political cults, or become nihilists. Others have just stopped feeling, going through life like robots. Yet they live in one of the most affluent civilizations in history.

As previous chapters have shown, this feeling of disenchantment is no accident. It's the subjective side of an objective historical reality—the Great Disconnect caused by certain trends in religion, politics, and economics that have reinforced each other for centuries.

The Great Disconnect started in the 11th century with the onslaught of institutional Christianity against magical Christianity. After the triumph of the former, internecine battles between the Church of Rome and Protestantism undermined both the moral standing and the political power of institutional Christianity.

The ensuing Age of Reason and the Industrial Age pulled the rug out from under institutional Christianity as the West's great meaning-giver. The state and the business corporation tried on occasion to fill the vacated role but failed. The people, long discouraged by institutions from creating meaning for themselves, saw meaning retreat from their lives as the validating institutions lost their legitimacy.

Faced with the historical decline of powerful institutions as meaning givers, how can we recover meaning in our lives through our own efforts? This is a critical question that must now be faced by all thoughtful people in the modern world.

Reconnect!

The road to recovery consists of rebuilding lost connections—with our own inner selves, our neighborhood, our culture, the human family, the planet, and the cosmos. Great institutions have broken the connections and atomized us. When we reconnect, we put the many diverse experiences of our lives into encompassing wholes that give them context, purpose, and value.

As with any major enterprise, the creation of meaning requires experience, knowledge, and art. The more skillful we become in connecting things into larger experiential contexts, the more meaning our lives will have. The ever-growing fabric of meaning that we weave for ourselves through years of artful connecting is the magic of life insofar as each of us experiences it.

Square One

Because patriarchal-industrial society has denigrated the unifying skills needed to create meaning, we moderns have to start from square one when making the Great Reconnect. We can't just plug into a rich network of supportive practices that the dominant culture has made ready and waiting for us, as is the case in indigenous societies.

They typically put great effort into training their members in the integrative skills needed to create meaning. The tools they use for doing so are myth, dance, song, ceremony, the arts in all their forms, and sex. People learn to use them for that end at an early age, and continue to develop their skills with them throughout their lives. The result is a spiritual power that pervades their culture.

We, however, are latecomers to the craft of meaning creation, and basically self-taught. As such, we may be prone to costly missteps that could be avoided, if only we had some practical guidance from those who are more experienced. But since we usually don't, we have to be careful.

One of the biggest pitfalls is the common belief that meaning creation (or spiritual growth, as it is often called) is something impractical and other-worldly. Nothing could be farther from the truth. Indigenous societies anchor the creation of meaning to the most practical activities in their lives: cultivating crops, raising and slaughtering animals, making clothes, building houses, having sex, adapting to the seasons.

This practical focus doesn't mean that indigenous societies lack cosmic consciousness, as we call it. Far from it. But they come to cosmic consciousness from the ground up, not from the top down. They would laugh at anybody in their society who claimed to have a spiritual overview of the universe as a whole but who was inept in dealing with plants, animals, or other people.

The lesson for us, the spiritual newbies of modernity, is to be skeptical of anybody who pushes cosmic consciousness through methods that are impractical, other-worldly, or escapist. That path only leads to self-delusion and superstition. If your spiritual growth isn't rooted in the practical activities of your own daily life, you're designing a house without a foundation. It can be fun to dream of a fantasy house hanging in the air, but we should bear in mind Glinda's warning in

The Wizard of Oz: "You have no power here. Be gone before somebody drops a house on you, too!"

Depression

If you want meaning, then you'll have to deal with your life as it is right now, and how you feel about it. That's where you do have some power. For example, consider this question: Are you depressed? Many people in modern society are. In fact, depression has reached epidemic proportions in modernity, cutting across all social classes.

The depression epidemic has given rise to an entire industry. Private hucksters and corporate schemers can be found everywhere, promising relief from depression, if only we buy their products. The most insidious are the big pharmaceutical companies. They have convinced an entire generation of doctors to casually prescribe antidepressant drugs to their patients. Although some cases of depression are pathological and do require drug treatment, most exist because the patients' conditions of life are, in fact, depressing.

If you're depressed, your psyche is sending you a message that something is amiss in the way you live, and needs to be corrected. The situation is akin to physical pain, which is a message that something in your body is amiss and needs attention. Drugs can block the suffering for a while and may be appropriate in certain circumstances. However, the healthier response is to identify the underlying problem and take steps to correct it.

The root cause of depression is usually a lack of power in an oppressive situation or the blockage of a natural need. Examples: a suffocating job, an abusive spouse, lack of supportive friends, sexual starvation, a degraded neighborhood, blocked artistic expression, nature deprivation.

The answer in these cases is to identify the oppressor or the blockage, and come up with a plan to outmaneuver or remove it. Examples: look for a better job, divorce your spouse, make new friends, get laid, organize your neighbors against the drug thugs, explore your own artistic talents, spend time in the countryside or forest.

These efforts to deal with life's frustrations are fairly obvious. Why even mention them here? The point is their connection to the creation of meaning, which is a matter of reconnecting with self, community, and cosmos. The reconnecting starts at the most basic level, with the personal needs of daily life. Ignore these needs, and your quest for meaning will lead you into a spiritual ditch. Deal with these needs, and the doors of meaning will start to open in your life.

The Spirituality of Place

The basics of our lives involve not only personal needs but also personal geography—the specific physical places in which we eat, sleep, have sex, read, walk, drive, and work. The Great Reconnect requires that we be mindful of these places and devote thoughtful action to them.

Do you walk around in your room, apartment, house, or encampment in a daze, inattentive to details of cleanliness and order? Are you indifferent to the condition of the street in front of your home? Do you block out the sights that pass by as you walk, bicycle, bus, or drive? Are you unheeding of the look, feel, sound, and smell of the office, factory, store, or farm where you work?

If so, you have lost your place in the world. You are adrift in a sea of disconnectedness. You have nowhere to stand, to be rooted. Without being rooted, you cannot grow spiritually, just as a rootless tree cannot grow physically.

To have a place in the world is to be mindful of the specific spaces in which we move, however humble or stark, and to take some responsibility for investing them with goodness, order, and beauty, however little we can do. That means caring that our homes, neighborhoods, highways, and workplaces be safe, clean, peaceful, and welcoming.

In the process, we invest meaning in the physical contours of our lives. We discover that there is a spirituality of place.

The Spirituality of Time

The basics involve not only personal needs and geography but also time—the repetitive cycles that we follow, whether consciously or unconsciously, when pursuing our daily activities. The Great Reconnect requires that we be mindful of these repetitive cycles and devote thoughtful action to them.

Do you get up in the morning in a hurry, eat a skimpy breakfast, or skip it all together, and gulp down coffee to wake up? Do you bolt out the front door, only to push your way into a packed subway car, or else curse other drivers on the freeway? Do you spend eight hours at a job that deadens your soul? Do you come home in the evening, heat up a frozen dinner, wash it down with beer, and spend your free time watching TV or DVDs? Do you fall asleep at night feeling indifferent to all but yourself, or nursing resentments?

If so, you have run out of time. You have failed to see that every repetitive cycle in your life is a kind of meditation that either infuses time with meaning or bleeds it. By continually reinforcing deadening cycles in your life, you have lost time as a friend and turned him into an enemy. He has become a vampire that slowly sucks away the joy of living.

To have time as a friend is to take care that repetitive cycles be healthy ones. That means pausing and feeling thankful for the gift of life when you wake up each morning. It means eating healthy, balanced meals, and giving a moment's thought, before each meal, to the labor and sacrifice that has produced the food that keeps you alive. It means doing work during the day that you enjoy and that provides a needed service to the world. It means using some of your free time every day to develop your mind and creative skills. It means drifting off to sleep at night with feelings of gratitude for the good that others have done.

By living this way, we invest meaning in the temporal contours of our lives. We discover that there is a spirituality of time.

Why Care About Meaning Anyway?

All this is fine and dandy, you may say, but not everybody has the luxury to devote such delicate attention to reconnecting things in his or her personal needs, geography, or time. What about desperately poor people, living under crushing oppression, just barely surviving from day to day? They have to grab what they can for themselves, by whatever means, without thinking about larger patterns of connectedness. Otherwise, they may perish.

At the other extreme, what about aggressive self-promoters who are fighting their way up the great pyramids of wealth and power? They compete fiercely with each other in high-stake games of power, where one misstep could be ruinous. They can't let themselves be distracted by larger concerns of connectedness. Otherwise, they'll give the other sharks in the pool an opening to move in for the kill.

It's true that meaning creation is not the only goal in human life. Survival and self-advancement are powerful motivators, too. In fact, compared to them, meaning creation seems pretty feeble, at least in the short run.

But don't overlook the long run. With the passage of time, meaning (or its lack) can emerge as the decisive difference in a person's life. What will happen if the desperately poor person eventually concludes that survival is not worth struggling for? What will happen if the rich and powerful person eventually concludes that his or her life is empty, despite having acquired many material goods?

Both groups are less likely to find themselves in this fix if they have put at least some effort over the years into meaning creation. Admittedly, the importance of meaning varies at any particular moment in a person's life, depending on changing circumstances. Nonetheless it's a mistake to think that meaning can be discounted indefinitely, with no consequences for survival and happiness.

Keep yourself alive and get ahead, to be sure. But don't neglect meaning, or you may feel empty and disconnected at the end, even if you have material fullness. And even in terms of self-advancement, remember that a lack of concern for the larger picture can be costly. People with this lack commonly undermine their own health, alienate potential allies, and overlook both opportunities and dangers. Meaning is a consequence of awareness, and awareness promotes survival and success.

But Why Start Small?

Granted that meaning contributes to long-term psychological fulfillment, why must we start with the pedestrian needs, spaces, and times of our everyday lives? Sure, indigenous societies do that. But they live in their own little worlds, unconcerned about what happens thousands of miles away, in other cultures.

We, by contrast, have global concerns because of the very nature of our existence. Great issues of war and peace, the environment, and social justice are at stake, with consequences that affect everyone. Aren't these concerns, above all, the proper arenas where meaning creation should come into its own? Shouldn't we enter the global arenas at the outset?

It's true that meaning has a global side. And, yes, we can work to create meaning on a social scale without first attending to all the details of our own personal lives. In fact, the personal and the social efforts to create meaning can develop in tandem, or else by turns, one after each other, in a way that reinforces both.

But you're kidding yourself if you think you can save the world if your own personal life is a mess. Personal issues can be postponed for a time. However, if you divert attention away from them for too long, you run the risk of becoming hypocritical or dysfunctional, or both.

You claim you want to save the Amazon rain forest from being overrun by corporate plunderers. A noble concern. But why should anybody take you seriously when you don't care that your own neighborhood is being overrun by drug dealers?

You claim you want to see city hall adopt "progressive values" in making public policy. A noble concern. But why should anybody take you seriously when you resort to name-calling against anybody who disagrees with you politically?

You claim your church has a message that will save humanity from sin. A noble concern. But why should anybody take you seriously when you contribute money to an archdiocese that has covered up sexual abuse by its priests?

The most effective way to influence the values and thinking of others is through behavior that is self-consistent, honorable, and practical. You will never attain the solidity of character that is needed to make the world better if you have neglected to ground meaning in the depths of your own personal life. The branches of the tree of meaning may eventually sway impressively in the heavens above, but their nourishment comes from the plain soil below.

Beyond the Basics

Let's say you've attended to the basics. You are rooted in the geography of where you live, travel, and work. That means you have a place in the world. You are also attentive to the cycles that occur in your life activities. That means time is your friend. You are honest, practical, and consistent in your dealings with yourself, your spouse and family, your neighbors, your friends, and your co-workers. That means you have developed solidity of character. Having a place in the world, time as your friend, and a solid and consistent character, you are ready to expand the circle of meaning in your life.

Expanding the circle means connecting with others who are also rooted in space, time, and character, and to interact with them in ways that help make the world a more meaning-friendly place. This step is essential. Once you realize the importance of meaning creation, you will be easily demoralized if you just keep to yourself; even more so, if you spend a lot of time with people who are blind or hostile to meaning creation. Much of the machinery of modern life is fueled by the destruction of meaning. Kindred spirits in the quest for meaning are necessary in order to create protective oases amid the ambient emptiness.

Note that "kindred spirits" doesn't necessarily mean people who have the same opinions as you, or the same lifestyle, race, gender, sexual orientation, or class background. Another factor is more important—respect.

All people who are open to meaning creation have a certain degree of respect. They respect themselves enough to want to make their lives meaningful. They respect others enough to realize that creating meaning involves reaching out beyond themselves. Look for the manifestations of respect in any segment of the human spectrum, and there you will find kindred spirits.

A simple, but important way, to connect with kindred spirits is through dialogue. For this purpose, it's enough to find people who share similar interests, such as reading books, or going to movies or plays or sports events. Enjoy these activities together as a group, and discuss among yourselves what you've read or seen or done.

During discussions, make a note of the underlying values that come into play, both yours and others'. Examine these values for consistency, and note which are more basic. This process of value clarification through dialogue on matters of shared interest is valuable for its own sake. It enriches people as much as the particular subjects that are discussed.

A more potent way to connect with kindred spirits is by participating in a group that creates something. For example, if you can play a musical instrument, then form, or join, a group that makes music. Even rank amateurs who just play for their own amusement create circles of meaning that enrich their lives.

The most potent way to connect with kindred spirits is to join with others in common actions that make the world more beautiful, healthy, orderly, or just. For example, you can do volunteer work for a group that provides free AIDS counseling to the public. Or join a group working to make your neighborhood cleaner, safer, and more beautiful. Or join a political club to elect reform-minded candidates to office. Involvement of this nature leaves a legacy of positive changes that outlives its creators. It advances from one generation to the next, changing the world for the better.

Disagreements with Comrades

Once you join with others to change the world for the better, in whatever way, you will encounter disagreements with your comrades. That's ironic because your goal is to connect, not divide. But disagreement is inevitable. People naturally have different views about what constitutes the common good.

In fact, two individuals who are intelligent, sincere, and caring can bitterly disagree with each other on how to improve their neighborhood, their city, and the world. Such differences can be a roadblock that sidetracks and even destroys a common effort to create meaning. But they can also be a challenge that stirs people to develop greater skills of interacting with each other in positive ways, and thus grow spiritually.

The problem is usually that each person sees only part of the situation, while overlooking the other parts that others see. In addition, much of what we think we know, we don't, while some of the things we know best, we lose sight of when we act. We also forget that no program of reform can ever do justice to the complexities and ironies of human life. Every bumper sticker is at best a half-truth.

The right approach is to remain open to good-faith dialogue. Avoid becoming too righteous, and keep a sense of humor. Don't be afraid to act decisively when you have to, but first weigh every voice that should be heard, with an ear for the syllable of truth it may speak. As in chess, so in life: That game is played best where each side sees the board through the opponent's eyes. Nonetheless, the players are forced to move without the benefit of complete knowledge. In the game of life, good will, empathy, and humor help make up for that lack.

Resistance to Oppression

Not all opposition arises from the disagreement of comrades acting together in good faith. There is also the entrenched opposition of those who benefit by keeping others down or making the world ugly. When money or power are at stake, such people commonly resort to deceit, intimidation, and violence. The situation gets worse when they control great institutions. Intimidation and violence become cultivated and systematic. They develop a momentum of their own and become part of the institution's ethos.

Most human beings believe in standards of right conduct toward others and make a reasonable effort to live by them. A minority, however, have little regard for such standards. They devote themselves to aggrandizing their own money, fame, or power. They don't care about the harm they do to others, or the planet, along the way. They easily adapt themselves to the bullying ethos of great institutions. In fact, they're a perfect fit. They're the ones most likely to become the world's presidents, prime ministers, popes, media moguls, and CEOs.

Sooner or later, those who work to make the world better will encounter opposition from bullying institutions. The more power the great institutions have, the more ruthless they will become in crushing anyone who questions their methods. Previous chapters have shown the horrors that can result when any institution develops a near monopoly on power, as the Catholic Church did in certain periods of European history. Given sufficient power, any institution, whether religious or secular, will follow that precedent.

Luckily, there is a division of power in most modern societies. The great institutions have the will for complete domination but are impeded because they plot against each other, and none is dominant. Individuals and small groups can play the institutions off against each other (state against church against corporation) in order to gain breathing space.

The best hope of success in battling an overwhelming institution is to appeal to the basic sense of decency found in most human breasts. Those working for a better world have to find a way to arouse that sense in as many people as possible and channel it into practical programs of reform.

At the same time, the reformers have to be careful not to lower themselves to the moral level of their oppressors. The first great danger facing reformers is being crushed by their opponents; the second is becoming like their opponents. History has witnessed many instances of both kinds of failure.

The moral awakening that reformers strive to create in the public, even when united with the savviest of political tactics, may not be enough to bring them success. But if the moral dimension is lacking, or falters, no other kind of effort will make things better, even if it attains great power. The likely outcome will be the supplanting of one oppressive system by another. Czar Nicholas II of Russia was a tunnel-vision autocrat. So was Lenin, who replaced him. The tunnel of oppression remained. What changed were the portraits on its walls.

Living a meaningful life adds to the reservoir of moral energy available for making the world a better place. Ironically, though, it cannot provide, by itself, any guarantee of success. Integrity, vision, and principled struggle can all end in crushing defeat, and often do.

This irony is the stony soil from which both the majesty and the pathos of human life grow. We must settle for doing what we can, however little it may be, using the smartest methods we can devise, and motivated by the noblest goals. But there are no guarantees of success, while the possibilities for failure are many.

Cosmic Consciousness

Nonetheless, rewards remain for people who work with each other to make the world more beautiful, healthy, orderly, or just. As we have just seen, they connect with each other. That in itself is a great benefit in a society that thrives by undermining connectedness. But they also win something else—an expanded and deepened sense of self, one that results from interacting creatively with the larger world.

Making the Great Reconnect necessarily deepens and expands the lives of the people doing the reconnecting. They become more open to learning from other people's personal experiences, the cultural richness of humanity, and the wonders of the natural world.

If they invest enough of themselves in the world, they will no longer experience it as an alien presence of external, lifeless objects, disconnected from their own inner needs, feelings, and identity. Instead, they will come to experience both themselves and the world as mutually engaging parts of a larger, organic whole.

Eventually, if their spiritual growth goes far enough, they will feel personally addressed by the world, and seek to respond to the world's address as they would to a person's. They will understand what playwright Archibald MacLeish has a character say in his play *J.B.*:

Under the wind there was a word.

This understanding—that all things are interconnected in a great, encompassing, living unity—is what is meant by the term "cosmic consciousness." It's "consciousness" because it results from reflections on our experiences. It's "cosmic" because it expands more and more into the larger world as we ourselves become more interconnected. It involves a "living unity" because the universe constantly transforms and perpetuates itself with stunning creativity, like a great living organism, and because the universe is one.

This is how Walt Whitman put it:

A vast similitude interlocks all,
All spheres, grown, ungrown, small, large, suns, moons, planets,
All distances of place however wide,
All distances of time, all inanimate forms,
All souls, all living bodies though they be ever so different, or in
    different worlds,
All gaseous, watery, vegetable, mineral processes, the fishes, the
    brutes,
All nations, colors, barbarisms, civilizations, languages,
All identities that have existed or may exist on this globe, or any
    globe,
All lives and deaths, all of the past, present, future.
This vast similitude spans them, and always has spann'd,
And shall forever span them and compactly hold and enclose
    them.

CREATIVITY

Cosmic consciousness stimulates creativity among the individuals who cultivate it. Because of its emphasis on connectedness, it motivates people to integrate the tactile, conceptual, and emotional parts of their lives into an experiential whole.

When this integration is achieved, bodily movements, thoughts, and feelings all flow in tandem and resonate with each other's energies. The resulting synergy opens up the channels of creativity. At best, when the flow is perfected and artfully articulated, the individual's whole being—material, intellectual, sexual—becomes a unified conduit for the electricity of creativity.

This is an energy that invites company. As it moves through a person, it creates a field of psychological adhesiveness about itself, like the magnetic field created by electricity moving through a wire. It stimulates and attracts other people, in both body and soul, with an energy that can be both erotic and spiritual.

Walt Whitman called the phenomenon "the body electric":

> I sing the body electric,
> The armies of those I love engirth me and I engirth them,
> They will not let me off till I go with them, respond to them,
> And discorrupt them, and charge them full with the charge of
>   the soul.

If, finally, the ambient society nurtures and reinforces the energy flow, the creative outcome can be spectacular. Witness the glorious expressiveness in dance, song, narrative, bodily display, and sexuality that pervades every-day life in the world's indigenous cultures.

Here is where we find the font of the magic of life, for that font is people themselves when self-integrated, flowing with expressive creativity, and connected in body and spirit to each other and the cosmos. Here the boundaries of the self expand, and its windows open outward to the goodness and beauty of the whole, which it takes in with exuberance. From this place onward, life becomes a transformative and magical journey on an ever-opening road.

As usual, Walt Whitman said it best:

> I inhale great draughts of space.
> The east and the west are mine, and the north and the south are
>   mine.
> I am larger, better than I thought.
> I did not know I held so much goodness.

Afterword

Hal Offen

rthur Evans and I were dear friends for forty years. We had a great meet-up story. I was in my final year of college at CCNY, and drove a taxi part-time. One spring morning in 1971, I was taking a fare down Park Avenue when I came upon a demonstration in front of an office building. To my astonishment, I saw Gay Liberation slogans on the signs.

As soon as I discharged my passenger, I raced back to the scene, ditched the cab, and joined the onlookers gawking at this new kind of demonstration. It turned out to be the Gay Activists Alliance (GAA) protesting the policy of Household Finance Company (HFC) of refusing to sell life insurance to known gay people because, they explained, we were more likely to kill each other off to collect on the policies. (Were that in fact true, we should only have been charged higher premiums!) I grabbed a sign and joined my first Gay Rights protest.

Almost immediately, Arthur, who was leading the demonstration, approached me and said, "You just joined us. Good for you!" I recognized him from his appearance a few months earlier on the Dick Cavett Show, one of the first openly-Gay spokespeople to make the case for LGBT rights on national TV.

The demonstration out front ended abruptly and to my surprise, I was swept up in a (planned) rush into the elevators and up to the top floor for a "zap" of the CEO's offices. Loud, angry shouting about the absurdity of HFC's homophobia, cowering executives, and the arrival of the police culminated in half a dozen arrests for trespassing, including Arthur's.

GAA's zap tactics usually included volunteers who were willing to be arrested when the cops asked everyone to leave, extending the media coverage of the issue with court appearances—most ending with charges dismissed.

Although he missed the Stonewall Riots in June, 1969, a few weeks later, he and his then partner, Arthur Bell, joined the newly-formed Gay Liberation Front (GLF,) which proudly proclaimed itself to be Gay, countercultural, and revolutionary. It was within GLF, that Arthur and others created a cell called *The Radical Study Group* to examine the historical roots of sexism and homophobia, sparking an interest that would culminate in *Witchcraft and the Gay Counterculture*.

A number of GLF members, including Evans, soon became dissatisfied with the organization, complaining that it lacked a coherent, ongoing program of street activism. At the suggestion of GLF members Jim Owles and Marty Robinson, about twelve people met in Arthur Bell's Manhattan apartment on December 21, 1969, and founded The Gay Activists Alliance (GAA). Arthur wrote the group's statement of purpose and much of its constitution. He was one of the group's founding officers.

Acting on the principle that the personal is the political, GAA held homophobes who were in positions of authority personally accountable for the consequences of their public policies. Accordingly, Marty, Jim and Arthur, developed the tactic of "zaps." These were militant (but non-violent) face-to-face confrontations with outspoken homophobes in government, business, and the media. Arthur was often arrested in such actions, participating in disruptions of local business offices, political headquarters, local TV shows, and the Metropolitan Opera.

In effect, GAA created a new model of Gay activism, highly theatrical while also eminently practical and focused. It forced the media and the political establishment to take gay concerns seriously as a struggle for justice. Previously the media treated Gay life as a peripheral freak show. The new Gay activism inspired Gay people to act unapologetically from a position of gay pride. This new model inspired other gay groups across the country.

GAA was a pioneer in many of the issues the community would tackle in years to come, including repeal of the sodomy laws, passage of anti-discrimination laws, and marriage equality. In spring of 1971, Arthur led a take-over of New York's marriage license bureau, commandeering the telephone and informing callers that only same sex couples would be granted marriage licenses that day (Check out the video on YouTube!) In addition, GAA members founded the national organizations NGLTF, Lambda Legal and PFLAG, all of which continue to thrive today.

Arthur's doctoral studies in philosophy at Columbia University were curtailed by his leadership role and immersion in the gay movement, but his scholarship would express itself in the contribution he would make to LGBT history over the decades to come. In 1973, be began to publish his earliest research in the journals *Out* and *Fag Rag*. In the fall of the 1975, Arthur formed a new pagan-inspired spiritual group, the Faery Circle, after relocating to San Francisco. It combined countercultural consciousness, gay sensibility, and ceremonial playfulness. It sparked another movement.

In 1978, the first edition of *Witchcraft and the Gay Counterculture* was published. Prior to publication in 1976, Arthur presented an eight-part lecture series, Faeries, at one of the early and most beloved LGBT community centers in San Francisco, at 32 Page Street.

Each lecture covered a chapter of the new book and was accompanied by performances from local queer artists. The community's response was electric. We were thirsty for a context in which to understand the still relatively new gay liberation movement, immersed, as we were, in a blissfully-ignorant pre-AIDS euphoria.

As the successes of the movement made it safer for more LGBT people to declare themselves and lead open lives, Arthur grew disturbed by the burgeoning phenomena of what he dubbed the "Castro clone." A new stereotype emerged in the mid 1970s of a young, masculine, gym-toned, party-focused, anxious-to-conform, straight-identified, mustachioed Gay man, often dismissive of the Gay Rights movement that had made their lifestyle possible.

Arthur adopted the nom de plume *The Red Queen*, penned his first of many satirical commentaries—"Afraid You're Not Butch Enough?"—which, in a pre-internet era, he posted all over the Castro and the Haight. Never afraid to provoke controversy, Arthur's coining the term "clone" prompted a community discussion on whether the movement was about the right to be different or the right to be the same.

Around this time, Arthur and I went into business together. For eight years, we owned and operated a Volkswagen repair shop we called *The Buggery*. It was an unlikely turn of events, given our academic backgrounds, but we enjoyed providing a service to the community, and we took the summers off to head up to New Sodom, the forty acres of spectacular forest wilderness Arthur bought with partners on the Canadian border in eastern Washington State. They had hoped to homestead and enjoy a life in nature, but it ultimately proved too isolating for Arthur.

The business also allowed us to carve out time to remain active in the movement, especially during the rise of the nationwide anti-gay backlash, reflected in California by the Briggs Initiative on the state ballot that would have made it illegal for LGBTs (and straight allies who spoke out on our behalf!) to teach. The defeat of the Briggs Initiative may have been the first ever ballot victory for LGBT rights. Our euphoria was short-lived when Harvey Milk and Mayor George Moscone were murdered three weeks later.

While marveling at a double rainbow at the edge of a cliff at New Sodom, Arthur's then partner, Jacob Schraeter, asked him what he thought it meant. Arthur responded, "We're in the right place at the right time." That might describe Arthur's life experience. He found himself, part by chance and part by intention, at the heart of many of his generation's most significant countercultural and LGBT milestones.

In the 1960s, Arthur participated in many anti-war protests, including the celebrated upheaval at Columbia in the spring of 1968. In the same year, he participated in the protests at the Democratic National Convention in Chicago. In addition to being an early member of GLF, the first group formed to harness the energy of Stonewall, his leadership role in the groundbreaking GAA, and his founding of the Faery Circle, Arthur was active in many of San Francisco's LGBT activist organizations, including Bay Area Gay Liberation (BAGL) and the Harvey Milk LGBT Democratic Club, renamed for the slain leader.

He was an active participant in the White Night riots, protesting the slap on the wrist given to the murderer of Milk and Moscone, and was arrested more than once protesting the government's failure to address the AIDS epidemic.

When Arthur was diagnosed with an outsized aortic aneurism—perhaps a result of childhood exposure to secondhand smoke from his chain-smoking parents—he remained loyal to his values as an independent thinker that characterized his

69 years. He refused the surgery that doctors wanted to perform immediately. He learned that there was a great risk of devastating complications, and spent the last eleven months of his life enjoying himself, in minimal discomfort, only rarely seeing a doctor.

When I asked him if he was afraid, he said only of being a prisoner in his own body, not of dying. He was grateful to have had a good life and the opportunity to make a contribution. He remained happy and engaged until the end. We continued our weekly chess nights until a few days before a thankfully quick heart attack took him in the middle of the night, much as he hoped it would. Even in a crisis of mortality, Arthur was a role model for living on his own terms.

With his passionate embrace of justice, Arthur offered an articulate, insightful analysis of homophobia and the political strategy to combat it. Typically at meetings of LGBT activist organizations, Arthur would listen quietly as different opinions were expressed. When he eventually rose to speak, the room would grow silent in anticipation of what he had to say. He often made a comment about process and added perspectives that hadn't been considered, usually employing his witty sense of humor. Even as a young man, Arthur's intellect was admired and he was treated with the respect earned by elder statespersons.

Arthur was a role model for righteous indignation and an inspiration to countless budding activists. Most LGBT people in the early days had to deal with internalized homophobia. Instead of wallowing in self-hatred, Gay activists learned to direct years of pent-up rage against oppressive institutions and individuals. It was invigorating.

As a result, not only would there be political victories, but the emotional well-being of the community would be transformed. GAA joked that "a zap a day keeps the shrink away." By living authentically, proudly and openly Gay, early activists became each other's heroes and role models, none more so than Arthur.

We challenged the myths about us—including, and especially, that we don't fight back, and exposed hypocrisy, often with ridicule. The strategy was to become such a nuisance and public relations headache that it would become easier for homophobes to acquiesce to our reasonable and just demands than to continue their harmful policies.

Progress was slow at first, but then small victories ushered in larger ones, and laid the foundation for much of the remarkable change we've seen in the last half century. Few others played as significant a role as Arthur did in launching the modern gay liberation movement. May his name be for a blessing.

Cited Sources

Alford, Violet, and Rodney Gallop, "Traces of a Dianic Cult from Catalonia to Portugal," in *Folk-Lore*, vol. 46, Dec. 1935, pp. 350-361

Anacreon, *Fragments*

Anglo, Sydney, ed., *The Damned Art: Essays in the Literature of Witchcraft*, Routledge & Kegan Paul, London, 1977

Ankarloo, Bengt, "Sweden: The Mass Burnings (1668-1676)" in Ankarloo, Bengt, and Gustav Henningsen, eds., *Early Modern European Witchcraft: Centres and Peripheries*, Clarendon Press, Oxford, 1990, pp. 285-317

Ankarloo, Bengt, and Gustav Henningsen, eds., *Early Modern European Witchcraft: Centres and Peripheries*, Clarendon Press, Oxford, 1990

Apuleius, *The Golden Ass*

Aristotle, *On the Life Principle* [*De Anima*]

Bailey, Derrick, *Homosexuality and the Western Christian Tradition*, Archon Books, 1955; reprinted 1975

Baroja, Julio Caro, "Witchcraft and Catholic Theology," in Ankarloo, Bengt, and Gustav Henningsen, eds., *Early Modern European Witchcraft: Centres and Peripheries*, Clarendon Press, Oxford, 1990, pp. 19-43

Barstow, Anne Llewellyn, *Joan Of Arc: Heretic, Mystic, Shaman*, Edwin Mellen Press, Lewiston, 1986

Barstow, Anne Llewellyn, *Witchcraze: A New History of the European Witch Hunts*, Pandora, 1994

Barstow, Anne Llewellyn, *Witchcraze: A New History of the European Witch Hunts*, Pandora, 1994

Bauer, Walter, *A Greek-English Lexicon of the New Testament and Other Early Christian Literature*, 2nd revised edition, University of Chicago Press, Chicago, IL, 1979

Bautier, R.H. "L'hérésie d'Orléans et le mouvement intellectuelle au début du XIe siècle," *Acts du 95e Congrès National des Sociétés Savantes* (Rheims, 1970): Section philologique et historique (Paris, 1975), vol. I, pp. 63-88

Becker, Raymond de, *The Other Face of Love*, trans. by Margaret Crosland and Alan Daventry, Bell Publishing Company, New York, 1964

Benko, Stephen, "The Libertine Gnostic Sect of the Phibionites According to Epiphanius," in *Vigiliae Christianae*, vol. 21, 1967, pp. 103-119

Berger, Eric, "Original Texans? Austin-Area Find Adds to Debate Over Early Man," *Houston Chronicle*, Nov. 25, 2001

Berger, Pamela, *The Goddess Obscured: Transformation of the Grain Protectress from Goddess to Saint*, Beacon Press, Boston, 1985

Bethune, Brian, "Mystery of the First North Americans," *Maclean's*, March 19, 2001

Bondì, Claudio, *Strix: medichesse, streghe e fattucchiere nell'Italia del Rinascimento*, Lucarini, Roma, 1989

Boniface VIII, Pope, *Unam Sanctum*

Bonomo, Giuseppe, *Caccia alle streghe: la credenza nelle streghe dal secolo XIII al XIX con particolare riferimento all'Italia*, Palumbo, Palermo, 1959

Borst, Arno, *Die Katharer*, Schriften der Monumenta Germaniae Historica, vol. 12, Stuttgart, 1953

Branston, Brian, *The Lost Gods of England*, Oxford University Press, New York, 1974

Brewster, David, *Memoirs of the Life, Writings and Discoveries of Sir Isaac Newton, Vol. II*, T. Constable and Co., Edinburgh, 1855

Briffault, Robert, *The Mothers*, three volumes, 1927, reprint by George Allen & Unwin, London, 1969; Johnson Reprint Corporation, New York, 1969

Briggs, Robin, *Witches & Neighbors: The Social And Cultural Context Of European Witchcraft*, Viking, New York, 1996

Broad, William J., "In an Ancient Wreck, Clues to Seafaring Lives," *The New York Times*, March 27, 2001

Burland, Cottie, "Africa, South of the Sahara," in Philip Rawson, ed., *Primitive Erotic Art*, G.P. Putnam's Sons, New York, 1973

Burland, Cottie, "North America," in Philip Rawson, ed., *Primitive Erotic Art*, G.P. Putnam's Sons, New York, 1973

Centini, Massimo, *Le schiave di Diana: stregoneria e sciamanismo tra superstizione e demonizzazione*, Edizione Culturali Internazionali Genova, Genoa, 1994

Cervantes, Fernando, "The Devil's Encounter with America," in Barry, Jonathan, Marianne Hester, and Gareth Roberts, eds., *Witchcraft In Early Modern Europe: Studies In Culture And Belief*, Cambridge University Press, Cambridge, 1996, pp. 119-144

Chadwick, Nora K., *The Druids*, University of Wales Press, Cardiff, 1966

Chambers, E.K., *The Medieval Stage*, 1903

Childs, Brevard, *The New Testament as Canon*, Fortress Press, Philadelphia, 1984

Clark, Stuart, *Thinking With Demons: The Idea Of Witchcraft In Early Modern Europe*, Clarendon Press, Oxford, 1997

Cohn, Norman, *Europe's Inner Demons*, Sussex University Press, London, 1975

Cohn, Norman, *The Pursuit of the Millennium*, Essential Books, Fairlawn, NJ, 1957

Comnena, Anna, *The Alexiad*, Barnes & Noble, New York, 1967

Congregation for the Doctrine of the Faith, "The Message of Fatima," Vatican City, June 2000

Corradi Musi, Carla, *Shamanism From East To West*, English text revised by Paul Davis, Akadémiai Kiadó, Budapest, 1997

Crapanzano, Vincent, "Saints, *Jnun*, and Dreams: An Essay in Moroccan Ethnopsychology," in *Psychiatry*, vol. 38, 1975, pp. 145-59

Cyprian, St., *De unitate catholicae ecclesiae*

Cyprian, St., *Epistle 72*

De Riencourt, Amory, *The Rising American Empire*, Delta, New York, 1968

Dodds, E.R., *Euripides' Bacchae*, The Clarendon Press, Oxford, 1960

Dubos, René, *Mirage of Health: Utopias, Progress, and Biological Change*, orginally published 1959; reprint by Harper Colophon Books, San Francisco, 1979

Eliade, Mircea, "Some Observations on European Witchcraft," *History of Religions*, vol. 14, No. 3, 1974, pp. 140-72

Eugenius IV, Pope, *Cantata Domino*

Euripides, *Medea*

Evans, Arthur, *Critique of Patriarchal Reason*, White Crane Press, San Francisco, 1997

Evans, Arthur, *The God of Ecstasy*, St. Martin's Press, New York, 1988

Evans, Arthur, *Witchcraft and the Gay Counterculture*, Fag Rag Books, Boston, 1978

Fell, Barry, *America B.C.: Ancient Settlers in the New World*, Quadrangle/New York Times Book Co., New York, 1976

Fell, Barry, *Bronze Age America*, Little, Brown, Boston, 1982

Fell, Barry, *Saga America*, Times Books, New York, 1980

Fellini, Federico, *8½* [movie],

Freke, Timothy, and Peter Gandy, *The Jesus Mysteries: Was the "Original Jesus" a Pagan God?*, Harmony Books, New York, 1999

Gallino, T. Giani, ed., *Le grandi madri*, Milan, 1990

Gibbon, Edward, *The Decline and Fall of the Roman Empire*, three volumes, reprinted by Modern Library, New York

Gilbert, Felix, *et al.*, *The Norton History of Modern Europe*, W.W. Norton, New York, 1971

Ginzburg, Carlo, "Deciphering the Sabbath,"in Ankarloo, Bengt, and Gustav Henningsen, eds., *Early Modern European Witchcraft: Centres and Peripheries*, Clarendon Press, Oxford, 1990, pp. 121- 137

Ginzburg, Carlo, "Folklore, magia, religione," in *Storia d'Italia*, vol. 1, Torino, 1974

Ginzburg, Carlo, *Clues, Myths, and the Historical Method*, trans. by John and Anne C. Tedeschi, Johns Hopkins University Press, Baltimore, 1989

Ginzburg, Carlo, *Ecstasies: Deciphering the Witches' Sabbat*, trans. by Raymond Rosenthal, London, 1992; translation of *Una decifrazione del sabba*, Turin, 1989

Ginzburg, Carlo, *The Cheese And The Worms: The Cosmos Of A Sixteenth-Century Miller*, trans. by John and Anne Tedeschi, Routledge & Kegan Paul, London, 1980

Ginzburg, Carlo, *The Night Battles: Witchcraft & Agrarian Cults In The Sixteenth & Seventeenth Centuries*, Johns Hopkins University Press Baltimore, 1983; trans. of *I Benandanti*, Giulio Einaudi Editore, Turin, 1966

Given, James, *Inquisition and Medieval Society: Power, Discipline, and Resistance in Languedoc*, Cornell University Press, Ithaca, NY, 1997

Grimm, Jacob, *Deutsche Mythologie*, 4th edition, vol. I, Wissentschaftliche Buchgesellschaft, Berlin, 1875

Gugliotta, Guy, "Earliest Americans Seen as More Diverse," *Washington Post*, July 31, 2001, Page A01

Harner, Michael, *Hallucinogens and Shamanism*, Oxford University Press, New York, 1973

Hastrup, Kirsten, "Iceland: Sorcerers and Paganism," in Ankarloo, Bengt, and Gustav Henningsen, eds., *Early Modern European Witchcraft: Centres and Peripheries*, Clarendon Press, Oxford, 1990, pp. 383-401

Hatt, Jean-Jacques, *Celts and Gallo-Romans*, Nagel, Geneva, 1970

Heikkinen, Antero, and Timo Kervinen, "Finland: The Male Domination," in Ankarloo, Bengt, and Gustav Henningsen, eds., *Early Modern European Witchcraft: Centres and Peripheries*, Clarendon Press, Oxford, 1990, pp. 319-338

Hemmerlin, Felix, *Tractatus de credulitate daemonibus adhibenda*, in *Opuscula*, Basil, 1497

Henningsen, Gustav, "'The Ladies from Outside': An Archaic Pattern of the Witches' Sabbath," in Ankarloo, Bengt, and Gustav Henningsen, eds., *Early Modern European Witchcraft: Centres and Peripheries*, Clarendon Press, Oxford, 1990, pp. 191-215

Henningsen, Gustav, "The Ladies from Outside: An Archaic Pattern of the Witches' Sabbath," Ankarloo, Bengt, and Gustav Henningsen, eds., *Early Modern European Witchcraft: Centres and Peripheries*, Clarendon Press, Oxford, 1990, pp. 191-215

Hester, Marianne, *Lewd Women and Wicked Witches: A Study of the Dynamics of Male Domination*, Routledge, London, 1992

Hope, A.D., *A Midsummer Eve's Dream*, Viking, New York, 1970

Hughes, Pennethorne, *Witchcraft*, Penguin, Baltimore, 1965

Hutton, Ronald, *The Pagan Religions of the Ancient British Isles*, Blackwell Cambridge, MA,1991

Hutton, Ronald, *The Rise and Fall of Merry England*, Oxford University Press, New York, 1994

Hutton, Ronald, *The Stations of the Sun: A History of the Ritual Year in Britain*, Oxford University Press, New York, 1996

I Ching or Book of Changes, trans. by Richard Wilhelm, 3rd Edition, Princeton University Press, Princeton, NJ, 1968

James, Grace, *Joan of Arc*, Methuen & Co., London, 1910

Kahk, Juhan, "Estonia II: The Crusade Against Idolatry" in Ankarloo, Bengt, and Gustav Henningsen, eds., *Early Modern European Witchcraft: Centres and Peripheries*, Clarendon Press, Oxford, 1990, pp. 273-284

Kicza, John E., *The Peoples and Civilizations of the Americas Before Contact*, American Historical Association, Washington, DC, 1998

Kieckhefer, Richard, *European Witch Trials*, University of California Press, Berkeley, 1976

Klaits, Joseph, *Servants Of Satan: The Age Of The Witch Hunts*, Indiana University Press, Bloomington, IN, 1985

Klaniczay, Gábor, "Hungary: The Accusations and the Universe of Popular Magic," in Ankarloo, Bengt, and Gustav Henningsen, eds., *Early Modern European Witchcraft: Centres and Peripheries*, Clarendon Press, Oxford, 1990, pp. 219-255

Kligman, Gail, *Calus: Symbolic Transformation in Romanian Ritual*, University of Chicago Press, Chicago, 1981

Kors, Alan C., and Edward Peters, eds., *Witchcraft in Europe, 1100-1700: A Documentary History*, University of Pennsylvania Press, Philadelphia, 1972

Kramer, Heinrich, and James Sprenger, *The Malleus Maleficarum*, ed. and trans. by Montague Summers, Dover Publications, New York, 1971

Kristeller, Paul Oskar, *Renaissance Thought: The Classic, Scholastic, and Humanist Strains*, Harper Torchbooks, New York, 1961

Lambert, Malcolm, *Medieval Heresy: Popular Movements from the Gregorian Reform to the Reformation*, 2nd ed., Blackwell, Oxford, 1992

Le Roy Ladurie, Emmanuel, *Montaillou: The Promised Land of Error*, trans. by Barbara Bray, Vintage Books, 1979

Lea, Henry Charles, *Materials Toward a History of Witchcraft*, vol. I, University of Pennsylvania Press, Philadelphia, 1939

Lea, Henry Charles, *Materials Toward a History of Witchcraft*, vol. II, Thomas Yoseloff, New York, 1957

Lecouteux, C., *Fées, sorcières et loups-garous au Moyen Age. Histoire du double*, Imago, Paris, 1992

Legman, G., *The Guilt of the Templars*, Basic Books, New York, 1966

Lerner, Robert, *The Heresy of the Free Spirit in the Later Middle Ages*, University of California Press, Berkeley, 1972

Levack, Brian P, *The Witch-Hunt In Early Modern Europe*, 2nd ed., Longman, New York, 1995

Lewis, Chartlon, and Charles Short, *A Latin Dictionary*, The Clarendon Press, Oxford, 1966

Liddell, Henry George; Robert Scott; and Henry Stuart Jones, *A Greek-English Lexicon*, 9th edition, The Clarendon Press, Oxford, 1966

Lightbody, Charles W., *The Judgements of Joan*, Harvard University Press, Cambridge, 1961

Loos, Milan, *Dualist Heresy in the Middle Ages*, Martinus Nijhoff, The Hague, 1974

Lucretius Carus, Titus, *On the Nature of Things*

MacLeish, Archibald, *J.B.*, Houghton Mifflin Co., 1956

Markale, Jean, *Women of the Celts*, Gordon Cremonesi, 1975

Mather, Cotton, *Wonders of the Invisible World*, 1692

McGowan, Margaret M., "Pierre de Lancre's *Tableau de l'inconstance des mauvais anges et demons*: The Sabbat Sensationalised," in Sydney Anglo, ed., *The Damned Art: Essays in the Literature of Witchcraft*, Routledge & Kegan Paul, London, 1977, pp. 182-201

Mimnermus, *Elegies*

Momigliano, A., ed., *Conflitto tra paganesimo e christianesimo nel secolo IV*, Turin, 1975

Monter, E. William, *Witchcraft in France and Switzerland: The Borderlands During the Reformation*, Cornell University Press, Ithaca, NY, 1976

Moore, Robert I., *The Formation of a Persecuting Society: Power and Deviance in Western Europe, 950-1250*, Basil Blackwell, Oxford, 1990

Muraro, L., *La signora del gioco: Episodi di caccia alle streghe*, Feltrinelli, Milan, 1977

Murray, Margaret, *The God of the Witches*, Oxford University Press, Oxford, 1931; paperback reprint 1970

Murray, Margaret, *The Witch-Cult in Western Europe*, Oxford University Press, Oxford, 1921

Murray, T. Douglas, *Jeanne d'Arc*, McClure, Phillips & Co., New York, 1902

Nettleship, Henry, J.E. Sandys, and Oskar Seyffert, *Dictionary of Classical Antiquities*, The World Publishing Company, Cleveland, OH, 1966

Niebuhr, Gustav, "The Bible, as History, Flunks New Archaeological Tests," *The New York Times*, July 29, 2000.

Noble, David F., *A World Without Women: The Christian Clerical Culture of Western Science*, Alfred A. Knopf, New York, 1992

Nye, Andrea, *Words of Power: A Feminist Reading of the History of Logic*, Routledge, New York, 1990

Obolensky, Dmitri, *The Bogomils: A Study in Balkan Neo-Manichaeism*, Cambridge University Press, 1948

Origen, *In Jesu nave homiliae*

Ovid, *Metamorphoses*

Oxford English Dictionary, 2nd ed., Clarendon Press, Oxford, 1989

Partride, Burgo, *A History of Orgies*, Crown Publishers, New York, 1960

Peters, Edward, ed., *Heresy and Authority in Medieval Europe: Documents in Translation*, University of Pennsylvania Press, Philadelphia, 1980

Pico della Mirandola, Giovanni, *Oration on the Dignity of Man*, trans. by A. Robert Caponigri, Regnery Gateway, Chicago, 1956

Piette, Édouard, and Julien Sacaze, "La montagne d'Espiaup," *Bulletins de la Société d'anthropologie de Paris*, 1877, pp. 225-251

Pius IX, Pope, *Syllabus errorum*

Pius XII, Pope, *Mystici corporis*

Plato, *Defense of Socrates*

Plato, *Theaetetus*

Purkiss, Diane, *The Witch In History: Early Modern and Twentieth-Century Representations*, Routledge, New York, 1996

Quispel, G., "Gnosticism and the New Testament," *Vigiliae Christianae*, vol. 19, 1965, pp. 65-85

Rawson, Philip, "Early History of Sexual Art," in Philip Rawson, ed., *Primitive Erotic Art*, G.P. Putnam's Sons, New York, 1973

Robbins, Rossell H., *The Encyclopedia of Witchcraft and Demonology*, Crown Publishers, New York, 1959

Roper, Lyndal, *Oedipus and The Devil: Witchcraft, Sexuality, and Religion in Early Modern Europe*, Routledge, London, 1994

Roscoe, Will, *The Zuni Man-Woman*, University of New Mexico Press, Albuquerque, 1991

Runciman, Steven, *The Medieval Manichee*, Cambridge University Press, 1947

Russell, Jeffrey, *Witchcraft in the Middle Ages*, Cornell University Press, Ithaca, NY, 1972

Sacaze, Julien, "Le culte des pierres dans le pays de Luchon," *Association française pour l'avancement des sciences, compte rendu*, vol. 7, 1878, pp. 900-905

Sagan, Carl, *Billions and Billions: Thoughts on Life and Death at the Brink of the Millennium*, Random House, New York, 1997

Sappho, *Fragments*

Scott, George R., *Phallic Worship*, Mental Health Press, Westport, CT, n.d.

Scott, W. S., *Trial of Joan of Arc*, The Folio Society, London, 1956

Scribner, Robert W., "The Reformation, Popular Magic, and the 'Disenchantment of the World,'" in C. Scott Dixon, ed., *The German Reformation: The Essential Readings*, Blackwell, Oxford, 1999, pp. 262-279

Shakespeare, William, *A Midsummer Night's Dream*

Shakespeare, William, *A Midsummer Night's Dream*

Showerman, Grant, "The Great Mother of the Gods," in *Bulletin of the University of Wisconsin, Philology and Literature Series*, vol. 1, No. 3, 1898-1901

Simpson, Jacqueline, "Margaret Murray: Who Believed Her, and Why?", *Folklore*, 105 (1994), pp. 89-96

Spina, Bartolomeo, *Quaestio de strigibus*, Rome, 1576

Summers, Montague, *A Popular History of Witchcraft*, E.P. Dutton, New York, 1937

Tartarotti, D., *Del congresso notturno delle lammie*, Rovereto, Venice, 1749

Taylor, G. Rattray, *Sex in History*, Vanguard Press, New York, 1954

Theocritus, *Idylls*

Trevor-Roper, H.R., *The European Witch-Craze of the Sixteenth and Seventeenth Centuries, and Other Essays*, Harper & Row, New York, 1956

Tyson, Joseph, *The New Testament and Early Christianity*, The MacMillan Co., New York, 1984

Van Alstyne, R.W., *The Rising American Empire*, Quadrangle, Chicago, 1960

Vanggaard, Thorkil, *Phallós*, International Universities Press, New York, 1972

Verga, Ettore, "Intorno a due inediti documenti di stregheria milanese del secolo XIV," in *Rendiconti del Reale Istituto Lombardo di Scienze e Lettere*, ser. II, 32, 1890, 156 ff.

Virgil, *Aeneid*

Vivan, Itala, *Caccia alle streghe nell'America puritana*, Milan, 1972

Wakefield, W.L., and A.P. Evans, *Heresies of the High Middle Ages*, Columbia University Press, New York, 1969

Wakefield, Walter L., *Heresy, Crusade and Inquisition in Southern France 1100-1250*, University of California Press, Berkeley, 1974

Walker, D.P., *Spiritual and Demonic Magic From Ficino to Campanella*, University of Notre Dame Press, 1975

Warner, Marina, *Alone of All her Sex: the Myth and Cult of the Virgin Mary*, New York, 1976

Whitman, Walt, *Leaves of Grass.*

Williams, Walter L., *The Spirit and the Flesh: Sexual Diversity in American Indian Culture*, Beacon Press, Boston, 1986

Williams, William, *The Contours of American History*, New Viewpoints, New York, 1973

Wright, Thomas, "The Worship of the Generative Powers During the Middle Ages of Western Europe," in *Sexual Symbolism: A History of Phallic Worship*, The Julian Press, New York, first published in 1866, reprinted 1957

ARCHUR EVANS
GENERAL BIBLIOGRAPHY

AA.VV., *Le streghe siamo noi. Il ruolo della medicina nella repressione della dona,* Rome, 1980

Abels, Richard, and Ellen Harrison, "The Participation of Women in Languedocian Catharism," *Mediaeval Studies,* vol. 41, 1979, pp. 215-51

Acosta, Joseph de, *Historia naturale e morale delle Indie,* Venice, 1596; translation of original, in 1590 [Accounts of native Indian religions in Peru and Mexico as Devil worship]

Acquaviva, Sabino S., *The Decline of the Sacred in Industrial Society,* trans. by Patricia Lipscombe, Oxford, 1966; revised 1979 [Catholic account]

Agnoletto, A., "Maria e la strega," in T. Giani Gallino, ed., *Le grandi madri,* Milan, 1989

Alderfer, E.G., *The Ephrata Commune,* University of Pittsburgh Press, Pittsburgh, 1985 [Double monastery, with Gnostic tinges, established in Lancaster County, PA]

Alford, Violet, and Rodney Gallop, "Traces of a Dianic Cult from Catalonia to Portugal," in *Folk-Lore,* vol. 46, Dec. 1935, pp. 350-361

Alford, Violet, *Introduction To English Folklore,* London, G. Bell and Sons, 1952

Alford, Violet, *Pyrenean Festivals, Calendar Customs, Music & Magic, Drama & Dance,* Chatto and Windus, 1937

Alic, Margaret, *Hypatia's Heritage,* Beacon Press, Boston, 1986

Allen, Paula Gunn, "Lesbians in American Indian Cultures," *Conditions,* 7, 1981, 67-87

Anderson, Bonnie, and Judith Zinsser, *A History of Their Own: Women in Europe,* 2 vols., Harper & Row, New York, 1988

Anglo, S., ed., *The Damned Art: Essays in the Literature of Witchcraft,* London, 1977 [P. de Lancre's mention of sodomy at sabbat, pp. 182-201]

Angus, Samuel, *The Mystery Religions and Christianity,* University Books, New Hyde Park, NY, 1966; reprint of 1925 edition.

Ankarloo, Bengt, & Stuart Clark, eds., *Witchcraft and Magic in Europe in the 18th and 19th Centuries,* U. of Penn., 1999

Ankarloo, Bengt, and Gustav Henningsen, eds., *Early Modern European Witchcraft,* Clarendon Press, Oxford, 1990

Anonymous, *Cultus arborum,* Privately printed, 1890

Anson, John, "The Female Transvestite in Early Monasticism: the Origin and Development of a Motif," *Viator*, vol. 5, 1974, 1-32

Apuleius, *The Golden Ass*, Loeb Classical Library, G.P. Putnam's Sons, New York, 1928

Asad, Talal, "Medieval Heresy: An Anthropoligical View," *Social History*, vol. 11, 1986, pp. 354-62

Aurand, Ammon Monroe, 1895-1956, *The "Pow-Wow" Book; A Treatise On The Art Of "Healing By Prayer" And "Laying On Of Hands", Etc., Practiced By The ...*, Harrisburg, Pa., Priv. print. by the Aurand press, 1929

Auvray, L., ed., *Les régistres de Grégoire IX*, Paris, 1896
[For text of *Vox in Rama*]

Bachofen, Johann Jakob, *Myth, Religion, and Mother Right*, trans. by Ralph Manheim, Routledge & Kegan Paul, London, 1967; abridged translation of original of 1926

Bagemihl, Bruce, *Biological Exuberance: Animal Homosexuality And Natural Diversity*, New York, St. Martin's Press, 1999

Bagemihl, Bruce, *Lesbian Gulls and Gay Giraffes: the Natural History of Homosexuality*, Harper Collins, San Francisco, 1997

Bahn, Paul G., and Jean Vertut, *Images of the Ice Age*, Windward, Leicester, 1988

Bahn, Paul G., and Jean Vertut, *Journey Through The Ice Age*, Berkeley: University of California Press, c1997

Bailey, Derrick, *Homosexuality and the Western Christian Tradition*, Archon Books, 1955; reprinted 1975

Bakhtin, Mikhail, *Rabelais and his World*, trans. by Hélène Iswolsky, Cambridge, MA, 1968
[Witches' rites as subversive, 74-83 & 273-7]

Balure, E., ed., *Capitularia regum francorum*, Paris, 1967
[Text of *Canon Episcopi*, under capitularies of Louis II, p. 867]

Bamberger, Joan, "The myth of Matriarchy: Why Men Rule in Primitive Society," in M. Rosaldo and L. Lamphere, eds., *Woman, Culture and Society*, Stamford University press, Cambridge, 1974, pp. 263-80
[Critique of matriarchal theories]

Barb, A.A., "The Survival of Magic Arts," in *The Conflict Between Paganism and Christianity*, ed. by A. Momigliano, Oxford, 1963

Barber, Malcolm, "The Plot to Overthrow Christendom in 1321," *History*, 66, 1981, 1-17

Barber, Malcolm, *The Trial of the Templars*, Cambridge, 1978

Barber, Malcom, [Article on Templars], *Nottingham Medieval Studies*, vol. 17, pp. 42-57
[New material on Templars]

Barnett, Walter, *Sexual Freedom and the Constitution: An Inquiry into the Constitutionality of Repressive Sexual Laws*, University of New Mexico, Albuquerque, 1973

Barrett, W.P., *Trial of Jeanne d'Arc*, Gotham House, London, 1932
[Good for trial documents, per Barstow]

Barry, Jonathan, and Marianne Hester, and Gareth Roberts, eds., *Witchcraft In Early Modern Europe, Studies In Culture And Belief*, Cambridge, New York, Cambridge University Press, 1996

Barstow, Anne Llewellyn, *Joan Of Arc: Heretic, Mystic, Shaman*, E. Mellen Press, Lewiston, 1986

Barstow, Anne Llewellyn, *Married Priests And The Reforming Papacy: The Eleventh-Century Struggle*, New York, E. Mellen Press, c1982

Barstow, Anne Llewellyn, *Witchcraze, A New History Of The European Witch Hunts*, San Francisco, CA, Pandora <1994>

Barstow, Anne, *Married Priests and the Reforming Papacy*, Edwin Mellen Press, New York, 1980

Basilov, V.N., "Vestiges of Transvestism in Central-Asian Shamanism," in V. Diòszegi and M. Hoppál, eds., *Shamanism in Siberia*, trans. by S. Simon, Akadémie Kiado, Budapest, 1978, pp. 281-89

Bataille, Georges, ed., *Les procès de Gilles de Rais: Les documents*, Paris, 1965

Baumann, Hermann, "Der kultische Geschlectswechsel bei Naturvölkern," *Zeitschrift für sexuale Forschung*, I, , 1950, 259-297

Baumann, Hermann, *Das doppelte Geschlecht: Ethnologische Studien zur Bisexualität in Ritus und Mythos*, Dietrich Reimer, Berlin, 1955

Baumann, Hermann, *Das doppelte Geschlecht: Studien zer Bisexualität in Ritus und Mythos*, Reimer, Berlin, 1955

Bautier, R.H. "L'hérésie d'Orléans et le mouvement intellectuelle au début du XIe siècle," *Acts du 95e Congrès National des Sociétés Savantes* (Rheims, 1970): Section philologique et historique (Paris, 1975), vol. I, pp. 63-88

Bechtel, Guy, *La sorciere et l'Occident, la destruction de la sorcellerie en Europe des origines aux grands buchers*, [Paris], Plon, c1997

Becker, Raymond de, *The Other Face of Love*, trans. by Margaret Crosland and Alan Daventry, Bell Publishing Company, New York, 1964

Bede, *Works*, ed. by J. A Giles, 1983

Beik, William, "Popular Culture and Elite Repression in Early Modern Europe," *Journal of Interdisciplinary History*, vol. 1, 1980, 97-103

Bell, Susan Groag, "Christine de Pisan: Humanism and the Problem of a Studious Woman," *Feminist Issues*, vol. III (1979), p. 183

Ben Hamza, Kacem, "The Cave Dwellers of Matmata," doctoral dissertation, Bloomington, 1977, chapter 4; published in French as "Croyances et pratiques en Islam populair: Le cas de Matmata," *Revue de l'institute des belles lettres arabes*, June 1980, pp. 87-109 [Berber *jnun* as fairies, and their rituals]

Benedetti, Jean, *Gilles de Rais*, Stein and Day, New York, 1972

Benko, Stephen, "The Libertine Gnostic Sect of the Phibionites According to Epiphanius," in *Vigiliae Christianae*, vol. 21, 1967, pp. 103-119

Bennett, J.M., "Misogyny, Popular Culture, and Women's Work," *History Workshop Journal*, vol. 31, 1991, pp. 166-88

Benoist, J., *Histoire des Albigeois et des Vaudois*, Paris, vol. I, 1691, pp. 283-86 [Authentic 12th century Bogomil book, per Loos]

Berger, Pamela, *The Goddess Obscured: Transformation of the Grain Protectress from Goddess to Saint*, Beacon Press, Boston, 1985

Bergquist, A., and T. Taylor, "The Origin of the Gundestrup Cauldron," *Antiquity*, vol. 61, 1987, pp. 10-24 Some issues available online through ProQuest Direct at: http://www.umi.com/pqdauto

Berlioz, Jacques, *"Tuez-les tous, Dieu reconnaitra les siens", le massacre de Beziers (22 juillet 1209) et la croisade contre les Albigeois ..*, [Portet-sur-Garonne], Loubatieres, 1994

Berman, Morris, *The Reenchantment of the World*, Cornell University Press, Ithaca, NY, 1981

Bernauer, James, and David Rasmussen (eds.), *The Final Foucault*, MIT Press, Cambridge, Mass, 1988, c1987

Bethe, E., "Die Dorische Knabenliebe; Ihre Ethik und Ihre Idee," *Rheinisches Museum für Philologie*, vol. 62, 1907, pp. 438-475

Beza, M., *Paganism in Roumanian Folklore*, Dutton, New York, 1928

Blackwood, Evelyn, "Sexuality and Gender in Certain Native American Tribes: The Case of Cross-Gender Females," *Signs: Journal of Women in Culture and Society*, 10, 1984, 27-42

Blanchet, Regis, *Les heresies medievales face a l'Inquisition*, Rouvray, Editions du Prieure, c1995

Bleibtreu-Ehrenberg, Gisela, "Homosexualität und Transvestismus im Schamanismus," *Anthropos*, 65, 1970, 189-228

Bleibtreu-Ehrenberg, Gisela, *Der Weibmann: Kultischer Geschlechtswechsel im Schamanismus*, Fischer, Frankfurt am Main, 1984

Bloch, Iwan, *Anthropological Studies in the Strange Sexual Practices of All Races in All Ages*, Falstaff Press, New York, 1933

Blum, Richard, and Eva Blum, *The Dangerous Hour: The Lore of Crisis and Mystery in Rural Greece*, London, 1970 [Nereids as a form of fairies, pp. 112-18; Mediterranean fairies, pp. 358-75]

Bober, P.F., "Cernunnos: Origin and Transformation of a Celtic Divinity," *American Journal of Archaeology*, vol. 55, 1951, pp. 13-51

Boccaccio, Giovanni, *Decameron* [9th tale of 8th night: secret society that holds orgies]

Bogin, Meg, *The Women Troubadors*, Norton, New York, 1980

Boglioni, Pierre, et al., *La culture populaire au moyen âge*, Montreal, 1979

Bogoras, W., *The Chuckchee, Part II. Memoirs of the American Musuem of Natural History*, vol. 11, G.E. Steckert & Co., New York, 1907

Bolton, B., "Tradition and Temerity: Papal Attitudes to Deviants, 1159-1216," *Studies in Church History*—vol. 9, *Schism, Heresy and Religious Protest*, ed. by D. Baker, Cambridge, 1972, pp. 19-91

Bondì, Claudio, *Strix: medichesse, streghe e fattucchiere nell'Italia del Rinascimento*, Lucarini, Roma, 1989

Bonomo, Giuseppe, *Caccia alle streghe: la credenza nelle streghe dal secolo XIII al XIX con particolare riferimento all'Italia*, Palumbo, Palermo, 1959 [P. 17: Pierina de Bugatis; pp. 65-67] [Revised edition forthcoming]

Bord, Janet, and Colin Bord, *Earth Rites: Fertility Practices in Pre-Industrial Britain*, Granada Publishing, 1982

Bordonove, Georges, *La tragedie cathare*, Paris, Pygmalion, c1991

Bornstein, Diane, ed., *The Feminist Controversy of the Renaissance*, Delmar, NY; Scholars' Facsimiles and Reprints, 1980

Borst, Arno, *Die Katharer, Schriften der Monumenta Germaniae Historica*, vol. 12, Stuttgart, 1953
[Good doctrinal account, per Lambert; sexual charges against Cathars, pp. 180-183]

Bossy, John, "Moral Arithmetic: Seven Sins into Ten Commandments," in E. Leites, ed., *Conscience and Casusistry in Early Modern Europe*, Cambridge, 1988, 215-30

Bossy, John, "The Counter-Reformation and the People of Catholic Europe," *Past and Present*, vol. 47, May 1970, pp. 51-70
[Effects of Counter-Reformation on suppression of sexuality]

Bossy, John, *Christianity in the West, 1400-1700*, Oxford, 1985
[Connection between new moralities of Reformation and Counter-Reformation, and the persecution of witches]

Boswell, *Christianity, Social Tolerance, and Homosexuality*, University of Chicago Press, Chicago, 1980

Boswell, J., *Christianity, Social Tolerance and Homosexuality*, Chicago, 1980

Bouget, Henri, *An Examen on Witches*
[Role of homosexuality in witchcraft, p. 234]

Bourdieu, P. *Esquisse d'une theorie de la pratique*, Geneva, 1972
[Similarities between Cathars and Kabylie in Algeria; cf. Shah, Indries, *The Sufis*]

Bourgeois of Paris, *A Parisian Journal: 1405-49*, trans. by Janet Shirley, Oxford, 1968
[Interesting comments about Joan of Arc; originally *Le journal d'un bourgeois de Paris*, ed. A. Tuetey, Paris, 1881]

Boyer, Paul, and Stephan Nissenbaum, *Salem Possessed*, Harvard University Press, Cambridge, MA, 1974

Boyer, Paul, and Stephan Nissenbaum, *Salem Village Withcraft: A Documentary Record of Local Conflict in Colonial New England*, Wadwsworth, Belmont, CA, 1972

Branston, Brian, *The Lost Gods of England*, Oxford University Press, New York, 1974

Braude, Ann, *Radical Spirits*, Beacon Press, Boston, 1989
[Spiritualism and movement for women's rights and educational reform]

Bray, A., *Homosexuality in Renaissance England*, Gay Men's Press, London, 1982

Brednich, Rolf Wilhelm, *Volkserzählungen und Volksglaube von den Schicksalsfrauen*, Helsinki, 1964
[Extensive comparative study of eastern European fairy beliefs]

Brenon, Anne, *Le vrai visage due catharisme*, Portet-sur-Garonne, 1988

Brenon, Anne, *Les cathares, vie et mort d'une eglise chretienne*, Paris, J. Grancher, c1996

Brenon, Anne, *Les femmes cathares*, Paris, 1992
[According to Lambert, vivid account based on inquisition evidence]

Briffault, Robert, *The Mothers*, three volumes, 1927, reprint by George Allen & Unwin, London, 1969; Johnson Reprint Corporation, New York, 1969

Briggs, Katharine Mary, *Pale Hecate's Team*, New York, Arno Press, 1977, c1962

Briggs, Robin, *Witches & Neighbors, The Social And Cultural Context Of European Witchcraft*, New York, Viking, 1996

Brody, Jerry J., *The Anasazi: Ancient Indian People of the American Southwest*, Rizzoli International Publications, New York, 1990

Bronner, Simon J., *Popularizing Pennsylvania, Henry W. Shoemaker And The Progressive Uses Of Folklore And History*, University Park, Pennsylvania State University Press, c1996

Brown, Judith, *Immodest Acts: the Life of a Lesbian Nun in Renaissance Italy*, Oxford University Press, New York, 1986

Brown, Peter, "Sorcery, Demons and the Rise of Christianity from Late Antiquity into the Middle Ages," in Mary Douglas., ed., *Witchcraft Confessions and Accusations*, London, 1970, pp. 17-45

Brown, Peter, *The Body in Society*, Columbia University Press, New York, 1988

Brown, Sanger, II, *The Sex Worship and Symbolism of Primitive Races: An Interpretation*, Richard G. Badgen, Boston, 1916

Bullough, Vern L., "Transvestites in the Middle Ages," *American Journal of Sociology*, vol. 79, n. 6, May 1974, pp. 1381-1395

Bullough, Vern, and James Brundage, eds., *Sexual Practices and the Medieval Church*, Prometheus Books, Buffalo, 1982

Burg, B.R., *Sodomy and the Perception of Evil: English Sea Rovers in the Seventeenth Century Caribbean*, New York University Press, New York, 1983

Burke, Peter, *Popular Culture in Early Modern Europe*, Harper & row, New York, 1978

Burland, Cottie, "Africa, South of the Sahara," in Philip Rawson, *Primitive Erotic Art*, G.P. Putnam's Sons, New York, 1973

Burland, Cottie, "Middle America," in Philip Rawson, *Primitive Erotic Art*, G.P. Putnam's Sons, New York, 1973

Burland, Cottie, "North America," in Philip Rawson, *Primitive Erotic Art*, G.P. Putnam's Sons, New York, 1973

Burr, George, Lincoln, *Narratives of the Witchcraft Cases, 1648-1706*, Charles Scribner's Sons, New York, 1914

Burton, Richard, "Terminal Essay," in *Sexual Heretics*, ed. by Brian Reade, Coward-McCann, New York, 1970

Bynum, Caroline W., "Was There a Female Subculture Among Women Religious in the Later Middle Ages?", paper delivered at Barnard College, Nov. 1, 1980

Bynum, Caroline W., *God the Mother: Studies in the Spirituality of the High Middle Ages*, University of California Press, Berkeley, 1982 [Visions of women religious in the Middle Ages]

Caporael, Linnda, "Ergotism: The Satan Loosed in Salem?", *Science*, vol. 192, 1976, pp. 21-26

Carbasse, Jean-Mari, "'Currant nudi': La répression de l'adultère dans le Midi médiéval," in *Droit, histoire et sexualité*, ed. by Jacques Poumarède and Jean-Pierre Royer, Lille, 1987, pp. 83-102

Cardin, Alberto, *Guerreros, chamanes y travestis, indicios de homosexualidad entre los exoticos*, Barcelona, Tusquets, 1984

Carpenter, Edward, *Intermediate Types Among Primitive Folk: A Study in Social Evolution*, George Allen & Col, Ltd., London, 1914

Castellan [?], *De festis graecorum*

Catlin, George, *Letters and Notes on the Manners, Customs, and Condition of the North American Indians*, Vol. 2, 4th edition, Wiley & Putnam, New York, 1842

Cavalli-Sforza, Luca, and F. Cavalli-Sforza, *The Great Human Diasporas: the History of Diversity and Evolution*, trans. by Sarah Thorne, Addison-Wesley, Reading, MA, 1995

Cavalli-Sforza, Luca, *Genes, People and Languages*, 2000

Centini, Massimo, *Le Schiave Di Diana, Stregoneria E Sciamanismo Tra Superstizione E Demonizzazione*, Genova, ECIG, 1994

Cervantes, F., *The Idea of the Devil and the Problem of the Indian: The Case of Mexico in the Sixteenth Century*, London, 1991

Chadwick, Nora K., *The Druids*, University of Wales Press, Cardiff, 1966

Chambers, E.K., *The Medieval Stage*, 1903 [Condemnation of feast of fools by U. Paris in 1414)

Champion, Timothy, et al., *Prehistoric Europe*, Academic Press, London, 1984

Childs, Brevard, *The New Testament as Canon*, Fortress Press, Philadelphia, 1984

Cipolla, Carlo M., ed., *The Fontana Economic History of Europe, Vol I: The Middle Ages*, Fontana Books, London, 1972

Cipolla, Carlo M., ed., *The Fontana Economic History of Europe, Vol II: The Sixteenth and Seventeenth Centuries*, Fontana Books, Glasgow, 1974

Claassen, Cheryl, and Rosemary A. Joyce, eds., *Women In Prehistory: North America And Mesoamerica*, Philadelphia, University of Pennsylvania Press, c1997

Clark, G., "The Beguines: a Medieval Women's Community," in Quest, ed., *Building Feminist Theory*, Longmans, London, 1981 [Inquisition's concern with sexual matters]

Clark, Stuart, *Thinking With Demons, The Idea Of Witchcraft In Early Modern Europe*, Oxford [England], Clarendon Press, New York, Oxford University Press, 1997

Clasen, Claus Peter, *Anabaptism: A Social Hisotry 1525-1618*, Ithaca, NY, 1972 [Sacramental sex among the Blood Friends, pp. 136-9]

Cocchiara, Giuseppe, *Preistoria e folklore*, Palermo, Sellerio, 1978

Cohn, Norman, *Europe's Inner Demons*, Sussex University Press, London, 1975

Cohn, Norman, *The Pursuit of the Millennium*, Essential Books, Fairlawn, NJ, 1957

Comnena, Anna, *The Alexiad*, Barnes & Noble, New York, 1967

Congregation for the Doctrine of the Faith, "The Message of Fatima," Vatican City, June 2000

Conway, Anne, *Principles of the Most Ancient and Modern Philosophy* [17th century; critical of dualism and mechanism; often falsely attributed to Francis Mercury van Helmont]

Corradi Musi, Carla, *Shamanism From East To West*, Akadémiai Kiadó, Budapest, 1997

Crapanzano, Vincent, "Saints, Jnun, and Dreams: An Essay in Moroccan Ethnopsychology," *Psychiatry*, vol. 38, 1975, pp. 145-59 [Moroccan jnun like faeries]

Cunliffe, B., ed., *The Oxford Illustrated Prehistory of Europe*, Oxford University Press, Oxford, 1994

Cunliffe, Barry, *The Celtic World*, McGraw-Hill, New York, 1979

Czaplicka, M.A., *Aboriginal Siberia*, Clarendon Press, Oxford, 1914

Daly, Mary, *Gyn/Ecology*, The Women's Press, London, 1979

Dandolo, T., *La Signora di Monza e le streghe del Tirolo*, Milan, 1855

Davis, Natalie Zemon, *Society and Culture in Early Modern France*, Stanford, 1975 [Importance to older Europe of societies of adolescent males; pp. 96-124, 152-89]

Davis, Philip, *Goddess Unmasked*, Spence Publishing, New York 1998 [Debunking critique of goddess thesis]

de Waal, F.B.M., "Bonobo Sex and Society," *Scientific American*, vol. 272, no. 3, 1995, pp. 58-64

Deacon, A.B., *Malekula, a Vanishing Race in the New Hebrides*, London, 1934 [Homosexual practices]

Deierich, A., *Mutter Erde*, 3rd edition, Leipzig and Berlin, 1925

Dekker, R., and Van de Pol, L.C., *The Tradition of Female Transvestism in Early Modern Europe*, Macmillan, Basingtoke, 1989

Delcambre, E., *Les devins-guérisseurs dans la Lorraine ducale: Leur activité et leurs méthodes*, Nancy, 1951

Deleuze, Gilles, *Foucault*, edited by Sean Hand. London: Athlone, 1988

Deleuze, Gilles, *Foucault*, translated by Sean Hand; foreword by Paul Bove. Minneapolis: University of Minnesota Press, c1988

Delporte, Henri, *L'Image de la femme dans l'art préhistorique*, Picard, Paris, 1993

Demos, John P., *Entertaining Satan: Witchcraft and the Culture of Early New England*, Oxford, 1982

DeShong Meador, Betty, trans., *Inanna, Lady of Largest Heart*, University of Texas Press, Austin, 2001

di Leonardo, M., *Gender at the Crossroads of Knowledge: Feminist Anthropology in the Postmodern Era*, University of California Press, Berkeley, 1991

Dieckwisch, Heide, *Altagsgeschichte*, [forthcoming] [Every-day life in early modernity]

Dodds, E.R., *Euripides' Bacchae*, The Clarendon Press, Oxford, 1960

Domhoff, G. William, *Who Rules America? Power And Politics In The Year 2000*, 3rd ed, Mountain View, Calif.: Mayfield Pub. Co., c1998

Dömötör, Tekla, "The Cunning Folk in English and Hungarian Witch Trials," in Newall, Venetia, ed., *Folklore Studies in the Twentienth Century*, Totowa, 1981, 183-7

Dondaine, A., *Un traité neo-manichéen du XIIIe siècle: le Liber de duobus principiis, suivi d'un fragment de rituel cathare*, Rome 1939

Dorsey, George A., *Traditions of the Caddo*, Carnegie Institute of Washington, Washington, DC, 1905

Dorson, Richard Mercer, ed., *Peasant Customs And Savage Myths*, [Chicago] University of Chicago Press [1968]

Douglas, M., ed., *La stregoneria: Confessioni e accuse nell'analisi di storici e antropologi*, Turin, 1979 [Link between witchcraft and shamanism]

Drachmann, A.B., *Atheism in Pagan Antiquity*, Ares Publishers, Inc., Chicago, 1977; reprint of 1922 edition

Driver, Tom F., *The Magic of Ritual: Our Need for Liberating Rites That Transform Our Lives and Our Communities*, Harper San Francisco, 1991

Dronke, Peter, *Women Writers of the Middle Ages*, Cambridge U. Press, 1984

Duffy, E., *The Sripping of the Altars*, New Haven, 1992

Duffy, Maureen, *The Erotic World Of Faery*, London, Hodder and Stoughton, 1972

Dulaire, Jacques-Antoine, *The Gods of Generation*, trans. of *Des divinités génératrices*, Panurge Press, New York, 1933; originally published 1804

Dupont-Bouchat, Marie-Sylvie, et. al., *Prophètes et sorciers dan le pay-Bays, XVIe-XVIIIe sièle*, Hachette, Paris, 1978 [Jesuits denouncing folklore practices as witchcraft, pp. 137-38; connection between witchcraft and sex, 142-144]

Dupouy, Edmund, "Prostitution in Antiquity," in Lee Alexander Stone, ed., *The Story of Phallicism*, vol. 2, Pascal Covici, Chicago, 1927

Durham, Mary Edith, *High Albania*, Virago, London, 1985 [Women who live as men in Albanian society]

Duvernoy, J., *Le Catharisme I: la religion des Cathares*, Toulouse, 1976; and II: L'Histoire des Cathares, 1979

Duvernoy, Jean, ed., *Le Registre d'Inquisition de Jacques Fournie, evêque de Pamiers (1318-1325)*, Toulouse, 1965, 3 vols., from Latin MS 4030, Vatican Library

Easlea, Brian, *Witch Hunting, Magic, and the New Philosophy: An Introduction to Debates of the Scientific Revolution*, Atlantic Highlands, NJ, 1980

Economou, George, *The Goddess Nature in Medieval Literature*, Harvard U. Pr., 1972

Ehrenberg, Margaret R., *Women in Prehistory*, British Museum Publications, London, 1989

Ehrenreich, B., and English, D., *Witches, Midwives and Nurses*, Writers and Readers, Longon, 1976

Eliade, M., *Lo schiamanismo e le tecniche dell'estasi*, Rome, 1951

Eliade, Mircea, "Some Observations on European Witchcraft," *History of Religions*, vol. 14, No. 3, 1975, pp. 140-72

Elias, Norbert, *The Civilizing Process: Sociogenetic and Psychogenetic Investigations*, trans. by Edmund Jephcott, 2 vols., Oxford, 1978, 1982 [Vol. 1: *The History of Manners* Vol. 2: *State Formation and Civilization*] [The opposite of Michel Foucault; emphasis on the biologic basis of sexuality]

Ellero, P., "Superstizioni volgari in Friuli," in *Scritti minori*, Bologna, 1875 [p. 32: Juxtaposition of the company of the Good Lady with the witches' sabbat]

Ellis, Peter B., *Celt and Roman: The Celts in Italy*, St. Martin's Press, New York, 1998

Evans-Pritchard, E., "Sexual Inversion Among the Azande," *American Anthropoligist*, vol. 72, No. 6, 1970, pp. 1428-34

Ewen, L.C., *Witch Hunting and Witch Trials*, Frederick Miller, London, 1971

Faderman, L., *Surpassing the Love of Men*, Junction Books, London, 1981 [Drag kings]

Fauvel, John, et al., eds., *Let Newton Be!*, Oxford University Press, 1988

Fell, Barry, *America B.C.: Ancient Settlers in the New World*, Quadrangle/New York Times Book Co., New York, 1976

Fell, Barry, *Bronze Age America*, Little, Brown, Boston, 1982

Fell, Barry, *Saga America*, Times Books, New York, 1980

Ferguson, Margaret, et al., eds., *Rewriting the Renaissance*, University of Chicago Press, Chicago, 1986

Ficker, G., *Die Phundagiagiten*, Leipzig, 1908 [pp. 1-86: text of letters of Euthymius re Bogomilism]

Flandrin, Jean-Louis, "Repression and Change in the Sexual Life of Young People in Medieval and Early Modern Times," in Wheaton, Robert, and Tamara Hareven, eds., *Family Sexuality in French History*, Philadelphia, 1980

Flint, Valerie I.J., *The Rise of Magic in Early Medieval Europe*, Oxford, 1991

Fogel, Edwin Miller, *Beliefs And Superstitions Of The Pennsylvania Germans*, Philadelphia, American Germanica Press, 1915

Force, James E., and Richard H. Popkin, eds., *Essays on the Context, Nature, and Influence of Isaac Newton's Theology*, Kluwer Academy Publishers, Dordrecht, 1990

Ford, Clellan, and Frank A. Beach, *Patterns of Sexual Behavior*, Harper & Row, 1951

Foucault, Michel, *Discipline And Punish: The Birth Of The Prison,* translated from the French by Alan Sheridan. 1st American ed. New York: Pantheon Books, c1977

Foucault, Michel, *Madness And Civilization: A History Of Insanity In The Age Of Reason*, translated from the French by ... New York: Vintage Books 1988, c1965

Foucault, Michel, *Power/Knowledge: Selected Interviews And Other Writings*, 1972-1977 Pantheon Books, c1980

Foucault, Michel, *The Archaeology Of Knowledge*, translated from the French by A. M. Sheridan Smith. London, Tavistock Publications, 1972

Foucault, Michel, *The History Of Sexuality*, Pantheon Books, c1978-

Foucault, Michel, *The History Of Sexuality*, translated from the French by Robert Hurley. Vintage Books ed. New York: Vintage Books, 1990

Foucault, Michel, *The History Of Sexuality*, translated from the French by Robert Hurley. New York: Vintage Books, 1980

Foucault, Michel, *The History Of Sexuality*, translated from the French by Robert Hurley, New York: Pantheon Books, c1978

Foucault, Michel, *The Order Of Things; An Archaeology Of The Human Sciences*, Vintage Books, 1973, c1970

Fraser, Jill Andresky, *White-Collar Sweatshop: The Deterioration of Work and Its Rewards in Corporate America*, W.W. Norton, 2001

Fulton, R., and S.W. Anderson, "The Amerindian 'Man-Woman': Gender, Liminality, and Cultural Continuity," *Current Anthropology*, vol. 33, no. 5, 1992, pp. 603-10

Gallino, T. Giani, ed., *Le grandi madri*, Milan, 1990

Garrett, Clarke, "Witches and Cunning Folk in the Old Regime," in Beauroy, Jacques, et al., eds., *The Wolf and the Lamb*, Saratoga, CA, 1976, pp. 53-64

Gibbon, Edward, *The Decline and Fall of the Roman Empire*, Vols. I & II, Modern Library, New York

Gilbert, Felix, *et al.*, *The Norton History of Modern Europe*, W.W. Norton, New York, 1971

Gimbutas, Marija, *The Civilization of the Goddess*, Harper Collins, San Francisco, 1991

Gimbutas, Marija, *The Goddesses and Gods of Old Europe: Myths and Cult Images*, Thames and Hudson, London, 1982

Gimbutas, Marija, *The Language of the Goddess*, Thames and Hudson, London, 1989

Ginzburg, Carlo, "Folklore, magia, religione," in *Storia d'Italia*, vol. 1, Torino, 1974

Ginzburg, Carlo, *Clues, Myths, And The Historical Method*, translated by John and Anne C. Tedeschi, Baltimore, Md.: Johns Hopkins University Press, c1989

Ginzburg, Carlo, *Ecstasies: Deciphering the Witches' Sabbat*, trans. by Raymond Rosenthal, London, 1992

Ginzburg, Carlo, *I Benandanti*, Giulio Einaudi Editore, Turin, 1966

Ginzburg, Carlo, *Storia notturna. Una decifrazione del sabba*, Turin, 1989

Ginzburg, Carlo, *The Cheese And The Worms: The Cosmos Of A Sixteenth-Century Miller*; translated by John and Anne Tedeschi, London: Routledge & Kegan Paul, 1980

Ginzburg, Carlo, *The Night Battles: Witchcraft & Agrarian Cults In The Sixteenth & Seventeenth Centuries*; Baltimore, Md.: Johns Hopkins University Press, 1983

Given, James Buchanan, *Inquisition And Medieval Society, Power, Discipline, And Resistance In Languedoc*, Ithaca, N.Y., Cornell University Press, 1997

Glendinng, Chells, "Notes Toward a Neo-Luddit Manifesto," *Utne Reader*, March/April 1990 *The Utne Reader*

Godbeer, R., *The Devil's Dominion: Magic and Religion in Early New England*, Cambridge, 1992

Goodrich, Michael, *The Unmentionable Vice: Homosexuality in the Late Medieval Period*, Dorset Press, New York, 1979

Goody, J., *Literacy in Traditional Societies*, Cambridge, 1968

Gordon, Mary, *Joan Of Arc*, Lipper/Viking, New York, 2000

Gossen, Gary H., and Miguel Leon-Portilla, eds., *South And Meso-American Native Spirituality: From The Cult Of The Feathered Serpent To The Theology Of Liberation*, Crossroad, New York, 1993.

Gratian, *Decretum, Part II, causa 26, quaestio 5, capitulum 12 Episcopi. Corpus iuris Canonici*, ed. E. Friedberg, Leipzig, 1879, vol. 1, cols. 1030-31, English translation, Lea, Materials, vol. 1, 178-80 [Text of *Canon Episcopi*]

Greenleaf, Richard E., *Zumárraga and the Mexican Inquisition*, Washington, DC, 1961

Greenleaf, Rirchard E., *The Mexican Inquistion of the Sixteenth Century*, Albuquerque, 1969

Grim, John A., *The Shaman: Patterns of Siberian and Ojibway Healing*, University of Oklahoma Press, Norman, OK, 1983

Grimm, Jacob, *Deutsche Mythologie*, 4 vols., Berlin, 1981 [Connection between Diana and various Germanic goddesses, i, 221-6; and iii, 87-9]

Grimm, Jacob, *Teutonic Mythology*, trans. by J.S. Stallybrass, vol. I, London, 1880 [Pages 259-262, Abbot Rudulf's description of pagan agrarian ritual with wagon in 1133]

Grinsell, L.V., "Witchcraft at Some Prehistoric Sites" in Venetia Newall, ed., *The Witch Figure*, Routledge & Kegan Paul, Boston, 1973, pp. 72-79

Gui, Bernard, *Practica inquisitionis heretice pravitatis* ed. by Célestin Douais, Paris, 1886 [See French translation: *Manuel de l'inquisiteur*, trans. by G. Mollat, 2 vols., Paris, 1926-27]

Guibert of Nogent, *De vita sua*, ed. by Bourgin
[Bk III, p. 215: homosexuality of Bucy heretics]

Gutiérrez, Ramón A., *When Jesus Came, The Corn Mothers Went Away: Marriage, Sexuality, And Power In New Mexico, 1500-1846*, Stanford, Calif.: Stanford University Press, 1991.

Halliday, W.R., *The Pagan Background of Early Christianity*, Hodder & Stoughton, London, 1925

Halperin, David, *et al.*, *Before Sexuality: The Construction of Erotic Experience in the Ancient Greek World*, Princeton University Press, 1990

Hamilton, B., *The Medieval Inquisition*, London, 1981
[View that anti-heretical impetus came from the common people, not authorities; criticized by Moore.]

Hamilton, K.B., "An Account of the Remains of the Worship of Priapus Lately Existing at Isernia in the Kingdom of Naples," in *Sexual Symbolism: A History of Phallic Worship*, originally published 1786, reprinted by the Julian Press, New York, 1957

Hammer-Purgstall, Joseph von, *Fundgraben des Orients*, vol. 6: *Mysterium Baphometis revelatum, seu fratres militiae Templi, qua Gnostici et quidem Ophiani apostasiae, idoloduliae et impuritatis convicti per ipsi eorum monumenta*, Vienna, 1818
[The Templars as practitioners of erotic gnosticism]

Hammer-Purgstall, Joseph von, *Mémoire sur deux coffrets gnostiques du Moyen Âge, du Cabinet de M. le Duc de Blacas*, 1832

Harding, M.E., *Women's Mysteries*, Longman's Green, 1935
[Etymology of *virgo*]

Harnack, Adolph, *Militia Christi: The Christian Religion and the Military of the First Three Centuries*, trans. by David M. Gracie, Fortress Press, Philadelphia, 1981

Harner, Michael, *Hallucinogens and Shamanism*, Oxford University Press, New York, 1973

Harrison, Michael, *The Roots of Witchcraft*, London, 1973
[Murray-like approach

Harrison, Tom, "Equatorial Islands of the Pacific Basin," in Philip Rawson, ed., *Primitive Erotic Art*, G.P. Putnam's Sons, New York, 1973

Harrison, Tom, *Savage Civilization*, London, 1937
[Account of homosexuality among Malekula by homophobic author]

Hartmann, Heidi, "Capitalism, Patriarchy, and Job Segregation by Sex," in *Women and the Workplace: The Implications of Occupational Segregation*, ed. by Martha Blaxall and Barbara Reagan, University of Chicago Press, Chicago, 1979

Hatch, Nathan O., *The Democratization of American Christianity*, Yale University Press, New Haven, CT, 1989

Hatt, Jean-Jacques, *Celts and Gallo-Romans*, Nagel, Geneva, 1970

Hawkes, Jacquetta, & Leonard Woolley, *History of Mankind*, vol. I: *Prehistory and the Beginnings of Civilization*, Harper and Row, New York, 1963

Heaton, Herbert, *Economic History of Europe*, Revised Edition, Harper & Row, New York, 1948

Hege, Marianne, *Die steinerne Fee, Idealisierung und Damonisierung weiblicher Kraft*, Weinheim, Beltz, c1985

Heinsohn, Gunnar, and Otto Steiger, "The Elimination of Medieval Birth Control and the Witch Trials of Modern Times," *International Journal of Women's Studies*, Vol. 5, No. 3, May-June 1982, pp. 193-214

Heisch, A., "Queen Elizabeth I and the Peresistence of Patriarchy," *Feminist Review*, vol. 4, 1980

Henningsen, Gustav, "The Greatest Witch-Trial of Them All: Navarre, 1609-1614," *History Today*, November 1980, pp. 36-39

Henningsen, Gustav, and John Tedeschi, eds., *The Inquisition In Early Modern Europe: Studies On Sources And Methods*, Dekalb, Ill.: Northern Illinois University Press, 1986.

Henningsen, Gustav, *The Witches' Advocate: Basque Witchcraft and the Spanish Inquisition*, University of Nevada Press, Reno, 1980
[Male homosexuality, p. 154]

Herbig, Reinhard, *Pan, der griechische Bockgott*, Vittorio Klostermann, Frankfurt am Main, 1949

Herves, Gordon W., "Cultural Continuity from the Paleolithic Onward," *Comparative Civilizations Bulletin*, vol. 10, no. 2, Summer 1981, pp. 5-9

Hester, Marianne, *Lewd Women and Wicked Witches*, Routledge, London, 1992
[Shows connection between persecution of witches and sexual allegations; lesbianism, 182-83]

Heurgon, Jacques, *The Rise of Rome to 264 B.C.*, University of California Press, Berkeley, 1973

Hill, Frances, *The Salem Witch Trials Reader*, Da Capo Press, 2000

Hill, W.W., "The Status of the Hermaphrodite and Transvestite in Navaho Culture," *American Anthropologist*, 37, 1935, 275-76

Höffler, *Kultische Geheimbünde der Germanen*, Frankfurt-am-Main, 1934
[Ritual associations of young males and shamanic experiences; influenced by Nazi ideology, stressing warfare at cost of agriculture; yet has some value, per Ginzburg]

Hooks, Bell, *Talking Back: Thinking Feminist and Thinking Black*, Sheba, London, 1989

Hope, A.D., *A Midsummer Eve's Dream*, Viking, New York, 1970

Hopkin, Charles Edward, *The Share of Thomas Aquinas in the Growth of the Witchcraft Delusion*, Philadelphia, 1940
[pp. 174-79: all conjuration presupposes a pact with the Devil]

Hoppál, Mihály, "Traces of Shamanism in Hungarian Folk Beliefs," in Hoppál, ed., *Shamanism in Eurasia*, Göttingen, 1984

Horsley, Richard, "Who Were the Witches? The Social Roles of the Accused in the European Witchcraft Trials," *Journal of Interdisciplinary History*, Vol. 9, No. 4, Spring 1979, pp. 689-715

Howard, Clifford, *Sex Worship: An Exposition of the Phallic Origins of Religion*, published by author, Washington, DC, 1897

Howard, Michael, *The Sacred Ring*, Capell Ban, 1995. [According to Hutton, ignores the new view that is critical of the pagan-survival thesis.]

Hoy, David Couzens, *Foucault: A Critical Reader*, Oxford, UK; New York, NY, USA: B. Blackwell, 1986

Hutton, Ronald, *The Pagan Religions of the Ancient British Isles*, Cambridge, Mass.: B. Blackwell, 1991

Hutton, Ronald, *The Rise and Fall of Merry England*, New York: Oxford University Press, 1994

Hutton, Ronald, *The Stations of the Sun: A History of the Ritual Year in Britain*, Oxford University Press, New York, 1996

Hyde, H. Montgomery, *The Love that Dared Not Speak its Name: A Candid History of Homosexuality in Britain*, Little, Brown & Co., Boston, 1970

Imhoff, Arthur E., "From the Old Mortality Pattern to the New: A Radical change from the Sixteenth to the Twentieth Century, *Bulletin of the History of Medicine*, vol. 59, no. 1, Spring 1985 [Separateness of male and female life in European peasant society, p. 13]

Irving, John Treat, Jr., *Indian Sketches Taken During an Expedition to the Pawnee Tribes*, reprint of 1835 edition, ed. by John Frances McDermott, University of Oklahoma Press, Norman, 1955

Jacobus, Dr. [pseudonym], *Untrodden Fields of Anthropology*, vol. II, Falstaff Press, Inc., New York, 1937

Jalby, Robert, *Sorcellerie, medecine populaire et pratiques medico-magiques en Languedoc*, Nyons, Editions de l'Aygues, 1974

James, Edwin O., *Seasonal Feasts and Festivals*, New York, 1962

James, Grace, *Joan of Arc*, Methuen & Co., London, 1910

Johnson, Kenneth, *Witchcraft and the Shamanic Journey: Pagan Folkways from the Burning Times*, 2nd edition, Llewellyn Publications, St. Maul, MN, 1998 [Author: Kenneth Johnson, c/o Llewellyn Worldwide, PO Box 64383, Dept. K379-4, St. Paul, MN 55164-0383]

Josephy, Alvin M., Jr., and Frederick E. Hoxie, eds., *America In 1492: The World Of The Indian Peoples Before The Arrival Of Columbus*, Knopf , New York, 1992

Kahk, Juhan, "Estonia II: The Crusade Against Idolatry" in Ankarloo, Bengt, and Gustav Henningsen, eds., *Early Modern European Witchcraft: Centres and Peripheries*, Clarendon Press, Oxford, 1990, pp. 273-284

Kamen, Henry, *Inquisition and Society in Spain in the Sixteenth and Seventeenth Centuries*, Indiana University Press, Bloomington, IN, 1985

Kamen, Henry, *The Spanish Inquisition: A Historical Revision*, New Haven, Conn.: Yale University Press, 1998.

Karlen, Arno, "The Homosexual Heresy," *Chaucer Review*, vol. 6, 1971

Karlsen, Carol F., *The Devil in the Shape of a Woman: Witchcraft in Colonial New England*, Norton, New York, 1987 [Implicit lesbianism of witches, p. 136] [Construction of new, bourgeois gender of women as undermining decline in witch hunts.]

Karsch-Haack, Ferdinand, *Das gleichgeschlechtliche Leben der Naturvölker*, Reinhard, Munich, 1911

Kassiola, Joel Jay, *The Death of Industrial Civilization*, State University of New York Press, Ithaca, NY, 1990

Kelly, L., *Surviving Sexual Violence*, Pluto Press, London, 1988 [Wide extent of violence against women]

Kicza, John E., *The Peoples And Civilizations Of The Americas Before Contact*, American Historical Association, Washington, D.C., 1998.

Kieckhefer, Richard, *European Witch Trials*, University of California Press, Berkeley, 1976

Kieckhefer, Richard, *Magic in the Middle Ages*, Cambridge,, 1990

Kieckhefer, Richard, *Repression of Heresy in Medieval Germany*, University of Pennsylvania Press, Philadelphia, 1979

Kirchner, Audrey Burie, *In Days Gone By, Folklore And Traditions Of The Pennsylvania Dutch*, Englewood, Colo., Libraries Unlimited, 1996

Kirk, Robert, *Secret Commonwealth*

Kittredge, George Lyman, *Witchcraft in Old and New England*, Harvard University Press, Cambridge, MA, 1929

Klaits, Joseph, *Servants Of Satan: The Age Of The Witch Hunts*, Bloomington, IN: Indiana University Press, c1985 Grad Svcs BF1566.K531 1985 [Persecution of homosexuals, heretics, p. 19]

Klaniczay, Gábor, "Benandante-kresnik-zduhac-táltos," *Ehnographie*, 94, 1983, 116-33

Klaniczay, Gábor, "Shamanistic Elements in Central European Witchcraft," in Mihály Hoppal, ed., *Shamanism in Eurasia*, Göttingen, 1984, pp. 404-22

Kligman, Gail, *Calus: Symbolic Transformation in Romanian Ritual*, University of Chicago Press, Chicago, 1981

Knight, Richard Payne, "A Discourse on the Worship of Priapus and Its Connection with the Mystic theology of the Ancients," in *Sexual Symbolism: A History of Phallic Worship*, originally published 1786, reprinted by the Julian Press, New York, 1957

Knüsel, C.J., and K. M. Ripley, "The Berdache or Man-Woman in Anglo-Saxon England and Post-Roman Europe," in A. Tyrell and B. Frazer, eds., *Social Identity in Early Medieval Britain*, forthcoming

Koch, Gofftried, *Frauenfrage und Ketzertum im Mitelalter*, Forschungen zur mittelalterlichen Geschichte, Berlin, 1962 [Women among the Cathars; pp. 113-121: libertinism]

Kors, Alan C., and Edward Peters, eds., *Witchcraft in Europe, 1100-1700: A Documentary History*, University of Pennsylvania Press, Philadelphia, 1972

Kramer, Heinrich, and James Sprenger, *The Malleus Maleficarum*, ed. and trans. by Montague Summers, Dover Publications, New York, 1971

Kristeller, Paul Oskar, "Learned Women of Early Modern Italy: Humanists and University Scholars," in Patricia A. Labalme, ed., *Beyond their Sex: Learned Women of the European Past*, New York University Press, New York, 1980

Kristeller, Paul Oskar, "The Contribution of Religious Orders to Renaissance thought and Learning" in Paul Oskar Kristeller, *Medieval Aspects of Renaissance Learning*, Duke University Press, Durham, NC, 1974

LaChapelle, Dolores, *D.H. Lawrence: Future Primitive*, Denton, Tex.: University of North Texas Press, c1996

LaChapelle, Dolores, *Earth Wisdom*, Guild of Tutors Press, Boulder, 1978 X-SFPL

Lambert, Malcolm D., *Medieval Heresy: Popular Movements from Bogomil to Hus*, Holmes & Meier Publishers New York, 1977, c1976

Lambert, Malcolm D., *The Cathars*, Blackwell Publishers Oxford, 1998

Lambert, Malcolm, [Forthcoming book on the Cathars]

Lambert, Malcolm, *Medieval Heresy: Popular Movements from the Gregorian Reform to the Reformation*, 2nd ed., Blackwell, Oxford, 1992

Lancre, Pierre de, *Tableau de l'inconstance des mauvais anges et démons*, Paris, 1612

Lang, Sabine, *Men as Women, Women as Men: Changing Gender in Native American Cultures*, trans. from the German by John L. Vantine, University of Texas Press, Austin, 1998

Larner, Christina, *Enemies of God: The Witch-hunt in Scotland*, Chatto & Windus, London, 1981
[Stresses importance of misogyny in witch-hunts, per Anne Barstow]

Larner, Christina, *The Thinking Peasant: Popular And Educated Belief In Pre-Industrial Culture*, Glasgow, Pressgang, c1982.

Larner, Christina, *Witchcraft and Religion: the Politics of Popular Belief*, Oxford, 1984

Lawson, John Cuthbert, *Modern Greek Folklore and Ancient Greek Religion*, Cambridge, 1910
[Leaving food out for Fates to eat, p. 125]

Le Roy Ladurie, Emmanuel, *Carnival in Romans*, trans. by Mary Feeney, New York, 1979

Le Roy Ladurie, Emmanuel, *Montaillou: The Promised Land of Error*, Random House, New York, 1979
[Separate lives of the sexes in European peasant families;
Survival of paganism;
oppression of the Cathars;
Medieval Christian piety as the attribute of the elite, p. 305]

Lea, Henry Charles, "The Innocence of the Templars," in G. Legman, *The Guilt of the Templars*, Basic Books, New York, 1966

Lea, Henry Charles, *A History of the Inquisition of the Middle Ages*, vol. III, The Harbor Press, 1955

Lea, Henry Charles, *Materials Toward a History of Witchcraft*, vol. I, University of Pennsylvania Press, Philadelphia, 1939
[Old accounts of nightly activity of witches, vol. I, pp. 170-98, 201-5]

Lea, Henry Charles, *Materials Toward a History of Witchcraft*, vol. II, Thomas Yoseloff, New York, 1957

Lea, Henry, *A History of Sacerdotal Celibacy*, Williams and Norgate, London, 1907

Lecouteux, C., *Fées, sorcières et loups-garous au Moyen Age. Histoire du double*, Imago, Paris, 1992

Leff, G., *Heresy in the Later Middle Ages*, Manchester, 1967
[Believes that some of the charges against the Free Spirit were true]

Legman, G., *The Guilt of the Templars*, Basic Books, New York, 1966

Legman, G., *The History and Psychology of Religio-Sexual Orgies*
[unclear whether ever published]

Lenman, Bruce, and Geoffrey Parker, "The State, the Community, and the Criminal Law in Early Modern Europe" in Lenman, Bruce, and Geoffrey Parker, eds., *Crime and the Law*, V. Gatreel, London, 1980
[Change in nature of European justice in 12th century]

Lerner, Robert, *The Heresy of the Free Spirit in the Later Middle Ages*, University of California Press, Berkeley, 1972

Levack, Brian P, *The Witch-Hunt In Early Modern Europe*, 2nd ed., London, New York, Longman, 1995

Levack, Brian P., ed., *Anthropological Studies Of Witchcraft, Magic, And Religion*, New York: Garland Pub., 1992

Levack, Brian P., *Witchcraft In The Ancient World And The Middle Ages*, New York: Garland Pub., 1992

Levack, Brian P., *Witchcraft, Women, And Society*, New York: Garland Pub., 1992

Levi, Peter, *The Frontiers of Paradise: A Study of Monks and Monasteries*, Weidenfield and Nicolson, New York, 1987

Liber Sancti Johannis
[Extant Bogomil document]

Licht, Hans [pseudonym for Paul Brandt], *Sexual Life in Ancient Greece*, Barnes & Noble, New York, 1952

Liddell, Henry George; Robert Scott; and Henry Stuart Jones, *A Greek-English Lexicon*, 9th edition, The Clarendon Press, Oxford, 1966

Lightbody, Charles W., *The Judgements of Joan*, Harvard University Press, Cambridge, 1961

Lindberg, David C., and Ronald L. Numbers, eds., *God and Nature*, University of California Press, Berkeley, 1986

Liversidge, Douglas, *The Luddites*, Franklin Watts, London, 1972

Long, George, *The Folklore Calendar*, [London] P. Allan, 1930

Loomis, R.S., "Morgan la Fée and the Celtic Goddesses," in *Speculum*, vol. 4, 1945

Loos, Milan, *Dualist Heresy in the Middle Ages*, Martinus Nijhoff, The Hague, 1974

Lot-Falk, E., *Psychopathes et chamanes yakoutes*, Paris, 1979
[Erotic links between shamans and helper spirits]

Lucian [?], *Treatise on the Syrian Goddess*

Maccullock, J.A., "Folk-Memory in Folk-Tales," *Folklore*, vol. 60, 1949, pp. 307-315
[Prehistoric contents of folk tales]

Macey, David, *TheLives of Michel Foucault: A Biography*, New York: Vintage Books, 1995, c1993

MacFarlane, A., *Witchcraft in Tudor and Stuart England*, a Regional and Comparative Study, Routledge & Kegan Paul, London, 1970
[Social deviance as the most common cause of witch accusations, pp. 226-227]

MacKinnon, C., *Toward a Feminist Theory of the State*, Harvard University Press, London, 1989

Maclean, Ian, *The Renaissance Notion of Women*, Cambridge University Press, 1980

Macrobius, Ambrosius, *Saturnaliorum conviviorum libri septem*
[III, 8: male, female transvestism in worshipping bisexual Aphrodite]

Manselli, [?], *Eresia*
[Sexual charges against Cathars: p. 201]

Manselli, Raoul, *La religion populaire au moyen âge*, Montreal, 1975

Map, Walter, *Walter Map's Book De Nugis Curialium (Courtiers' Trifles)*, tr. by M.B. Ogle and Frederick Tupper, London, 1924
[Stories of night riders with Diana]

Markale, Jean, *Women of the Celts*, Gordon Cremonesi, 1975

Marshall, Sherrin, ed., *Women in Reformation and Counter-Reformation Europe*, Indiana University Press, Bloomington, 1989

Mather, Cotton, *Magnalia Christi Americana*, vols. I & II, Silas Andrus, Hartford, CN, 1820

Maury, A., *Les fées au Moyen Age*, Paris, 1843

Mayer, Anton, "Erdmutter und Hexe," in *Historische Forschungen und Quellen*, begr. v. Jos. Schlecht, heraus. v. Anton Mayer in P. Ruf. XII Heft, 1936

McKibben, Bill, *The End of Nature*, Doubleday, NY, 1990

McNeill, John T., "Folk Paganism in the Penitentials," *Journal of Religion*, vol. 13, 1933, pp. 450-66

Meaden, George Terence, *The Goddess of the Stones: the Language of the Megaliths*, Souvenir Press, London, 1991
[Early farming communities as egalitarian and goddess-centered]

Meier, M.H.E., *Histoire de l'amour grec dans l'antiquité*, Stendhal et Compagnie, Paris, 1930

Mellinkoff, Ruth, *Outcasts: Signs of Otherness in Northern European Art of the Late Middle Ages*, 2 vols., Berkeley, 1993

Menius, Justus, *Von den Blutfreunden aus der Widertauff*, Servasius Sthümer, Erfurt, 1551
[Sacramental sex among the Blood Friends]

Meskell, L., "Goddesses, Gimbutas, and 'New Age' Archaeology," *Antiquity*, vol. 69, 1995, pp. 74-86

Middleton, C., "Women's Labour and the Transition to Pre-industrial Capitalism," in L. Charles and L. Duffin, eds., *Women and Work in Pre-Industrial England*, London, 1985

Midelfort, H.C. Erik, "Heartland of the Witchcraze: Central and Northern Europe," *History Today*, vol. 31, 1981, 27-31

Mizruchi, Ephraim, *Regulating Society: Beguines, Bohemains, and Other Marginals*, University of Chicago Press, Chicago, 1987

Mizruchi, Ephraim, *Regulating Society: Marginality and Social Control in Historical Perspective*, The Free Press, New York, 1983

Momigliano, A., ed., *Conflitto tra paganesimo e christianesimo nel secolo IV*, Turin, 1975

Monter, E. William, "La Sodomie à l'époque moderne en Suisse romande," *Annales: Économies-Sociétés-Civilisations*, vol. 29, 1974, pp. 1023-33

Monter, E. William, ed., *European Witchcraft*, New York, 1969
[Contains translation of Le Roy Ladurie's *Les Paysans de Languedoc*, stressing folkloric interpretation of witchcraft]

Monter, E. William, *Frontiers Of Heresy: The Spanish Inquisition From The Basque Lands To Sicily*, Cambridge; New York, NY: Cambridge University Press, c1990.

Monter, E. William, *Ritual, Myth, And Magic In Early Modern Europe*, Athens, Ohio: Ohio University Press, 1984, c1983.

Monter, E. William, *Witchcraft in France and Switzerland*, Cornell University Press, Ithaca, NY, 1976
[According to Anne Barstow, a rare early study that emphasizes the importance of gender to the witch hunts; Monter discusses persecution for sodomy, pp. 196-98; witchcraft persecution the result of increasing patriarchal power, 119, 196-98, & nn. 14, 141; Sodomy & witchcraft, pp. 135-36]

Moore, R.I., *Origins of European Dissent*, 2nd Edition, Oxford, 1985
[Early heresies]

Moore, R.I., *The Formation of a Persecuting Society: Power and Deviance in Western Europe, 950-1250*, Basil Blackwell, Oxford, 1990
[Role of the new European state in persecuting homosexuals]

Moore, Robert I., *The Birth of Popular Heresy*, London, 1975

Morgan, Robin, "Theory and Practice: Pornography and Rape," in L. Lederer, ed., *Take Back the Night: Women on Pornography*, Bantam, New York, 1982

Muchembled, Robert, "The Witches of Cambrésis: The Acculturation of the Rural World in the 16th and 17th Centuries," in Obelkovich, James, ed., *Religion and the People, 800-1700*, University of North Carolina Press, Chapel Hill, 1979
[Witch hunts as a cultural war]

Muchembled, Robert, "Witchcraft, Popular Culture, and Christianity in the Sixteenth Century ...," trans. by Patricia M. Ranum, in *Ritual, Relgion, and the Sacred*, ed. by Robert Forster and Orest Ranum, Johns Hopkins University Press, Baltimore, 1982

Muchembled, Robert, *Popular Culture and Elite Culture in France*, 1400-1750, Baton Rouge, 1985
[Role of peasant women as transmitters of popular culture, pp. 66-71.]

Müller, C.O., *The History and Antiquities of the Doric Race*, John Murray, London, 1839

Muller, Daniela, *Frauen vor der Inquisition, Lebensform, Glaubenszeugnis und Aburteilung der deutschen und franzosischen Katharerinnen...*, Mainz, Verlag Philipp von Zabern, 1996

Mundy, John Hine, *Men and Women at Toulouse in the Age of the Cathars*, Toronto, 1990
Pontifical Institute of Mediaeval Studies

Mundy, John Hine, *The Repression of Catharism at Toulouse*, Toronto, 1985

Muraro, L., *La signora del gioco: Episodi di caccia alle streghe*, Feltrinelli, Milan, 1977

Murray, Alexander, *Reason and Society in the Middle Ages*, Oxford University Press, Oxford, 1985

Murray, Margaret, *The God of the Witches*, Oxford, 1931

Murray, Margaret, *The Witch-Cult in Western Europe*, Oxford University Press, Oxford, 1921

Murray, T. Douglas, *Jeanne d'Arc*, McClure, Phillips & Co., New York, 1902
[Trial records]

Nauert, C.G., *Agrippa and the Crisis of Renaissance Thought*, Urbana, IL, 1965

Nelli, R., *L'Érotique des troubadours*, Tolouse, 1963

Nelli, R., *La vie quotidienne des cathares du Languedoc au XIIIe siècle*, Paris, 1969

Neri, F., "Le tradizione italiane della Sibilla," in *Fabrilia*, Turin, 1930

Newall, Venetia, ed., *The Witch Figure*, Routledge & Kegan Paul, Boston, 1973

Niebuhr, Gustav, "The Bible, as History, Flunks New Archaeological Tests," *The New York Times*, July 29, 2000

Noble, David F., *A World Without Women: The Christian Clerical Culture of Western Science*, Alfred A. Knopf, New York, 1992

Noble, David, *The Masculine Millennium*
[Forthcoming; about technology]

Nye, Andrea, *Words of Power: A Feminist Reading of the History of Logic*, Routledge, New York, 1990

Obelkevich, James, ed., *Religion and the People, 800-1700*, Chapel Hill, 1979

Oberman, H.A., *Masters of the Reformation*, Cambridge, 1981

Obolensky, Dmitri, *The Bogomils: A Study in Balkan Neo-Manichaeism*, Cambridge University Press, 1948

Oldenbourg, Zoe, *Massacre at Montségur*, Pantheon, New York, 1961

Oplinger, Jon, *The Politics Of Demonology, The European Witchcraze And The Mass Production Of Deviance*, Selinsgrove, [Pa.], Susquehanna University Press, London, Associated University Presses, c1990

Osborne, Harold, "Central Andean Region," in Philip Rawson, ed., *Primitive Erotic Art*, G.P. Putnam's Sons, New York, 1973

Oxford English Dictionary, 2nd ed., Clarendon Press, Oxford, 1989

Ozment, Steven, ed., *Religion and Culture in the Renaissance and Reformation*, Kirksville, MO, 1989

Pagel, Walter, *Paracelsus*, S. Karger, Basle, Switzerland, 1958

Pagels, Elaine, "What Became of God the Mother? Conflicting Images of God in Early Christianity," *Signs*, vol. 2, no. 2 (1976), p. 298

Parinetto, Luciano, *Streghe e potere: il capitale e la persecuzione dei diversi*, Rusconi, Milan, 1998

Paris, G., *Légendes du Moyen Age*, Paris, 1904, 2nd ed.
[Sibyl, p. 70 ff.]

Parker, Geoffrey, "Some Recent Work on the Inquisition in Spain and Italy," *Journal of Modern History*, vol. 54, no. 3, September 1982, pp. 519-32

Parker, Thomas W., *The Knights Templars in England*, University of Arizona Press, Tucson, 1963

Partner, Peter, *The Murdered Magicians: The Templars and Their Myth*, New York, 1982

Partridge, Burgo, *A History of Orgies*, Crown Publishers, New York, 1960

Payer, Pierre, *Sex and the Penitentials*, University of Toronto Press, Toronto, 1984

Peacock, J., "Symbolic Reversal and Social History: Transvestites and Clowns of Java," in B. Babcock, *The Reversible World*, Cornell University Press, Ithaca, 1978, pp. 209-224

Pernoud, Régine, *Joan of Arc, by Herself and her Witnesses*, Stein & Day, New York, 1966
[Good slection of original documents, per Barstow]

Pernoud, Régine, *Retrial of Joan of Arc*, trans. by J.M. Cohen, Methuen, London, 1955

Peters, Edward, ed., *Heresy and Authority in Medieval Europe: Documents in Translation*, University of Pennsylvania Press, Philadelphia, 1980

Peters, Edward, *The Magician, the Witch and the Law*, Philadelphia, 1978
[Per Moore, demonstrates role of learned culture in using witch accusations to consolidate legal power of state and church]

Peuch, H.-C., and A. Vaillant, *Le traité contre les Bogomils de Cosmas le Prêtre*, Travaux publ. par l'Inst. d'Ét. slav., 21, Paris, 1945

Pico della Mirandola, Giovanni, *Oration on the Dignity of Man*

Piette, Édouard, and Julien Sacaze, "La montagne d'Espiaup," *Bulletins de la société d'anthropologie de Paris*, 1877, pp. 225-251

Piggott, Stuart, *The Druids*, Praeger, New York, 1975

Pinies, Jean-Pierre, *Figures de la sorcellerie languedocienne, breish, endevinaire, armier*, Paris, Editions du CNRS, c1983

Pitrè, Giuseppe, *Usi e costumi, credenze e pregiudizi del popolo siciliano*, Palermo, 1889
[*Donna di fuora*, v. iv, p. 153, 163 ff.]

Porete, Marguerite, of Hainault, *The Mirror of Simple Souls*, in Guarnieri, ed., *Achivo Italiano per la storia della pietà*, vol. 4, pp. 513-635; also, Kirchberger, C., ed., *The Mirror of Simple Souls*, New York, 1927

Potts, Thomas, *The Wonderfull Discoverie of Witches in the countie of Lancaster*, Chatham Society, London, 1845 [Account of the Lancashire witches, Old Demdyke and Old Chattox, most detailed account of an English witch trial]

Powers, Richard Gid, *Secrecy and Power: The Life of J. Edgar Hoover*, The Free Press, NY, 1987

Prem, Hanns J., *The Ancient Americas: A Brief History And Guide To Research*, translated by Kornelia Kurbjuhn, University of Utah Press, Salt Lake City :, c1997.

Preston, James, ed., *Mother Worship*, Chapel Hill, 1982

Puech, H.C., and A. Vaillant, *Le Traité contre les Bogomils de Cosmas le Prêtre*, Paris, 1945

Purkiss, Diane, *The Witch In History: Early Modern And Twentieth-Century Representations* , London; New York: Routledge, 1996

Quaife, Geoffrey Robert, *Godly Zeal And Furious Rage, The Witch In Early Modern Europe*, London, Croom Helm, c1987

Quicherat, Jules, *Procès de condamnation dt de réhabilitation de Jeanne d'Arc dite la Pucelle d'Orléans*, 5 vols., Renouard, Paris, 1841-49; Johnson Reprint Corporation, New York, 1965

Quispel, G., "Gnosticism and the New Testament," *Vigiliae Christianae*, vol. 19, 1965, pp. 65-85

Rabbinowitz, Jake, [New book on witchcraft, from a neo-pagan perspective]

Randolph, Vance, *"Unprintable" Ozark Folk Beliefs*, manuscript, 1954

Ranke, Friedrich, "Das Wilde Heer and die Kultbünde der Germanen," in his *Kleine Schriften*, ed. by H. Rupp and E. Studer, Bern, 1971, 380-408

Rashdall, Hastings, *The Universities of Europe in the Middle Ages*, Oxford University Press, 1985

Rawson, Philip, "Early History of Sexual Art," in Philip Rawson, ed., *Primitive Erotic Art*, G.P. Putnam's Sons, New York, 1973

Redstockings, "Redstocking Manifesto," in R. Morgan, ed., *Sisterhood is Powerful*, Vintage Random House, New York, 1970

Regino of Prüm, *De disciplinis ecclesiasticis et religione christianae*, Baluze, Paris, 1671 [Text of *Canon episcopi*, vol. II, col. 364]

Restall, Matthew B., *The Maya World: Yucatec Culture and Society, 1550-1850*, Stanford University Press, Stanford, 1997 [Advances in understanding Mayan civ, based on Mayan language documentation]

Reuss, R., *L'Alsace au 17e siècle*, Paris, 1898 [The Devil as a sodomite]

Ridley, Matt, *The Red Queen: Sex and the Evolution of Human Nature*, Viking Penguin, London, 1993 Bioscience GN365.9.R53 1994

Robbins, Rossell H., *The Encyclopedia of Witchcraft and Demonology*, Crown Publishers, New York, 1959

Roper, Lyndal, *Oedipus And The Devil, Witchcraft, Sexuality, And Religion In Early Modern Europe*, London, New York, Routledge, 1994

Roper, Lyndal, *The Holy Household: Women and Morals in Reformation Aubsburg*, Oxford, 1989

Roquebert, Michel, *Les Cathares: De La Chute De Montsegur Aux Derniers Buchers*, [Paris]: Perrin, c1998

Roscoe, Will & Stephen O. Murray, eds., *Boy-Wives And Female-Husbands, Studies In African Homosexualities*, New York, St. Martin's Press, 1998

Roscoe, Will, *Changing Ones, Third And Fourth Genders In Native North America*, New York, St. Martin's Press, 1998

Roscoe, Will, ed., *Living The Spirit, A Gay American Indian Anthology*, New York, St. Martin's Press, c1988

Roscoe, Will, *The Zuni Man-Woman*, Albuquerque, University of New Mexico Press, 1991

Rose, Elliot, *A Razor for a Goat: A Discussion of Certain Problems in the History of Witchcraft and Diabolism*, University of Toronto Press, Toronto, 1962

Ross, Anne, "Celtic and Northern Art," in Philip Rawson, *Primitive Erotic Art*, G.P. Putnam's Sons, New York, 1973

Ross, Anne, "The Divine Hag of the Pagan Celts" in Venetia Newall, ed., *The Witch Figure*, Routledge & Kegan Paul, Boston, 1973, pp. 139-164

Ross, Anne, *Everyday Life of the Pagan Celts*, G.P. Putnam's Sons, New York, 1970

Ross, Anne, *Pagan Celtic Britain*, Columbia University Press, New York, 1967

Rossi, Paolo, *Philosophy, Technology, and the Arts in the Early Modern Era*, Harper & Row, New York, 1970

Rottenwöhrer, G., *Der Katharismus*, Bad Honnef, 1982
[Account of rituals in I (in 2), II (in 2), per Lambert]

Roy, Philippe, *Les Cathares, histoire et spiritualite*, Paris, Editions Dervy, c1993

Runciman, Steven, *The Medieval Manichee*, Cambridge University Press, 1947

Runeberg, Arne, *Witches, Demons, and Fertility Magic, Societas Scientiarum Fennica, Commentationes Humanarum Litterarum*, vol. 14, no. 4, Helsingfors, Helsinki, 1947
[Stress of folklore evidence]
[Meals put out for healing faeries, p. 154]

Russell, Diana, *Rape in Marriage*, Macmillan, New York, 1982

Russell, Jeffrey B., *Religious Dissent in the Middle Ages*, John Wiley & Sons, New York, 1971

Russell, Jeffrey Burton, *A History Of Witchcraft, Sorcerers, Heretics And Pagans*, London, New York, Thames and Hudson, c1980

Russell, Jeffrey Burton, *Dissent And Order In The Middle Ages, The Search For Legitimate Authority*, New York, Twayne Publishers, Toronto, Maxwell Macmillan Canada, c1992

Russell, Jeffrey, *Il diavolo e l'enferno tra il primo e il quinto secolo*, Milan, 1986
[Possibly a translation of *The Devil: Perceptions of Evil from Antiquity to Primitive Christianity*]

Russell, Jeffrey, *Il diavolo nel medioevo*, Bari, 1987
[Possibly a translation of *Satan: The Early Christian Tradition*]

Russell, Jeffrey, *Satan: The Early Christian Tradition*, Ithaca, 1981

Russell, Jeffrey, *The Devil: Perceptions of Evil from Antiquity to Primitive Christianity*, Ithaca, 1977

Sacaze, Julien, "Le culte des pierres dans le pays de Luchon," *Association française pour l'avancement des sciences, compte rendu*, vol. 7, 1878, pp. 900-905

Sahlins, Marshall, *Stone Age Economics*, Aldine, Chicago, 1972

Salisbury, Neal, *Manitou and Providence: Indians, Europeans, and the Making of New England*, 1500-1643, Oxford University Press, New York, 1982

Sanday, Peggy Reeves, *Female Power and Male Dominance: On the Origins of Sexual Inequality*, Cambridge University Press, 1981
[Importance of myth in nature societies as validator of women's hight status]

Sannita, W.G., "Induzione farmacologia ed esperienze psichiche, medicina popolare e stregoneria in Europa agli inizi dell'età moderna," in M. Cuccu & P.A. Rosse, eds., *La strega, il teologo, lo scienziato*, Genoa, 1986 [Use of hallucinogens among witches]

Saslow, James M., *Ganymede in the Renaissance: Homosexuality in Art and Society*, Yale University Press, New Haven, 1986

Schiebinger, Londa, *The Mind Has No Sex? Women in the Origins of Modern Science*, Harvard university Press, Cambridge, MA, 1989

Scott, George R., *Phallic Worship*, Mental Health Press, Westport, CT, n.d.

Scott, H., *The Feminisation of Poverty*, London, 1984

Scott, W.S., *Trial of Joan of Arc*, The Folio Society, London, 1956

Scribner, Robert W., "Ritual and Popular Relgion in Catholic Germany at the Time of the Reformation," *Journal of Ecclesiastical History*, vol. 35, 1984, pp. 47-77

Scribner, Robert W., "The Reformation, Popular Magic, and the 'Disenchantment of the World,' in C. Scott Dixon, ed., *The German Reformation: The Essential Readings*, Blackwell, Oxford, 1999, pp. 259-279

Segal, Robert A., ed., *Anthropology, Folklore, And Myth*, New York, Garland Pub., 1996

Segalen, Martine, *Love and Power in the Peasant Family*, trans. by Sarah Matthews, University of Chicago Press, Chicago, 1983
[Separate lives of the sexes in European peasant families]

Seznec, J., *The Survival of the Pagan Gods*, New York, 1961

Shah, Indries, *The Sufis*, Anchor, New York, 1991
[p. 232 ff, influence of North Africa on later European witchcraft]
[See also P. Bourdieu, *Esquisse*]

Showerman, Grant, "The Great Mother of the Gods," in *Bulletin of the University of Wisconsin, Philology and Literature Series*, vol. 1, No. 3, 1898-1901

Shumaker, Wayne, *The Occult Sciences in the Renaissance: A Study of Intellectual Patterns*, University of California Press, Berkeley, 1972

Sidky, H., *Witchcraft, Lycanthropy, Drugs, And Disease, An Anthropological Study Of The European Witch-Hunts*, New York, Peter Lang, c1997

Silverblatt, I., *Moon, Sun, and Witches: Gender Ideologies and Class in Inca and Colonial Peru*, Princeton, 1987
[Witches as political subversives, pp. 195-96]

Simpson, Jacqueline, "Margaret Murray: Who Believed Her, and Why?", *Folklore*, 105 (1994), pp. 89-96 [Sharp critique of Murray]

Sjöö, M., and B. Mor, *The Ancient Religion of the Great Cosmic Mother*, Trondheim, Norway, 1981

Sjöö, M., and B. Mor, *The Great Cosmic Mother: Rediscovering the Religion of the Earth*, Harper & Row, San Francisco, 1987

Söderberg, H., *La religion des Cathares: études sur le gnosticisme de la basse antiquité et du moyen age*, Uppsala, 1949 [Good on Cathar doctrine, per Lambert]

Spanos, Nicholas P., and Jack Gottlieb, "Ergotism and the Salem Village Witch Trials," *Science*, vol. 194, 1976, pp. 1390-94

Spierenburg, Pieter, *The Broken Spell: A Cultural and Anthropological History of Preindustrial Europe*, London, 1991

Spindler, Konrad, *The Man in the Ice*, Weidenfeld and Nicholson, London, 1994 [Ancient European body recovered from ice]

Spretnak, Charlene, *Lost Goddesses Of Early Greece: A Collection Of Pre-Hellenic...*, Berkeley, Calif.: Moon Books, c1978

Spretnak, Charlene, *States Of Grace: The Recovery Of Meaning In The Postmodern Age*, HarperSanFrancisco, c1991

Spretnak, Charlene, *The Politics Of Women's Spirituality: Essays On The Rise Of Spritual Power Within The Feminist Movement*, Anchor Books, 1982

Spretnak, Charlene, *The Resurgence Of The Real: Body, Nature, And Place In a Hypermodern World*, Reading, Mass.: Addison-Wesley, c1997

Spretnak, Charlene, *The Spiritual Dimension of Green Politics*, Bear, Santa Fe, 1986

Steiner, Stan, *The Islands: The Worlds of the Puerto Ricans*, Harper Colophon Books, New York, 1974

Stevenson, Mitilda C., *The Zuñi Indians: Their Mythology, Esoteric Fraternities, and Ceremonies*, 23rd Annual Report of the Bureau of American Ethnology, 1901-1902, 1-608, Government Printing Office, Washington, DC, 1904

Steward, Charles, "Nymphomania: Sexuality, Insanity and Problems in Folkore Analysis," in Alexiou, M., and V. Lambropoulos, eds., *The Text and Its Margins: Post-structuralist Approaches to Twentieth-century Greek Literature*, New York, 1982, pp. 219-52 [Greek & Mediterranean fairy beliefs]

Stoyanov, Yuri, *The Other God: Dualist Religions from Antiquity to the Cathar Heresy*, Yale, 2000

Summers, Montague, *A Popular History of Witchcraft*, E.P. Dutton, New York, 1937

Sumption, H., *The Albigensian Crusade*, London, 1978

Symonds, John A., *A Problem in Greek Ethics*, 1873, reprinted Areopagitica Society, London, 1908

Tartarotti, D., *Del congresso notturno delle lammie*, Rovereto, Venice, 1749 [Identifies witches with worship of Diana, as late as 18th century]

Taylor, G. Rattray, *Sex in History*, Vanguard Press, New York, 1954

Taylor, Timothy, *Prehistory of Sex*, Bantam, New York, 1996
New York: Bantam Books, c1996

Teyssèdre, B., *Nascita del diavolo*, Genoa, 1992

Thilo, J., *Codex apocryphus Novi Testamenti*, Leipzig, 1832 [pp. 884-96: authentic 12th century Bogomil book, per Loos]

Thomas Aquinas, Excerpt from *Summa contra gentiles* pertaining to conjuration, in Alan C. Kors and Edward Peters, eds., *Witchcraft in Europe, 1100-1700: A Documentary History*, Philadelphia, 1972 [pp. 53-62: all conjuration presupposes a pact with the Devil]

Thomas, George, *Studies in Ancient Greek Society: The Prehistoric Aegean*, originally published 1949, Citadel Press, New York, 1965

Thomas, Keith, *Religion and the Decline of Magic*, Penguin, London, 1973
[Chap. 7: pagan influences in village life

Todorov, Tzvetan, *The Conquest of America: The Question of the Other*, Harper & Row, New York, 1984, 1987

Trevor-Roper, H.R., *The European Witch-Craze of the Sixteenth and Seventeenth Centuries, and Other Essays*, Harper & Row, New York, 1956

Turcan, Robert, *Les religions de l'Asie dans la vallée du Rhône* in *Études préliminaires aux religions orientales dans l'Empire romain*, vol. 30, E.J. Brill, Leiden, 1972

Tyson, Joseph, *The New Testament and Early Christianity*, The MacMillan Co., New York, 1984

van Gennep, Arnold, *The Rites of Passage*, University of Chicago Press, 1960

Vanggaard, Thorkil, *Phallós*, International Universities Press, New York, 1972

Vasey, P.L., "Homosexual Behavior in Primates: A Review of Evidence and Theory," *International Journal of Primatology*, vol. 16, no.2, 1995, 173-204
[According to Timothy Taylor, most up-to-date info on primate homosexuality]

Verga, Ettore, "Intorno a due inediti documenti di stregheria milanese del secolo XIV," in *Rendiconti del Reale Istituto Lombardo di Scienze e Lettere*, ser. II, 32, 1889, pp. 166 ff.
[Concerning Pierina de Bugatis and the society of Diana]

Vicaire, Marie-Humbert, "Les Cathares albigeois vus pare les polémistes," in *Cathares en Languedoc*, pp. 105-28

Vivan, Itala, *Caccia alle streghe nell'America puritana*, Milan, 1972
[Salem witch hunt as reacting against Indian and Black rituals]

von Cles-Reden, Sibylle, *The Realm of the Great Goddess*, Prentice-Hall, Englewood Cliffs, NJ, 1962

Wakefield, Walter L., and Austin Evans, *Heresies of the High Middle Ages*, Columbia University Press, 1969
[Good source material for early 11th century heresy trial; sexual charges against Cathars: pp. 46-47]

Wakefield, Walter L., *Heresy, Crusade and Inquisition in Southern France 1100-1250*, University of California Press, Berkeley, 1974

Walby, S., *Theorising Patriarchy*, Blackwell, Oxford, 1990

Walker, D.P., *Spiritual and Demonic Magic From Ficino to Campanella*, University of Notre Dame Press, 1975

Wappler, Paul, *Die Täuferbewegung in Thüringen von 1526-1584*, Jena, 1913
[Sacramental sex among the Blood Friends, pp. 189-206, 408-94]

Warner, Marina, *Alone of All her Sex: the Myth and Cult of the Virgin Mary*, New York, 1976, 1983
[pp. 318-19: Mary called "high goddess"]

Warner, Marina, *Joan of Arc: The Image of Female Heroism*, New York, 1981

Waugh, Scott L., and Peter D. Diehl, eds., *Christendom and Its Discontents: Exclusion, Persecution, and Rebellion, 1000-1500*, Cambridge, 1996

Weber, Max, *The Protestant Ethic and the Spirit of Capitalism*, trans. by Talcott Parsons, New York, 1958
[p. 105: intro. of term Entzauberung der Welt]

Weeks, Jeffrey, *Sexuality and Its Discontents: Meanings, Myths, and Modern Sexualities*, London, 1985
[View that homosexuality is a modern construct]

Wellnhofer, M., "Die Thrakischen Euchiten und ihr Satanskult im Dialoge des Psellos: *TimÒqeoj À per˘ tîn daimÒnwn*," *Byzantinische Zeitschrift*, vol. 30, 1929-30, pp. 477-84

Werner, E., "Adamatische Praktiken im spätmittelalterliche Bulgarien," vol. 20, 1959, pp. 20-27

Wessley, Stephen E., "The Thirteenth-Century Guglielmites: Salvation Through Women," in Derek Baker, ed., *Medieval Women*

West, R.H., *Reginald Scot and Renaissance Writings on Witchcraft*, Boston, 1984

Weyer, Johann, Witches, *Devils and Doctors in the Renaissance: Johann Weyer, De praestigiis daemonum*, ed. by G. Mora, trans. by J. Shea, Binghampton, NY, 1991

Wilbur, Ken, *The Eye of Spirit*, Boston, Shambhala, 1997

Williams, Walter, *The Spirit and the Flesh: Sexual Diversity in American Indian Culture*, Beacon Press, Boston, 1986

Wood, Gordon, *The Radicalism of the American Revolution*, New York: A.A. Knopf, 1992, c1991

Wright, L.B., *Middle Class Culture in Elizabethan England*, University of North Carolina Press, Chapel Hill, NC, 1935
[Attacks on butch women and fem men, pp. 496-7]

Wright, Thomas, "The Worship of the Generative Powers During the Middle Ages of Western Europe," in *Sexual Symbolism: A History of Phallic Worship*, The Julian Press, New York, first published in 1866, reprinted 1957

Wunderer, Richard, *Erotik Und Hexenwahn; Eine Studie Der Entstehung Des Hexenwahns In Der Vorchristlichen Zeit Bis Zu Den Pogromen... 3. Aufl.*], Stuttgart, Weltspiegel [1963, c1962]

Yates, F., *The Occult Philosophy in the Elizabethan Age*, London, 1979

Yates, Frances A., *Giordano Bruno and the Hermetic Tradition*, Chicago, 1964

Zika, Charles, "Fears of Flying: Representations of Witchcraft and Sexuality in Early Sixteenth-Century Germany," *Australian Journal of Art*, vol. 8, 1989-90, pp. 19-48

Zilsel, Edgar, "The Sociological Roots of Science," *American Jounral of Sociology*, vol. 47, 1942

Index

When originally preparing the index, I first made a card for every name appearing anywhere in the text, but in the end I decided to use only the following personal names in the index: (1) the name of any known Lesbian or Gay man; (2) the name of any person accused of heresy or sexual "crime." Consequently, all the names have been dropped of inquisitors, theologians, most kings, and all except one Pope. A. E.

N.B. In additions to the entries Arthur Evans indexed in *Witchcraft and the Gay Counterculture*, this edition of *The Evans Symposium* includes index entries for *Moon Lady Rising* for Evans' search terms.

www.gaywisdom.org

• THE WHITE CRANE WISDOM SERIES •

White Crane Institute's guiding principle: "fostering the gathering and dissemination of information about the critical role sexuality and gender plays in the development of cultural and spiritual traditions and to provide a nurturing environment for the continuation and expansion of those explorations for the greater good of all society."

As Gay people we bear wisdom. As Gay people we create culture. White Crane is proud to present these valuable treasures through our Gay Wisdom Series. Our aim is to provide you with fine books of insight, discernment and spiritual journey. White Crane Institute is a 501(c)(3) educational corporation, committed to the certainty that gay consciousness plays a special and important role in the evolution of life on Earth. White Crane Institute published White Crane, the Journal of Gay Wisdom & Culture and Daily GayWisdom, an almanac of LGBT history. Contributions and support are tax-deductible to the fullest extent of the law.

White Crane Institute
22 County Route 27 • Granville NY 12832
www.gaywisdom.org • editor@gaywisdom.org

www.ingramcontent.com/pod-product-compliance
Lightning Source LLC
Chambersburg PA
CBHW031459270326
41930CB00006B/159